American Catholic Etiquette

American Catholic Etiquette

by *Kay Toy Fenner*

The Newman Press
WESTMINSTER, MARYLAND
1963

First published, 1961
Second printing, 1962
Third printing, 1962
Fourth printing, 1963

Nihil obstat: EDWARD A. CERNY, S.S., S.T.D.
          Censor Librorum

Imprimatur: FRANCIS P. KEOUGH, D.D.
          Archbishop of Baltimore

Date: September 22, 1961

Acknowledgments

THE AUTHOR wishes to acknowledge her enormous indebtedness to the Reverend Joseph P. Conway, Vice Chancellor of the Diocese of Albany, without whose advice and assistance this book could not have been written.

Grateful thanks are also due to:

Lavinia Finin (Mrs. William G.) for permission to use material previously published by her, in the chapter entitled "Making Your Wedding More Catholic."

Dr. Paul Popinoe, Director of the American Institute of Family Relations and the American Newspaper Syndicate, copyright holder, for permission to quote from two of his newspaper columns entitled "Your Family and You."

Dr. Margaret Mead and Editorial Projects for Education, copyright holder, for permission to quote from an article entitled "Marrying in Haste in College."

Sister Catherine Francis, C.S.J., President of the College of St. Rose, and the Reverend Barnabus Abele, O.F.M., Librarian of Siena College, for permission to use the libraries of these two colleges.

Finally, Dr. Doris Grumbach (Mrs. Leonard) for editorial and marketing help and for unfailing encouragement and inspiration.

KAY TOY FENNER

Contents

❖❖❖❖❖

Contents

Contents   xiii

Contents

Introduction

THE TWENTIETH CENTURY has been a period of steadily increasing informality in dress, entertaining, and manners. Some people, confusing correct behavior with outmoded ceremoniousness, have concluded that there is no longer a standard code of polite conduct and have been content to rely upon their native taste as a guide to proper behavior in any set of circumstances.

They are wrong. There are still acceptable and unacceptable ways of dealing socially with our fellow men, whether those dealings be ceremonial or informal. To know and thus to be able to choose the right way is to free oneself from dozens of minor problems.

A book of etiquette is like a road map. One should be able to consult it to learn the accepted and graceful way to conduct oneself in any unfamiliar social scene exactly as one refers to a map to plan a trip into unknown country. One *could* make the trip relying on road signs and inquiries, but only at the risk of error, delay, or inconvenience. One *could* trust one's instincts on the social scene, but to do so courts the danger of appearing gauche or even unkind. Why pretend to omniscience? To consult an authority on a subject with which one is not thoroughly conversant is simple prudence, and requires no defense.

But, the reader may properly ask, why *Catholic* etiquette? Is correct Catholic behavior wholly different from that of non-Catholics? Certainly not. In many phases of daily living—in business, in sports, and in much of our social behavior—our code is that of any well-bred American of any creed. Since advice on these matters is readily obtainable in standard works of etiquette, no useful purpose would have been served by including them in this volume, and they have therefore been omitted.

But the code of behavior for Catholics does differ at some points
from that of non-Catholics. Mother Church has given us seven sacraments to give us grace and help us to earn Heaven. The reception of
most of them has some social connotations and accompanying social
functions. The newborn baby is baptized and becomes "a child of God
and heir of Heaven." The occasion requires the parents to do a number
of things correctly in a social as well as a spiritual sense; for the reception of a sacrament is a ceremony, and a ceremony is the very essence
of formal behavior. Formal means "with strict attention to outward
forms and ceremonies" says the dictionary. Thus to be wrong or incorrect in any part of the performance of a ceremony is not to be
formal at all. It is not size or elaborateness that determine formality;
it is correctness.

Penance, extreme unction, and the ordinary reception of the Holy
Eucharist might be called "private" sacraments, with the reception of
which no one is concerned but the recipient; but all the others are
social as well as religious ceremonies. Our burial rites, too, are occasions of great ceremoniousness which must be correctly performed. It
thus becomes the duty of all good Catholics to know and to perform
the social duties and privileges accompanying these occasions of
churchly ceremony. These social duties are secondary to the spiritual
duties and privileges also involved, but only to them.

The primary purpose of this book, therefore, is to define and explain for laymen the social duties and privileges entailed in the reception of the sacraments and in the social functions accompanying them.
It is not in any sense intended to be a spiritual guide, as the author is
not qualified to write such a volume; but due cognizance has been
taken of the fact that what is acceptable socially often stems from what
is spiritually licit. Therefore, in this description of social duties a brief
account is given of the spiritual obligations also. The author has
attempted to stress the point—which cannot be made too often—that,
in all the matters discussed, the opinions and preferences of the
reader's own pastor and the customs of his parish and diocese are to
be preferred and followed whenever they differ in some respects from
the very general rules laid down in this book.

The sacraments of the Catholic Church according to the Roman
Rite are the same everywhere—else the Church would not be true to
Her title of Universal. (The Roman Rite is the only one dealt with in
this book because the very great majority of Americans follow the
Roman Rite.) Around the reception of these sacraments each nation
and each people have woven an embroidery of customs and pious

practices peculiar to each and characteristic of them. A Polish wedding is quite different from an Italian one. Our Canadian and Mexican neighbors are much stricter in observing mourning customs than we in the United States. The material in this volume is an attempt to gather between two covers the currently acceptable social practices employed by Catholics of taste in the United States.

There is also a reason why the general code of behavior of Catholics differs at some points from that of our non-Catholic friends. This is because, wherever we go and whatever we do, our behavior is judged as *the behavior of a Catholic*. Always and everywhere, we are ambassadors from our Church to the world. Non-Catholics, rightly or wrongly, form their opinions of the Church, not from the ideals She holds up to us, but by our individual success or failure in living up to them.

A Catholic who publicly flouts the laws of abstinence renders them meaningless and pharisaical to non-Catholic observers. A Catholic athlete who loses his temper and clouts an opponent not only commits the capital sin of anger but bears witness to all observers that "those Catholics" do not take the capital sins very seriously. Thus the very fact of our Catholicism imposes upon us an obligation to behave courteously, honorably, and *in a wholly Catholic manner at all times*. To help you to do so is the second purpose of this book.

The third subject covered here springs from the fact that we American Catholics are well-integrated members of our various communities. All of us include among our friends Protestants and Jews whom we dearly love, and who love us. These friends often wish to share our joy, to demonstrate the fact that they do at our christenings, weddings, ordinations etc., and to offer us sympathy in a time of bereavement. Sometimes they are prevented from doing so through lack of knowledge as to what they may acceptably do within the framework of our Faith. Catholics are sometimes prevented from sharing in the lives of our non-Catholic friends for the same reason.

Therefore this book attempts to tell members of each of the three great American religious communities what they may do for one another on some of these occasions—not only what is acceptable and unacceptable, but why. To know is to understand. It is the author's dear hope that these brief practical explanations will clear up a number of current misunderstandings and help all of us to live together happily, with love and forbearance.

American Catholic Etiquette

1

Baptism

All power in heaven and on earth has been given to me. Go, therefore, and make disciples of all nations, baptizing them in the name of the Father, and of the Son, and of the Holy Spirit, teaching them to observe all that I have commanded you; and behold, I am with you all days, even unto the consummation of the world (Matthew 28:18–20).

BAPTISM OF INFANTS

Time

A healthy child should be baptized during his first two weeks of life. Usually the ceremony is performed on the second Sunday after birth. It should not be delayed except for grave reasons and upon consultation with one's pastor.

The hour for the ceremony is determined by the custom of the parish to which the family belongs. Many parishes set the hour for baptisms directly after the latest Sunday Mass, but this is not always the case. One should not ask to have the ceremony performed at a special hour to suit one's convenience, but should concur in the custom of the parish. One should notify the parish office in advance of the date on which one intends to have the child baptized.

Place

A child should be baptized in his own parish church except under unusual circumstances. This is standard practice, and has a number of practical advantages: it enrolls the child in his parish, aids in making the parish census, and provides a permanent repository for the baptismal record and the information that it contains, which is of value in later years. The child may need the certificate for "proof" of birth and will certainly need it to receive First Communion, confirmation, and the sacrament of matrimony.

Some exceptions to this rule are: if the child is born while the parents are living in a summer home or out of the parish because the father is on military duty. If the child has an uncle or other relative who is a priest in another local parish, permission might be requested to let the relative baptize the child in that parish, but the more common practice is to ask for permission to allow him to perform the baptism in the child's parish church.

Officiating Priest

The priest who performs the ceremony is the pastor or any of his assistants to whom he may delegate the duty for that day. If one has a relative or very intimate friend in holy orders whom one wishes to officiate, one asks permission for him to do so from one's pastor. Such permission is almost always granted, but if it is withheld, the parents must acquiesce cheerfully and without comment. This is a matter that lies wholly within the province of one's pastor.

Godparents

Canon law requires that a child have one baptismal sponsor, who may be either a man or a woman, without regard to the sex of the infant to be baptized. It *permits* a child to have two sponsors at most; when there are two, one shall be a man, the other a woman. Common American practice is to employ two sponsors.

The godparents must be Catholics. Objection to this point may be raised by the non-Catholic partner in a mixed marriage, who wishes to have one of his non-Catholic relatives as a godparent. But such an objection can come only from a lack of understanding of the duties of a baptismal sponsor. To ask a relative or a friend to be a godparent to a child does not confer a social honor; rather, it asks the prospective sponsor to assume an obligation which cannot be entered into lightly. When anyone agrees to become a child's godparent, he takes upon himself the responsibility to see to it that the child is brought up a good Catholic. If the parents are themselves good Catholics who do their duty toward their child, the sponsor's obligation is a slight one. But one can never depend upon its being so. The parents may fall away from their Faith. They may die, and the child's upbringing be entrusted to non-Catholics. They may hold their responsibilities too lightly. In these cases, and in *all* cases where the godparent feels that the child is being neglected in the spiritual realm, he must assert his rights and perform his duties as the spiritual parent of the child. This can be an unpleasant or even painful task. One should be aware that all this is implicit whenever one is asked to become a godparent.

Parents should bear all this in mind when selecting godparents. One should not ask mere acquaintances to accept such an obligation. One should ask only devout practicing Catholics who are friends of long standing or relatives.

The father, mother, wife, or husband of the person to be baptized cannot be his sponsor, nor can children under the age of fourteen, except with permission of the pastor. It is imprudent to choose an elderly person for sponsor, as it is reasonable to assume that he might not live long enough to fulfill his duty to his godchild.

A true spiritual relationship exists between godparent and godchild, but not between the two godparents. A godparent and godchild may not marry without a dispensation.

Often parents wish to have for godparents for the child relatives or friends who live at a distance, who cannot come for the ceremony. The parent writes the friend and asks him to be the child's godparent. The friend accepts, also in writing. His name appears on the baptismal certificate as godparent, and all the obligations, rights and duties of the position are his. To act for the real godparent at the ceremony, the parents, with the approval of the true godparent, may ask any Catholic friend or acquaintance. This proxy has no duties beyond those on the baptismal day, when he attends the ceremony and, if a woman, holds the child, or, if a man, makes the responses in place of the actual godparent. No spiritual relationship is considered to exist between the child and the proxy godparent, and the proxy assumes no spiritual responsibility for the child, even if his true godparent should die. But the consent of the true godparent to act in that capacity must be obtained in writing, so that it can be shown to the officiating priest when the baptismal certificate is made out.

Among Protestants an invitation to be a godparent is an honor that must be accepted. A refusal is socially impossible. Among Catholics, this is not true. If for any good reason one feels unable to fulfill the obligations of a godparent, it is not only proper to decline but one is bound in conscience to do so. Some valid reasons would be: serious ill-health, of which the world may not know; a position which will require one to live abroad; a decision to take holy orders, etc. One need not give the actual reason. An explanation that for "personal reasons one cannot yet divulge, one does not feel qualified to accept," is sufficient. The parents accept such a refusal without comment. In such cases, which are of course quite rare, it is a pleasant gesture to send a substantial present to the baby, if one is able.

Naming the Baby

The Church desires that the name of a saint be given a child in baptism, in order that the child may imitate his virtues and have him for a protector and intercessor in Heaven. It is an ancient custom, stretching back into the early days of the Church, and a beautiful one, which should be acceded to as a matter of course. This is the sole spiritual requirement in naming a baby.

Quite often the saint's name which one selects for one's child is also the name of a relative and is chosen for that reason. But whatever the reason for selecting the saint-name, it is a worthy custom for the parents to familiarize themselves with the life of the saint in question, with his virtues, sufferings and trials, and to teach the child about "his" saint's life when the child is old enough to comprehend it. It is well to teach him to ask for his namesake's intercession in time of trouble or need.

There are many names which have been borne by several saints— Francis, Catherine, Teresa, John, etc. In such cases, decide which saint it is you wish to honor—and what a hard choice it will be! Who could choose between Francis of Assisi, Francis de Sales, and Francis Xavier! In these cases, it would be advisable to familiarize oneself with the life stories of all the saints who had borne the name in question, to emphasize for the child how noble is the name he bears. But one should still choose one of these great souls and designate him the child's name saint.

To the saint's name may be added a second name, which may be, but does not have to be, a saint's name. American children seldom have more than two given names; many have only one. In the discussion about selecting names which is to follow, some names will be discussed which are not saint's names. In all such cases, we are considering their use as second names, to be joined with a saint-name.

On the question of taste in selecting a name, one could write volumes! Parents should give consideration to the fact that a name is perhaps one's most intimate possession, and that its suitability, or lack of it, is believed to exercise a profound influence upon the child.

Care should be taken that no name is chosen which could be used to ridicule. Avoid names that lend themselves to silly puns, particularly when they are to be combined with surnames which are also common nouns (Walker, Post, Coward, Dresser, etc.). "Iva" and "Ima" are the worst offenders in this respect. A child was named Iva French, which seems harmless enough. She had, however, the misfortune to marry a man named Cook! "Rose" as a second name is sometimes awkward; one should remember that "rose" is also a verb.

Names which result in initials that spell a word or anything silly can also cause a child misery. Carol Ann Thomas is a sensible name, but any girl so named will be called a "C.A.T." by her teasing friends. W.O.W., U.G.H., and P.O.P. are similarly unfortunate.

Some baptismal names have unpleasant connotations. "Reginald," "Guy," and "Percy" are considered "sissy" in America, although they are suitable for English boys. "Hiram," 'Silas," "Erastus," and "Samantha" are currently regarded as "rube" or comic names. "Mary Ann" and "Maria" were once so considered, but are recovering their respectability. Maria must be correctly pronounced with a short "i."

Families with common surnames like "Miller," "Dwyer," and "Johnson" should give some thought to choosing distinctive baptismal names, merely as a means of identification. It is sometimes a good idea to use the mother's maiden name for the second baptismal name. William Robert Johnson is sure to have a duplicate in almost any community; William *Rice* (the mother's maiden name) Johnson is less common. But watch out for pitfalls in using family names too: John McAfee McSorley is impressive, but who wants "J. McA. McS." for initials?

Families with surnames that reflect unmistakably their national origin should choose baptismal names that are plain English, or are of the same origin. "Gretchen Schwartz," "Moira FitzPatrick," or "Angelina Bellontoni" are suitable, but "Gretchen FitzPatrick," "Angelina Schwartz," and "Moira Bellontoni" are not! "Michelle Murphy" is affected; "Michelle Patnaude" is not.

Refrain from being whimsical or humorous in naming your baby. Always remember the frightful example of the prominent Texan who actually named his daughters Ima and Iva Hogg! This should prevent persons named Bull from calling their children "John" or "Lotta." The Joneses should not name a child "Casey"; the Hoods should avoid "Robin"; the Monroes should not select "Marilyn."

Famous names of any kind, even though dignified and selected because of admiration for the originals, are usually a burden. George Washington Smith and Woodrow Wilson Miller probably wish they had been named William or Henry.

If one is a direct or collateral descendent of a distinguished person, there are special factors to consider. Family pride and affection plead for continued use of the famous name. But even here, taste and euphony must be weighed. Peter Schuyler TenEyck sounds strong and dignified, but Napoleon Bonaparte Nesselrode is a dreadful mouthful!

There are pitfalls, too, in selecting one's saint-name. Americans do not call their children "Jesus"; the name is held too sacred to give to a human child. But among Mexicans this is a favorite name. One nation avoids it; the other employs it, both for the same reason: to honor our Savior! "Lazarus" and "Magdalene" are saints' names, but because of their connotations they are not a happy selection. The mothers who named their daughters "Ava Maria McNulty" and "Madonna Dommermuth" intended to honor the Blessed Mother. But the names fall so oddly upon American ears that their bearers are sure to be teased. Better to call both girls Mary; it fulfills the same purpose without making the children suffer for it.

Let the name be easy to say, easy to understand, and euphonious. "Emily Esthyr Estabrook" is hard to say, but "Kevin Kenneth Kelly" comes *too* trippingly off the tongue. It is better to be trite (Mary Jane Smith) than pretentious (Lucretia LaVerne Smith) but try not to be either. Avoid names that are fashionable; they will not always be so, and they tend to "date" their owner. Avoid alliteration; it sounds theatrical.

Some other points to consider: do not use three one-syllable or three two-syllable names, like Paul James Walch, or Sárah Éllen Dóty. There is nothing wrong with any of these names, but when so combined they sound like a soldier clumping along in heavy boots. Three three-syllable names, especially if all accented on the same syllable, sound like a waltz. (Chrístopher Wórthington Dóolittle.) Do not use names which repeat one consonant, or the same vowel sound, as in Eleanor Julia Ellington (too many "l"s) or Candace Ann Brannigan (too many "an" sounds).

Be careful with nicknames. *Never* call a boy Junior, even though he is. It is in the worst possible taste. Do not call children Baby, Buzzie, Sister, Buddie, Sonnie, Toots, etc. The names will be outgrown, but may not be shaken off. If you do not intend to call your child by either of his baptismal names (really the sensible thing to do), then at least select and use, from infancy onward, a nickname which will not be absurd or undignified when he grows up.

Naming a boy for his father is frequently done. Some problems occasionally arise from so doing, which are caused mainly by a confusion that seems to exist concerning the correct use of "senior" and "junior."

A man named Michael Francis Ward has a son who is named for him. The man's name continues to be Michael Francis Ward; his son's name, as long as his father lives, is Michael Francis Ward, Jr., or junior. (If *junior* is written in full, it is not capitalized; if it is abbreviated, it is always capitalized.) The older man is never properly referred to as Michael Francis Ward, senior, especially in writing. He may be so referred to in common speech, to differentiate him from his son, particularly when the son becomes an adult and the two are in business together. But such a usage is never correct. It is better to say "the senior Mr. Ward" if one wishes to make a distinction.

Upon the death of his father, Michael Francis Ward, Jr., becomes Michael Francis Ward. If his father leaves a widow, a problem arises. The widow's correct name continues to be Mrs. Michael Francis Ward. But this is now also the correct name of her daughter-in-law who was formerly Mrs. Michael Francis Ward, Jr. To avoid confusion, the elder woman may have her charge accounts made out to Mrs. Michael Francis Ward, senior, and employ this usage in all business relationships. But it is never employed socially, and should never be engraved on a card or invitation. Socially, the older woman may be addressed simply as Mrs. Ward, or as Mrs. Michael Francis Ward, despite the danger of confusion. A widow is never addressed as Mrs. Martha Ward, either socially or in business.

If during his father's lifetime Michael Francis Ward, junior, has a son who is named for him, the distinction is as follows: the grandfather is Michael Francis Ward. His son is Michael Francis Ward, Jr. The grandson is Michael Francis Ward III, because he is the third bearer of that name. When the grandfather dies, his son becomes Michael Francis Ward, and the grandson becomes Michael Francis Ward, Jr., during his father's lifetime.

A boy named for a living relative *not* his father is Michael Francis Ward II. This is the only time when the numeral "II" may correctly be used. The child is the second of that name but is not "junior." Usually the child so called has been named for a grandfather (but his father is not a "junior") or an uncle or granduncle. Upon the death of the relative for whom he is named, the child becomes Michael Francis Ward.

If in later years other relatives of the original—and still living— Michael Francis Ward wish to give another child his name, that child is called Michael Francis Ward III, or even IV or V. But the practice is an unfortunate one, because, upon the death of the elder Michael Francis Ward, all the others become simply Michael Francis Ward, and the confusion resulting is bound to be frequent and annoying. Sons of Michael Francis Ward II, III, or IV who are named for their father are, during his lifetime, each called Michael Francis Ward, Jr. The difficulties created when a single family persists in repeatedly using one name are very real, and cannot be obviated by the various members continuing to use II, III, etc., after the death of the common ancestor for whom all were named. We do not have family dynasties in America, and to use these numerals after the proper time for so doing has passed is considered affected.

The title "junior," and the numerals just discussed, are never used by an unmarried woman, even though she is named for her mother or grandmother. One is never Harriet Catherine Swallow, Jr., or Mildred Louise Trombley, II. But one is correctly Mrs. Michael Francis Ward, junior, if one's husband is named for his still-living father.

Baptismal Robes

It is traditional for infants of both sexes to wear baptismal robes, usually long-skirted and lavishly trimmed with embroidery or lace. This is the one time when a baby may be so dressed without violating the canons of good taste. White is better than a pastel color. Fine lawn, nainsook, unstarched organdy, handkerchief linen, or even very fine white silk are suitable materials. Chiffon, satin and taffeta are not. Ideally, the robe and its accompanying petticoat and bonnet should be handmade. Any lace that trims it should be handmade also, and any embroidery should be handwork. When this is not possible, the dress should be of a fine delicate material, made very simply. The nicest robe of all is the one that is handed down through the generations and has been worn by many family babies. In time, such a robe is a treasure.

Recently boy babies have worn white suits and "manly" caps. The effect is rather droll, but it may be a fashion that will pass. Certainly it violates tradition, so is not recommended.

The child should be suitably dressed for protection against the weather. Coat and bonnet should be removed for the ceremony, and the neck of the robe should be unbuttoned, so that the priest may easily anoint the breast and back of the baby.

Guests

It is necessary only for the godparents and the father of the child to attend the baptismal ceremony. The mother may go if she feels well enough. Grandparents and other close relatives may attend if they wish, but if several babies are being baptized, all save the godparents should remain in the body of the church and not crowd the space around the font.

Attire of Guests

Guests at the baptismal ceremony or the party that follows it wear the same kind of clothes that they would wear to High Mass. For women, this means suits or modestly cut dresses, always with hat, stockings and gloves. Men do not wear sport clothes, but in summer may wear white linen or dark summer suits. White shirts and conservative ties are always worn. It is also correct for men to wear the so-called "informal" type of afternoon attire: black or oxford-gray single-breasted coat, striped trousers, with the customary accessories; but this is really quite formal, and is seldom seen nowadays.

The Offering

The father of the infant to be baptized makes an offering to the priest who performs the ceremony. An impression seems to have arisen that the offering should be made by the child's godfather, but this is not correct. *The offering is made by the child's parent.* It is placed in a plain white envelope with the parent's calling card and is handed unobtrusively to the priest before the group leaves the church. This offering is not a fee but an expression of gratitude for the pastoral care given a congregation by its pastor. The offering is therefore always turned over to the pastor of the church where the ceremony occurs, even though the ceremony was performed by an assistant priest or a family friend or relative in holy orders. In the latter case, if one wishes also to make an offering to the priest actually performing the ceremony, two offerings should be prepared and placed in two envelopes, one bearing the pastor's name, the other that of the priest performing the baptism. The offering should be commensurate with one's income and with the manner in which one is celebrating the occasion.

Photographs

Most families like to have a pictorial record of this occasion. Most churches permit pictures to be taken during the baptism. On this, as on all churchly occasions, the photographer should do his work as inconspicuously as possible, and should be dressed as the guests are.

The Christening Party

There is no social precedent that requires entertaining following a baptismal ceremony. Often the young mother does not feel strong enough to attempt to entertain. Money problems frequently loom large at this time. But many people feel that a simple celebration of important family happenings—baptisms, birthdays, First Communions— makes for a happy and united family life. Sometimes the effort looms mountainous to a harassed young mother, but in the end the results seem well worth it.

A traditional christening party is basically simple. The parents of the child invite to their home, directly after the ceremony, the officiating priest and the godparents. They may add any others they care to include—grandparents, spouses of godparents—but the priest and godparents are the only ones who must be asked. The priest is seldom free at such a time to accept the invitation, but it must always be proffered to him.

To the guests the parents serve a small, white cake, iced like a bridal cake, called a baby cake, and champagne or champagne punch to toast the health of the little new Christian. This is all that is required, and if kept to this minimum, it is really not much trouble or expense.

Young people who live informally and are not in the habit of drinking or serving wines may wonder why champagne is specified for this occasion. It is because this party is in itself a little ceremony, and champagne is the traditional drink with which to observe it. Only a glass or two is offered to the guests; this is drunk as a toast. Guests and host alike should remember that they are celebrating the reception of a sacrament, and should behave accordingly. Sherry, port, or madeira may be served, but champagne is put at the head of the list because it is the most festive of wines and, when served in small quantities, costs little more than the others.

If one wishes, one may celebrate far more elaborately. In addition to, or in place of the baby cake, many people serve the type of food offered at cocktail parties. This includes anything that may be eaten with the fingers—salted nuts, olives, small, open-faced sandwiches, potato chips, carrot sticks, tidbits on toothpicks, etc.

Either set of grandparents may give the baptismal party if the parents are willing; it usually makes for a happy occasion, as it relieves the new mother of the strain of entertaining at this time. If the baptism is held in the morning, it may be followed by a luncheon, if in the afternoon, by a tea, or the grandparents may choose to give the traditional type party just described.

In any case, the guest of honor is always any priest who may attend. If more than one is present, one's pastor is the first honored guest, the other priest, the second. A bishop or monsignor, of course, has precedence over any other priest. Otherwise the precedence between two priests is determined by their seniority in holy orders. If no clergy are present, the godparents are the honor guests at any entertaining at which the parents are hosts. If the grandparents are hosts, the parents of the child are the honor guests.

The question of whom to honor is unimportant if the entertaining is the traditional christening party, or a tea, or a luncheon served buffet style; but at a seated luncheon the precedence must be determined to decide who occupies the seats of honor at the right of the host and hostess.

The refreshments and style of service follow the customary forms for luncheons and teas, except that the service of intoxicants is held to a strict minimum; usually the champagne toasts are served just before, during, or after the food.

Baptismal Gifts

Godparents always give their godchild a baptismal gift. If the sponsors are a married pair, they may give one present, but it should be of more value than one of the gifts when two are given. If the sponsors are not a married couple, each gives a gift. The traditional ones are a silver mug and a silver porringer. A silver knife, fork, and spoon in a child's size is also a popular gift. One may of course give anything one wishes; the value of the present depends upon the financial status of the giver and his relation to and affection for the child. If one is able, a really substantial present should be made. Less expensive ones which are suitable for the occasion are: gold baby pins, gold or sterling silver religious medals, a statue of the Blessed Mother or the Infant Jesus, a crucifix, a baptismal bonnet, a baby blanket or a carriage robe. More valuable presents might be: a gold cross and chain, a painting with a religious subject suitable for the nursery, the baptismal robes, the start of a pearl necklace, a savings account in which a substantial deposit has been made, stocks or bonds, or an endowment insurance policy.

No one save the godparents is obligated to give a child a present at the time of baptism, but proxy godparents usually do and so do grandparents. If they gave the baby a valuable present at birth, the baptismal gift may be a trifle. But many Catholic grandparents wait until the baptismal day to give their present, and then it is something substantial. Traditionally, a baptismal gift should be something lasting that the child can enjoy in later life, like most of the things mentioned above. But the grandparents may, if they prefer, give a baby carriage or nursery furniture, or some similar item for immediate use.

Any friend or relative who wants to do so may of course give the baby a baptismal gift. Almost anything considered suitable for a birth present is suitable for this occasion. If the present has a religious connotation, all the better, but this is not a requirement.

EMERGENCY BAPTISM

An infant who is in danger of death prior to having received the sacrament of solemn baptism should be baptized privately at once. Unbaptized adults in danger of death who have at any time indicated a desire for baptism should also be privately baptized immediately. Any man, woman or child, Catholic or not, who is physically and mentally capable of doing so may administer private baptism in case of emergency, but parents should not baptize their children under such circumstances if there is present anyone else who can do so.

Such a baptism is administered by pouring ordinary water on the forehead of the person to be baptized, while saying at the same time, "I baptize thee in the name of the Father, and of the Son, and of the Holy Spirit." The act of pouring and the saying of the words should be simultaneous and the same person must do both.

Regular reception of the sacrament of baptism is called solemn baptism, and is a more elaborate ceremony. Parents of a child who has received a private baptism while in danger of death are obligated to see to it, if the child subsequently recovers his health, that he is taken to church to receive the supplemental ceremonies of solemn baptism that are omitted in a private baptism.

An adult who has been privately baptized while in danger of death and subsequently recovers is personally obligated to receive the supplemental ceremonies of solemn baptism.

ADULT BAPTISM

The Ceremony

Adult baptism is usually the baptism of a convert and is his reception into the Faith. The theological problems involved are intricate; each case must be judged on its particular circumstances and will be so judged by the priest who has given the convert his instructions, by the pastor who baptizes him, or both.

It must first be determined whether or not the convert has ever been baptized. This apparently simple fact is sometimes difficult to ascertain. If it can be determined, without question, that he is unbaptized, regular solemn baptism is administered, as in the case of cradle Catholics. Original sin and all the sins of his past life to that moment are removed by the reception of the sacrament of baptism; the convert may receive Holy Communion immediately, without making a confession.

No one may receive the sacrament of baptism more than once. Therefore, in the case of a convert who has been baptized outside the Church, the validity of the ceremony in the eyes of the Church must be determined. Since the validity of such a baptism is often difficult to determine due to the passage of time and a number of delicate theological problems, the Church usually takes care of the problem by administering conditional baptism.

In such a case, the convert first makes a profession of faith after which he is baptized conditionally. The convert then makes his first confession and is given *conditional* absolution. This absolution is conditional because if the conditional baptism is valid the convert has just been cleansed of original sin and all the sins of his past life to that moment, and thus had no need of absolution. But if the earlier baptism was valid, then the sins which he has since committed must be absolved by confession before he can receive Holy Communion.

Sponsors

An adult convert has sponsors, just as a child does. A wife, husband, father, mother, or fiance may not be a sponsor because of the spiritual relationship contracted.

Saint-Name

An adult takes a saint's name in baptism, just as a child does. If he already has a saint's name as one of his legal names, he may chose to take that one; if not, he chooses one. He is not obligated to take this name by legal process, nor to use it, if he does not wish to. It will appear on the baptismal record, but not on subsequent church records —wedding certificate, death notice, etc.—unless he so chooses.

Entertaining

The reception of baptism by an adult is usually an occasion of profound joy to the recipient, who may have reached this point in his life after a period of spiritual travail. Sometimes this feeling is so deep that he does not want any social observance of the occasion. This is socially correct, if he so chooses. But frequently, too, the newly-baptized soul is overflowing with joy and wishes his loved ones to "rejoice with me." The convert may properly act as his own host. His parents, mate, children, or other close friends may properly entertain in honor of the occasion, in the fashion described under "The Christening Party." The "baby" cake should be omitted, unless one wishes to serve it as symbolic of the birth of his life in the Church. Let all remember that this party is a ceremony, that any intoxicants should be served and drunk as toasts, as symbols of rejoicing, and should be indulged in with great moderation.

NON-CATHOLIC BAPTISM

It sometimes happens that the child of a mixed marriage is baptized outside the Church. This can only occur when the Catholic parent ignores his responsibilities and the non-Catholic parent is faithless to his vows to rear the child in the Church. A helpless infant is thus robbed of his spiritual birthright. The matter can only be an occasion of deep sorrow to any Catholic relatives or friends of the family. Neither the ceremony nor any entertaining to follow may be attended by Catholics, nor may the occasion be marked as a happy one by the sending of a present.

Regarding the Protestant baptism of the child of Protestant parents: a Catholic cannot be a sponsor or official witness to a Protestant baptism, and Catholics may not attend the baptismal service.

Under certain special circumstances, a Catholic may attend a christening party following such a service, and even give a gift of a secular nature, as follows:

a) When the Catholic (a convert) is related to the child being baptized.

b) When the Catholic is a business partner or a very intimate friend of the Protestant family.

2

Penance and Extreme Unction

PENANCE

The disciples therefore rejoiced at the sight of the Lord. He therefore said to them again, "Peace be to you." . . . When he had said this, he breathed upon them, and said to them, "Receive the Holy Spirit; whose sins you shall forgive, they are forgiven them; and whose sins you shall retain, they are retained" (John 20:20–23).

Introduction

The sacraments of penance and extreme unction are the only ones which have no social rites attached to them. That is why both are discussed in this chapter. Nothing need be said of them here except to give a brief account of the spiritual requirements for valid reception and the proper behavior involved.

Spiritual Requirements

The spiritual requirements for worthy reception of the sacrament of penance are:

a) Examination of conscience.

b) Sorrow for our sins.

c) A firm purpose of not sinning again.

d) Confession. This means confession to a duly ordained priest of all the mortal sins committed since the last confession and such venial sins as one may recall; it includes the number of times such offenses have been committed.

e) Willingness to perform whatever penance the priest imposes. The usual penances require the recitation of a number of prayers. In the case of very serious offenses, the penance may also consist of fasting and almsgiving, or other acts of charity.

One may ask to receive the sacrament of penance at any reasonable

time. This is particularly true in any spiritual emergency, or "dark
night of the soul." Parishes have regular hours for hearing confessions,
and it is best to go to confession at this time, if possible, out of consideration for the heavy working schedules of our priests. But this is
not to be interpreted as meaning that one may not ask to have one's
confession heard at any time that one's spiritual welfare requires it.

The usual place for receiving the sacrament of penance is in the
confessionals provided in all parish churches. For the benefit of non-
Catholic readers, it may be of interest to explain that a confessional is
merely two small cubicles adjoining one another but separated by a
wall in which there is a small screened opening to talk through. The
confessor sits on one side; the penitent kneels on the other. Some
churches include an earphone for the hard of hearing. In others a
special confessional in a secluded spot, such as the sacristy, is provided
to allow the priest to speak loudly to the deaf penitent.

Behavior

A penitent should take time properly to examine his conscience and
to determine what he has to say to his confessor before entering the
confessional. This is for his own soul's good, as it enables him to make
a worthy confession. It is also good manners, as it prevents him from
staying too long in the confessional, taking up the priest's time and that
of waiting penitents.

A penitent should, while awaiting his turn to go to confession, stand
far enough from the confessional so as to be unable to hear anything
that may be said in it.

A penitent should *never* push his way ahead of others waiting to
be heard. This is not only inexcusably bad manners, it is also, considering the place and the purpose, uncharitable and unchristian. But if
someone should push his way into the waiting line ahead of you, do
not glare and show your displeasure. "Offer up" this little trial to our
Lord as a sacrifice, and be both a good Catholic and a gentleman.

A penitent should always behave quietly and reverently, remembering Who is present on the altar. School-children going to confession sometimes forget this and giggle and whisper among themselves
or tramp about noisily. Parents should caution their children about this.

In the confessional, the penitent should speak in the lowest audible
tone. Should one inadvertently overhear any part of what is said to or
by another in Confession, one must *never* repeat it, and should endeavor to forget it immediately.

Out of consideration for others, one should avoid choosing the time
of one of the great feasts, such as Easter or Christmas, for making a

general confession. Since a general confession takes so much longer than an ordinary confession, it imposes a hardship on the busy priest and the many other waiting penitents. This does *not* mean that a general confession is forbidden at such a time, and one may certainly be made on such an occasion if one feels that one's spiritual health requires it. It merely means that it is a courteous act to defer it to a less crowded occasion if one may safely do so.

Dress

The proper costume for going to confession is the same as on all other occasions when one is entering the church. When possible, one should be dressed both neatly and formally. When not possible, school or working clothes are permissible. A handkerchief or bit of tissue on the head are in the worst possible taste. Women should buy and keep in their purse the small prayer veils now available, for unplanned visits to church. But if the only alternatives are wearing a handkerchief on the head or staying away from confession, a handkerchief may be worn.

EXTREME UNCTION

> Is any one among you sick? Let him bring in the presbyters of the Church, and let them pray over him, anointing him with oil in the name of the Lord. And the prayer of faith will save the sick man, and the Lord will raise him up, and if he be in sins, they shall be forgiven him (James 5:14–15).

Spiritual Requirements

All baptized Catholics who have attained the use of reason (seven years or more) and who are in danger of death from illness or accident should receive extreme unction. The patient need not be—preferably should not be—*in extremis.* He need only be gravely ill, or seriously injured, so that there is a danger of death resulting. To receive extreme unction worthily, one must have the intention of so receiving it, and be in a state of grace. Because of this latter requirement, extreme unction is preceded by confession whenever the physical condition of the patient permits it. This is why it is preferable whenever possible to send for a priest to administer extreme unction before a patient has lapsed into unconsciousness.

If the sick person is unconscious when the priest is called, so that intent cannot be determined nor his confession heard, the sacrament of extreme unction is administered conditionally.

In case of sudden death a priest should always be called. Absolution and extreme unction can be administered conditionally for several hours after signs of life have ceased, because we are not sure of the moment when the soul leaves the body.

A healthy person in danger of death, such as a soldier about to go into battle or a man condemned to death, may not receive extreme unction. The soldier may prepare for battle by penance and Holy Communion; the condemned man may do the same, and is further sustained by prayers for the dying just prior to his execution. But the sacrament of extreme unction is administered only to give health and strength to the soul and sometimes to the body when we are in danger of death from illness, accident, or old age.

Preparations for Extreme Unction

Whenever time permits, the sickroom of the person about to receive extreme unction should be in perfect order, and the patient should be bathed and wearing fresh night clothing. A woman patient's costume should always be modest. Near the sickbed there should be a table covered with a white cloth and holding a crucifix, two lighted blessed candles, a vessel of holy water, a spoon, a dish with five or more bits of cotton, and a damask napkin.

If the priest comes bearing the Blessed Sacrament, as he will if the patient is conscious, he should be met at the door by a person bearing a lighted blessed candle and be conducted to the sickroom. If the patient is able to make a confession, he should be left alone with his confessor to do so. But all the family who are at home should be present in the sickroom for the anointing, the Viaticum, the Apostolic Benediction, and the prayers for the dying which follow extreme unction.

Viaticum is the name for Holy Communion given as part of extreme unction. It requires no eucharistic fast, and if the patient cannot take food, only a small particle of the Host is administered.

Whether an offering may be made to a priest who has administered extreme unction is the province of the bishop of the diocese. In some it is permitted; in many others it is discouraged as being unbecoming to the nature of the occasion. (See chapter on Holy Eucharist: Receiving Communion at Home.)

Request to Non-Catholics

A non-Catholic who is caring for a Catholic invalid in possible danger of death will be performing an act of Christian charity if she sends for a priest to attend the patient before he lapses into unconsciousness. A non-Catholic present at the scene of a serious accident to a Catholic can help him most by sending for *both* a priest and a physician.

Catholics should carry about with them at all times a card stating that they are Catholic, and requesting that a priest be called to attend them in case of accident. This is another good reason for wearing always a religious medal of some kind, since it will not be easily lost, and will identify one as a Catholic.

In a Catholic home the telephone number of the parish rectory should be posted in a conspicuous place, along with that of the fire and police department, and the family doctor, so that a stranger may find it quickly.

3

Holy Eucharist

❖❖❖❖❖

And while they were at supper, Jesus took bread, and blessed and broke, and gave it to his disciples, and said, "Take and eat; this is my body." And taking a cup, he gave thanks and gave it to them, saying, "All of you drink this; for this is my blood of the new covenant, which is being shed for many unto the forgiveness of sins" (Matthew 26:26–28).

SPIRITUAL REQUIREMENTS

Mother Church lays down two requirements for the valid reception of the sacrament of Holy Communion. They are:

1. The communicant must be in the state of grace, that is, free from mortal sin. This condition is fulfilled by making a worthy confession prior to the reception of the Eucharist. As long as one remains in the state of grace one may continue to receive the sacrament of Holy Communion without making another confession. When the reception of the Eucharist is not immediately preceded by confession, it is prudent to make an examination of conscience, to make sure one is free from mortal sin and to recall and ask forgiveness for any venial sins one may have committed. When some time has elapsed since receiving the sacrament of penance, pious people sometimes go to confession even though they are still in the state of grace. While such caution is commendable, it must be stressed that it is not required by the Church for worthy reception of Holy Eucharist: *the only requirement is that one be in the state of grace.*

2. Proper observance of the eucharistic fast. On March 25, 1957, the late Pope Pius XII issued new regulations for the eucharistic fast which made profound changes in and superseded the rules formerly governing it. These new rulings now bind the entire Roman Catholic world. They are:

23

a) Abstention from solid food and alcoholic beverages for three hours prior to the reception of Holy Communion.

b) Abstention from all liquids, other than water, for one hour prior to the reception of Holy Communion. This means that liquids such as tea, coffee, soft drinks, and even such nourishing beverages as clear broth and nonalcoholic eggnog may be taken up to one hour before receiving.

c) Water is not considered to break the fast, and may be taken at any time. This includes tap water, mineral water and carbonated water, but nothing to which flavoring or sugar may have been added.

d) People who are ill, even though not confined to bed, may take medicine in either liquid or solid form at any time, even though the medicine may contain alcohol. The ill or infirm may also take all nonalcoholic beverages before Holy Communion without any time limit. No special dispensation is required for these privileges.

e) These rules are the same for all Masses—morning, evening (after twelve noon) or midnight. One may not receive Holy Communion more than once in a single day, reckoning a day as from midnight to midnight.

f) These rules apply to all the faithful, including children more than seven years of age who are making their First Holy Communion. They are identical for all, except that priests are obliged to reckon their fasting as prior to the hour at which they begin to say Mass, while the laity may measure it as prior to the time at which they receive the sacrament.

Brushing one's teeth does not break the fast. Neither does smoking, taking snuff, nor chewing tobacco, but, while these practices are not forbidden, one is urged to eschew them during the fasting period.

THE EASTER DUTY

Church law requires all who are seven years of age or more to receive Holy Communion at least once a year during the Easter season. The term is usually considered to mean the time between the first Sunday in Lent and Trinity Sunday.

FIRST HOLY COMMUNION

The Church desires that a baptized child who has reached the age of reason shall be permitted to make his first confession and receive Holy Communion. The age of reason is usually considered to be about seven years, although it may vary from child to child. He should be able to understand the significance of the sacraments and the instructions which he receives to prepare him for them. It is the solemn duty of both parents to see to it that the child receives the instructions and the sacraments when he has reached the proper age.

In parishes large enough to maintain a parochial school, the matter is a simple one. Regular First Communion classes are usually held twice a year, in the spring and fall. The Sisters who teach in the school give the instructions. Parochial school children receive them as a part of their daily instruction; a special class is held out of school hours for children not attending the school.

In smaller communities and remote areas the problem is more difficult but can always be resolved. In such localities parents should consult their pastor whenever a child reaches the age of reason and make arrangements for his instruction and reception of the sacraments.

Before discussing the social aspects of First Communion here are a few suggestions to mothers. Try to remember, as you are raising your family, that children's attitudes and opinions are formed almost wholly upon your own. The school and the views of their contemporaries have some weight; but until they reach the teen years it is *your* opinions, and *your* reactions that they value and imitate.

It is you, therefore, who can bring home to them the wonder and the joy of the great sacramental occasions. Do everything within your power to make the day of First Holy Communion meaningful. You do this by putting emphasis on the reception of the sacrament, and its significance. Help them to realize that it makes them a living temple of their Savior; that penance and the Holy Eucharist place in their own hands, for the remainder of their life, the power to obtain forgiveness of their sins and reunion with their divine Lord.

It is the sacraments that are important, far above their costumes, their gifts, or any entertaining you may do in honor of the occasion. But, once you have made sure that you have stressed the vital aspect of the day, you may do everything within your means, in the way of special clothing, gifts, and entertaining, to make it more memorable for your child.

Clothing

It is natural on this great day for parents to wish to dress their children, particularly their daughters, as handsomely as they can, always bearing in mind that, in ceremonial clothing for children, one should strive for delicacy and simplicity. If you are pressed for funds and cannot buy your daughter the expensive clothing you would like, do not let her be aware that this is the case. She will be perfectly happy with a simple costume, even one "inherited" from an older sister or cousin, if you appear pleased with it. But if you belittle it or apologize for it, she will be unhappy. Whatever your circumstances, remember this and act accordingly.

The parish church usually designates some sort of special costume for the little First Communicants, to enhance the importance and add to the beauty of the ceremony. This costume varies from parish to parish. Boys may wear blue suits and eton collars, or all-white suits. Little girls wear white dresses and veils. In recent years some parishes have had the children wear all-white replicas of their school uniforms, so that there would be no distinction between rich and poor. Still another recent innovation is for the children to wear little white academic caps and gowns, which may be rented. This is done to save the parents work and expense. Whatever the choice of the parish, the parents should acquiesce in it, regardless of their personal preferences in the matter. Here is another occasion on which the children's attitudes will be formed by those of their elders.

The costumes most commonly worn in this country are white blouses and dark blue shorts for boys and white dresses and veils for girls. The veils are often purchased in quantity and are identical; the dresses are individually selected. Lawn, handkerchief linen, organdie, voile, dotted swiss, and net are suitable materials. So is very soft taffeta, if trimmed only with smocking or picoting, but satin and tulle are not. Whether you can choose a costly costume or an inexpensive one, it is always good taste to keep it simple. This applies to the accessories also.

In Spain and other Catholic countries, well-to-do families have a charming custom which might well be adopted by families of means in our own land. In these countries, a wealthy family will dress its own child in an inexpensive costume and will completely dress a poor child in the same First Communion class. The gift is made anonymously.

In our fortunate country few families are so poor as to be unable to spend anything at all for their child's Communion clothing. But the custom could be adopted thus: consult the Sister in charge of the First Communion class and find out if any children in it are underprivileged. Arrange with her to make a secret gift of a sum of money—enough, say, to buy a pair of shoes—for one or several of these children. Do not let the recipients or anyone save the Sister know who made the gift.

Tell your child what you have done in her name and that the money was saved by buying her a simple costume, so that she may learn young that true charity, which is Christian love, is both a privilege and a personal sacrifice. If you feel, however, your child is too young to keep such a matter secret, do not tell her about it until she is old enough to understand it.

Entertaining

In some parishes a First Communion breakfast for children and parents is held in the church hall or school cafeteria. Women of the church societies prepare the breakfast and the parents of the children provide the funds for it. This is a pleasing custom, as it means that every child in the class will share in a celebration.

If this is not done in your parish, you should have a celebration breakfast of your own; or you might like to have a "special" dinner that evening, to which you invite the child's godparents, grandparents, and other favorite relatives. There is no social obligation to do this, but it is a nice thing to do for the child's sake. Grandparents sometimes like to be the hosts for this meal, and this is quite correct. If "Grandpa" wants to give the dinner at his club or at a restaurant, this would be a fine treat for the child also.

Gifts

No one is socially obligated to give a child a First Communion gift, but parents, godparents, grandparents, and other relatives and friends usually do so.

Some appropriate gifts are: First Communion rosary, prayer book, gloves, veil, shoes, underclothing, cross and chain, religious medal, book of Bible stories, picture book of the life of Christ, small holy water font for the bedside, crucifix to hang over the bed, statue of Jesus, Mary, or Joseph, or the child's name saint. In selecting a statue, make sure that the colors are not garish, and the carving or molding not too crude. One can now buy lovely statues carved of natural wood. Secular gifts appropriate to the child's age are also correct. A Protestant friend may offer a gift at this time if he wishes; in this event he might prefer to make a secular gift, such as a storybook, fountain pen, or camera.

FIRST COMMUNION OF CONVERTS

The First Holy Communion of converts is usually received directly after their baptism—or on the day following it. In either case, the two are so closely joined that they are celebrated, in the secular sense, together. The adult costume for First Holy Communion, as for baptism, is the same sort as one would wear to High Mass: hat, stockings, gloves, and a suit or modest dress for women. If a dress is worn, it must not have a low-cut neck, and must have some kind of sleeve, even in the warmest weather. Men wear conventional business suits. Sports clothing is not permissible, but a white or plain dark summer suit is. A man may also wear morning clothes with a short jacket, not a cutaway, but this is very formal, and not often seen.

RECEIVING COMMUNION IN THE HOME

Spiritual Requirements

Those who are confined through illness, injury, or infirmity, may, with their pastor's permission, receive Holy Communion in their home. If their condition requires it, the rules of fasting for the ill and infirm may be further relaxed; but this requires special dispensation from the pastor and need not be discussed here.

Preparing the Home for a Visit from Our Lord

It is a great privilege for everyone in the household when the Blessed Sacrament is brought into it. Unless the occasion is an emergency which does not allow for proper preparation one should demonstrate one's awareness of this by having one's home "swept and garnished."

The sickroom should be in perfect order. The patient should be bathed and wearing fresh clothing. The bed should be neat. Near it should be a small table covered with a clean white linen cloth. On this should be a crucifix, two lighted blessed candles, a small empty glass bowl, a vessel of holy water, and a white linen or damask napkin.

Proper Behavior

The priest who brings the Blessed Sacrament to the home should be met at the door by someone carrying a lighted blessed candle. (This may be one of the two which are to be on the table in the sickroom.) If possible, this person should be accompanied by another, to open the door and assist the priest in removing his outer coat and hat. If no second person is in the house, the one bearing the candle may set it down and assist the priest with his wraps. No one speaks, out of reverence for the Sacred Presence.

The priest is then taken to the sickroom, where he will at once prepare to give the Eucharist. If the sick person needs assistance in raising up to receive the sacrament, the lay person should give it. If he does not, all present kneel, and behave just as one does when Communion is offered at Mass. All who are in the home should be present in the room and kneeling when the sick person receives the sacrament.

After the sacrament has been given, and a proper period allowed for recollection and thanksgiving, the head of the house, the sick person, and others present, greet and thank the priest. One may offer him breakfast, but the offer will probably not be accepted, as he may have other duties requiring his immediate attention. Sometimes, if requested in advance, the priest will serve Communion to others present, but this is a rare privilege, and should be so regarded.

The Offering

Most Catholics, having had the Holy Eucharist brought into their home, feel a strong impulse to make an offering to their priest in gratitude for the blessing conferred upon them and in recognition of the personal inconvenience to which he may have been put. This is particularly true when one has an invalid in the home, to whom the priest may have brought the sacrament many times.

This is a matter that falls within the province of the bishop of the diocese; and in a few places it is permitted.

In many others it is frowned upon. The coming of the Holy Eucharist into a home is a treasure for which no man on earth can make adequate recompense; it is also a privilege to which the poorest and humblest Catholic is entitled as a child of the Church. To make an offering at this time for such a service is therefore distasteful to many and is not encouraged. The gesture, while not forbidden, is considered unbecoming.

COMMUNION AT MASS

Any question of manners or dress that might arise in connection with reception of Holy Communion at Mass, in the fashion in which one customarily receives it, is covered in the chapter "Behavior at Mass." It may be well, however, to include here one point from that section.

One should, if at all possible, be neatly and even formally dressed in one's best for attendance at Mass and reception of the Blessed Sacrament. But if one is going to or returning from school or work, it is both proper and commendable to receive in the costume suitable to the activity in which one is about to be, or has been, engaged, even though it is not such as one would have worn by choice to receive the sacrament. Thus a high school girl whose costume includes socks and a babushka may go to Communion so dressed, even though she would otherwise have worn stockings and hat. The same is true of a boy in blue jeans and jersey or a young child in a snowsuit. A nurse or waitress may wear her uniform. So may a bus driver or postman, and a laborer may properly receive in his working clothes, even though they are soiled by his day's labors.

It is, of course, always wrong to come to church in soiled clothes of any sort if one has had an opportunity to change into proper dress. But if the choice lies between receiving in soiled work clothes and not receiving, one should always choose to receive.

Willfully to choose to wear soiled, sloppy or overly-informal clothing is always wrong; so is immodest dress of any nature. The safe test in a doubtful case is to remember that our Lord can always read our hearts; if our intent is to honor Him and unite with Him in the holy sacrament, He looks beneath all outward symbols.

4

Confirmation

Now when the apostles in Jerusalem heard that Samaria had received the word of God, they sent to them Peter and John. On their arrival they prayed for them, that they might receive the Holy Spirit; for as yet he had not come upon any of them, but they had only been baptized in the name of the Lord Jesus (Acts 8:14–16).

SPIRITUAL SIGNIFICANCE

Confirmation is the sacrament through which the Holy Spirit comes to us in a special way and enables us to profess our faith as strong and perfect Christians and soldiers of Jesus Christ. The word *confirmation* means "a strengthening." A Catholic who is confirmed becomes a soldier of Christ, always ready to profess his faith openly and practice it fearlessly, and ready to suffer anything, even death, rather than deny Christ.

The usual minister of confirmation is the bishop. Two exceptions to this rule are made to fit special cases. They are:

Those in danger of death from sickness, accident, or old age may be confirmed by their pastor or parish administrator.

Priests in missionary lands are sometimes delegated by the Holy Father to administer confirmation. Most priests of the Eastern Rites also have this privilege. But the ordinary minister is still the bishop of one's own diocese.

ELIGIBILITY

A candidate for confirmation must be a baptized person in the state of grace. Canon law requires bishops of each diocese to provide for the administration of the sacrament in every parish in their diocese at least once every five years. An American child is usually confirmed upon the first occasion that the sacrament is administered in his parish after he has reached the age of seven. He may thus be anywhere between seven and twelve when he actually receives the sacrament, and is usually about age ten. A baptized person of more than seven years cannot, without sin, neglect to receive confirmation when the opportunity presents itself. It is also the solemn duty of parents to see to it that a child of more than seven years is confirmed at the earliest opportunity.

SPIRITUAL REQUIREMENTS

A candidate for confirmation must be baptized, must have been thoroughly instructed in the truths of our religion, and must be in the state of grace when he receives the sacrament. A person not in the state of grace when he receives the sacrament commits the sin of sacrilege and receives no grace from it. He nonetheless receives the sacrament validly; if and when he regains the state of grace, he will then receive the graces of confirmation.

SPONSORS

A confirmand has a sponsor of his own sex. The sponsor must be a baptized, confirmed Catholic who was not his godparent at baptism. The other requirements are the same as for a baptismal sponsor. A spiritual relationship is contracted between the confirmed person and the sponsor, who must provide for the confirmand's further Christian education if his natural parents fail to do so. Each confirmand usually has his own sponsor.

CONFIRMATION NAME

A child to be confirmed chooses a saint's name other than the one he already bears and is confirmed in this name. Like his baptismal name-saint, this saint becomes his patron.

CONFIRMATION DRESS

Correct dress for confirmands is similar to that prescribed for first communicants. The average age of the children is usually between nine and eleven. Most parishes permit boys to wear any type or color of suit with a jacket, and a white shirt and plain tie. The tie is sometimes white. Girls usually wear delicate white dresses, sometimes with veils, but not always. Sometimes a wreath of flowers or smilax is substituted, or a white hat or cap of the beret type. Whatever the headdress selected, it is usually identical for all girls. White academic gowns for both boys and girls are more frequently used for confirmation than for First Communion. Some parishes prefer white replicas of the school uniform. All the advice given in this book about the clothing for first communicants applies to confirmands also. (See pp. 25–26.)

ENTERTAINING

There is no social obligation to entertain for a confirmand, but most Catholic parents are eager to observe this day, like the other great religious days in a child's life, with some sort of family celebration. Confirmations often are held on Sunday afternoon. A little reception immediately after the ceremony is a convenient way of entertaining for this occasion. One may invite grandparents and other relatives, the sponsor and his wife or husband, family friends. It may be in the nature of an open house, with all fellow confirmands, or a selected group of them, invited to drop in.

The refreshments should be the kind served for a tea. They may be served buffet style and should include food and drink suitable for children. Adults may be offered intoxicants in the form of a ceremonial toast. As on all sacramental occasions, intoxicants should be served and taken with great moderation. This is particularly true for confirmation, however, as this is frequently the occasion upon which children take a pledge to abstain from intoxicants until they are twenty-one.

GIFTS

Only a sponsor has a social obligation to give the confirmand a present. Parents, grandparents and other relatives frequently do. Godparents sometimes do. Friends, both Catholic and non-Catholic, may do so if they wish. Some suitable presents are: Missal, silver rosary, biography of his confirmation patron saint, the New Testament, some of his clothing for the occasion. Also secular gifts, such as billfold, money clip, jewelry, cuff links, chemistry set, sewing box, fountain pen.

ADULT CONFIRMATION

Adult confirmation is not always the confirmation of adult converts. Cradle Catholics sometimes fail to be confirmed in their childhood at the proper age for a number of reasons that need not be discussed here. When the failure to be confirmed has resulted from circumstances beyond his control, the unconfirmed person has not sinned. But a baptized person of proper age cannot, without sin, neglect to receive confirmation when the opportunity offers itself. If the neglect to receive confirmation arises from a contempt for the sacrament, the sin is grave. Adult converts should be confirmed at the first opportunity after their reception into the Church.

Therefore Catholics who did not receive confirmation at the customary age should and often do receive it during their adult life. Confirmation is usually administered to adults, both converts and unconfirmed Catholics, in a parish at the same time that confirmation is scheduled for the children of the parish. In some dioceses, adult confirmations are held once or twice yearly in one church in a community for all adults of that community who desire confirmation. In cities which are the seat of the diocese, these are usually held in the cathedral church.

Adult confirmands have sponsors just as children do, and their confirmation is in all respects similar to that of child confirmands. Adult confirmands wear clothing similar to that worn at High Mass. A party similar to a christening party may be held in honor of the occasion, with the confirmand, his sponsor, or his family acting as hosts. The occasion need not be marked by a party if the confirmand does not wish it.

5

Holy Orders

For every high priest taken from among men is appointed for men in the things pertaining to God, that he may offer gifts and sacrifices for sins. He is able to have compassion on the ignorant and erring, because he himself also is beset with weakness, and by reason thereof is obliged to offer for sins, as on behalf of the people, so also for himself. And no man takes the honor to himself; he takes it who is called by God, as Aaron was (Hebrews 5:1–4). The Lord has sworn, and he will not repent: "You are a priest forever, according to the order of Melchisedec" (Psalm 109:4). With all thy soul fear the Lord, and reverence his priests (Ecclesiasticus 7:31).

HOLY ORDERS

Holy orders is the sacrament through which men receive the power and grace to perform the sacred duties of bishop, priest, and other ministers of the Church. The ceremony which bestows the powers of the priesthood is called *ordination*. The further ceremony which raises a priest to a bishop is called *consecration*.

A man called to the priesthood advances through seven degrees before he is ordained. The first is received at conclusion of first year of clerical studies and is called *tonsure*. It signifies that he has dedicated himself to the service of God. He further advances through the minor orders, which are *porter*, *lector*, *exorcist*, and *acolyte*, and the major orders of *subdeacon* and *deacon*, before he is ordained a priest. There is by Church law a period of time between the reception of the various degrees.

ORDINATION

A layman invited to attend an ordination is usually a relative of one of the candidates for the priesthood. This is because the limitations of space in any building usually make it impossible to ask as guests any save the ones dearest to the candidates.

Costume

When attending such a ceremony, a woman wears formal day attire such as is suitable for High Mass: modest dress or suit, hat, gloves and stockings. Men usually wear business suits, white shirts, and plain ties. Black shoes are preferred. In summertime a white suit or dark summer suit may be worn, but never sports clothes. Formal daytime wear for men is seldom seen nowadays at these occasions, but is quite correct. If one were an honor guest at such a ceremony—such as a mayor or governor, the holder of a papal title, or the head of a Catholic organization—a cutaway and its accessories would be the correct attire.

FIRST SOLEMN MASS

A newly ordained priest customarily says his first Solemn Mass in the church of the parish in which he was raised, or in which his family currently resides. This is not true of priests in the cloistered orders, such as the Cistercians, but it is of all others. It is to this first Solemn Mass that the young cleric and his parents invite relatives and friends; it is immediately following this ceremony that any reception or social celebration of the occasion is held.

The term "First Mass," as used here and in common speech, means the new priest's First Solemn Mass. He may have said low Mass several times between his ordination and the Solemn Mass. But the term "First Mass" is the one customarily employed in referring to the ceremonial occasion.

For the newly ordained priest and his parents, the day of his First Mass is one of profound joy. It is similar to a wedding in this respect, but outranks even this, as the priestly calling outranks the marriage vocation. Parental rejoicing is unalloyed. One may question the wisdom of one's child's choice of a mate, or his fitness for the marriage state. But a priest has been so tested and weighed in preparing for a priestly life that when the pinnacle is reached there are no doubts existing to becloud the moment.

There is also a mundane difference. Wedding observances have developed over the centuries, through tradition and custom, into established practices which may be difficult to observe but are easy to ascertain. In the social realm, all choices remain firmly in the hands of the bride and her parents; but in a First Mass and its accompanying celebration, many are concerned. There are rules laid down by the man's seminary or religious community. There are the customs and rules of his diocese. There are the practices and preferences of the pastor of his home parish to be followed. Even civic customs sometimes are involved. Difficult it may be for a young priest's family to determine the correct procedure in his particular case; it is harder still to generalize about them sufficiently to attempt to cover them in a book of this nature!

The priest's family will be instructed well in advance of the occasion in the practices of his seminary or his order. His home pastor should be consulted at the earliest possible occasion to learn his preferences and the degree of his participation. The pastor will also instruct in any diocesan rules which govern the occasion, or will advise where to learn such rules. The parents follow all such practices strictly as outlined to them. To learn all about these things as early as possible is the paramount duty of the parents at this time.

Invitations

The form and style of invitations to a First Solemn Mass are often determined by the officials of the seminary the young priest attends and are identical in style for all the men in a class. When this is so, they are purchased in quantity, with each family paying for the ones used by their son. When this is not the case, the young priest and his family have some latitude of choice, as in the case of a wedding invitation. Unlike the latter, an invitation to a First Mass may be printed rather than engraved or embossed to save expense; but, whenever possible, engraving or embossing is to be preferred. The invitation to any entertaining following the First Mass may be made part of the First Mass invitation if all invited to the Mass are to be invited to the reception, or it may be on a separate enclosure card like a reception card in a wedding invitation. In the latter case, one sends the invitation to all invited to the church, adding the enclosure card to those bid to the entertaining to follow.

Here are some samples of First Mass Invitations.

Dr. and Mrs. Vincent R. Reilly
announce the
Ordination to the Sacred Priesthood
of their son
The Reverend Donald J. Reilly
to be conferred by
His Excellency
The Most Reverend George W. Ahr, S. T. D.
Bishop of Trenton
on Saturday, the twenty-sixth of May
Nineteen hundred and fifty-six
at nine o'clock
Saint Mary's Cathedral
Trenton, New Jersey
and cordially invite you to offer with him his
First Solemn Mass
Trinity Sunday, the twenty-seventh of May
at twelve-fifteen o'clock
Our Lady of Refuge Church
Ocean and Foster Avenues
Brooklyn, New York

Reception, Sunday afternoon
four-thirty until six-thirty
Hotel St. George, Clark Street

The Reverend James Aloysius McKeough
of the Society of Jesus
announces his
Ordination to the Holy Priesthood
and cordially invites you to offer with him his
First Solemn Mass
Sunday, the twentieth of June
Nineteen hundred and fifty-four
at eleven o'clock
The Church of Saint Vincent de Paul
Nine hundred Madison Avenue
Albany, N. Y.

Reception: three until five o'clock
New Crystal Room
DeWitt Clinton Hotel
Albany, N. Y.

Guest List

The guest list is made up just as for a wedding in the family, but should also include all the young men in the ordinand's seminary graduating class and their parents. Invitations are sent to distant relatives and friends who cannot attend, to notify them of the great occasion, as well as to those who will be expected to come. Such an invitation is a compliment to the receiver—an acknowledgment that he is esteemed by the family and remembered at this joyous time. Because of this, the entire family should be consulted as to those invited and the list checked and rechecked for possible omissions.

All relatives, in-laws, and "connections" must be remembered. To overlook anyone is a serious social slight. For example, all the adult members of the family of a priest's sister-in-law—her parents, sisters, and brothers, both married and unmarried, even though some of them are not personally known to the ordinand and his family—must receive an invitation.

This extensive guest list applies only to the First Solemn Mass, not necessarily to the entertaining to follow. It is the First Mass invitation that is the compliment, and that ceremony transcends in importance any entertaining to follow. Anyone receiving such an invitation should so regard it. The reception invitations may be restricted in number because of the family's financial position, the health of the ordinand's mother, the rules of the diocese or parish, the size of his family, or any number of factors that have nothing to do with their wish to invite many people. Thus no one should feel slighted at not being asked to the reception if invited to the First Mass.

Parish Invitation

The First Mass of a priest is a matter of interest to all in his home parish, whether or not they are acquainted with him. All are happy that a "parish boy" has been so elevated. Recognizing this, the pastor will announce the date and hour of the First Mass during parish services shortly before the Mass is to occur and will issue a general invitation to all members of the parish. This is a bonafide invitation, and may be accepted by all who care to do so; in fact it is a compliment to the family to attend. Far more important, it redounds to one's spiritual welfare to receive the new priest's blessing on the occasion of his First Solemn Mass.

Acknowledging First Mass Invitations

An invitation to a First Mass which does not include an invitation to the reception requires no acknowledgement, as one's presence or absence will make no difference in the arrangements. An invitation that includes the reception must be acknowledged promptly, and in the formal style in which the invitation is issued. The acceptance (or regrets) is addressed to the person in whose name the invitation was issued, either the priest or his parents. A double fold of plain white writing paper is used. It may be monogrammed or carry an engraved address. The small sheets known as informals may not be used. The acknowledgment is handwritten on the front of the double fold, then folded once horizontally when inserted in the envelope. It must be expressed in the third person and spaced and worded as the invitation is. Following is an example of an acceptance (it must be handwritten):

Mr. and Mrs. George Robert Burns

accept with pleasure

the kind invitation

of

The Reverend James Patrick Gerrity

to offer with him his First Solemn Mass

and to attend

the reception to follow

on Saturday, the eighteenth of May

Nineteen hundred and fifty-nine.

Refusals are similarly worded except that they say, "Mr. and Mrs. George Robert Burns decline with regret the kind invitation, etc." No reason for a refusal need be given. For further discussion of formal correspondence, see the chapter on "Wedding Correspondence and Printed Forms."

Arrangements for First Mass

In arranging the details of a First Mass, one must work closely with the church pastor. The date and hour will be determined by him. He will see to it that altar boys are selected for the occasion and that they are drilled, scrubbed and shining! He will alert the church choir months in advance to practice special music for the day.

Sometimes a young priest wishes to have the choir of his seminary furnish the music for his First Mass, or to have special friends as soloists, as at a wedding. This is a delicate point. The pastor's consent must be obtained, and should be asked for months ahead of the ceremony. Even so, he may regard it as a "slur" on his own choir; and the choir members may also feel slighted, particularly if they have already begun to practice for the occasion.

Neither choir nor pastor *should* feel so, but it is very natural and human to do so. The point is raised here to warn a young priest that by asking permission for special musicians he may be creating a problem. It is, of course, permissible for him to do so. He will abide by the pastor's decision without question.

Details of First Mass

The Altar Society will provide at least the regular Sunday display of flowers. Parents may, if they wish, offer to provide these or add to them, but even if the pastor consents the Society should be consulted, as its members may have planned a special display to honor the occasion. Canopy and carpet are never used.

A number of the front pews are reserved for the priest's family and invited guests. When announcing the occasion, the pastor will ask the rest of the parish to occupy rear pews. The front seats are not marked off by flowers or ribbons, as at a wedding.

In most parishes the family may, if they wish, designate a couple of relatives or friends of the young priest to act as ushers to those who have received invitations. Usually they are brothers or cousins, but may be merely friends. These ushers dress as for a wedding: in formal day attire if the priest's father is so dressed, otherwise in dark business suits, white shirts, black shoes, and plain matching ties.

The ushers escort only those formally invited. These guests indicate their status by waiting in the rear of the church to be shown to a seat. The seating order is not so strictly observed as at a wedding. Parents and close relatives sit in the first pews on the epistle (right) side of the church. Other relatives and friends sit behind them. On the gospel side sit any nuns and religious brothers attending, also the officers or members of any Catholic society attending the Mass officially as society members. The officers of all parish clubs might so attend, as might Knights of Columbus, etc., but none will necessarily do so. Any priests present always sit in the sanctuary.

At the Communion, the priest's parents are the first to receive; usually they kneel alone at the rail to receive Holy Communion from their son's hands for the first time. They are followed by the rest of the family, invited friends, and the remainder of the congregation in that order. This is also the order in which the young priest's blessing is received at the end of Mass. In both cases, parish members should wait until they are sure that all relatives and invited friends have preceded them before they approach the altar. It is *very, very* discourteous to push ahead of those who take precedence over one at this time. A thoughtless rush to the altar by all present can make a shambles of a beautiful ceremony. Family and guests should also be permitted to leave the church before the rest of the congregation does so.

Non-Catholic Guests

A young priest and his family may have a number of non-Catholic friends whom they will invite to the First Solemn Mass. Such guests may sit quietly in their seats without attempting to take part in the service, or they may stand, sit and kneel when the congregation does. The latter is perhaps friendlier, and certainly less conspicuous; but if religious scruples prevent them from appearing to take part in the service they may sit as observers. Non-Catholic guests will not, of course, join in receiving Holy Communion, as this sacrament is reserved to Catholics. But they may go to the altar rail at the conclusion of the Mass to receive the young priest's blessing, if they wish. One merely walks to the altar rail, kneels there, receives the blessing, and departs.

Costume

The mother of the new priest dresses as for a family wedding except that her clothing should never be conspicuous or high fashion. A widow or an elderly woman who habitually wears black may do so on this occasion, but, in general, color is a better choice. Shades of blue, green, beige, violet, gray, the wine tones or a rose color are suitable. Yellow, pink, red and orange are to be avoided. Since these ceremonies almost always take place in early summer, a white suit is correct—or any type of dressmaker suit of lightweight material, like linen, tussah silk, etc. If a dress that does not have its own jacket is worn, it should have long or bracelet-length sleeves. Hats that are very large or elaborately trimmed are not in good taste, nor are elaborate shoes with much openwork. Classic pumps are best. Gloves are always worn. The mother may wear flowers if she choses.

The priest's father may wear morning clothes if he wishes to do so, and if the tone of the entertaining to follow warrants it. If he does, the ushers should be similarly dressed. Brothers and brothers-in-law of the priest should dress in the manner that the father selects. Dark business suit, white shirt, black shoes, and sober tie is the costume most generally worn nowadays. Very informal attire such as jacket and trousers that do not match is not correct.

Guests at a First Mass wear clothing suitable for weddings, christenings, etc., as outlined in several other sections of this book.

Children

Children old enough to behave properly may be allowed to go to a First Mass, because it is a religious ceremony carrying special spiritual benefits from which they should be not excluded. They should not be taken to the reception unless they have been specifically invited. This prohibition applies to all invitations parents receive, from an impromptu barbecue to ceremonial entertaining; one should never bring one's children of any age, unless they have been named in the invitation. If in any doubt in the matter, do *not* ask the hostess to clarify the invitation—it may place her in an awkward position. Simply leave the children at home. Better that they miss some function which they might have attended, than that they be taken where they are not wanted and should not be.

Presents

An invitation to a First Mass, even including the reception to follow, does not require the receiver to send the young priest a present. For example: a young man on military duty in an uncivilized country might find it difficult to procure a present. An old couple living on a small fixed income might find it a financial burden. But, in general, persons so invited wish to mark the occasion with a present of some sort. It may be substantial or trifling, according to one's own wishes.

Diocesan priests may accept and keep for their own use such presents as may be regarded as necessary for ordinary modern living. A diocesan priest may accept fountain pens, wallets, scarves, gloves, books, handkerchieves, a wristwatch, cuff links, luggage, etc. He may also have his own chalice, pyx, vestments, sickcall kit, and other impedimentia of his calling. He may accept moderate sums of money. Sickcall kits and stoles are a too-common choice; most young priests are given more of them than they need. It is always sensible to consult the young man's parents before choosing a present.

A priest of a religious community, such as the Jesuits, Franciscans, or Dominicans, is in a different position. Not only is he bound by a vow of poverty, but great emphasis is laid upon the fact that the men of the order are a band of brothers, holding all things in common.

Thus a young priest of a religious community turns in or offers to turn in to the common holdings all presents made to him, whatever their nature. The offer may be accepted, and he may be allowed to keep for his own use none of the presents that were made to him. The equivalent, from the common holdings, might be given to him by his superiors, or it might not. Or the superiors might grant him permission to retain for his own use some or all of the presents he has received. This holds true for money as well as other presents. Because of this it is very wise to consult the priest's parents before selecting a gift to a man in a religious community. He may prefer that you make a gift directly to his order—perhaps altar equipment for a new house of studies. Or he may prefer that you make a money gift to the order in his name. Money given to any young priest should *not* be accompanied by a request to have Masses said by him, as it then becomes a Mass stipend. Any present made to a new priest should be delivered in advance of the occasion, like a wedding gift. Such presents are *not* brought to the reception.

Acknowledging Ordination Gifts

One of the basic laws of society is the one that requires all who receive a present to acknowledge it with a prompt and grateful hand-written note of thanks. Men appear to regard the fulfillment of this duty as a hardship; they strive to avoid it by persuading their mothers or wives to write for them. This duty is *not* transferable: he who receives the present must write the letter of thanks.

Within the month following his ordination, the new priest must acknowledge all his ordination presents with such a note. It must be handwritten on plain white writing paper or paper carrying his address. Mention the present by name (wallet, stole, pyx, check, etc.) and express gratitude. Any holy cards issued to commemorate the occasion may be enclosed with such a letter, if desired. A sample:

> MY DEAR MRS. TOBIN,
>
> *It was most kind of you and Mr. Tobin to send me such a generous check in commemoration of my ordination. Thank you very much. I think I shall use it to buy some of the reference books I shall need in my library. When I use them I will think of the good people who made it possible for me to get them.*
>
> *I will continue to remember you in my prayers at the altar, as I hope you will remember me in yours.*
>
> *Affectionately,*
> FATHER JOSEPH (Joey) POWELL

Sometimes when the ordination or First Mass invitations are being engraved for a class of ordinands, the seminary will order engraved cards of thanks for the new priests to send in place of a note. This does not mean that the seminary superiors are placing their approval on sending such cards; it merely means that they recognize how careless and dilatory young men are about writing proper letters of thanks. Their reasoning is that it is better for the givers of presents to receive a card of thanks than no acknowledgment at all! Nevertheless it must be respectfully pointed out that such cards of thanks are never socially correct. The young ordinands should be urged to write proper notes.

RECEPTION

There is no obligation on the family of a young priest to follow his First Mass with any kind of entertaining. It is only within the last quarter century that it has been done. In some dioceses, bishops are limiting the nature and degree of lavishness of such entertaining lest it overshadow in common minds the First Mass, which is the truly momentous occasion. In other dioceses no such limitations are laid down.

Parents who wish to entertain should first consult their pastor to learn whether there are any diocesan rules governing such entertaining. In some dioceses all receptions must be held in the parish halls. Sometimes there are other limitations. Whatever their nature, they must be observed. Other than diocesan regulations or such as a religious order may set up, there are no restrictions on the type of entertaining save family preference.

At Home

The simplest reception is in the family home on the afternoon of the day of the First Mass. This might merely be a large family style dinner, served either at the table or buffet style, to which relatives are invited, or a reception which may include a larger number of people. A dinner for relatives may be followed by a reception for friends.

The atmosphere of such a gathering is friendly and informal. The entrance door may be left open or ajar, and guests may let themselves in without ringing to announce their arrival. A family member or friend may be stationed in the hall to open the door and direct the guests to the cloakroom. The priest's mother and the young priest stand near the entrance to the living rooms. They greet the arriving guests and the priest may give them his blessing at that time if he wishes. As at wedding entertaining, the father does not receive but mingles with the guests and sees that they are introduced. Conversation provides the only entertainment.

Refreshments are offered buffet style, and may be as simple or elaborate as one chooses. They may range from small iced cakes and punch to an assortment of meats, cheeses, aspic, finger sandwiches, and champagne. A nonalcoholic drink should always be served for those who do not care for anything else. Any intoxicants should be served and indulged in with circumspection, bearing in mind the nature of the occasion. Guests will be coming and going throughout the hours indicated for the reception. One should not make a prolonged stay at such a party.

Outside the Home

A reception held in a club or hotel may be as formal or informal as one wishes and may be for any number; but usually such functions are more formal because they are larger. Only the formal type will be discussed here. One should take care that the room selected is suitable for the number invited, neither too small to accommodate all, nor so large as to appear half-filled. Arrangements should be made well in advance of the date of the party.

Luncheon

The reception is usually preceded by a luncheon or breakfast for family and relatives, similar to a wedding breakfast. An invitation to the luncheon is extended either by a note or by word of mouth. The luncheon invitation must be promptly acknowledged so that the priest's mother can plan the seating arrangements without last minute confusion. Usually the luncheon guests are all priests who were present at the First Mass, and close relatives. The number invited is optional with the priest's parents, except for the clerical guests who must be included.

Seating

The seating arrangement is also like a wedding. If there is a table of honor, the new priest, his parents, and other priests present are seated there. If there are not many clerical guests, the new priest's grandparents, if living, or his adult brothers and sisters may sit at the honor table. But no brothers and sisters should be so seated unless all can be.

A long rectangular table is better than a round one, as it makes the seating arrangements simpler. At such a table, the young priest, acting as his own host, sits in the middle facing outward toward the rest of the guests. On his right is his mother. On his left is his father. On his mother's right is the cleric whom they most wish to honor, and this should be determined as follows:

a) A bishop, if present.
b) A monsignor, if any present. If more than one is present, the man first raised to monsignor occupies the seat of honor, unless one of them is the pastor, in which case he is honored.
c) The pastor in whose church the First Mass was said. If the pastor be not present, the oldest priest at the luncheon is given the precedence.

On the father's left is seated the priest who deserves the second place of honor, determined as above, then the remaining clergymen in order of importance. Because of the lack of women at such a table, the usual seating arrangements of man-woman-man must be disregarded. If grandparents are seated at such a table, they might sit at the head and foot of it, in the places sometimes occupied by host and hostess. Otherwise guests sit only on one long side of such a table, facing toward the other guests.

These other guests may be seated at two long tables running out like arms from either end of the table of honor to form a U or at small round tables throughout the room. All such tables are placed in front of the table of honor. No order of precedence is observed at any save the honor table. The priest's mother merely attempts to see that guests are seated in congenial groups. If the luncheon is small, all might be seated at one large table with guests seated "below" the honored clergy, as stated above.

The usual decoration for an honor table is a centerpiece of white flowers. Because the guests at the other tables will want to be able to see the honor guests, the centerpiece should be low; and if a long rectangular table is used, the flower arrangement should be long and narrow. If the table is very long, the central piece might be supplemented by two smaller ones farther down the table. No candles should be used. If the other guests are seated at long tables at right angles to the honor table, similar arrangements are used on these. If they are seated at round tables, a small center bouquet is used on each in which case the arrangement may be taller. Colored flowers may also be used on these tables. They should all be alike, or very similar.

Toasts and Speeches

The young priest's father makes the first toast at this occasion. Sometimes it is the only one made. The young priest is the next speaker. His remarks usually take the form of a touching tribute to his parents. Usually another priest—the one, perhaps, who gave the sermon at the First Mass—then makes a speech or offers a toast. This usually takes the form of a discussion of the steps by which the young priest was led to the priesthood, his life in the seminary, his bright future prospects, etc. Other priests may also be called upon to speak.

Menus

Menus for a First Mass luncheon are similar to a wedding luncheon. Not more than four or less than three courses are served. Champagne or some white wine is usually served for the toasts. If served, the glasses are never refilled more than once, and are often not refilled at all. Some typical menus:

Fresh fruit cup
Chicken Eugenie   Asparagus, butter sauce
Strawberry mousse

Jellied consomme
Rock game hen   Wild rice
Endive Salad
Meringues glaces

Melon
Lobster newburg   Green peas and mushrooms
Cucumbers in tomato aspic
Orange Ice   Petits fours

Green turtle soup
Virginia ham   Potato puffs
Cesar salad
Profiteroles   Chocolate sauce

Details

Whenever possible, the luncheon should be served in a room other than that in which the reception is to take place. Otherwise, the luncheon guests must stand about awkwardly while the luncheon is cleared away, the tables removed, and the room prepared for the reception. But if two rooms cannot be engaged, the priest's mother should make sure that the hour for the beginning of the reception is set late enough so that no reception guests will arrive before the luncheon is over and housekeeping details are taken care of.

At any reception in a public place, a cloakroom with an attendant should be provided so that wraps may be checked. If it is held in a club, the club members attending the reception do not tip the attendant. Other guests do.

Receiving

After luncheon the new priest and his mother stand near the entrance to the reception room and greet all arriving guests. His father may receive with them if he wishes, but he is better employed moving about the room, introducing guests to one another and making sure everything is going smoothly. Usually there is no one else in the receiving line, but it would be proper to include grandparents if they wished to greet all guests. Also, if some of the young priest's classmates are present, he might like to have them in the line to meet all who come.

Refreshments

Refreshments are set up on a buffet and are of the same type as described for home receptions, but drinks are usually served by waiters who move among the guests with trays. Champagne punch is often served, but other beverages may be offered. Drinking must be very moderate.

Music

A string quartet is sometimes engaged to play at the reception, but this is not common. There is no dancing.

Decorations

The reception room may be decorated with palms and flowers if the parents wish it.

HOUSING GUESTS

As at a wedding, parents are in some measure responsible for the lodging of out-of-town relatives and intimate friends who come to the Solemn Mass of their priest-son. They may, if it is convenient, arrange for them to stay at the homes of local relatives and friends. If this is not possible, reservations should be made for them at a hotel. The parents are responsible for making the reservation, but not for the bill for the lodgings. This is paid by the person occupying the room.

In the case of priest-guests, the parish pastor *may* offer to lodge them, or some of them, at the rectory, but he is under no obligation to do so and in any case is seldom able to provide for more than one or two. Secular priests correctly may be lodged also in the homes of friends or relatives, or hotel accommodations may be found for them. In this latter case, the new priest's parents pay for the lodgings.

Housing of men who are members of a religious community is governed in part by the rules of their community. In arranging housing for such guests, one should consult them to learn what is the proper arrangement.

CORRECT USAGE OF "FATHER" AND "THE REVEREND"

In speaking to a priest, one addresses him as "Father," or "Father Powell." This method of address is to be preferred to all others. Young men who have done military service sometimes call their chaplains "Sir" because the chaplain is an officer, and may even carry the practice into civilian life and address all priests as "Sir"; but this is not proper. Chaplains as well as priests in civilian life are called "Father" by the men with whom they serve.

When writing to a priest, the address properly reads, "The Rev. Joseph Powell," or "The Reverend Joseph Powell." The correct salutation in a letter is "My Dear Father Powell." In writing to a priest who is a member of a religious community, his name is followed by the initials of his community, thus: "The Rev. Joseph Powell, S.J." (the Jesuits), "The Rev. Pierre Duval, C.S.C." (Congregation of the Holy Cross).

When referring to a priest in the third person, as in a formal invitation or a newspaper article, the correct usage is "The Reverend Joseph Powell." In introducing a priest as a speaker, one says "Our speaker for the day is the Reverend Joseph Powell, who, etc.," and concludes with, "Ladies and gentlemen, Father Powell."

The title "Reverend" is never properly used as a term of direct address for either priest or minister, although one frequently hears it so employed. The title "Reverend" is never used under any circumstances unless preceded by "the."

In introducing or identifying himself, as in a telephone conversation, a priest usually says, "This is Father Powell." If a priest were to say, "This is Joseph Powell," the average listener would have trouble in realizing that he was speaking to Father Joseph Powell.

A priest may sign letters to intimates "Father Joseph" or "Father Joe." Personal correspondence of a less intimate nature may be signed "(Father) Joseph Powell." Clerical papers such as baptismal certificates are signed "The Rev. Joseph Powell." Business correspondence other than clerical matters, personal checks, etc., is signed "(The Rev.) Joseph Powell."

Confusion seems to exist, even in the minds of some Catholics, as to the precise status of men and women in religious communities who are commonly known as brothers and sisters. Such persons are *not* in holy orders. Holy orders is the sacrament by which a man is given the power and grace for the performance of sacred offices, as described at the beginning of this chapter.

Brothers and sisters are men and women living in religious communities for the purpose of following as perfectly as possible the evangelical counsels of our divine Lord. The evangelical counsels enjoin vows of poverty, perpetual chastity, and obedience.

Many of the religious communities for men include both priests and brothers. The priests in such orders have not only received the sacrament of holy orders but have also taken vows of poverty, chastity, and obedience. The obedience of priests who are members of religious communities is to their superiors in the community.

Secular priests are the great body of men in holy orders who serve God and shepherd the laity in the parish churches of the world. They take vows of perpetual chastity and obedience to their superior, who is the bishop of their diocese. Secular priests voluntarily lead lives of self-denial and poverty, but do not take a vow of poverty.

A Catholic woman cannot receive holy orders, but she can assume the obligations of the evangelical counsels by making the vows of the religious life, which is called the life of perfection. This does not mean that those who follow the religious life become perfect, but that they assume the obligation of striving for perfection in a special way. The terms "nun" and "sister" are used interchangeably to describe women in religious life. All are addressed as "Sister" and the distinction is of no concern to laymen.

In addition to following the evangelical counsels, brothers and sisters serve God in two other ways. In the cloistered orders, they retire from the world and devote themselves to prayer. They do this not merely for their own souls' good, but to make reparation to our Lord for those who never pray to Him, and to call down His blessings upon His people in various ways. They pray for peace, for the spread of faith, for help for priests in their high calling, for the welfare of orphans, aged and afflicted. Only God knows how many ills the world has been spared through the prayers of these devoted men and women.

In religious communities which are not cloistered, the members devote themselves to the spiritual and corporal works of mercy. They care for the ill, the insane, the aged, the orphan and the destitute. They teach in schools and colleges. Some of them are lifelong students, pursuing knowledge in chosen fields. Their ranks include saints and savants, mystics and philosophers. Most dear and familiar to Americans is the little parochial school sister, devoting all the days of her life to her efforts to help our children to become well-informed citizens, patriotic Americans, and devout Catholics.

After a period of testing and learning called the novitiate, a candidate formally enters the religious life by assuming the responsibilities of the state through a free and public profession of the vows of poverty, chastity and obedience. Because of space limitations, the ceremony is seldom open to the general public. Usually only the nearest relatives of the young religious can be invited.

The ceremonies of religious profession vary so widely between the different communities that it would serve no useful purpose to discuss them here. They have almost no social connotations. Friends do not make gifts to the newly professed religious. Some communities will allow friends to send flowers to the convent or monastery to help decorate it for the great day of profession, but this is not always so. One should call or write the community for permission before doing anything of the kind.

There is one social gesture which friends can and should make: they should send a note of congratulation to the parents of the young religious on the occasion of his profession, or offer their congratulations in person. Parents whose children are led to the religious life have been greatly favored by God, and this fact should be acknowledged by their friends and relatives.

6

Funeral, Burial, and Mourning Etiquette

"I am the resurrection and the life; he who believes in me, even if he die, shall live; and whoever lives and believes in me, shall never die" (John 11:25–26).

FOR THE FAMILY OF THE DECEASED

Introduction

The hours immediately following the death of a loved one impose a triple burden upon the family survivors. They must struggle to learn to bear their private grief and personal loss; they must make hurried and costly decisions about funeral and burial arrangements; they must strive to perform with absolute correctness the religious and social rites by which the Church and the world bid a soul farewell. During this sad time, members of the family must endeavor to control their emotions and behave with dignity, holding fast to the consolations of the Faith.

Upon the death of a child or spouse the responsibility for the funeral decisions falls naturally upon the surviving parents or mate. In other cases the line of authority is shadowy; several survivors may have equal claim to the right to make the necessary funeral arrangements. In such a situation, the ideal solution is for the survivors to select one among them to act for all. If such a choice can be made easily and with unanimity, much friction is avoided. But if this solution is not practicable, the survivors must share the decisions, with as much kindliness and respect for one another's preferences as possible. A bereavement can be a time of rasped nerves, tender feelings, and intense emotionalism—all prime ingredients for a bitter family row. The primary responsibility of the mourners, therefore is: bear and forebear. Love one another, and *maintain family unity.*

The Funeral Director

The first consideration in the selection of a funeral director is to choose one who knows exactly how to conduct a Catholic funeral. In areas where there is a large Catholic population it is safe to assume that all directors are so informed. A Catholic director in any community would, of course, possess this information. In sections where the Catholic population is small and there is no Catholic director, it is wise to consult one's pastor to determine which of the men available are qualified.

The next consideration in the choice of a funeral director is his honesty and competence. The men who enter this profession are, in the main, conscientious and well-qualified. Unfortunately, in this calling as in all others, there are a minority who are unwilling to uphold the standards of the craft. It is a simple matter for an unscrupulous funeral director to take advantage of his clients, who are dazed by grief, to lead them into unnecessary or excessive expense. Sadly enough, this is the more apt to happen to families of very small income. A bewildered widow or orphan is sometimes induced to spend the insurance which may be the sole estate of the deceased upon a lavish funeral. It is vital, therefore, to choose a director of fine reputation.

The natural choice is a director who is a friend or acquaintance. Failing this, one might choose a man who has served his community for many years, or one who advertises his membership in a professional association of funeral directors. These associations try to police their membership and maintain a high ethical standard. Of course, one may always consult one's pastor, or the family doctor.

Funeral Expenses

Clients should tell a funeral director at first meeting what they can afford to pay for his services. An honest director will try to satisfy his patron's requirements and please his taste at a price within his means. But in this, as in all business matters, the client should watch out for his own interests by making sure he understands the transaction and by using reasonable care in checking details.

Broadly speaking, "the price of the casket is the price of the funeral." This means that the price quoted for any casket is a flat fee which includes the cost of a number of services: embalming, use of funeral parlors (if desired), use of a set number of motor cars, engraved cards to acknowledge condolences. The funeral director also serves by: obtaining legal burial permits, sending paid announcements and obituary notices to the newspapers, arranging with the church for the hour of the funeral, hiring musicians for the funeral. He will, if desired, file information for Social Security benefits, insurance claims and veterans' claims. Sometimes his fee covers the cost of a metal burial vault, but this is not always the case.

The quoted price does not include: fees paid for newspaper announcements, cemetery fee for opening the grave, cost of the musicians for the funeral, the offering for the Mass. If interment is to be made in an out-of-town cemetery, an extra fee is charged for the trip.

In making funeral arrangements one should exercise care on two points: to understand what financial obligations he is incurring and to plan obsequies in accord with his usual style of living. Simplicity and moderation are always good taste.

Place of Funeral

The funeral may be held from the home or from funeral parlors. In urban communities, no social stigma attaches to holding funerals from the director's parlors, and they are held there far more frequently than from one's home. There are several advantages to this: the parlors are centrally located and easy for friends to reach; calling hours may be announced in the newspapers and will then be observed by all; greater crowds may be accommodated than in the average home; flowers may be displayed to better advantage; the grief and strain of the occasion are removed from the home, thus sparing small children, old people, and invalids.

In rural areas and small communities, home funerals are still more generally seen. This may be because the homes are larger, or the funeral parlors not so conveniently located for all. Whatever the reason, this difference of taste does exist. However, from the point of view of correctness, either is proper. The choice is based upon the preference of the bereaved family.

If the decision is for a home funeral, the director will come at once to the home and prepare the remains to repose in the person's own bed for twelve hours, during which time the family is not officially receiving. No one should call at the house at this time except relatives. After this the coffin will be placed in the living room, and the family will prepare to receive condolence calls.

If the funeral is to be from the parlors, the director will immediately take the remains there, and within twelve hours all will be ready to receive visitors.

Place of Burial

The question of the place of burial is another which must be promptly decided. If the family has clear title to a plot in a Catholic cemetery, no problem exists. But in some cases unusual problems arise. Title to a cemetery plot differs from ordinary land title. The plot holder is always bound by the rules of the cemetery association. Title to a plot cannot always be inherited, at least beyond the second generation. You may always have assumed your family's right to be buried in "Grandpa's plot," and find you have no such right.

> The title of a lot-holder in a cemetery is rarely a title in fee simple. The right of burial conveyed by a written instrument in a cemetery or churchyard is either an easement or a license, and never a title to a free-holder (*Catholic Encyclopedia* on Burial).

Only the baptized can have Christian burial. It is denied to "pagans, Jews, infidels, schismatics, apostates and excommunicants." Also to "duelists, suicides of sound mind, notorious unrepentant sinners and those who express a desire for cremation" (*Catholic Encyclopedia*, as above). Where any doubt exists as to the right of Christian burial, the pastor of the deceased person is consulted.

On the other hand, burial in a Catholic cemetery is both the right and the duty of a Catholic.

> According to canon law, every man is free to choose the [Catholic] burial ground in which he wishes to be interred. If no choice has been expressed by the deceased, it is assumed to be any place belonging to the family, or the parish or cemetery of his place of residence (*Catholic Encyclopedia*).

When the family of the deceased own no lot, therefore, the simple and proper thing to do is to purchase one in the Catholic cemetery with which one's parish or community is affiliated. There are, of course, still large sections of our country in which the Catholic population is too small to maintain a Catholic cemetery. In such regions, the pastor will tell the family how he takes care of this problem, and where they may properly purchase a lot.

Cremation

It should not be necessary to say that Catholics are not cremated. But, since books of this nature are frequently referred to in settling disputes: let it be said!

> The Church has forbidden cremation not because it is wrong in itself nor because it is contrary to divine law but because it is in opposition to the Jewish and Christian tradition and has been advocated by anti-Christians with the express purpose of destroying belief in the immortality of the soul and the resurrection of the body. The Fathers of the Church defended the custom of burial by reason of the doctrine of the resurrection of the body and the respect due it as the temple of the Holy Ghost.
>
> During great pestilences when it is impossible to bury the dead in time to prevent the spread of contagion, the Church permits mass cremation because it is neither wrong in itself nor expressly forbidden by divine law (*Baltimore Catechism*, Revised Edition, Number 3, p. 154).
>
> There is nothing actually opposed to any dogma of the Church in the practice of cremation and . . . if the heads of this sinister movement [cremation] ever so far control the governments of the world as to make the custom universal, it would not be a lapse in her [the Church] if she were obliged to conform (*Catholic Encyclopedia* on Cremation).

Notifying Relatives

While some members of the family are busy with the funeral arrangements, one or two others should be chosen to prepare a list of out-of-town relatives and friends who must be invited to attend the obsequies. This must be done promptly, and great care should be taken that no one is overlooked. Anyone so neglected will, quite properly, regard the oversight as a social affront. Family opinion will decide which relations, connections, in-laws, and friends are to be notified. A standard message should be prepared, and wired or telephoned to all on the list.

A typical message sent at this time might read:

Very sorry to tell you Aunt Lucy died early this morning.

Funeral Wednesday at nine o'clock. Please let us know
if you can come and probable hour of arrival.
(Signed) Cousin John Daley

Local relatives and close friends are notified at once by telephone. The persons sending these messages and calls should be held responsible for keeping track of the replies received to them.

The Paid Newspaper Announcement

The general public learns of a death through the paid newspaper announcement; hence it is important that the notice be sent to the papers at the earliest possible date. It appears in all local papers, in each edition between the time of the first notice and the day of the funeral. If the deceased person has lived in more than one place, a notice should be sent to the newspapers of all the communities in which he has lived. These matters will ordinarily be taken care of by the funeral director, but he will need to be told which out-of-town papers to notify and will need family help in assembling the information to be included.

Such notices generally give the date of death, place of residence of the deceased, close surviving relatives and their place of residence (if not local). The first notice may not give the date and hour of the funeral, as it may not yet have been determined, but includes the place (home or funeral parlors) and the hours for receiving condolence calls. A typical first notice follows:

> MCCLURE, LEONARD D. At his home, 14 Hollywood Ave., after a brief illness, April 6, 1958. Husband of Gretta Murphy McClure, son of Mrs. Thomas McClure of St. Louis, Mo., father of Jane, Ellen and Leonard, Jr., brother of Mrs. Arthur Gardiner of Framingham, Mass. Also survived by several nieces and nephews. Friends may call at the Radcliffe Brothers Funeral Home Wednesday and Thursday afternoon and evening, 1–4 and 7–9 o'clock. Notice of funeral hereafter.

The later notices would read as above, with the notice of funeral added, to read:

> Funeral from the Radcliffe Brothers Funeral Home Friday morning at nine o'clock, and from St. Agnes' Church at nine-thirty, where a Solemn Mass of Requiem will be celebrated. Interment in St. Lucy's Cemetery.

The Obituary

Speaking in very general terms, it may be said that in cities with a population of more than a million people, no obituary notice other than the paid newspaper announcement is published unless the deceased was in some respect prominent or well-known. In smaller communities a brief obituary of all respectable people is usually published. The funeral director will be able to tell you the custom of the community and will write the obituary from the information you furnish him. Sometimes the local newspaper furnishes a printed sheet to be filled in, covering place of birth, education, marriage, surviving relatives, place of employment, general nature of work, club and church affiliations, date and place of death, funeral, and interment.

But the survivor who prepares this material should remember that almost everyone has done some small thing in his lifetime of which he was proud, and for which he would have liked to be remembered. Try to see that this salient fact is included, even if no place appears for it on the newspaper form. It is correct to say "Mr. Smith served in World War I in the battles of the Argonne Forest and Belleau Wood," or "He was graduated from Georgetown University in 1916, and was a member of the football varsity for two of his college years," or even, "Mr. Smith was well-known in local bowling circles and was for two terms secretary of the local chapter of the League of American Bowlers." Here are two sample obituaries, the first of an obscure person, the second of a prominent one:

MRS. THOMAS NOONAN

Mrs. Thomas Noonan of 308 Douglass Street died today in St. Clare's Hospital after an illness of several months. The former Maria Kelly was born in Syracuse, the daughter of Mrs. Charles Kelly and the late Mr. Kelly. She was educated in the parochial schools of that city, and was graduated from Cathedral High School as salutatorian of her class.

In 1910 she married Thomas Noonan and moved to this city, where she resided thereafter. She was a communicant of St. Joseph's Church and a member of its Altar and Rosary Society. She was one of the founders and a charter member of St. Clare's Hospital Guild.

Surviving besides her mother and husband are three children: John, Mrs. Edward Fay, and Thomas Jr., now serving with the Armed Forces in Germany; a brother,

Charles Jr., of Houston, Texas; a sister, Mrs. Robert Wilson of Pasadena, Cal.; four grandchildren and several nieces and nephews.

The funeral will be held from her late home at nine o'clock Wednesday, and at nine-thirty from St. Joseph's Church, where a Solemn Mass of Requiem will be sung. Burial will be made in St. Mark's Cemetery, Syracuse.

FRANCIS X. DILLINGHAM

Francis X. Dillingham, 68, founder and chairman of the board of Eastern Drop Forge and Tool, died at his home, 77 Parkway East, early this morning after an illness of several months.

Mr. Dillingham was born in Boston, Mass., and was the elder son of the late Martin and Clara Peabody Dillingham. The Senior Mr. Dillingham was a well-known philanthropist and contractor.

Francis Dillingham was educated at Xavier Academy, Lenox, Mass., and at Massachusetts Institute of Technology, from which he was graduated in the class of 1911. For several years thereafter he worked for a number of large steel companies, and in 1916 he came to this city and founded Eastern Drop Forge and Tool. Later in the same year he married Miss Mary Louise Fitz Patrick, of this city. His company grew rapidly, due in part to Mr. Dillingham's successful experimentation on new methods of annealing.

At the outbreak of World War I he put his company in charge of his associate and brother-in-law, Patrick Fitz Patrick, and enlisted in the Army Engineers, being discharged a major. He never lost his interest in the Armed Forces, and served on the local Draft Board in World War II.

His company continued to prosper and now gives employment to more than 1200 people. Mr. Dillingham retired in 1949, and the firm is now headed by his sons, Martin and Patrick.

Mr. Dillingham was long active in the civic life of the community. He was at various times Chairman of the Community Chest, Chairman of Red Cross drives, director of Henley Museum and President of the Boy's Club. His clubs include the Fort William, Edgewood Golf Club, American Engineering Association, National Association of Manufacturers, Don Brown Post, American

Legion, and the New York Athletic Club. He was also a
member of the First Friday Club and the Nocturnal
Adoration Society. He was a communicant of the
Cathedral of the Assumption, and a member of the Holy
Name Society of that church, and a trustee of St. Mary's
Hospital.

Surviving besides his wife and sons are two daughters: Theresa, now Sister Mary Paula of the Sisters of
Charity of St. Vincent de Paul, presently stationed in
Buffalo, and Mrs. Paul Lafferty of Boston. Also one
brother, John F., of Boston, and two grandchildren.

The funeral will be Saturday morning at ten o'clock
from the Hale Funeral Home, and at ten-thirty from the
Cathedral of the Assumption, where a Solemn Mass of
Requiem will be celebrated by the Rt. Rev. Lawrence
Murphy. Men of the Holy Name Society will form a
guard of honor for the procession at the church and
cemetery. Senior boys from St. Cyril's Home will act as
pallbearers. The honorary pallbearers will be: Judge
George M. Brackett, Dr. Brian Sexton, Senator Samuel
Beckstein, Gregory Havilland, Edwin Phelps, Dean of
Xavier School, and Professor Thomas Wills of Massa-
chusetts Institute of Technology.

Interment will be made in the family plot in St.
Martha's Cemetery.

The Wake

It is no longer customary for mourners to sit up throughout the night
during the interval between death and burial, as was done for many
years. The old-fashioned "wake," which originated in a wish to show
respect for the dead and to console the bereaved, imposed an intolerable strain upon the family. Accompanied, as it occasionally was, by
immoderate drinking, it even gave rise to maudlin or irreverent behavior. It was an old-world custom not worthy of being perpetuated.
Present-day practice is to end the visiting hours at nine or ten o'clock.
All the family then retire for the rest they so sorely need.

Occasionally the survivor of an aged couple insists that an old-
style wake be held for the departed mate. Such a wish should be
acceded to. But it should be the duty of younger and more alert members of the family to see to it that those invited to sit up through the
night be few in number and prudent and stable in character. Any
excess in eating and drinking should be out of the question. The time

should be passed in prayer, quiet conversation, or silence. Better yet, as soon as can be, let the custom fall into "innocuous desuetude."

Although the custom has lapsed, the term "wake" survives as a quick and easy way of referring to the period of receiving condolence calls between the time of death and the funeral. The word will be so used hereafter in this volume and will be meant in the sense just explained.

Mourning Costume

All relatives who are so closely related to the deceased as to be receiving condolence calls wear mourning costume throughout this period and the funeral. For women, this consists of an all-black costume, save for hose. Black hose are currently so unfashionable that they are not obligatory even at this time, but they may be worn if preferred. A wristwatch or plain brooch that serves a purpose may be worn but it is better taste to eschew all jewelry at this period. If the weather is very cold, a dark brown fur coat may be worn to the funeral. Dark coats of any shade may be worn to save expense. Often there are kind friends to loan a black coat if one does not own one. Widows, mothers, and daughters of the deceased person usually wear mourning veils to the funeral. This is not an obligation; it is an accommodation, to protect them from curious glances in a time of travail.

The correct costume for men is a charcoal gray, oxford, or black suit, black shoes, white shirt, black tie. For the funeral they should add black top coat, black or gray hat, gray gloves. If money problems make this impracticable, the male mourner wears the soberest clothes he owns, always with a white shirt and black tie. Sometimes a mourning band is worn on the left sleeve of the suitcoat, but this is less seen than formerly.

Mourning wear for children under fourteen is no longer considered fitting. But a child younger than this might be allowed to wear an all-white costume to the funeral of a parent if it occurs in the summertime, when the attire would not be conspicuous. All-white, like all-black, is full mourning.

Receiving Condolence Calls

Catholic and Protestant funeral customs seem to be diverging more and more in recent years. Many Protestants seem to prefer privacy and seclusion to the strain of receiving condolence calls. The funeral itself is often private. Respecting this attitude, friends express their sympathy by sending flowers and notes of sympathy rather than by calling. This attitude is quite correct socially and, for Protestants, who do not believe in praying for their dead, in the religious sense also. But for the Catholic, it is impossible.

> Our Lord expressly taught that one can earn the eternal reward of Heaven by performing the corporal works of mercy, and that those who deliberately refuse to perform such works will be barred from heaven. . . . That Almighty God is pleased to reward those who bury the dead is distinctly taught in the book of Tobias. To visit a house of mourning or to attend a funeral is a mark of respect to the dead and a consolation to the relatives of a deceased person (*Baltimore Catechism*, revised edition, no. 3, p. 152).

It naturally follows that the bereaved Catholic has an obligation to receive those who come to offer their respects quite as binding as that requiring his friends to visit him. To refuse to do so offends in three ways: (1) it denies the caller the privilege of performing a corporal work of mercy; (2) it belittles his offer of sympathy; (3) it may deprive the departed soul of prayers for his repose.

In meeting this requirement, moderation may be observed. The aged, the ill, and the very young may be excused from seeing anyone. If hours for visiting have been announced, callers should confine their visits to these hours, and one who comes at another time should not be offended if told the mourners are "not at home" or "resting."

All healthy adult members of the bereaved family should be present during some of the announced visiting hours. Some principal members of the family should receive during all visiting hours. A male member of the family stands near the entrance to greet all arrivals and direct them to the particular member of the family whose friend they are. A family member should be appointed to find out which callers will be attending the funeral and to arrange with the funeral director for motor accommodation for them. Throughout the whole sad period, the family members should strive to control their emotions and behave with dignity and courage.

During this period of condolence calls, the family must attend to a number of details. Someone is given the duty of keeping a record of all flowers, Mass offerings, prayer enrollments, notes, cards of sympathy, and telegrams. The funeral director will try to keep such a list, but because he is not always aware of some of these offerings the responsibility for keeping a record is a family one. The list should include a description of each floral offering, the gist of long-distance telephone conversations, the names of neighbors who send in food, and of those who performed such kindnesses as looking after children, running errands, and housing relatives. This record serves as a guide for the writing of thank-you notes; it is also a permanent record of kindnesses bestowed in a time of trouble.

Displaying Flowers

Cards are removed from flowers displayed at the time of mourning. The director may say that they may be left on or not, as one chooses. If left on, donors may identify their offering and make sure it is satisfactory. This is an instance in which "commercial" advice on etiquette is wrong. It is of no consequence to visitors who sent what. When cards are left on bouquets, an otherwise beautiful floral background takes on the appearance of a flower show, and some ill-bred persons are sure to walk about peering at them with heartless curiosity and creating an irreverent atmosphere. *Do not leave cards on flowers.*

Funeral Procession

The night before the funeral, the director will need family help in mapping the order of the funeral procession. By this time the family should know which relatives and friends will attend the funeral, and also any religious who will be present. They should have determined whether there will be delegations from places of business, clubs, religious societies, or civic bodies, and any religious or governmental dignitaries who will be present. The procession is then arranged as follows: Pallbearers, honorary pallbearers; Priests, religious Brothers, Sisters; immediate members of the family; other relatives; officials, in order of rank (governor, mayor); delegations; friends; servants, tenants, employees. In the case of these latter, consideration must be given to the intimacy of their association with the deceased. Devoted family servants or long-time employees may follow directly after the family if the family wishes them to be placed there. Otherwise the order is as given above.

Pallbearers

Unless the deceased person had at some time named those whom he wished to have as pallbearers, the selection of those to fulfill this duty is made by the family during the wake. Catholics seldom employ professional bearers, although it is perfectly proper to do so if they wish. It might be necessary if the deceased was an aged man whose surviving friends are too feeble for the task. Usually, distant relatives, family connections, or friends are asked. The writer once attended the funeral of an aged man whose adult grandsons were his pallbearers. While it is not usual to employ such close relatives, it seemed both fitting and touching that these tall strong youths should perform this last service for their grandparent.

Honorary pallbearers are not a necessary part of a funeral. Many people do not choose to have them. Their sole function is to form a guard of honor for the bier as it enters the church, and as it is carried to the grave. Honorary pallbearers add solemnity to a funeral and give the family an opportunity of honoring a number of men who may have been associated with the deceased in various phases of his life's activities. They may be government officials, fellow clubmen or classmates, or associates in business or philanthropy.

Pallbearers and honorary pallbearers need not be Catholics to serve in this capacity at a Catholic funeral. Catholics may act as pallbearers at a non-Catholic funeral also.

Housekeeping Details

A time of mourning is particularly hard for the family housekeeper. Mourners must eat; out-of-town relatives must be housed; children continue to need attention. Fortunately, in most American communities large and small, neighbors and friends maintain the custom of helping if they can. Usually the larder fills rapidly with salads, casseroles, pies, and cakes from neighbors. Occasionally a considerate person will send a baked ham or turkey. This is a time in one's life when it is proper to accept all offers of help. If a former servant volunteers to return to her place in the kitchen, accept with thanks. If a neighbor offers to help with the children, feel free to let her do so. If a cousin puts herself and her car at your disposal, let her be your errand boy. By permitting them to help, you are enabling them to perform a cardinal work of mercy which redounds to their good. It does not obligate you, except to return such favors in kind when sorrow comes to one of your helpers.

Even when taking advantage of all the aid offered, there is much to do. Out-of-town relatives are housed in the home of the deceased when possible. Other local relatives or friends may throw open their homes. When such arrangements are not practicable, hotel reservations should be made. In this latter case, the hotel accomodations are paid for by the individual occupying them, not by the family of the deceased.

The Funeral and Requiem Mass

On the morning of the funeral those who are to attend gather at the home or funeral parlor a few moments before the appointed hour. If a priest, Brother or Sister is present, he or she leads the assemblage in prayers. If no religious are present, the funeral director may lead the prayers. Then the funeral cars are called and the mourners file out in the order described under "Funeral Procession," with this exception: the pallbearers stay behind to carry the casket to the hearse. This is done after all present have entered their cars.

The procession drives to the church in the same order in which it was formed. The Mass celebrant, any other attending priests, and the altar boys meet the remains at the rear of the church. The casket has been placed on a bier, and is guided up the main aisle by the pallbearers. Then follow the honorary pallbearers, Brothers and Sisters, the immediate family, etc., as described above.

The bier is left at the head of the main aisle. The family sit in the pews on the epistle side (right) of the church, just to the rear of the casket. The pallbearers sit in the pews on the left and right side in front of the bier. Behind them on the left sit honorary pallbearers, religious Brothers or Sisters, civic dignitaries, and official delegations. Attending priests always sit in the sanctuary. Friends sit behind the family on either side of the church. The recessional follows the same order of precedence, save that now the immediate family files out directly behind the bier.

Burial

No one is socially obligated to accompany the bereaved family to the place of burial except pallbearers and honorary pallbearers, but usually all relatives and very intimate friends do so.

Honorary pallbearers form a path from the roadside to the grave as a guard of honor. The space around the grave is reserved for the immediate family. Others stand a little distance away to afford them privacy at this difficult time. Following the committal prayers, pallbearers sometimes cast into the grave the gloves furnished them by the funeral director, but this is not always done. All present leave the cemetery privately; no set order is observed.

If the interment is to be made in a community other than the one in which the Mass is said, the journey is made directly after the funeral. Should the distance be a long one, pallbearers may be excused from making it. In this case professionals hired by the director replace them at the grave. Only the immediate family go to such a committal; certainly there is no obligation for any others to attend.

If death occurred in midwinter and the body is to rest in a cemetery vault for the time being, a brief service in the cemetery chapel is substituted for the committal service.

Children and Funerals

There are no rules that define the propriety of children attending or absenting themselves from the funerals of relatives. Some families excuse children up to the age of twelve from the funeral rites of a parent on the theory that attendance would be too painful for them. Many parents excuse children up through the teen years from making condolence calls or attending the funerals of anyone, the feeling being that it is not required of the children by the laws of propriety and that the duty can therefore be postponed until they are adults.

Such a position is correct socially, but to shield children from contact with death and mourning is surely unwise, unnatural, and un-Catholic. Death, like birth, is one of the major realities of life. Catholics know that it is the door that opens the way to eternal life, for which our earthly existence is but a preparation. A bereaved family at time of death suffers the pangs of loss and loneliness, but the *fact* of death is not, and should not be, in itself, fearful or shocking.

Considering all this, one may conclude that a child of more than eight years might be allowed to make an earthly farewell to the remains of a grandparent, aunt or even closer relative, always having been prepared for it by the gentle reminder that this is but the earthly envelope of the beloved, that the soul which animated it has gone to its heavenly reward, where we will one day be able to join it. Children over eight may also be allowed to attend the funeral of a relative, to see the loving ceremony with which the family and the Church consign the dead to God's care.

In the loss of a parent, consideration must be given to the temperament of the child. Obsequies are painful. But consider: a small child is suddenly told "Father has gone to heaven to live with God." The parent was here. He is gone, with no preparation, no farewell, no ceremony. How is the child to understand that the rest of his family will not similarly be snatched away without warning? What fearful imaginings may he not substitute for the ceremonies he was not allowed to witness? Surely this is the more traumatic experience.

Children of fourteen and over should be expected to make condolence calls, thus learning at the proper age how to perform the duties which will be required of them as adults.

After the Funeral

Following a funeral it is a custom, quite generally observed, for the nearest of kin to offer luncheon to all relatives before they go their separate ways. This is not an obligation and may be wholly omitted if circumstances warrant. But it is a gracious practice that promotes family loyalty and solidarity.

Catholics do not grieve "as those who have no hope." At such a time, hearts are heavy with loneliness, sore with loss. But the mourners know that this parting is not final. Their loved one has gone before them to "a place of refreshment, light and peace," to be for them a powerful intercessor in the court of heaven. Daily they will remember him in their prayers, speak of him to one another, recall him to their children in loving reminiscence. This final meal together is for the living, to strengthen family ties—ties that form, not a net, to bind and constrict, but a warm garment to protect from a cold outer world, a garment woven of loving, caring, and sharing. Through it the joys and consolations of the Faith run like a golden thread.

Ideally, this meal is served in the home of the departed soul. Old friends or former servants may offer to prepare it there and have all ready for a buffet luncheon when the family returns from the services. A local relative may offer to give it in her home. Failing this, the family homemaker may plan to serve the luncheon with the help of a caterer, or arrange for the luncheon in a private dining room of a restaurant. Sometimes the titular head of the family assumes the expense for this meal, or it may be shared by the group.

Acknowledgments

Condolence calls require no written acknowledgment, it being presumed that callers are thanked for their visit at the time it is made. All other expressions of sympathy require prompt written acknowledgment. Pallbearers are thanked in writing for their services. Flowers, Mass offerings, prayer enrollments, notes of sympathy, gifts of food, personal services, use of cars, are acknowledged by a brief handwritten note from the nearest of kin. If these latter—wife, mother, etc.—are too overcome to write their own acknowledgments, another near relative may do so in their name.

The engraved cards which the funeral director furnishes to the bereaved family are a bare minimal response which are acceptable only in a few special cases. Well-bred people will exert themselves to write short notes for all kindnesses received. The cards are proper only in the following cases:

a) The death of a public official or religious dignitary, whose family receives hundreds of expressions of sympathy. Use of the cards to acknowledge some of them is then proper, but cards should not be sent to relatives or personal friends.

b) The sole survivor is an aged person who would be overtaxed by writing notes.

c) The sole survivors are young children.

d) The sole survivor is someone who lived elsewhere, to whom those who offered sympathy are not personally known.

e) There are no actual survivors and acknowledgment is made by the deceased's estate office or lawyer.

f) To acknowledge mere cards of sympathy.

Notes of acknowledgment are written on small, double sheets of all-white or black-bordered note paper. Some examples follow:

> DEAR JOHN,
>   *Thank you for serving as a pallbearer for my father. Your kindness will be long remembered.*
> > Sincerely,
> > ALTHEA WHITE

> DEAR ELINOR,
>   *The spray of lilies which you sent when Mother died was so beautiful. Your kindness was deeply felt by all of us.*
> > Affectionately,
> > LAURA

> MY DEAR MR. WELCH,
>   *Thank you most profoundly for the Masses which you and the others of my late husband's associates have arranged to have offered for his repose. The children and I will never forget your kindness.*
> > Sincerely,
> > LYDIA JAMES

> DEAREST JANE,
>   *I cannot find words warm enough to thank you and Howard for the flowers, Masses, and innumerable other*

kindnesses which you offered me when Fred left us. I hope you can read my heart. Please drop in whenever you can.

Devotedly,
CYNTHIA

DEAR LEONARD,
Your letter moved me more than I can say. How well you knew and appreciated Vincent! I shall save your letter to show the children when they are older.

Gratefully,
PATTY

DEAR MRS. DOUGLASS,
My mother asks me to convey to you her heartfelt thanks for the Masses you are having said for my Aunt Rachel. When Mother is feeling a little better, she will thank you personally.

Sincerely,
EDNA REILLY

DEAR MRS. PUGH,
Thank you so much for having enrolled my mother in the Perpetual Mass Association of the Congregation of the Holy Cross. It was a beautiful thought—and so like you.

Gratefully,
MARGARET MCMAHON

The Funerals of Children

Children who have attained the age of reason (considered to be seven years old or thereabouts) receive the last rites of the Church in the form of a Requiem Mass, just as adults do, on the assumption that, having been capable of distinguishing between right and wrong, they were also capable of sinning, and are thus in need of the supplication of the Requiem Mass.

The mourning period and the funeral itself are in general similar to that of adults. The coffin is white; the child is robed in white; white flowers are sent to the house of mourning by friends. Taste dictates the other details. High school children sometimes have classmates for pallbearers.

It is sensible to keep all details of a child's funeral very simple. The period for receiving calls should be brief: one day and evening is enough.

For children too young to have reached the age of reason, no Requiem Mass is sung. Since they died before having become capable of sinning, the supplication of the Requiem Mass is not required for them. But the Church permits the funerals of little ones to be performed in church with a Mass of the Angels, the Mass of the day, or a votive Mass being celebrated. The Church does not *require* this to be done; She merely permits it where the parents so desire.

For children who die in infancy, it is perhaps better merely to bury the child with the customary services at the grave, that is, to omit receiving condolence calls and the Angel's Mass, because it is such a harrowing experience for all concerned and is not needed for the little soul's welfare. All baptized children, however young, are buried in consecrated ground.

Unbaptized children have no funeral services and are not buried in consecrated ground, but in a decent place.

Following is a résumé of the Church's position about the "Burial of Little Ones":

a) Unbaptized infants may not be buried in a blessed place; but their corpses should be buried, without prayers, in a decent place.

b) Baptized little ones who possessed the use of reason, although they had not attained their seventh year, should be buried after the manner of little ones.

c) Baptized little ones who have died before attaining the use of reason or the years of discretion should be buried after the manner of little ones. Under the name of "little ones" are included all over seven years of age who have been insane all their life.

The Ritual says nothing about the Mass to be celebrated at the burial of little ones. But the piety of the faithful has introduced in some places the custom of celebrating a votive Mass of the Angels. This Mass, however, enjoys no privileges and it must therefore be celebrated according to the rubrics for private votive Masses. Whenever the Rubrics do not permit this Mass, the Mass of the feast occurring in the calendar may be celebrated.[1]

[1] Wuest, Rev. Joseph, *Matters Liturgical.*

The custom of celebrating the votive Mass of the
Angels has been approved by the Church, provided that
a votive Mass may be said on that day. The Mass of the
day or any other votive Mass may be said. The Requiem
Mass is forbidden, since the child, having died before it
reached the age of reason, has no need of supplication.[2]

Living In Mourning

a) *Mourning Attire*   The wearing of mourning costume following
the funeral has become, with Americans, so much a matter of personal
preference that it is difficult to lay down rules about it. Mourning is
an outward expression of inner sorrow—or, ideally, it should be so.
For the new mourner, mourning attire is a protection. Clerks, taxi
drivers, all casual contacts are kind and obliging to one in full mourning. Acquaintances refrain from idle chat; friends do not ask one to
parties or unsuitable gaieties.

On the other hand, mourning is seldom worn to business, the feeling being that it is improper to obtrude one's personal loss upon business connections. Since so very many of us, both men and women, now
go to business, the question arises: must one have a full set of mourning clothes to wear while not at work, and another wardrobe for one's
working day? This is beyond the means of so many that all the old
rules about the wearing of mourning carry less and less weight.

Elderly widows sometimes wear mourning for the rest of their lives.
Elderly women sometimes wear mourning or half-mourning for life
upon the death of a grown child. Most widows and mothers wear
mourning or half-mourning for a year. Mourning for aged parents is
often limited to six months and reserved for ceremonial occasions such
as church services. Adult sisters and brothers seldom wear mourning
following the funeral. The wearing of mourning by children under
fourteeen is no longer considered proper, regardless of the degree of
relationship. From fourteen to eighteen, mourning is worn from three
to six months for a parent only.

Since men spend so much time in the business world, they tend to
wear mourning less and less, regardless of the severity of their loss.
Widowers should wear mourning for a year, but the fact that they may
not do so is no longer considered any reflection upon their devotion to
their late wife. It is usually a matter of finances.

Mourning attire is always a material of dull finish that gives a

[2] O'Connell-Schmidt, *The Book of Ceremonies.*

somber appearance. Broadcloth, serge, gabardine, wool, wool jersey, flannel, silk crepe and unlustered faille are mourning; tulle, tweed, satin, net, taffeta and silk jersey are not. Mourning clothes are never trimmed with embroidery, beading or lace. Full mourning requires an all-black costume and no jewelry. All-white is also full mourning, and may be worn in the country where all-black is unsuitable. A child under fourteen may also be properly dressed in all-white for mourning, although a child so young would never be dressed in black. Black with white touches, or white with black touches, is half-mourning.

b) *Mourning Behavior* The rules governing social behavior following a bereavement seem to be quite as outmoded—or disregarded —as those about wearing mourning. But it is still true that the behavior of a bereaved person is regarded as an indication of his feelings. If a mourner's heart is full of grief, he willingly avoids all large gatherings and scenes of gaiety; if it is not, he may mingle in society as much as he chooses and flaunt his indifference to the world. One should remember that one will be so judged, to avoid giving the wrong impression.

One in mourning does not go to large public functions, balls or large dinner parties. He does not dine out in gay restaurants or go to night clubs. He does not entertain at all during the mourning period. He may dine with a few friends in their home, or go alone or with a small party to the opera, a concert, or the motion pictures. He may dine at his club, but not take guests there, other than his immediate family. He may continue such sports as he has always played—golf, bowling, etc. His sports costumes should be dark-colored but suitable to the game he is playing. If he is a member of a regular bridge foursome, he continues to play, but if it is a bridge club of two or more tables, he withdraws from it temporarily.

A widow or widower should not accept or offer attentions to the opposite sex for a year. If he disregards this rule, he should leave off all mourning garb and drop all pretense of being withdrawn from society.

Children who have lost a parent continue to take part in such school activities as sports events (as player, not spectator), recitals, club meetings, glee club and orchestra. They may attend church functions such as Sodality or Holy Name meetings. But they do not go to dances, teas, receptions, fraternity or sorority functions, dinner or birthday parties. They should observe at least a three-months mourning period.

Children and teen-agers go into mourning only for parents. But this attitude may be carried to extremes. Sometimes a parent says, "I shall let Sally go to the dance next weekend, even though dear Grandma has just died. The child has been looking forward to it for so long; and Grandma would have been the last person in the world to deny her a little pleasure."

Such an attitude merely teaches Sally to be heartless, shallow, and ill-bred, and to regard her pleasures as more important than respect for her grandparent's memory. If Sally is to develop the kind heart and loving ways that are the true attributes of a lady, she should be allowed her share in her parent's sorrow for the loss of a parent, and be expected, as a matter of course, to show it by denying herself the pleasures of the dance. To shield or exempt children, particularly teen-agers, from all that is sad, irksome, or burdensome in family life is to deprive them of the means of learning how to grow into maturity.

Veterans' Burial Rights

In any family in which a service veteran dies, one should check immediately with the nearest regional office of the United States Veterans' Administration to learn the rights of the deceased. A veteran who served with any of the Armed Forces in war time is entitled to an allowance of $150 towards his burial expenses. There are a number of benefits for both war and peacetime veterans, and as these vary in individual cases, a check with the Administration office is the safe way to get the facts.

Spare Your Family!

It must be obvious to one who has read this chapter how greatly the difficulties of the bereaved family are multiplied by the many decisions so quickly required of them. How much they are spared if the departed soul has anticipated these difficulties and obviated them! A sensible man does not balk at insuring his life or making a will. Why should he not purchase a cemetery plot at his leisure while he is in good health? And it is surely a trifling task to write down one's wishes about one's last rites: the amount to be spent, the director one prefers, the pallbearers, such material as one wishes included in one's obituary, etc. There is nothing that would be a greater help in a house of mourning than to find, filed away with will and insurance policies, the departed loved one's wishes about his funeral. It would surely be a final proof of his care for and love of his family.

MOURNING AND FUNERAL ETIQUETTE FOR FRIENDS

Letters of Condolence

Letters of condolence should be handwritten on white personal writing paper. A seal, monogram, or printed address on the paper is allowable, but colored paper is not. Generally speaking, such letters should be brief, dignified, and sympathetic. Their tone and content varies, of course, with the degree of acquaintance between writer and recipient. A note similar to the one given below satisfies all the social requirements:

> DEAR MRS. BANNISTER,
> *My husband and I were much grieved to hear of your*
> *sad loss. Please accept our most profound sympathy.*
> *Sincerely yours,*
> *Wednesday*   IDA HUMMEL

Such a note satisfies the social requirements because it takes due notice of the bereavement, expresses sympathy, does not harrow the feelings of the recipient, and is not maudlin or overstrained. It is, however, very formal and impersonal. It is suitable to send to casual or business acquaintances, and, if one does not trust one's ability to say more, it will do for a more intimate acquaintance. If one has any felicity of expression at one's command, however, and if one feels any personal sorrow at the bereavement, one should attempt to say more. The line here is hard to draw. Here are some examples of actual notes received in the writer's family during a time of bereavement, which are tactful and consoling. The deceased was an aged man who had borne the cross of blindness for many years with courage and cheerfulness.

From a neighbor:

> DEAR EUNICE,
> *In all the distress of the present hour, it must comfort*
> *you to remember that human love does not die but is, in*
> *some mysterious and beautiful way, transmuted into the*
> *Eternal.*
> *The love and care you gave your father during the*
> *long years of his illness have been a constant inspiration*
> *to me.*
> *With deepest sympathy,*
> CAROLYN COX

From a family friend:

> DEAR EUNICE,
> *Please accept my sympathy in the loss of your father.
> The way he accepted his cross in life was a splendid ex-
> ample to all of us. How fortunate you were to have had
> him for so long!*
> *We who have suffered the loss of our loved ones
> realize how much our Faith means to us in our darker
> moments, and what a help it is in accepting God's Holy
> Will.*
> *With understanding sympathy and affection,*
> LAVINIA WILLS

From a distant niece:

> DEAREST AUNT FRANCES,
> *Oh, how I wish I could come to you to tell you how
> sorry I am to learn of Uncle John's passing! It is in times
> like these I most regret that a continent stands between
> us. Paul and Mary Ellen send you their sympathy also.*
> *I cherish the memory of the many happy hours I
> spent in your house as a child. Can it really be thirty
> years ago? I still tell my children some of the stories I
> first heard from Uncle John. He was a superb teller of
> tales. And do you remember how he would sit me on his
> lap and let me "help" him drive your big Franklin? That
> marvelous old car was a magic chariot to me.*
> *Aunt Frances, you know I will not forget. He will be
> remembered in my prayers every day—and so will you.
> My dear love and sympathy to you and the girls.*
> *Always, with deepest affection,*
> ANN MARIE

From a business associate of the deceased:

> MY DEAR MRS. WEBER,
> *For thirty years your late husband and I were busi-
> ness competitors. Although I have not had the pleasure
> of meeting you, I intrude myself upon you at this sad
> time to tell you how grieved I am to learn of his passing,
> and how profoundly he will be missed in the industry he
> did so much to promote.*
> *The high ethical standards which he applied to his*

*private life were precisely the ones which guided his
business activities. I never knew him to do a mean or
ignoble thing. If he had any enemies, he most certainly
did not deserve them.*

 *To you and your family I offer my heartfelt sym-
pathy. If I can serve you in any way, please feel free to
call on me.*

Sincerely yours,
JOHN EDWARD PARNELL

Letters such as these are treasured by the receiver and are a true
source of consolation. Since they must come from the heart, it is almost
impossible to lay down rules of composition for them. One can only
say: Be brief. Be natural. Be sincere. Do not express emotion you do
not feel; do not attribute to the departed soul virtues he did not
possess. *Never* attempt to harrow the receiver's feelings or impress him
with your writing skill. Always keep in mind your main purpose: to
condole and to console.

Between Catholics

Catholics have a dual religious obligation to offer some expression
of sympathy to a mourning family in a time of bereavement.

a) We believe in the efficacy of prayer for the soul of the dead,
because it helps satisfy God's justice, and may move Him in His
mercy to remit part of the temporal punishment for sin, which
the departed soul suffers in Purgatory. "It is therefore a holy
and wholesome thought to pray for the dead, that they may be
loosed from sin" (II Machabees 12:46).

b) To bury the dead is one of the corporal works of mercy by
which we strive to earn heaven. The phrase "bury the dead"
means, in its broader sense, any kindnesses or assistance offered
to a bereaved family to ease them in their time of suffering.
Thus a menial task, such as running errands, if offered up with
the correct intention, becomes a corporal work of mercy.

The religious obligation intensifies the normal impulse felt by all
well-bred people to offer sympathy to mourners; it also enlarges the
number of occasions on which one does so.

A Catholic may properly offer sympathy in the form of a note or a
visit of condolence to any other Catholic with whom he is acquainted,
whenever that Catholic has suffered the loss of any relative. He may
do this even though the deceased was wholly unknown to him. Conversely, a Catholic who loses a friend in death may properly express

sympathy to any of that friend's surviving relatives, even though the relatives were hitherto unknown to him.

The form this offering takes varies with the degree of acquaintance. A brief note is sufficient for casual or business relationship. A call at the home or funeral parlors (wherever the family have been announced as receiving) is correct whatever the degree of acquaintance. An offering of a Mass or an enrollment in a prayer or Mass association is the finest thing one can do for the deceased person, and is therefore a true consolation to his survivors.

It is currently fashionable to decry the sending of flowers as a "waste" of money. It is true that such an offering does not carry the religious benefits of a Mass, but it is socially correct to send them. Anyone who has ever attended a funeral to which no flowers have been sent values them more highly thereafter. In some intangible way their beauty *does* soothe and console, and provides a noble frame for a sad picture. If one is financially able to send both Mass offerings and flowers to the funeral of a relative, one should certainly do so.

There are a number of services which relatives, intimate friends, and neighbors can offer that are informal in character but are truly helpful and much appreciated. The custom of bringing food to a house of mourning still survives. This is the traditional offering from neighbor to neighbor, and one may correctly extend it even to one only slightly known. Meat dishes, casseroles, salads, desserts—anything that may be quickly served buffet style will be a real help to the housekeeper.

Help in caring for small children is highly valued. Intimate friends may offer the use of mourning veils, black clothing, etc., or may volunteer to shop for these items. One may offer the use of one's car for the funeral, with or without a driver. If such an offer is accepted, the car should be spotless.

Relatives and very intimate friends of the deceased person who live out of town should try to come to pay their respects during the period of condolence calls, or for the funeral. In deciding your obligation to be present, degree of relationship, degree of intimacy, the distance involved, and the expense are all factors to be weighed, as is the number of survivors. Thus if your Aunt May, the mother of five living children and the sister of six, dies in a town three hundred miles from you, you might feel that you could be excused from appearing. But if your grand-uncle Emmet dies a thousand miles from you, with few to mourn him, you should go if at all possible.

The best rule is: go if you can do so without serious hardship to yourself or family, without regard to other factors. It is a kindness which is deeply appreciated and long remembered, and it is a corporal work of mercy which will earn an eternal reward. Furthermore, such gatherings promote family solidarity, increase affection and maintain family ties.

Pallbearer

An invitation to act as pallbearer, or honorary pallbearer, may be refused only for the most serious reasons. Illness, incapacity because of age or ill-health, or absence from the city are the only acceptable excuses. It is proper for a Catholic to serve as bearer at non-Catholic funerals; it is equally proper for a non-Catholic to act in like capacity at a Catholic funeral.

Catholics do not customarily employ professional pallbearers. If one is asked to be a pallbearer, it usually means that one is expected to assist in carrying the casket. If one is to be an honorary pallbearer, it will be so stated. One's only duty then is to be part of a guard of honor when the remains are carried into the church. Either request is an honor; it is more of an honor to be an actual pallbearer than an honorary one, as it implies a closer degree of friendship.

From Catholic to Non-Catholic

A Catholic who wishes to offer sympathy to non-Catholic friends in a time of bereavement takes care that the nature of his offering is acceptable to the non-Catholic party by remembering that, to the non-Catholic, the expression of sympathy is a social duty, not a religious one. A note is always proper. So is a condolence call, unless the family is "not receiving," or attendance at the funeral services, if they have not been announced as private. Flowers are correct unless otherwise specified in the death notice. But the Catholic should bear in mind that the non-Catholic does not expect such attentions from casual acquaintances, nor upon the death of distant relatives.

Mother Church, in Her infinite mercy, will offer prayers for the repose of any departed soul. When a Protestant friend dies, a Catholic may arrange to have a Mass said for his repose as a final act of friendship, but he would do this without so notifying the friend's surviving relatives, lest the gesture offend them. If the non-Catholic deceased friend has surviving Catholic relatives, notice of a Mass offering should be sent addressed to the Catholic survivors only. To the Catholic survivors, such an offering would be precious. But, unless the deceased was a relative or very intimate friend, the Catholic had better confine his expressions of sympathy to the social type acceptable to non-Catholics. These expressions include the offering of food and services and other neighborly kindnesses if the degree of acquaintance warrants them.

Many Protestant and Jewish death notices say: "Contributions to the American Cancer Society (or the Heart Fund, or the Cerebral Palsy Society, whatever the family desires) are requested in lieu of flowers."

This means that the family of the deceased person feels that the money that is frequently spent for funeral flowers would be put to better use if offered to fight illness. Usually the request for a contribution is made on behalf of the ailment from which the dead person had suffered; the inference being that if contributions in his memory are made to help find a cure for the disease which killed him, others may be spared a similar death, and the loved one will not have suffered in vain.

In such a case, friends write to the local office of the chosen society and donate any sum of money they choose, to aid the cause. They give the name of the deceased person in whose memory they are making the contribution and also the name and address of the principal survivor, or the one with whom they are acquainted. The society will acknowledge the offering by a letter of thanks to the donor, and will also send a letter or printed card to the indicated survivor, stating that an offering has been made by the donor in memory of the deceased person.

From Non-Catholics to Catholics

The differences in the mourning customs of Catholics and those of other faiths stem mainly from two Catholic beliefs not generally understood by non-Catholics. They are:

a) The belief that to assist in any way in burying the dead is a corporal work of mercy which is pleasing to God, and which helps the doer to earn heaven. By "burying the dead" we mean any service or act of kindness offered to a bereaved family in their time of loss. We believe such acts find favor in God's sight, just as does care for orphans or the sick or homeless. Therefore such attentions are not merely a kindness to one's bereaved friends; they also redound to one's own spiritual good.

b) We believe that sincere sorrow for our sins and a worthy confession earns forgiveness for sin and saves us from being condemned to hell. But it does not always wipe out the temporal punishment for sin, which must be expiated in purgatory. The length of time we suffer in purgatory may be shortened, if God so wills it, by the prayers of living souls or of the saints. Since the noblest of all prayer is the Holy Sacrifice of the Mass, Catholics believe that the greatest kindness one can offer to a departed friend or loved one, is to arrange to have a Mass offered for the repose of his soul.

Most of the practices outlined in this section stem from these two beliefs.

It is correct to offer an expression of sympathy to any Catholic friend, business associate, or neighbor upon the death of any of his relatives, whether one was acquainted with the relative or not. It is correct to offer sympathy upon the death of a Catholic friend, business associate or neighbor, to his survivors, whether one is acquainted with the survivors or not.

A note or a call at the funeral parlor during visiting hours is correct for any degree of acquaintance. So are the usual kindnesses offered by neighbor to neighbor. Anything one might do for any Christian friend may be done for a Catholic, including attendance at the funeral itself.

Flowers are acceptable. They are sent to the home or funeral parlor (wherever the family is receiving) addressed to The Funeral Of ———————————— or The Family of ————————————. They are not sent to the church. No flowers appear at the church at a Catholic funeral, as, in the church, they are symbols of rejoicing, not of mourning. But they are displayed during visiting hours and are taken to the grave for the committal service.

To have a Mass or a number of Masses said for the respose of the soul of a Catholic friend is the finest thing one can do for him. Such masses are of two types, High or Low. A Low Mass is not sung. The date and hour are not announced; it is offered at the convenience of the celebrant. A High Mass is chanted by the priest, and sung by a soloist or choir. The hour and date are announced in the parish bulletin or at the Sunday Masses just prior to the date upon which they are to be celebrated. The two types of Masses have equal favor in God's sight and equal spiritual value, but in the case of the High Mass the family of the deceased are able to be present if they wish, because they have had public notification of the time at which it is to be celebrated.

To arrange for a Mass for a friend, one calls at any Catholic rectory and asks that such a Mass, or Masses, be said. One gives the full name of one's deceased friend and states the number of Masses one wishes to have offered, and whether one wishes a High or Low Mass. Most city rectories have printed forms, called Mass Cards, which the priest fills out. These cards state that "a Mass will be offered for the repose of the soul of ⸺⸺⸺⸺⸺, at the request of ⸺⸺⸺⸺⸺." One may also buy these cards at religious shops; one then takes them to the rectory at the time one requests a Mass; they will be filled out by the priest and returned to the donor. It is prudent to buy the form and bring it when one requests a Mass, for some rectories do not provide them. Such Mass cards may be mailed to the bereaved family or delivered personally when making a condolence call.

It is customary to make an offering when asking that Masses be offered. Such offerings may be as little as one dollar for a Low Mass. The offering for a High Mass is usually five dollars or more. Such an offering is not "pay" for the Mass. A Mass is beyond price, yet thousands of them are said every year for the destitute without any offering having been made. The offering is an expression of gratitude for service given, similar to the offerings made at a baptism or wedding.

A similar kindness one may perform for a Catholic friend that has great merit in his eyes is to enroll him in a prayer association. A number of religious communities such as the Franciscans, the Dominicans, and dozens of others have such associations. The priests of the order offer up a number of masses within a given period for all who are enrolled in the association. Any priest of the order which one selects can arrange for such an enrollment. One makes a donation to the good works of the order when asking for such an enrollment.

Non-Catholics sometimes hesitate to make a condolence call on Catholic friends because they are uncertain what is expected of them on such an occasion. This is unnecessary. The etiquette is the same as in making a similar call on a non-Catholic, with one exception. Catholics believe in the efficacy of prayer for the dead. Therefore a prie-dieu, or kneeling bench, is placed near the casket. Catholics customarily kneel here and offer a brief prayer for the departed soul. Non-Catholics may do so also, if they wish, but failure to do so will occasion no comment.

From Christian to Jew

The Jewish faith is divided into three denominations: Orthodox, Conservative, and Reformed. The Orthodox persuasion follows strictly the ancient, traditional observances of Jewry. The Reformed persuasion is the least strict; the Conservative lies between the two. As regards what is acceptable practice for Christian friends in offering sympathy in a time of mourning, there is not a great deal of difference between the three. Such differences as exist are included in this material.

The formal mourning period for all Jews before the funeral is brief, usually confined to the night prior to the funeral. After the funeral, all Jews observe for one week in their homes a formal mourning period. Therefore the following gestures of sympathy between Christian and Jews are acceptable:

a) A note of sympathy, couched in the usual terms.

b) Attendance at the funeral or committal service, or both.

c) A condolence call at the home during the post-funeral mourning period.

d) A bouquet of flowers (never a funeral "piece") sent to the home with a note of sympathy.

e) A basket of fruit sent to the home during the week of mourning. This is the traditional offering.

Such expressions of sympathy are correct for all three persuasions. When attending a Jewish funeral, a Christian man should notice whether the Jewish men present have removed or are wearing their hats, or skull caps, and should follow the custom of the congregation, as this practice differs in different congregations.

Orthodox Jews usually do not receive callers during the mourning period the night before the funeral, but some do. Conservative and Reformed Jews usually do receive callers at this time. Since there is no set rule about this, one should consult the death notice in the newspapers. If they are receiving, the notice will so state. Technically, Jewish mourning does not begin until after the funeral. The observance the night before the funeral is in the nature of an earthly farewell to the departed. It is for this purpose that one visits the funeral chapel at this time, rather than to condole with the mourners. If the deceased belonged to a lodge which holds services for the deceased members, this is the time at which they are held. No clergyman is present.

In the Jewish faith, flowers are a symbol of rejoicing. A funeral floral arrangement sent to the funeral chapel is seldom acceptable to an Orthodox or Conservative Jew. They are suitable in some cases to a Reformed Jew. Since the difference exists, it is best to avoid this type of offering. If one insists on attempting it, one should call the funeral director to find out whether it is acceptable.

Jews follow the practice that is also popular with Protestants of requesting a contribution to the Cancer or Heart Fund, or some similar medical group, in lieu of other offerings. If they wish this kind of remembrance for their dead, the funeral notice will say so.

Another Jewish custom is to request a contribution to the Tree Fund for Israel, which is one of the activities of Hadassah. This is especially suitable if the family are ardent Zionists, but is acceptable to all. The tree, as a symbol of Life Eternal, suits the occasion.

To make such a contribution, call the local Jewish National Fund, or Tree Chairman of Hadassah, and make an offering. She will then send a notice of the contribution to the bereaved family. Any local rabbi or Jewish funeral director can tell one who the local chairman is.

Another offering acceptable to all Jews is to make a contribution to the Book Fund of their synagogue. The money will be used to purchase Bibles, and will bear a bookplate stating that it was donated in memory of one's deceased friend. Catholics cannot make such an offering however, as it is a direct contribution to an alien faith, which is not licit.

Orthodox and Conservative Jews have Jewish pallbearers; Reformed Jews usually do also. But Christians are sometimes asked to be honorary pallbearers. Such an invitation cannot be refused, except for grave reasons, such as serious ill-health.

7

Engagement and Pre-Nuptial Entertaining

"Behold, the bridegroom is coming, go forth to meet him!" (Matthew 25:6–7).

DEFINITION

An engagement is a promise to marry at some future date, mutually given by the two contracting parties. It should be made freely, without reservations, and neither contracting party should have been subject to pressure, fear or duress. It may be terminated at any time prior to marriage by mutual consent.

Historically (and currently in several foreign countries), the Church has recognized engagements when they take the form of a formal espousal signed by the two parties and witnessed by their pastor or two lay witnesses. This practice has never taken root in America. Here the engagement of Catholics has been a wholly secular affair.

But since World War II a number of devout young Catholics, eager to invest the period of their engagement with a religious significance, have been contracting a kind of formal espousal called a canonical engagement. This practice will be discussed at length under the heading "Canonical Engagement."

SPIRITUAL SIGNIFICANCE

Even a secular engagement has much spiritual meaning of which the contracting parties should be aware. It should be preceded by a time of courtship in which the young couple learn to know one another and, if possible, become acquainted with one another's families. It should not be entered into quickly or lightly, nor with mental reservations. It should not be agreed to unless the parties concerned can marry a year or so after becoming engaged. It should not be so brief

87

as to fail to accomplish its purpose, which is to allow the young people to know one another well enough so as to be sure they truly wish to marry.

Engaged couples have privileges: they can spend more time together than before, spend more time alone, and focus their attention more exclusively upon one another. But an engagement is not a license for improper intimacies. The new status should impel the young woman to refrain from any freedom that might be an occasion of sin to her fiancé: the young man should cherish and respect his fiancée more than ever.

It is a time when hearts and minds should be opened freely. The young man and woman should strive to learn one another's true feelings about their Faith, children, the purpose of marriage, ideal family life, the duties of husband and wife, proper spending of the joint income, and all other matters that can be a source of friction after marriage. Now, above all, is the time for honesty. A girl who says she "adores" children when she really "hates the little brats" is deceiving her beloved. A man who says he is anxious to settle down into family living should not plan to continue to golf on Saturday, fish on Sunday, and play poker twice a week. If possible, learn to know one another's families. Remember that the prospective mother-in-law whom you now dislike may be a preview of your future bride thirty years hence!

FIRST DUTIES

In present-day America, an engagement is more solely the concern of the contracting parties than in any other country in any age. A young man often proposes and is at least tentatively accepted without either family's being consulted. Thereafter the young people sometimes announce it to their families as a settled thing, without any permission being asked or given.

The more old-fashioned way is the better one. Let the young man tell his family in advance that he intends to propose, and what his marriage plans are. Let him listen to his parents' opinions in the matter, especially if they know the girl. He may not—indeed, if he is of age, he need not—take their advice, but he should hear it, and try to weigh it dispassionately.

After proposing and being accepted, he should then call formally on his fiancée's father and ask his consent to the marriage. He should tell him what his present financial status is, how he intends to support a wife, and what his future prospects are. He should be able to tell him that there is nothing in his past life unknown to his future wife that could shame or injure her. If he cannot say this, he should confess any past misdeeds at once. Here we are talking of serious things, such as a prison record, the drug habit, etc.

If he fears that he has any tendency towards alcoholism, he should say so, and tell how he intends to combat the evil. He should be prepared to say that his health is good, or to admit to ill health.

Why should a young man do all this? To his prospective bride's father he is, more often than not, almost a stranger. He is asking that father to commit to a stranger's care a soul whom he helped bring into the world, to whose rearing, education, and nurturing he has devoted the best years of his life, whom he loves with a special feeling unlike any other. To ask his consent in this manly fashion immediately reassures the parent in two ways: it shows that the young man quite properly feels that his fiancée is a treasure whom he cannot snatch away without a by-your-leave, and that he is grateful for the years of devotion her father has lavished upon her. There is nothing a prospective fiancé can do that can create a better impression than this. There is nothing wiser a father can do than to require it.

A young couple should give serious consideration to objections made by either family. Such objections may be selfish, frivolous, based on jealousy or insufficient information, but they are not often so. Differences in religion are extremely serious, and will be discussed elsewhere. Differences in racial stock, education, background or aim in life may make a marriage more difficult. Immaturity is the worst hazard of all—and the hardest one for the contracting parties to recognize. If a couple are very young, or unable to support themselves, they should not consider marrying without parental consent, whether they may legally do so or not. The odds against a happy marriage are too high.

CANONICAL ENGAGEMENT

The canonical, or ecclesiastical, engagement is a custom that is part of a recent movement, fostered both by laymen and clergy, to weave the beauty and symbolism of our liturgy into our practice of our Faith and to invest all the important occasions of our life with a religious or sacramental character. Its purpose is to combat the unfortunate effect of the blatant secularism that surrounds us in all areas of living, and which promises to increase rather than decay.

A canonical engagement serves a further good purpose: It emphasizes the true purpose of an engagement as a time of serious and thoughtful preparation for the responsibilities and joys of marriage. It helps arm the young couple against sins against chastity and purity which tempt the best of us so powerfully and so attractively at this time in our lives.

The point must be made that there is no obligation on any Catholic to make his engagement a canonical one. Many pastors are not yet familiar with the custom. But it is indeed a beautiful and worthy one, deserving the strongest recommendation.

A canonical engagement is a promise to marry at some future date, made freely and without reservations before the altar of the Blessed Mother by the contracting parties, who further promise to guard against sins against purity and chastity at this time. It is signed by the pastor of the church. Like any engagement, it may be terminated at any time before marriage by mutual consent, or by any lawful impediment to marriage later discovered. If a priest is not available to sign such a contract, the signature of two lay witnesses may be substituted.

Following is a description of the suggested form of a canonical engagement, as prepared by the Rt. Rev. Martin Hellriegel.

The Ecclesiastical Engagement

The custom of canonical engagement is growing. We herewith print a suggestion for a program to follow for the event which may be adapted as circumstances indicate.

I. IN OFFICE OF RECTORY (a week or so before the actual engagement):

1. The pastor points out the purpose and spirit of ecclesiastical engagement.

2. He stresses the other promises, indicated on document. Like *four* great cornerstones:
   a) Frequent reception of holy sacraments and prayer
   b) Charity
   c) Mutual respect
   d) Chastity

3. He gives the young people a copy of document asking them to read it over carefully and bring it along on the day appointed.

II. BEFORE THE ALTAR OF THE BLESSED MOTHER, on the day appointed:

1. The pastor (in surplice and stole, with pen and parish seal on altar) gives brief instruction, once more emphasizing what he said in office.

2. The two to be engaged read aloud their promise (from document).
3. They approach the altar to sign it (man first).
4. The pastor signs it.
5. He blesses the ring (*Benedictio ad omnia*), sprinkles it with holy water.
6. The bridegroom-to-be places the ring on the finger of his bride-to-be, saying: "In the name of the Father, and of the Son and of the Holy Spirit Amen."
7. A word of encouragement is given by the pastor, admonishing them to make their time of preparation for marriage one of courtship, not shipwreck.
8. All kneel and say a prayer to our Blessed Mother, asking her for her blessing, help and protection.
9. The pastor congratulates the young people and reminds them of preparing a "Family History Book" (in which the engagement certificate will be the first entry).
10. If convenient, the couple may be asked to the parish house for a hearty chat and a little refreshment. (The greatest things of our Lord were done at the table!)

The following engagement contract form, handsomely printed in two colors on heavy board paper, may be obtained by writing to the Pio Decimo Press, St. Louis, Mo. It reads:

IN THE NAME OF OUR LORD JESUS CHRIST, AMEN:

Before Almighty God and His heavenly Court, and in the presence of the witnesses whose names are affixed to this document, we the undersigned promise to one another by this ecclesiastical engagement Marriage in Christ. We further promise that by the frequent devout reception of the holy sacraments, by prayer and charity, by mutual respect and chastity we shall assist one another in preparing worthily for the blessed day of our Marriage in Christ. We have made this promise before the altar of our most Holy Mother Mary. We humbly ask the Virgin Mother Mary to carry our promise to the throne of God, and to obtain for us His grace and blessing.

Signed: . . . . & . . . .

Church of . . . .

Date . . . .

Witnessed by . . . .

If a couple wish to have a canonical engagement, they should plan for it some time before the formal announcement of their engagement, to allow time for a visit with their pastor and for the ceremony itself. This should precede the engagement announcement.

FAMILY DUTIES

Immediately following an engagement and prior to the announcement of it, both families should express their pleasure in it to the contracting parties and to each other. The form this expression takes varies with the degree of previous intimacy and place of residence. A woman who has known and loved her prospective daughter-in-law from infancy would not write her a note. But one living out of town would write at once to her new "daughter" along these lines:

> MY DEAR ISABELLA,
> *Philip telephoned us last night to tell us the joyful news. We are so happy for you both! James and I are eager to know you better, and hope that you will be able to visit us soon.*
> *I have sent you a little present to commemorate the happy occasion. It should reach you soon.*
> *Please tell your parents how much we are looking forward to meeting them. Philip has told us so much about them.*
>
>   *Affectionately yours,*
> *Monday*   MARGARET BARR

A letter similar in tone should go from the bride's mother to the prospective bridegroom if he lives or works in another city or if they are not well acquainted.

If the parents live in different cities, and are not acquainted, the bride's mother should write along these lines:

> MY DEAR MRS. WELCH,
> *We are so pleased over the children's great news! Harry is a fine young man, whom we shall be proud to call our son. We feel the young people are ideally suited to one another.*
> *My husband and I are eager to know you and Mr. Welch. Can you not, sometime between the announcement and the wedding, plan on spending a weekend with us?*
>
>   *Sincerely yours,*
> *Saturday*   ALIDA CURTIS

If both sets of parents live in the same city but were hitherto un-acquainted or slightly acquainted, the man's mother should call the girl's parents and invite them and the girl to luncheon, dinner, or tea. This takes the place of the formal call the man's parents made on the young lady in former times. Whatever form this entertaining takes, both parent couples and the engaged pair should be present. Other family members may be included if desired.

No other relatives take any notice of the engagement prior to the formal announcement and often do not know of it. On the day of the public announcement, or just prior to it, the girl or her mother should tell her local relatives, either by a telephone call or a note, that it is to be announced so that they do not first learn of it through the newspapers. The bridegroom's mother does the same for their local relatives.

ANNOUNCING THE ENGAGEMENT

The public is informed of an engagement through an announcement sent to the local papers. The usual form is as follows:

> Mr. and Mrs. George Thatcher Price, 117 Aspinwall Road, announce the engagement of their daughter, Miss Monica Lynn Price, to Mr. William Walter Sims, son of Mr. and Mrs. Walter Douglas Sims, of Rochester.

If the man and girl are both local people, it would read, "son of Mr. and Mrs. Walter Douglas Sims, of 678 Cromwell Drive."

If the bride's parents are dead the engagement may be announced by her grandparents, any relative with whom she makes her home, or an older sister or brother. An example:

> Mr. and Mrs. William Fox Riordan, 322 Elizabeth Street, announce the engagement of her sister, Miss Monica Lynn Price, to Mr. William Walter Sims, son of Mr. and Mrs. Walter Douglas Sims, of 678 Cromwell Drive. Miss Price is the daughter of the late Mr. and Mrs. George Thatcher Price."

Either widowed parent may also announce an engagement. If any of the parents are dead, the fact should be noted. Example: "son of Mrs. Walter Douglas Sims, 678 Cromwell Drive, and the late Mr. Sims."

In many communities the society editor will request more information to accompany the announcement. One may properly add: "The wedding will take place in the fall" or "in April," etc. One may also mention where the two young people were educated. If either had prominent grandparents whose names will be recognized by many, they may be mentioned. Not much else is permissible. A photograph of the bride-to-be may be furnished if requested. Some sample forms:

> Mrs. George Thatcher Price, 117 Aspinwall Road, announces the engagement of her daughter, Miss Monica Lynn Price, to Mr. William Walter Sims, son of Mr. and Mrs. Walter Douglas Sims, of Rochester. Miss Price is the daughter of the late George Thatcher Price, and the granddaughter of Admiral Carl Chase and the late Mrs. Chase. She was graduated from Manhattanville College of the Sacred Heart in the class of 1959.
>
> Mr. Sims was graduated from Cranwell Preparatory School, and is a student at Georgetown University.
>
> The marriage will take place in October.

If the engagement is announced at a party, the public announcement may be made in a news item about it. This is less formal, but correct. An example:

> The engagement of Miss Monica Lynn Price, daughter of Mr. and Mrs. George Thatcher Price, 117 Aspinwall Road, to Mr. William Walter Sims, son of Mr. and Mrs. Walter Douglas Sims, of Rochester, was announced yesterday at a luncheon in the family home, for twenty of Miss Price's intimate friends.
>
> Miss Price is the granddaughter of Admiral Carl Chase and the late Mrs. Chase. She is a graduate of the College of Mount St. Vincent.
>
> Mr. Sims was graduated from Notre Dame University, and has recently returned from Germany, where he served in the Armed Forces as a lieutenant of artillery.

If the newly engaged girl has no living relatives to announce the engagement, the correct form would be:

> Announcement has been made of the engagement of Miss Monica Lynn Price, 22 Crestwood Arms, to Mr. William Walter Sims, son of Mr. and Mrs. Walter Douglas Sims, of Palo Alto, California. Miss Price is the daughter of the

late Mr. and Mrs. George Thatcher Price. She was graduated from Marymount College and has done graduate work at Columbia University. She is currently employed as a market research analyst by the Compton Marketing Research Corporation.

Mr. Sims was graduated from Loyola University of Chicago and Fordham Law School. He is a partner in the law firm of Tobin, Tyrell, Dormuth and Sims.

The marriage will take place in October.

Note that, in this announcement, Mr. Sims is mentioned as having been graduated from Loyola University *of Chicago*. This is necessary when there are several schools having the same name. Otherwise the location of the school is not mentioned.

When one of the engaged couple went to a school but was not graduated from it, the correct phrasing is: "Miss Price studied at the Sorbonne." Or, "Miss Price went to Our Lady of the Elms College." Do not say "attended"; it is pretentious.

If the young man's parents live in a different city than the bride-to-be, an announcement is usually sent to the papers of the town in which they live. In this notice, only the city in which the bride and her parents live is mentioned, and the street address of the bridegroom's parents is given, thus:

Mr. and Mrs. George Thatcher Price, Columbia, Missouri, announce the engagement of their daughter, Miss Monica Lynn Price, to Mr. William Walter Sims, son of Mr. and Mrs. Walter Douglas Sims, 1143 Windemere Parkway. Miss Price was graduated from Nazareth College, Louisville, Kentucky.

Mr. Sims is a graduate of Manhattan College. During his high school years he was an outstanding quarterback for St. Joseph's High School and is currently the club champion at Seven Oaks Golf Club.

If the engaged girl and her family lived for some time in another city than that in which they are presently living, an announcement may be sent to the papers in their former home. The form might be:

Mr. and Mrs. George Thatcher Price, Boston, announce the engagement of their daughter, Miss Monica Lynn Price, to Mr. William Walter Sims, son of Mr. and Mrs.

Walter Douglas Sims of Scranton, Pa. The bride-to-be
and her family are former residents of this city. She is
the granddaughter of Admiral Carl Chase, 15 Chestnut
Street, and the late Mrs. Chase, and of Mrs. Andrew
Everett Price, 587 Parkington Court, and the late Mr.
Price, who was mayor of this city from 1918 to 1926.

In small communities, and among unworldly people, no formal
announcement of an engagement need be made. The bride-to-be
simply wears her ring and shows it to friends. Otherwise the engaged
girl first wears her ring publicly on the occasion of her announcement
party, or after the newspaper announcement has appeared.

ENGAGEMENT RING

The custom of giving a ring as a pledge of betrothal is a very
ancient one. It was common among the Romans in the pre-Christian
era; the betrothal ceremony of those times consisted of a mutual exchange of promises to marry, after which the man sent his promised
bride an iron ring called *annulus pronobus.*

The practice thus has an ancient and honorable tradition behind it,
but it is in no sense obligatory in modern times, and may be dispensed
with if the couple so desire. Currently the diamond is a popular stone
for an engagement ring, but any other may be substituted to suit the
couple's taste. In the romantic nineteenth century, a young man usually
purchased the ring before he asked for the girl's hand and presented it
to her immediately after being accepted. In our practical era, the
young man often waits until he has been accepted; the couple then
select the ring together to suit the girl's taste and the man's pocket-
book.

The custom of giving one's bride-to-be an engagement ring which
contains a gem that has long been in the man's family is an old one
and still popular. In some families it is the custom for a man's mother
to give to her eldest son the ring that was her engagement ring, to
present to his fiancée when the son wishes to marry. This may seem
like a hardship for the mother, but if the custom is well-established in
a family, the mother probably received it in the same way from her
mother-in-law and understood that she would one day be required to
pass it on to a prospective daughter-in-law. The stone is sometimes
reset, sometimes not. Other family jewels than the mother's engagement ring may of course be used. In either case, the custom is a charming one, because it reminds the newly-engaged couple of the other
happy lovers who so plighted their troth and lived to enjoy many

fruitful years together, and it impresses them with a feeling of family unity and continuity. Regardless of her personal taste in jewels or the value of the gem in question, a bride-to-be should, for sentimental reasons, prefer such a ring to one newly purchased.

ENGAGEMENT PARTIES

Most people announce an engagement through the notice sent to the newspapers. Nothing further is required. Many, however, like to make the announcement to friends at a party. For such a party, the hosts are the girl's parents. No one else may properly give such a party unless the girl is an orphan, in which case another relative, such as grandparents or older brother, may give it for her. If she has no living relatives, the couple themselves may give the party. No one else may properly act as host at such an occasion.

Announcement may be made at a dinner, luncheon, or reception. Recently one hears of announcements being made at cocktail parties. If one wishes to invite a great many people in evening hours without large outlay, the cocktail party serves the purpose, but it is not in accord with conservative tradition.

The type of party selected depends somewhat on whom one intends to invite. If it is limited to relatives, a dinner is often chosen. If it is to be an intimate daytime affair to which only the bride's young women friends are to be bid, a luncheon is the choice. If it is to be a large group of both sexes, a late afternoon or early evening reception is best. Such a party in the afternoon may also be a tea.

There is one type of engagement entertaining which is in every respect unsuitable. This is a large evening party to which young men and women friends of the couple are invited. They are told in advance by a friend of the pair that it is to be an engagement party, and that they are to bring gifts. *This is wrong.* No gifts are required or expected of anyone on the occasion of an engagement announcement. None should be brought to such a party, as the announcement presumably is a surprise.

Stress is laid on the fact that this party is not in good taste because it does not accord with tradition and because there is a trend in modern life to require too much in the way of gift-giving from friends of a bridal couple. It is reaching unwarranted lengths, and must be discouraged.

FORM OF ANNOUNCEMENT

Some years ago it was customary to look for elaborate ways to announce the engagement at engagement parties. Today the usual method is a toast by the bride's father. At an all-women's luncheon, the bride's mother makes the toast, which merely announces the engagement and expresses the family's pleasure in it. Something like this is sufficient:

> Dear friends: I am very happy to tell you that this little gathering is to announce the engagement of my beloved daughter, Mary Rose, to Mr. Arthur Troxel. I am sure you will all agree with me that they seem ideally suited to one another. I ask you now to join with me in pledging them LONG LIFE AND HAPPINESS. (Raises glass and all toast the couple.)

If the host is a witty man and graceful speaker, he may, of course, say much more and say it better. This example merely indicates the essentials.

ENGAGEMENT PRESENTS

No one is obligated to give a present when an engagement is announced. Quite often the girl's parents choose that time to make her a present, usually part of her bridal linens, silver, or bedding. Sometimes the man's mother sends her a similar present—a dinner cloth or luncheon set. But all that is required is a loving note.

If the announcement is made at a party, the man's parents sometimes send flowers for the occasion, either a corsage for the girl to wear or a handsome floral arrangement to use as decoration. If the latter is selected, a tall piece that can stand on the floor or low table is a happy choice, as the bride's mother has probably already selected the luncheon table decorations.

Friends may also send flowers the day of the party if they are aware of the nature of it. Friends may also give the girl an engagement present at some time after the announcement has been made, if they wish to, but there is no obligation. Usually something for her bridal linens is selected.

Relatives of the bridegroom, such as aunts or grandparents, may, if they wish, write the bride-to-be an affectionate note after the announcement. This is not required, but is a nice gesture.

Such a note might read:

> MY DEAR MARY ROSE:
> *We were so pleased to hear the news about you and Arthur. My husband and I are so happy for you! Arthur*

is a fine boy, and very dear to us. We hope he will bring
you to see us soon, as we are longing to meet you.
                                        Affectionately,
                                        SUE MARY COX

The engaged girl answers such notes at once, if possible on the
day they are received. Her answer might say:

MY DEAR MRS. COX,
    Your warm and friendly letter pleased me very much.
    Arthur often speaks of "Aunt Sue and Uncle Jack." It
    makes me happy to know that there is a place waiting
    for me in the family circle.
                                        Sincerely,
                                        MARY ROSE CONNALLEY

All engagement presents are acknowledged by notes of thanks,
unless they are given in person. In such a case, if the gift has been
opened and admired in the presence of the giver, and hearty thanks
spoken, no note is necessary.

BREAKING THE ENGAGEMENT

Sometimes one or both parties to an engagement discover that they
have mistaken the degree of their affection, or that their feelings have
changed with the passage of time. Such a discovery is painful, and
creates an awkward situation for all concerned. But the primary purpose of an engagement is to allow a period of testing and weighing, to
enable the engaged pair to be sure they have made a proper choice of
marriage partners. If they discover that they do not, after all, wish to
marry, the engagement has served its purpose just as successfully as
though it terminated in marriage. Bearing in mind the indissolubility
of the marriage bond, one must realize that a broken engagement is
preferable to a lifetime of marital misery.

The termination of an engagement may, if the parties concerned
wish, be formally announced, just as the engagement was. The more
prominent the families or the nearer the wedding date, the more necessary the announcement becomes. If the engagement was not known to
many people, or if the wedding was still far in the future, an announcement may be dispensed with and word of the termination may be
spread by notes or word of mouth.

A public announcement appears in the newspapers in this form:
"Mr. and Mrs. Charles Austin, 13 Campus Hill, announce that the

engagement of their daughter, Miss Veronica Carson Austin, to Mr.
John Erwin Clausen, son of Mr. and Mrs. Roderick Clausen, of Topeka,
Kansas, has been terminated by mutual consent."

Regardless of which partner broke the engagement, all presents
which the formerly engaged pair have received or given one another
must be returned to the giver. This means that the engagement ring is
returned to the man, along with any other presents of value that he has
made to his fiancée. Similar presents she had given her prospective
bridegroom—watch, valuable camera, etc.—are returned.

Shower and wedding presents are also returned, if wedding plans
were so advanced that such presents had been received. These
presents, when returned, must be accompanied by a note of explanation along these lines:

> DEAR AUNT MARY,
>   *I am sorry that I must tell you that Charles and I
> have decided that our engagement was a mistake and
> have ended it by mutual consent. I am therefore return-
> ing the beautiful pin which you sent me to commemorate
> the occasion, with many grateful thanks, and the assur-
> ance that your kindness will not be forgotten.*
>
>   *Affectionately,*
>   *Tuesday*   EDITH

> MY DEAR MRS. QUINN,
>   *No doubt you saw the recent announcement that Mr.
> Anthony Wells and I have terminated our engagement
> by mutual consent. I am therefore returning to you with
> grateful thanks the beautiful luncheon cloth which you
> sent me to honor the occasion, with the wish that you
> and Mr. Quinn and all of Anthony's relatives will remem-
> ber me with the affection that I shall continue to feel
> for them.*
>
>   *Sincerely,*
>   *Tuesday*   EDITH AVERY

Regardless of which partner wished to dissolve the engagement,
convention decrees that both parties and all friends and relatives
behave as though the girl had ended it to spare her the embarrassment
of appearing to have been jilted.

No matter how wounded and angry one party to the engagement
may feel at its termination, it is best for all concerned that no public
indignation be displayed. Bear firmly in mind that a broken engage-

ment is always preferable to an unhappy marriage; thank God that the change of heart was discovered before it was too late. Try to understand that the partner who broke the engagement did so, not to injure the other, but to spare both future unhappiness. Members of both families should discuss the matter as little as possible. When some mention of it is necessary, regret may be expressed, but no rancour or resentment should be permitted to appear.

SHOWERS

After the engagement announcement and prior to the wedding, it is a custom to entertain for the prospective bride with showers. These are afternoon or evening parties at which the hostess is one of the bride's most intimate friends and the guests are women friends of her own age. Each guest brings a present, either something for the bride's trousseau or for her future home. Usually, at the request of the hostess, they are similar in nature—something for the kitchen, the linen closet, lingerie, etc. Sometimes the hostess asks each guest to contribute a small sum of money with which the hostess buys a single, more substantial gift.

Showers are popular all over our land. They have a long tradition; indeed they stem from our pioneer forbears, whose friendly neighbors chose this means to help a young couple set up housekeeping in regions where stores were scarce. They are informal and fun for all if moderation is observed. The primary duty of the hostess at such a party is to see to it that it stays within bounds. It should never be suggested that expensive presents are expected. Anyone offering to give such a present should be courteously discouraged from doing so. Proper presents are little accessories for home or trousseau—not the major components. One might give a hand towel, handkerchieves, spice holders, baking dishes, stockings, etc., depending on the type of shower. One does *not* give an electric toaster, vacuum cleaner, or negligee and matching gown. These things are entirely too expensive for such an occasion.

A shower hostess should also avoid asking a large number of guests, merely to swell the bride's "loot." Only intimate friends should be invited. A recent innovation is to ask older women—the bride's mother, prospective mother-in-law, aunts, family friends, etc. This can be awkward. A shower invitation is difficult to refuse, even when one does not wish to attend. Be sure that all you invite will come for the pleasure of the occasion, not from a sense of obligation.

Traditionally, showers are feminine affairs. Occasionally one hears of parties called "showers" to which both sexes are invited, and to which all bring presents. Avoid this. Another dreadful innovation is the holding of "liquor" and "money" showers. A liquor shower is in the worst possible taste. A money shower is plain and simple begging. It is hard to find terms strong enough to condemn such entertaining.

A knowledgeable hostess will give the traditional bridal shower, to which she will invite only the bride's intimate friends. A well-bred bride will not consent to any other type of shower. A thoughtful one will not agree to a great number of any sort, lest she burden her friends. Three or four are the most that should be given for any bride.

No relative of bride or bridegroom should give a shower. It makes them appear grasping. This advice is not intended to reduce the amount of entertaining given for a bride. Anyone may give a party in her honor to increase the gaiety of pre-nuptial days. A luncheon given by the bridegroom's mother to introduce the bride to relatives and family friends is a nice gesture. A tea is equally pleasant. Cocktail parties, dinners and receptions are delightful ways to entertain, and may be given by any relatives of the bridal couple. But they must not be showers.

There are two special cases in which a shower given by a relative might be permissible. They are:

When the bride's only wedding attendant is to be her sister. This sister might then give a small shower to which only the bride's most intimate friends are invited.

When the bride's sister is one of several wedding attendants, all of whom are to be cohostesses at a single shower, she may join the group as a hostess.

THE BACHELOR DINNER

Traditionally, the bridegroom-to-be is host for the bachelor dinner. This is usually held on the weekend prior to the wedding. Catholics never hold this party on the night before the wedding, as this time is reserved for the rehearsal. It may be given at a club, at home, or in a hotel.

The guests are the best man and the ushers. The man's father and future father-in-law may be invited, as well as brothers and cousins not in the wedding party, if the host wishes to do so. But he is obligated only to ask his wedding attendants. At this party the host presents his groomsmen with his wedding remembrance gifts to them. They are usually jewelry, such as handsome cuff links, a lighter, etc. His gift to his best man is always more valuable than those he gives his ushers. He may also give them their wedding ties and gloves, which are always a present from the bridegroom, but it might be a wise precaution to wait until the rehearsal to do this.

At this party also, the ushers present the host with the wedding present for him and his bride which they have jointly purchased. A modern innovation is to give a personal gift to the bridegroom, such as luggage, a portable radio or record player, etc., jointly purchased by all the guests. In this event the usher's joint wedding present is sent to the bride's home, like the other wedding gifts. This is allowable, but is another instance of the way in which the weddings of one's friends are becoming an increasing financial burden to all.

Another modern variation is to substitute for the bachelor dinner a party in honor of the bridegroom, at which he is the honor guest instead of the host. The best man, or all the male wedding attendants jointly, or all invited to the party, may bear the expense of it. In any event, the best man makes all the arrangements, including the selection of and inviting of the guests. Such parties usually include all the close friends and young male relatives of the bridegroom and the bride, as well as his attendants, and the best man consults both mothers as to whom to invite so that no one may be overlooked. A joint gift is given. The whole affair is informal and gay, the masculine counterpart of a bridal shower. Presumably it is a surprise to the honor guest, but practically this is hard to arrange.

If this party is substituted for the traditional bachelor dinner, the bridegroom waits until the party after the rehearsal to give his attendants their presents from him.

BRIDESMAIDS' LUNCHEON

It was formerly the custom for a bride to give her attendants a luncheon to correspond to the bridegroom's bachelor dinner. Sometimes, instead of a luncheon, it was a party on the night of the bachelor dinner. This practice is dying out because it is impractical for the bride's family to cram so much entertaining into the wedding period. It may, of course, be held, if the family wishes it. It is a simple affair, attended only by the women members of the bridal party and the bride's mother. Her prospective mother-in-law may be invited if desired.

At this party, the bride gives her attendants their wedding remembrance presents. That of the maid of honor is more valuable than those given to the bridesmaids. The bridesmaids' presents are identical in type, if not in design. Some suitable presents are: rosary beads, earrings, bracelets, vanity cases, silver picture frames, gold-mounted purse fittings such as combs or perfume bottles. Often they are engraved with the date of the wedding.

If this party is not held, the bride gives her attendants their presents at the rehearsal party.

THE REHEARSAL DINNER

Even the simplest Catholic wedding requires a rehearsal. If consulted in time, the church pastor or one of his assistants will arrange to hold this early in the evening—about seven or seven-thirty—of the night before the wedding. This is the ideal time, for some members of the wedding party often come from other communities and will not reach town until just prior to the wedding. Understanding this, the pastor will arrange to hold the rehearsal at this time if at all possible. If it is not possible, the attendants should arrange to be present at the time the pastor selects. This is another reason why one should consult one's pastor and make these arrangements well in advance of the wedding date.

The rehearsal is usually followed by a dinner or party at the home of the bride. It may, of course, be formal, if that accords with the style of living of the bride's parents and they wish to have it so. Practically, it is the worst possible time for the bride's family to attempt to give an elaborate party. The home is crowded with visiting relatives and bridal attendants, cluttered with wedding presents and wedding paraphernalia, and frequently rearranged and out of its normal routine in preparation for entertaining on the day of the wedding. And yet this is a party that should not be given in a club or hotel.

If the party is held at the bride's home, it is usually a simple one, either a buffet supper or a cocktail party at which hors d'oeuvres are substantial and plentiful. No one is invited but the members of the wedding party; it is over at an early hour out of consideration for the stresses of the day to come.

A newer and surely a better idea is to relieve the bride's mother of this entertaining. Custom decrees that the parents of the bridegroom shall be guests, and only guests, at the wedding of their son and the entertaining to follow. They can bear none of the expense and express no opinions as to its nature, however it may clash with their ideas as to what is suitable. This is a difficult position to be in, but it does relieve them of much expense and responsibility and it leaves them with far more leisure than the harried parents of the bride.

If, therefore, they live in the city in which the wedding is being held, the parents of the bridegroom may properly offer to hold the

rehearsal party in their home. It is a charming ges
one which will be appreciated; it gives them a sha *105*
usually longing to have in the wedding excitement
being burdensome to them.   ־, and

If the bridegroom's parents live in another commuare
offer to hold the rehearsal dinner, the maid of honor out
bridal attendants may offer to give it in their home. An a
bride may also offer to give this party if she wishes. The ᵦ
always the bridal party only, and it is always over at an early

Today it is usually at this party that the bride gives her atte.
their wedding remembrance gifts, and the bridegroom may giv
attendants theirs if he wishes to. It is also the time when he g.
them the identical ties and gloves for the wedding, which the briᵈ
groom traditionally buys for his groomsmen.

8

Wedding Correspondence and Printed Forms

A marriage took place at Cana of Galilee, and the mother of Jesus was there. Now Jesus too was invited to the marriage, and also his disciples (John 2:1–3).

WEDDING INVITATIONS

There is no detail of a wedding more strictly bound by custom and usage than the wedding invitation. Clear and precise rules for every detail concerning it have been laid down and observed for generations; the bride who attempts to deviate from them labels herself as socially inept.

The Senders

Wedding invitations are issued in the name of the bride's parents, if they are living. If the bride is half-orphaned, they are issued in the name of the living parent. If she is wholly orphaned, they may be issued in the name of any relative—grandparent, brother, sister, uncle, etc.—who is standing *in loco parentis* for her on this occasion. If she has no relatives to act for her, the invitations may be sent in her own name.

Under no circumstances may invitations properly be sent in the name of the bridegroom's parents, in that of any of his relatives, or in his own name. The reason for this distinction is that the wedding is always regarded socially as an event for which the bride or her parents are responsible and at which the bridegroom's family are honored guests, but merely guests.

Time of Sending

Invitations are sent three weeks before the date of the wedding. They should be ordered far enough in advance so that they will be delivered to the bride at least six weeks before the ceremony, to allow time for addressing them.

Guest List

The size of the guest list depends upon the elaborateness of the wedding and the entertaining to follow and upon whether the invitation invites to the wedding and to the reception or to the wedding only, with reception cards enclosed to those who are invited to the nuptial entertaining. It also depends upon the actual size of the church in which the ceremony is taking place. One could not invite large numbers of people to a ceremony in a tiny country church.

Where the invitation is to the church only and the ceremony is being held in a large church, one is free to invite all one's relatives and friends to be present.

The bride's mother is responsible for making the list of all relatives and friends of the bride. The bridegroom's mother is similarly responsible for the relatives and friends of the bridegroom. She should take pains to see to it that her list, which she will give to the bride's mother, includes the correct addresses for all who are named on it, for many of them will be unknown to the person who is addressing the invitations. In actual practice, of course, both mothers will consult with members of their immediate family to determine who shall be sent invitations.

Both the sender and the recipient of a wedding invitation should member that it is a compliment to the receiver. Catholics should remember that an invitation which desires their presence at one of the great sacraments of the Church is as distinguished a compliment as a friend can pay them, regardless of whether it includes an invitation to any entertaining that may follow the ceremony. The numbers bid to such entertaining may be limited by a number of factors unrelated to personal affection, but the wedding invitations are not. (For further discussion of this matter see chapter eight, under "Wedding Presents.")

Invitations may be freely sent to distant friends and relatives. Regardless of whether or not they may be able to attend, they should be included in the guest list.

Forms and Styles

Wedding invitations are inscribed on good quality paper, either white or ivory-colored, with a vellum or kid finish. The paper is a double sheet, folded vertically, with all the writing appearing upon the facing sheet. When folded thus, it traditionally measures about five by seven and one-half inches, although currently a slightly smaller size is fashionable. It may have an inch-wide plate mark for a border, or be left plain. For mailing, the double sheet is folded once, horizontally, and is inserted in two envelopes.

A formal wedding invitation is, ideally, always engraved. This is a process in which a copper plate is inscribed with the message and reproductions are made from it, which causes the lettering to stand out from the surface of the paper. When expense is no object, engraving may be preferred. Modern embossing, which is a kind of printing which produces letters similarly raised from the surface of the paper, gives a result almost indistinguishable from engraving and is considerably less expensive because no plate is required. When cost is a factor, the bride may consider substituting embossing for engraving. If the invitation is correct as to size, quality of paper, style of lettering and wording, there is nothing improper in the use of the embossing process. Straight printing may never be used.

Invitations are always inscribed in black ink. Gold or silver is not correct.

The bride has a choice in the matter of type face. Script is considered the most formal, traditionally, and is now extremely fashionable also. There are a number of script styles, known as London script, Dover script, Victorian, etc. Unfortunately, all engravers do not use the same names for these various styles, so there is no point in attempting to name them here. Your stationer can show you the various type styles, and point out which are script. Antique roman, shaded antique roman, and shaded modified roman are also popular type faces. Shaded modified roman is especially effective when embossing is substituted for engraving.

The traditional wording and spacing for a wedding invitation is as follows:

Mr. and Mrs. John Lester Sullivan

request the honour of your presence

at the marriage of their daughter

Joan Louise

to

Mr. Vincent Paul McGinty

on Monday, the fifth of June

one thousand nine hundred and sixty

at ten o'clock

Saint Ignatius' Church

South Bend, Indiana

In a large community, the street address of the church is sometimes given. All names are written in full, no abbreviations being permissible. If the bride's father or husband is "junior," the term is so engraved. "Jr." is beginning to be considered acceptable, but it violates the rule of no abbreviations in a wedding invitation. The use of numerals is also to be avoided, except in the case of an awkwardly long street address, such as "Four Hundred and Nineteen West One Hundred and Twenty-Fourth Street." This would be written "419 West One Hundred and Twenty-Fourth Street."

When the bride is an orphan, the variations in this form are as one would expect. When a widow is hostess the invitation reads:

Mrs. John Lester Sullivan

requests the honour of your presence

at the marriage of her daughter

Joan Louise

etc.

For a widowed mother who has remarried, the phrasing is:

Mr. and Mrs. Schuyler Worthington Hatt

request the honour of your presence

at the marriage of her daughter

Joan Louise Sullivan

etc.

For a widower:

Mr. John Lester Sullivan

requests the honour of your presence

at the marriage of his daughter

Joan Louise

etc.

For a remarried widower:

Mr. and Mrs. John Lester Sullivan

request the honour of your presence

at the marriage of his daughter

Joan Louise

etc.

Invitations issued in the name of a sister, brother, grandparent, etc., require similar changes in wording. In any case where the invitation is issued by one whose name differs from that of the bride, her full name is given, as in the illustration for the daughter of a remarried widow.

When the bride has no relatives to act for her and must issue invitations in her own name, the customary form is:

The honour of your presence

is requested at the marriage of

Miss Joan Louise Sullivan

to

etc.

Wedding of a Widow

Invitations to the wedding of a young widow who is remarrying are issued in the name of her parents, if they are living, and follow the conventional form except that the bride's name appears as "Joan Sullivan Ladd" (her deceased husband's surname). The more traditional form is "Joan Louise Ladd," not using her maiden surname, but friends of the bridegroom find this confusing, as they are unable to trace the relationship between "Mr. and Mrs. John Lester Sullivan" who are hosts at the wedding and "Joan Louise Ladd," the bride.

Older widows seldom issue formal invitations to their second marriage. When they do, the correct form is:

The honour of your presence

is requested at the marriage of

Mrs. Kenneth Bruce Ladd

to

etc.

Some widows feel that it is not fitting that the name of their first husband appear thus on the invitation to their second wedding. To avoid it they sometimes substitute "Mrs. Joan Sullivan Ladd." This is very bad form.

The title "Mrs." may only be used correctly before a surname ("Mrs. Ladd") or before a man's name ("Mrs. Kenneth Bruce Ladd"). It may *never* properly be used before a feminine name ("Mrs. Joan Sullivan Ladd"). This is perhaps the commonest of all errors in etiquette today. The usage is frequently seen in newspapers. It is also common in business. Business persons who receive a letter from an associate signed "Joan Sullivan Ladd" and who know the writer to be married but do not know her husband's name are obliged to respond by using "Mrs. Joan Sullivan Ladd." The usage in such a case is understandable, because there is no possible substitute. It is nevertheless incorrect, and is to be avoided whenever possible.

To employ such a form in correspondence as formal as a wedding invitation is unthinkable. There is no reason for a widow, particularly a Catholic widow, to avoid using the name of her first husband, as in her case there could be no question of the first marriage having terminated in divorce (always an unpleasant connotation in connection with a second marriage).

If the widow is determined to avoid using her late husband's full name, a possible substitute is to use her own name with no title, thus:

(See following page for sample.)

The honour of your presence

is requested at the marriage of

Joan Sullivan Ladd

to

etc.

This is not correct either, but it is certainly preferable to "Mrs. Joan Sullivan Ladd." If used, it is perhaps better to avoid using the title "Mr." before the bridegroom's name. This is occasionally done even in a conventional wedding invitation, but it is really very informal and not to be recommended except under special circumstances that might require it, as above.

Special Forms

For a wedding so small or so large that all invited to the church are to be invited to the entertaining to follow, the invitation may read:

(*See next page for sample.*)

Mr. and Mrs. John Lester Sullivan

request the honour of your presence

at the marriage of their daughter

Joan Louise

to

Mr. Vincent Paul McGinty

on Monday, the fifth of June

at ten o'clock

Saint Ignatius' Church

and afterwards at

Eleven Claremore Drive

Tulsa, Oklahoma

R. S. V. P.

In the example given above, the entertaining is to be in the house of the bride's parents. For a breakfast held in a club or restaurant a similar form may be used, but a difficulty arises: Traditionally, the bride's house address never appears on a wedding invitation, except when the reception is to be held at home. In such a case, the guests may send their acceptances to the address given in the invitation.

When the address given for the breakfast is "Wanneka Golf Club, Ten Western Boulevard," many of the friends of the bridegroom do not know and have no easy way of determining where to send their notes of acceptance or regret.

Because of this very real difficulty and because the tradition of omitting the bride's house address does not seem to be founded on any sensible reasoning, modern brides usually see to it that their house address is given on any invitation or reception card which asks for "the favour of a reply."

When the breakfast is not to be held at home, this means that an invitation would read as follows:

Mr. and Mrs. John Lester Sullivan

request the honour of your presence

at the marriage of their daughter

Joan Louise

to

Mr. Vincent Paul McGinty

on Monday, the fifth of June

at ten o'clock

Saint Ignatius' Church

and afterwards at

Wanneka Golf Club

Tulsa, Oklahoma

R. S. V. P.

22 Leslie Avenue

Where the club is sufficiently well-known as to require no street address, and where it is in the same city as the bride's house, so that a city address need be mentioned only once, all this material may appear in a wedding invitation without too much crowding. But when the club is in the suburbs, so that one need say "Wanneka Golf Club, Ardmore, Oklahoma," followed by "R.S.V.P. 22 Leslie Avenue, Tulsa, Oklahoma," the sheet begins to look over-written. The best solution to this problem is to use the conventional wedding invitation form and to enclose a reception card, even though all guests are to be bid to both occasions.

Some parishes require that a mixed marriage be solemnized in the church rectory. In such a case no wedding invitations can be issued. No one is present at the ceremony save the bridal party, both sets of parents and possibly one or two other relatives. There is not space for any more and, in addition, the practice of inviting a large group of guests to a rectory wedding is frowned upon. For such a ceremony, no ushers are required and sometimes there are none. But if such a wedding is to be followed by a large reception, the bridegroom sometimes asks a number of his friends to be "ushers" to balance the wedding party at the reception. In such a case the ushers attend the ceremony, but have no duties.

If one is following a rectory wedding with a large reception, the reception invitation is inscribed on a large sheet, exactly like the invitation to a church wedding. The invitation then reads:

Mr. and Mrs. John Lester Sullivan

request the pleasure of your company

at the wedding reception of their daughter

Joan Louise

and

Mr. Vincent Paul McGinty

on Monday, the fifth of June

at twelve o'clock

Onondago Yacht Club

Lakeside, Wisconsin

R. S. V. P.
Ten Mount Vernon Street
Madison, Wisconsin

Sometimes a wedding is held in a village church accommodating only a limited number, and is followed by a large reception to which more people are invited than can be asked to the church. In this case, the reception invitation is sent out in the form given above. Into the envelope with the reception invitation, to those invited to the church, goes a small enclosure card, like that customarily used for a reception, which reads:

Mr. and Mrs. John Lester Sullivan

request the honour of your presence

at the marriage ceremony

at eleven o'clock

Church of St. Francis Xavier

Madison, Wisconsin

Note that the reception invitation requests "the pleasure of your company" while the wedding invitation requests "the honour of your presence."

The forms just suggested are not ideal, as putting the wedding invitation on an enclosure card (or omitting it entirely, as must be done with a rectory wedding) seems to make the wedding ceremony appear secondary to the nuptial entertaining. But it is the only solution to the problem of "small church, large wedding reception," since an enclosure card can never be sent without the principal sheet which it is to accompany, while the principal sheet may be sent without an enclosure whenever desired.

For a further discussion of wedding invitations, see chapter entitled "Making Your Wedding More Catholic."

Sample Invitations

A sample of the conventional formal invitation:

Mr. and Mrs. David Edward Durst

request the honour of your presence

at the marriage of their daughter

Teresa Anne

to

Mr. Michael Augustus Ward

on Saturday, the twenty-fifth of June

at eleven o'clock

Holy Family Church

New Rochelle, New York

An invitation (reduced in size) issued by a widow:

Mrs. Julius Nagy

requests the honour of your presence

at the marriage of her daughter

Yolanda Anne

to

Mr. Richard Philip Landy

on Saturday, the eleventh of July

nineteen hundred and fifty=nine

at eleven o'clock

Saint Ann's Church

Bridgeport, Connecticut

Reception Cards

The great majority of brides who issue formal invitations to their wedding choose to use the traditional invitation quoted first in this chapter, with a reception card enclosed to those invited to the breakfast or reception. This is a stiff card, slightly smaller than is the wedding invitation when folded for mailing. The paper is the same color and finish as the wedding invitation and is inscribed in the same type style. The traditional ones read:

Mr. and Mrs. John Lester Sullivan

request the pleasure of your company

for breakfast

on Monday, the fifth of June

at one o'clock

Onondaga Yacht Club

Lakeview, Wisconsin

R. S. V. P.

This follows the strictest tradition in that, although it asks for a reply, it does not give the bride's house address. Modern brides usually feel that this is an affectation which causes a number of people wholly unnecessary effort in determining the bride's house address. Even when using the traditional form above, they will add, under the R.S.V.P., the house address; and they will include the city and state if the city is not the community in which the breakfast is to be held.

Becoming steadily more popular is a briefer form which allows more room for the club or hotel address and house address. Since the claims of ceremonial politeness have been fulfilled by the wording of the wedding invitation, the reception card says simply:

Reception

from two until five o'clock

Yahundasis Golf Club

722 Van Rensselaer Boulevard

Latham, Massachusetts

R. S. V. P.

17 Slade Street

Boston, Massachusetts

Reception card.

Reception

immediately following the ceremony

Fairfield Inn

Fairfield, Connecticut

Reception card with return address and R.S.V.P.

Reception

immediately following the ceremony

Westchester Country Club

The favour of a reply is requested
Biltmore Avenue
Rye, New York

The initials "R.S.V.P." are an abbreviation for the French phrase "Respondez, s'il vous plait," which means, "Please answer." If one does not wish to use the French form, the correct phrase is "The favour of a reply is requested." 'Please reply," which is occasionally seen, is considered by many to be too brusque.

Pew Cards

Pew cards or cards of admission to a church ceremony are almost never used today. Cards of admission are never correct for a Catholic wedding because, in theory at least, any Catholic church service is open to all who care to attend. Anyone who comes unbidden to a large wedding should seat himself on one of the side aisles of the church, in the rear.

For a Catholic wedding to which have been invited a number of government officials, who must be seated according to the rules of protocol, pew cards might be sent with the invitation. They are similar to reception cards, but smaller—about three and one-half by two and one-half inches. Engraved on them are the words "Pew Number" followed by a space in which the number of the pew is written by hand. When a wedding invitation contains such an enclosure, the guest brings it to the church with him and presents it to the usher.

A more attractive way of handling this problem is to enclose the visiting card of the bride's mother, with "Pew Number Sixteen" hand-written on it. But it must be emphasized that pew cards are used mainly to solve the problems of protocol. (For a further discussion of this matter, see the section on "Seating Arrangements" in the chapter on "Large Weddings.")

Response Cards

A recent innovation that one occasionally sees is the response card. This is a small card, about one and one-half by two and one-half inches which says "———————————— (space for signature of person to whom card is sent) Will (space left to check one or the other) attend the Will not

wedding reception." This is enclosed in an unsealed envelope on which the address of the bride's mother is printed. The envelope is stamped.

The reason that such cards are used is that many people fail to acknowledge a traditional invitation until the last moment, or not at all. The cards are sent to make it easy for people to reply and to enable the bride's mother to determine in advance how many guests to expect.

But such cards are in the worst possible taste. They assume that all the invited guests are too ignorant to reply promptly and in the correct form or so ill-bred as to fail to respond at all. They do not necessarily solve the problem of obtaining prompt responses. People so careless as to fail to respond in the proper form are quite capable of ignoring their responsibility to return even this type of card. And they contain printed matter (the bride's house address on the envelopes) which is always wrong in an invitation.

The author discussed this problem of response cards with the stationer in a large jewelry store. He said quite bluntly, "Of course we never recommend response cards to any one, as they are wholly improper. But if a customer asks for them, or desires to order them, we do not make any comment, as they substantially increase the size of the order!"

Therefore one can only say: Response cards are not correct. No bride who is concerned that all the details of her wedding be correct and who knows better will ever use them. But if one receives an invitation containing a response card, one should fill it out properly, indicating whether it is an acceptance or a regret, and return it promptly. Do not embarrass the bride or her mother by sending a proper acceptance. To do so would show that you are aware of and choose to use the correct form, but it also carries an implied criticism of the usage which the bride chose to employ and might wound her. Do nothing to detract from the happiness of a wedding. The basis of all etiquette is kindness and consideration in dealing with one's fellow man. Where kindness and propriety clash, kindness must be the first consideration.

Addressing and Mailing

Rules for the addressing of wedding invitations are precise. The invitations come from the stationer's unfolded. One first folds them in half vertically, with the message facing upward. Then each is folded in half horizontally and, along with any enclosure, such as a reception or pew card, is placed within two envelopes.

Outer Envelope

Wedding invitations are always addressed by hand, and, where possible, the stylized modified backhand used by social secretaries should be employed. When addressed by a social secretary or a firm of bridal consultants, the "secretary's hand" will be employed. When the invitations are addressed by the bride and her mother, this kind of handwriting need not be attempted; but the form of the address is precise:

Do not use abbreviations unless not to do so would be absurd. Numerals may be used, for street number and post office route number.

The style is always as follows:

> Mr. and Mrs. Paul David Robinson
> 25 East Sixty-Fourth Street
> New York 33
> New York

The straight margin is maintained on the *right* side of the envelope.

A single invitation may be sent jointly to several members of a family living in the same house as long as only one married couple is involved. For more than one couple, separate invitations must be sent. A couple and their adult children would be addressed so:

> Mr. and Mrs. John Charles Gruyter
> Miss Laetitia Gruyter
> Mr. John Charles Gruyter, junior

Children who are not adults are not named on an outer envelope. A brother and sister living together are addressed:

Miss Phyllis Ann Perkins
Mr. George St. John Perkins

Two adult sisters living together are addressed:

Miss Mary Jane Manning
Miss Rose Marie Manning

or

The Misses Mary Jane and Rose Marie Manning

In both cases the name of the elder sister is given first.

Inner Envelope

The inner envelope of a wedding invitation is left unsealed. In fact, it is usually manufactured with the edge not gummed. Some modern brides choose to leave this inner envelope unaddressed, but it really is better form to follow the traditional practice and address it:

Mr. and Mrs. Robinson   (for a couple)

Mr. and Mrs. Gruyter
Miss Gruyter   (a couple and adult
Mr. Gruyter, junior   children)

When one wishes to invite young children to a wedding, their names appear only on the inner envelope, thus:

Mr. and Mrs. Gruyter
Jo-Ellen, Kathy and Heidi

or

Mr. and Mrs. Gruyter
Miss Mary Ann Gruyter
Miss Diana Gruyter
Master Paul Fletcher Gruyter

Return Address

The outer envelope of an invitation does not, usually, bear a return address. This is in line with the tradition that a bride's house address never appears on an invitation unless the reception is to be held at home. But in practice this creates difficulties. Some invitations must be sent to addresses the correctness of which is doubtful (old friends who may have moved, etc.) If the invitations carry a return address, any improperly addressed will be returned, and the bride will know that they went astray. If no return address is given, the invitation will go to the dead letter office; and the bride will never know whether it was received. It seems more sensible, therefore, to place a return address on the envelope of the wedding invitations, at least in cases where one is not perfectly sure of the correctness of the address.

Acknowledging Wedding Invitations

An invitation to the wedding ceremony only does not require an acknowledgment. An invitation to the ceremony and any entertaining to follow is answered in due form, with acceptance or regrets, for both ceremony and entertaining. An invitation to the reception only is answered as such.

The writing paper used should be white or cream-color. The correct size is five and one-half by seven and one-half and may or may not carry the writer's house address, monogram, or crest. If plain writing paper is used, a slightly smaller size is allowable, but the paper is always a double sheet. The acknowledgment is written by hand on the facing sheet, in the form in which the invitation was couched, and is folded once horizontally before placing in the envelope.

Some examples:

Mr. and Mrs. Thomas Estabrook Bergan

accept with pleasure

the kind invitation of

Mr. and Mrs. Sullivan

to the marriage of their daughter

Joan Louise

to

Mr. Vincent Paul McGinty

on Monday, the fifth of June

Saint Ignatius' Church

and afterwards at

Eleven Claremore Drive

If the reception or breakfast is not to be held at home, the acceptance of it may read "St. Ignatius' Church and the reception to follow" without reference to the club or hotel address. But an invitation to the reception only is answered as follows:

Mr. and Mrs. Thomas Estabrook Bergan

accept with pleasure

the kind invitation of

Mr. and Mrs. Sullivan

to the wedding breakfast of their daughter

Joan Louise

and

Mr. Vincent Paul McGinty

on Monday, the fifth of June

at twelve o'clock

Onondago Yacht Club

Regrets are also couched in the same terms as the invitation to which they are a reply. No reason need be advanced for declining. The correct form:

Mr. and Mrs. Thomas Estabrook Bergan

regret that they are unable to accept

the kind invitation of

Mr. and Mrs. Sullivan

to the marriage of their daughter

Joan Louise

to

Mr. Vincent Paul McGinty

and the reception to follow

Informal Invitations

Formal invitations are not sent for small weddings. To these, guests are invited by notes or word of mouth. They are issued by the bride's mother. Notes (or telegrams) are sent to those at a distance; others may be invited verbally. It is a nice touch for the bride's mother to send notes to all of the bridegroom's guests. They are simple and informal. A sample:

To the bridegroom's grandparents; when they live out of town.

DEAR MRS. CROWE:

You no doubt know that Thomas and my daughter Elsa are to be married here in Philadelphia, June seventh, at ten o'clock in St. Catherine's Church. There will be a wedding breakfast immediately following at the University Club.

We hope so much that you and Mr. Crowe will be able to come for both. Thomas is eager to have you present for the great occasion, and we are all looking forward to meeting you.

Sincerely,

ELIZABETH DARNELL

Tuesday

To the bridegroom's aunt, living in town:

> DEAR LAURA,
>
> *Tom and Elsa are being married June seventh, at ten*
> *o'clock, in St. Catherine's, with a small breakfast at home*
> *immediately following. I hope you and Herbert and*
> *Dorothy, too, if she is to be in town, will be able to come.*
>
> *Sincerely,*
>
> Sunday   MARGARET CURTIS STEVENS

Written invitations to a small wedding always include an invitation to any entertaining that follows it. Those asked only to the church service are invited by word of mouth. Therefore no one out of town receives an invitation to a small wedding unless invited to the entertaining to follow.

Informal written invitations to a small wedding are acknowledged by handwritten notes phrased in a similar informal manner. Verbal invitations are verbally accepted or declined.

WEDDING ANNOUNCEMENTS

A wedding announcement is a formal notification that a wedding has taken place, which may or may not include the new address of the bridal couple. As in the case of a wedding invitation there are strict rules to be followed in connection with all phases of issuing announcements. They should be faithfully observed.

The Senders

The senders are the same as for an invitation—the bride's parents, or one living parent, or other relative acting *in loco parentis* for the occasion, but never any member of the bridegroom's family. When a bride has no relatives to act for her or is an older widow, the announcements are issued jointly in the name of the bride and bridegroom. But in this case, the bride is still the sender.

Time of Sending

Announcements are mailed on the day of the wedding, or on the next day. They should be ordered far enough in advance so that a careful list of recipients may be made and so that the bride will have time to have all properly addressed and ready for mailing on the wedding day.

Announcement List

For a wedding for which formal invitations are issued one does not send announcements. They are issued following a wedding to which the guests have been informally invited—usually, but not necessarily, a small wedding. The names one includes on an announcement list need not be limited by the size of the wedding nor the entertaining to follow, nor expense involved, nor any of the factors which might limit one in issuing invitations. Consequently one sends announcements to all relatives of the bride and groom, all "connections" of the two families, such as the in-laws of one's married sisters and brothers, all friends, and all business associates with whom one has a relationship that is social or personal.

Unlike a wedding invitation, no compliment is paid in sending an announcement. But, also unlike a wedding invitation, to fail to send an announcement to one who might be considered eligible to receive one is a snub and indicates that one considers the friendship over or the relationship no longer worth acknowledging. Because of this latter consideration, very great care must be taken lest one inadvertently overlook someone who should have been remembered.

Forms and Styles

An announcement is inscribed on good quality paper, either white or ivory colored, with a vellum or kid finish. The paper is a double sheet, folded vertically, with all the writing on the facing sheet. The size currently fashionable is four and one-half by six inches, although traditionally it may be a little longer—about seven inches. It may have a plate mark border, or be left plain. For mailing, the double sheet is folded again horizontally, and put in two envelopes.

The announcement may be engraved or embossed, always in black ink. Plain printing is not correct. The same script selected for wedding invitations is proper for announcements.

The traditional wording and spacing is as follows:

Mr. and Mrs. George Gerald Stark

have the honour of announcing

the marriage of their daughter

Joyce Geraldine

to

Mr. Charles Bennett Southard

on Tuesday, the tenth of October

One thousand, nine hundred and sixty

Church of The Blessed Sacrament

Dallas, Texas

A Catholic wedding announcement always gives the name of the church in which the marriage was performed. In the case of a mixed marriage performed in the rectory, one should find out from the pastor whether one says "St. Michael's Church" or "St. Michael's Rectory" in the announcements. Sometimes one is permitted to say church, rather than rectory, to indicate that the marriage was performed under Catholic auspices, but it is not always permitted. Either way, it should not be omitted, lest people assume that the marriage was not recognized by the Church.

The classic style of announcement:

Mr. and Mrs. James Warner Kellogg, junior

have the honour of

announcing the marriage of their daughter

Katharine Pierce

to

Mr. Gilbert Eugene Dannenberg

Saturday, the twenty-sixth of December

One thousand, nine hundred and fifty-nine

Our Lady of Lourdes Church

Utica, New York

To the form given above, the couple's new address may be added.
This is given in the lower right-hand corner, as follows:

At Home

after the sixth of November

22 Blandina Street

Miami, Florida

The above examples are the traditional style. A more modern form is:

Mr. and Mrs. George Gerald Stark

announce the marriage of their daughter

Joyce Geraldine

to

Mr. Charles Bennett Southard

etc.

This is the form now most used. But if there is any possibility that an inference might be drawn that the marriage was not pleasing to the bride's parents, the older form should be employed. To this announcement an "at home" card may be added. This is a stiff card of the same color and quality as the announcement and somewhat smaller than are the announcements when folded horizontally for mailing. This may say

Mr. and Mrs. Charles Bennett Southard

1224 Salinas Street

After the sixth of November   San Francisco, California

or merely

At Home

after the sixth of November

1224 Salinas Street

San Francisco, California

It is an excellent idea to include the new address of the young couple if it is to be a home in any sense permanent, even for a year. But if the young pair are to live temporarily with either family, or very briefly at an Army base, it is better to omit "at home" cards or any mention of their current address.

At home cards:

At home

after the eleventh of January

1807 Broadway

San Francisco, California

Will be at home

after the ninth of March

127 Ryckman Avenue

Albany, New York

The variation in wording when someone other than the bride's parents is making the announcements is the same as for wedding invitations, except when the bride has no family to make the announcement or is an older widow. In the first case, the form is:

Miss Joyce Geraldine Stark

and

Mr. Charles Bennett Southard

announce their marriage

on Thursday, the sixth of September

one thousand, nine hundred and sixty

Saint John's Church

Bakersfield, California

For an older widow, whose parents do not make the announcement, the form is:

Mrs. Orrin Theodore Pierson

and

etc.

If she is reluctant to have her first husband's name appear on the announcement of her second marriage, the only possible form is:

Joyce Stark Pierson

and

Charles Bennett Southard

etc.

This is not actually correct, but it is infinitely better than "Mrs. Joyce Stark Pierson." "Mrs. Orrin Theodore Pierson," is the correct form.

In any of these cases, "at home" cards may be used.

Addressing and Mailing

The rules for addressing both inner and outer envelopes of announcements and for their mailing are exactly as for wedding invitations, except that they are mailed on the day of the wedding or the day following.

Acknowledging Announcements

There are no social rules which require any acknowledgment of a wedding announcement. One may send a friendly note of congratulation if one is so inclined, but this is solely a matter of personal choice. No obligation exists. Concerning the sending of wedding presents, see the section on that subject in the chapter on "Large Weddings."

LETTERS OF THANKS

The bride's obligation to acknowledge a wedding present with a prompt, handwritten note of thanks couched in terms as graceful and as warm as she is capable of is one of the strictest which society imposes. There is no acceptable substitute. A card of thanks will not do.

Neither will a note from her mother or her husband. Perhaps if the bride were to fall seriously ill just after the wedding, one of these persons might write explaining the situation. But for a healthy bride in possession of her faculties there is no escape from this responsibility.

No well-bred bride will seek one. Anyone sending a wedding present is showing his affection for the bridal couple. One knows that the donor has spent time, effort, thought, and money to do so. A pleasant note of thanks is not too much to expect in return. Certainly all brides do not have equal felicity of expression, but every bride should strive to do her very best when writing her notes of thanks. In some cases it will be all the recipient ever has by which to judge her.

Writing to one's own relatives and friends is not difficult. One knows their tastes and personalities and is sure of the "tone" to adopt. It is the letters to the bridegroom's as yet unknown relatives and family friends that present the greatest difficulty. Yet, because your letter will be the first impression of you that they receive, it is imperative to make it correct, appreciative, and graceful. Here are some suggestions that may help:

a) Use your personal writing paper, which may be plain white or cream-colored and may or may not be headed by a monogram or house address. For letters written after the wedding, small sheets called "informals" in the trade are sometimes used. These are folded horizontally and have the bride's new name engraved in the center of the facing sheet. The letter is written on the inner side of the sheet.

b) Make sure the form of your letter—spelling, spacing, salutation, and closing—are correct.

c) Sign it correctly. Sign thank-you letters written before your wedding with your maiden name—"Mary" to intimates, "Mary Audrey Price" to all others. After the wedding, sign your thank-you notes to all save intimate friends "Mary Price Roberts," using your maiden name for a middle name to help identify yourself to the bridegroom's friends. Never sign any letter "Mrs. John Roberts." This is always wrong.

d) As you are writing the letter try to think of the present you are acknowledging as you would have had it been the only present you received. Express yourself with the enthusiasm and gratitude you would have shown under those circumstances.

e) Think of the donor in the act of selecting it—how she may have hesitated between the Haviland service plates and the silver

salver, trying to decide which would please you most. This puts
you in a frame of mind to be properly appreciative.

f) Refer to the present by its specific name: vase, tea set, goblets,
etc. Do not call it "your wedding present" or "gift."

g) If possible, discuss with pleasure one of its identifying charac-
teristics: "I am so fond of copper." "I have always longed to
own a Wedgewood urn." "There will be so many occasions on
which we can use a muffin rack." A little polite social fibbing is
permissible here. One can scarcely say, "I absolutely loathe
Toby jugs," or "Where on earth did you find that ghastly
mobile?" And it may be hard to express heartfelt thanks for
one's seventeenth clock, but one can express enthusiasm about
clocks in general, even though one is planning to return this one.

h) Talk to your husband or mother-in-law about his friends and
relatives who sent you gifts to determine the relationship and
what kind of people they are. You will then know whether you
are writing to an older woman who values formality or to a
casual young person.

Examples are not much use in these cases, but here are a few, all
presumed to be sent to persons not known to the bride:

> My dear Mrs. Van Gelder,
>
> *John and I are so delighted with the handsome Pem-
> broke table you sent us! It has been much admired by
> all who have come to see the wedding presents. I know
> exactly the spot in our new apartment where it will look
> best, and I hope the day is not too far off when you will
> come and see it there. Thank you most sincerely for
> remembering us so generously.*
>
>

Sincerely,
>
>
> *Wednesday*   Mary Price Roberts

> My dear Mr. McHose,
>
> *Thank you so much for the handsome inkstand. You
> could not have known that Georgian silver is a passion
> of mine; but it is, and this beautiful piece is something I
> shall always treasure. John likes it as much as I do, and
> says it is "exactly the sort of thing Uncle Bill would
> select."*

We are both happy to know you are coming for the wedding—John to renew old ties, I to meet someone about whom I have heard so many pleasant things. Until we do meet, I hope you will not think it forward of me to sign myself

Your affectionate neice-to-be

Wednesday   MARY AUDREY PRICE

MY DEAR MRS. GRAMLING,

John and I are so pleased with the beautiful crystal smoking set you sent us. The large ash trays are so handsome, and so practical, and the lighter works perfectly. Also, the set blends with the modern decor we are using in our new home. Thank you very much.

We are almost settled in our little place—settled enough, at least, to receive old friends—so we hope you will call on us soon.

Wednesday   Sincerely, etc.

THE USE OF "GREETING" CARDS

The use of engraved, printed or illustrated cards known in the trade as "greeting" cards has become so widespread that a discussion of their usage may serve a useful purpose. The use of the term "greeting" card is incorrect, except as a business term, but it is so much used, and any substitute is so awkward, that it is resorted to here.

Such cards may properly be sent at Christmas, Easter, Valentine's Day and birthdays. For any other occasion, and under any other circumstances, a card is not correct. A personal note is always to be preferred. This distinction applies even to "Get-well" messages. A note is always best. If a friend has a prolonged illness, so that one finally dispairs of finding anything new to say in a note, a series of cards might be sent, always remembering that they are very informal and not in the best taste.

The reason for the avoidance of cards is that they are a message prepared by the manufacturer, not by the sender, and so fail to carry the warmth and individuality of a personal note. In sending such a card one is saying, in effect, "I know a message of sorts is due you from me, but I am too lazy, or too unoriginal, or too indifferent, to write one of my own, so I shall fob you off with a card."

The use of a "thank-you" card of any kind is never proper. Even the use of small-sized writing paper that has "Thank you" engraved on the facing sheet, and space for a further message inside, is not proper. If you have *any* occasion to say "thank you," say it yourself, in your own handwriting, on your own writing paper.

Do *not* send cards of thanks for presents received on Christmas, birthday, anniversary, baptism, First Communion, confirmation, holy orders, engagement or wedding days. Do not send them as thanks for flowers, messages or presents received when ill. Do not send them to acknowledge flowers, mass cards, or messages of condolence in time of bereavement.

Do not send condolence cards or cards of congratulation to anyone on any of the occasions mentioned above, save Christmas and birthdays, except to children or to persons with whom you are on informal terms.

In selecting Christmas cards, remember that your name at the bottom of a message is really your signature, even when engraved. One therefore does not use "Mr. and Mrs. John Smith," any more than one would sign a letter that way. The correct signature is "John and Mary Smith," with the man's name first, as the wife is presumed to be the one who addresses and signs the cards.

A card that reads, "Mr. and Mrs. John Smith wish you a Merry Christmas and a Happy New Year" is correct, because the names are not a signature in such a message. This is the most formal type of card. Do not sign a card "Mr. and Mrs. John Smith and family," or even "John and Mary Smith and family." "And family" is poor usage and should be avoided. To those intimates on whose Christmas card you wish to include greetings from your children, strike out your own last name, if it is engraved on the card and add in ink: "and the children."

Modern thought inclines to the view that any sort of printed signature makes a Christmas card too impersonal. More and more people are signing their cards by hand. In this case, according to the degree of intimacy with the recipient, the card may be signed, "John and Mary Smith," "John and Mary," or "John, Mary, and the children."

9

Planning a Wedding

"Have mercy on us, O Lord, have mercy on us, and let us grow old both together in health" (Tobias 8:10).

SPIRITUAL REQUIREMENTS

The spiritual requirements for the wedding of two Catholics are the same regardless of the size or elaborateness of the wedding. The ceremony is performed in the bride's parish church, except for just cause. The young couple should call on the bride's pastor well in advance of the wedding date—two months in advance is not too soon.

If either party was baptized in another parish, he should bring with him a baptismal certificate not more than six months old. The young couple will be required to answer under oath to a questionnaire called *Examen nupturientum a parocho peragendum*. It covers simple matters, such as date and place of birth, parents' names, place of residence, reception of First Communion and confirmation, eligibility for marriage (no impediments), marrying of one's own free will, understanding of the marriage state, etc. The questionnaires are similar in all American dioceses.

The questionnaires are of fairly recent origin, and their purpose is not understood by some Catholics. They are asked for the protection of both the young people contemplating marriage and help to insure the validity and permanence of their union by endeavoring to uncover, before the ceremony takes place, any factors which, willfully concealed, might render it invalid.

If either of the contracting parties are hitherto unknown to the pastor, he may require some corroboration of their statements from a third party. Because the ceremony takes place in the bride's church, it is usually, but not always, the bridegroom who is a stranger to him, and about whom he may wish to inquire. In such a case, he may ask to talk with the bride's parents or one of the honor attendants. Such precautions are taken solely for the protection of the nuptial pair. No resentment should be felt at such precautions; certainly none should be displayed.

The bridal couple consult with the pastor when choosing the date and hour for the ceremony. Catholics are usually married with a nuptial Mass and solemn nuptial blessing. Since the solemn nuptial blessing is not usually given during Lent or Advent, Catholics do not often choose these times to be married. But they *can* be married in these seasons and may even be granted the nuptial blessing, if the pastor allows it. It is not common, however, and should not be attempted without a good reason.

In setting the wedding date and hour, one may find that one's tentative choice conflicts with that of another bridal already arranged for, or with the hours the church reserves for funerals, etc. In any such conflict, the bride changes her plans to concur with parish custom.

Arrangement is made at this time for the calling of the banns. Banns are called at the principal Mass in the bride's parish church on the three successive Sundays prior to the ceremony. They are also called in the bridegroom's parish church. Calling of the banns may be dispensed with for just cause. To determine when this may be done, one consults one's pastor.

The bride also asks her pastor at this time about any rules governing decoration of the church for the ceremony to make sure that her plans do not conflict with parish restrictions. The same is true of the use of a canopy and white carpet. If she wants extra music (such as violin or harp in addition to the organ) or wishes to employ any organist other than the church organist, she asks permission. In this latter case, if permission is granted, she may be required to pay the church organist's fee as well as that of the man whose services she actually employs. This is not true of vocal soloists; usually she may ask whomever she pleases to sing.

If the young couple wish to be married by any priest other than the pastor or his assistants, permission is now asked for this privilege so that the pastor may have time to obtain the proper papers of delegation. The date and hour for the wedding rehearsal may also be agreed upon at this meeting. Usually it is early in the evening on the night before the wedding.

WHAT KIND OF A WEDDING?

A newly-engaged girl about to make her wedding plans is apt to be in an unrealistic frame of mind. She loves and is loved; and the

world is a wonderful place. She plans a ceremony worthy of her love
and her luck, and ends up with a wedding similar in many respects to
the nuptials of Queen Elizabeth and Prince Philip. Then common
sense raises, very briefly, its unwelcome head, and she reluctantly
concludes that she cannot *really* wear a diamond tiara and a pearl
stomacher; but she is not ready to settle for much less.

This is normal. From early girlhood, "planning my wedding" is a
favorite game among the daughters of Eve. Indulging in this happy
dream, one is not hampered by questions of cost, suitability or effort
involved. When considering a real ceremony, a bride and her family
must weigh all three and use every particle of common sense that
they posess.

A wedding is many things in one. It is a sacrament of the Church.
It is a legal contract. It is a social function, weighted with traditions.
It is a sociological act which joins two families, hitherto unconnected,
and founds a new one. All of these aspects must be considered in
making wedding plans. The perfect wedding, in any given case, is the
one which best meets all the implied requirements in a framework of
judgment and taste.

The religious and legal requirements are easily determined. One
has the help of specialists—priests and civil authorities—in fulfilling
them. The sociological aspect is inherent in the wedding itself. All
that is further required sociologically is an attitude of mutual courtesy,
helpfulness, and good will by *all* members of both families. This is a
vital contribution to the happiness of the bridal couple. It sometimes
calls for forbearance, even for self-sacrifice. Sadly enough, relatives do
not always rise to the occasion. Advice, criticism, and instruction, given
unasked and unwanted by relatives and in-laws, create unnecessary
problems and may turn a happy bride into a harassed one.

But it is the wedding as a social function that creates the most
problems and demands a multitude of choices. There is no such thing
as an "informal" Catholic wedding ceremony. Formal means "with
strict attention to outward forms and ceremonies." Since all Catholic
weddings are so performed, they are all formal. Catholic weddings
may differ greatly, however, in their degree of elaborateness or
simplicity, and it is in choosing this precise degree that the bride
makes her primary decision about "what kind of a wedding."

Since World War II, people in all walks of life have been showing
a preference for large weddings and elaborate nuptial entertaining.
Many factors have contributed to this: the general high level of
income, the subtle but strong pressure exerted by business interests
concerned, and the unrealistic and romanticized attitude toward

marriage which permeates secular life. The most powerful influence of all is the unconscious desire to equal or outdo the weddings of friends, which induces many people to wedding display which is not really in accord with their own tastes and wishes. With these influences pressing her, a bride is apt to think of her nuptials as *the day*, outweighing in importance all the long, long days of her life to follow. It takes a levelheaded bride to consider how well and how happily she might spend, in those future days, money saved by a little circumspection in her wedding plans.

This nationwide trend toward extravagant weddings is causing concern among clergymen, educators, economists, and thoughtful people generally; and they would like to see it reversed. Twenty-five years ago, only people of wealth and social prominence were married with display and lavish nuptial entertaining, which was considered suitable to their position in the community. Those in more moderate circumstances celebrated more modestly. It was not at all unusual for a young couple to be married in their travelling costumes, accompanied only by their honor attendants. Such a ceremony was followed by a home dinner for the immediate families or a little home reception. Many a couple so married are learning, after a happy quarter-century together, that their daughter regards such wedding plans as pitiful, beneath contempt. They may well wonder, as they spend sums they cannot afford to give her a wedding she considers suitable, what this outlay will add to her future happiness to render it superior to theirs and make the wedding worth its cost.

These remarks should not be taken to mean that everyone should decide to be married as simply and inexpensively as possible. They are meant as a reminder that between the simple ceremony just described and the wildly elaborate ones all girls plan in fancy there are innumerable degrees of elaboration, both in the ceremony and in nuptial entertaining which one may choose, one of which is ideal in a given case. To consider and choose the one most suitable for *her* wedding, is the first duty of the bride and her family.

Now is the time for a happy though serious family council. The bride and her parents must examine the bride's wishes and ideal choices for her wedding, and try to align them with the total sum of money that her father feels he can spend upon it. They should also give some thought to their general style of living and that of the bridegroom and his parents. If they are quiet people not accustomed to giving or attending large formal parties, they might be ill at ease and uncomfortable in attempting a wedding of an elaborate nature.

Try to plan the ceremony so that it is on a level to which you and your friends are accustomed and can enjoy. Let it be your aim to have your wedding, whether large or small, correct in every detail. It will then be beautiful and memorable.

SOME POINTS TO CONSIDER

A wedding is the one occasion in the lives of most of us when we attempt to imitate, to some degree, the style and pomp of other days. Almost all phases of the occasion, therefore, are governed by tradition and established custom; it is usually a mistake to deviate from the norm. It is, in short, not the time to display one's originality or attempt to establish new precedents. The more elaborate the ceremony, the more one should attempt to follow the rules for it. The conservative bride will wear white or ivory color. The more daring might select very pale pink or very pale blue. Both brides would be correct. But the wearing of very pale green or deep yellow for a formal wedding would be criticized rather than admired. The same restraint must be exercised in all the choices that one must make. A good idea is to determine, first of all, what one may correctly choose in all the decisions one must make and then to exercise one's taste only within the limits of what is considered proper. Bear in mind that if your wedding is done in such a manner that the guests describe it as "most unusual" or "strikingly different," they are probably not intending their remarks as a compliment.

WEDDING EXPENSES

Since the amount one can spend is bound to affect one's wedding plans, it may be well to outline here who bears the various expenses of the wedding.

The bride or her family pays for:

Invitations or announcements
Gifts to bridal attendants
Any hired cars
Services of photographer
Floral decorations at church
Canopy and carpet
Fees to church musicians
Bridal gown and trousseau
Bridesmaids' bouquets
All nuptial entertaining, including rental of rooms for party, food, beverages, flowers and other decorations, musicians, wedding

cake, etc. Also for a present for the bridegroom, if desired. Also for the bridegroom's wedding ring, if the bride wishes. The bridegroom may buy it as one of a matched pair.

The bridegroom pays for:

Engagement and wedding rings

Marriage license

Offering to priest

Gift to altar boys

Bride's bouquet, also corsage bouquets for both mothers, if they wish to wear them.

Ushers' ties, gloves and gifts

Wedding gift to bride

All expenses of wedding journey

Members of bridal party pay for:

Their costumes for the wedding, with the exceptions noted above.

Travelling expenses to wedding, also lodging and meals if they are housed in a hotel.

From this résumé, it is apparent that wedding expenses are not equally apportioned but fall mainly upon the bride and her family. This division of costs is based on one of the oldest unwritten laws of western society: a man may not properly assume any of a young woman's expenses until they are man and wife, and may make her no expensive presents except her engagement ring and wedding present until they are married. The wedding and the entertaining that follows it are considered socially as entertaining done by the bride and her family, at which they are the hosts. The bridegroom's family, interested though they are in the event, have no part in it except as guests of the bride's parents.

Sometimes this is a hardship. A wealthy young man may be marrying a poor or orphaned bride. If his parents approve the match, they may long to give the pair a fine wedding at their expense. They may not properly do so. Even though they kept their share in the matter secret, the difference between the style of the wedding and the bride's means would be immediately apparent to the guests; and unpleasant comment would be the result. This is a basic rule from which one should never deviate: the cost of the wedding *must* be borne by the bride and her family, and must be limited to what they can afford. The only persons who can properly act as host at a wedding are: a) The bride's parents; b) Her grandparents or other blood relatives, if she is an orphan; c) The bride herself, if she is alone in the world. There is no permissible deviation from this rule.

This rule works a hardship in another way. It imposes great restraint upon the family of the bridegroom. Tastes do differ, always. No wedding a bride ever planned, elaborate or simple, corresponded in every detail to the wishes of the bridegroom's mother. If the bride is socially inexperienced and makes wedding plans that are not correct, the position of the bridegroom's mother is a painful one. Even under these circumstances, the older woman should not permit herself to make any unfavorable comment or to urge other arrangements upon the bride.

The bridegroom's mother demonstrates her awareness of the social niceties by gracefully agreeing to all the bride's choices far more than she would do by calling attention to her mistakes. If the mother is concerned about the possible impression the ceremony may make on her friends, she may console herself with the reminder that such of those friends as are themselves well-versed in the social amenities will be aware of her position and her primary responsibility. More important than this, by appearing to approve completely all of the bride's plans, she will be making her first contribution to amity and friendship between the two newly-connected families.

PREPARING FOR THE WEDDING

Professional Help

A wedding, even a simple one, is a lot of work for someone. It takes foresight, energy, taste, and strict attention to detail. Consequently people of means often engage a social secretary to help with the arrangements.

A second source of professional help is the bridal consultant, found in all large cities. These firms can take care of every detail from the engagement announcement to the reservations for the wedding journey. If the bride's mother is ill, elderly, or socially inexperienced, she may wish to employ these professional services. But there are drawbacks to doing so. Their suggestions in some details, may not always be in the best of taste for a Catholic wedding. The whole procedure takes on a high professional finish, too much like a fashion show, too little like a sacrament. It makes one's wedding too much like everyone else's because it lacks the personal touch which only the attention of the bride's family can give. One employing such a firm should carefully check the social and sacramental correctness of all the wedding plans and insist that everything be done in the proper manner.

Doing It Yourself

If you choose to arrange your own wedding, allow three months for preparation if possible. The larger the wedding, the more time is needed. Purchase a loose-leaf notebook, label it "Wedding Arrangements," and keep in it a careful account of all wedding plans and details. Include prices quoted to you for various services, dates on which deliveries have been promised, appointments for fittings— everything in connection with the wedding and any entertaining to follow. (Nuptial entertaining is discussed in another chapter.)

Here is a possible schedule of plans for arranging your wedding. All the points in it will be discussed at length in other chapters; this is a brief run-down of what must be covered for the largest and most elaborate wedding.

a) Choose month, day and hour of ceremony.
b) Make spiritual arrangements.
c) Invite wedding attendants to serve you.
d) Make out complete invitation or announcement list, with addresses.
e) Obtain similar list from bridegroom's mother.
f) Select and order invitations or announcements.
g) Select and order wedding dress, veil, slippers.
h) Select and order costumes for maid of honor and bridesmaids.
i) Both mothers select and order wedding costumes.
j) Engage photographer and plan pictures with him.
k) Engage church organist and other musicians if desired.
l) Plan music with organist and soloists.
m) Engage florist, plan church and reception decorations, select bouquets for bride and attendants.
n) Rent canopy and carpet, if desired.
o) Select trousseau.
p) Select and order gifts for attendants.
q) Choose wedding present for bridegroom, if desired. Not obligatory.
r) Fulfill civil obligations (health examination, license, etc.)
s) Select date to address invitations or announcements. Invitations are mailed three weeks before ceremony; announcements on day of wedding.
t) Make arrangements for nuptial entertaining: place, caterers, menu selected, beverages, wedding cake, decorations, music, guest list.

u) Note time and place of all pre-nuptial parties.

v) Reserve lodgings for out-of-town attendants and for out-of-town guests, as their acceptances are received.

w) Keep a record of all wedding presents, when received, from whom, brief description, date acknowledged with note of thanks.

x) Arrange for rehearsal and post-rehearsal dinner.

y) Arrange display of wedding gifts in home.

z) Arrange for bridesmaids' luncheon or dinner, if desired.

The bride should keep in mind that in addition to all these duties she will be selecting and purchasing her bridal linens, silver, and china, and, with her husband-to-be, will be searching for and furnishing their new home. It is wise, therefore, to take care of these other obligations well in advance of the wedding date. The weeks just prior to the wedding are bound to be hectic ones, no matter how forehanded she has tried to be.

Civil Arrangements

The bridegroom should determine in advance what the state and city require of a couple who want a license to marry, so that details, such as physical examinations, can be seen to some time before the wedding. Fees in connection with the license are paid for by the bridegroom.

WEDDING ATTENDANTS

Although the mother of the bride invites everyone else, the bride and bridegroom select and invite their own wedding attendants. This is an honor. If the bridegroom has a sister of the proper age, the bride usually invites her to be one of her attendants; if the bride has a brother who is old enough, the bridegroom usually includes him among his ushers.

The best man and maid of honor at a Catholic wedding should be Catholics. Permission for a non-Catholic to act as honor attendant and official witness at a Catholic wedding is granted only by the bishop, and then for a good reason. The situation usually arises only in connection with a mixed marriage, in which the non-Catholic party wishes to have his Protestant sister or brother as honor attendant. In such a case, permission may be given. Two Catholics being married should avoid creating such a problem by asking Catholic friends to be maid of honor and best man.

A Catholic asked to be best man or maid of honor at a non-

Catholic wedding must have the permission of his pastor to do so. Whether the permission will be granted depends on a number of circumstances too involved to discuss here. Whatever the pastor decides, the Catholic will agree without question.

The difficulty arises from the fact that the maid of honor and best man, because they are official witnesses, might be considered to take an active part in the ceremony. This is not true of ushers and brides-maids. Permission to have non-Catholic ushers or bridesmaids is usually granted, as is permission to act as bridesmaid or usher at a non-Catholic wedding, because this role in the proceedings is a passive one.

A bride may have any number of attendants, up to twelve, but more than eight is seldom seen. Four or six is more common. If one wishes to have children in the wedding party, one may have them as flower girl or ring bearer, but they should not be over six years old, as most children lose their picturesque babyishness at that age. One can never tell how children under six will behave under the stress of so much excitement. Also, children are natural scene-stealers. If included in a wedding party they are bound to attract attention to themselves and away from the bride, who should be the central figure of this occasion. For these reasons, children are not often seen in present-day wedding parties.

Bridesmaids

A bridesmaid has no actual duties except to look as pretty as possible on the great day. She should agree to whatever the bride selects as her costume and should seem to like it, whatever her private feelings. She pays for everything she wears except her flowers, which are furnished by the bride's father. Usually she gives a shower for the bride or joins a fellow-bridesmaid in giving one. If she lives in another community, she is relieved of this responsibility but must pay for her own transportation to the scene and lodgings while there.

Both married and single women may be asked to be bridesmaids, although formerly only single girls were asked. An expectant mother should never accept such an invitation unless her condition will not yet be apparent at the date of the ceremony. To consent to be part of a wedding party while in the last stages of pregnancy is in the worst possible taste because:

The purpose of a bevy of bridesmaids is to add to the beauty of the bridal scene. An attendant obviously pregnant strikes a false note, for neither her figure nor her carriage is beautiful to see.

The bride should be completely free to select gowns that suit her taste. She should not be limited to those suited to a mother-to-be.

The excitement and strain of wedding preparations and ceremony might adversely affect the health of the expectant mother.

The expense of a bridesmaid's costume is a heavy one, which most expectant mothers are happy to avoid at this time in their lives.

Ushers

Ushers have real responsibilities. They arrive at the church at least one half-hour before the ceremony. They meet all guests at the rear of the church and escort them to a seat. If the guest is a woman, the usher offers her his arm, which she takes, and escorts her to a seat. If the guests are a couple, the woman takes the usher's arm and her escort follows them down the aisle to a seat. If the guest is a man, or group of men, the usher precedes them down the aisle to a seat. If a family group comes together, the usher offers his arm to the wife, a daughter may follow on the arm of her father, and all are conducted together to their places.

Maid of Honor

The maid of honor is one of the two official witnesses to the marriage ceremony. Her other duties are to see that the bride's train and veil are properly arranged on entering and leaving the sanctuary, to hold her bouquet during the ceremony, and return it to her at the conclusion of the Mass.

Best Man

A best man is the other official witness to the marriage ceremony. He oversees all the ushers to see that they are properly dressed and arrive at the church in time to perform their duties, accompanies the bridegroom to the church, waits with him until it is time for the ceremony to begin, walks with him to the gates of the altar railing, follows him into the sanctuary, and stands near him before his own prie-dieu. At the proper moment, he hands the wedding ring to the altar boy, who hands it to the priest. If it is a double ring ceremony, he takes care of both rings. Following the recessional, he slips around to the rear of the church for his topcoat and hat and that of the bridegroom. Prior to the ceremony, he gives the altar boys their gifts—a moderate sum of money—in plain white envelopes containing the bridegroom's card. At some moment after the ceremony he must find the occasion to give the officiating priest the offering from the bridegroom. This is also in an envelope accompanied by his card. The best man should also be prepared to offer the first toast to the bride at any entertaining which follows the ceremony.

THE OFFERING

The offering made to a priest at a wedding ceremony should be commensurate with the style in which one is celebrating the occasion and should be as generous as one's means allow. When a couple is married at an elaborate ceremony, followed by a luncheon and reception for several hundred guests, an offering of one hundred dollars—or even five hundred—would not be unusual. At the more customary type of ceremony with a reception for two hundred, the offering should be at least fifty dollars. For simpler weddings, the amount may be scaled down—whatever one's conscience dictates. The offering should be put in a plain white envelope with the bridegroom's calling card. The best man takes charge of it, and gives it to the officiating priest either at the rehearsal, or just before or just after the ceremony.

ALTAR BOYS

If the bride or bridegroom has any young friends or relatives of the proper age who habitually serve on the altar of the church in which they are being married, they may ask the pastor to let them serve as altar boys for the wedding. Otherwise the pastor will select altar boys for the occasion.

While it is not required, it is a kind thing to remember these altar boys with a little tip or money present. It should not be large—one or two dollars is enough for each, and this too should be put into an envelope with the bridegroom's card, on which he may write "In remembrance of your assistance at a happy occasion" or some similar sentiment. The best man takes charge of these envelopes also, and gives them to the boys before the ceremony.

DISPLAYING WEDDING PRESENTS

Wedding presents will begin to arrive at the bride's home about two weeks before the wedding. Arrangements should therefore be made to display them prettily to the many friends who will be calling during this time. Select a convenient spot and set up tables, preferably long narrow ones that may stand against a wall. Several card tables may be used; the ping-pong table from the game room makes an excellent display table if you have room for it. Cover it with your finest damask cloths, lay them so that they hang to the floor in front.

If you do not have enough cloths, or they do not match well, use freshly laundered percale sheets, with the folds pressed out. In either case a little bridal decoration should be added. Take several strands of narrow white satin ribbon, drape them in swags that hang from the front edge of the table. Catch them up in knots or bows to which add a little cluster of artificial white forget-me-nots, lilies of the valley, or rosebuds. Arrange the presents attractively. If you receive many presents, reduce the display by showing only one place setting of your china, silver, and crystal, one glass of a set of cocktail glasses, etc. If your gifts are not unduly lavish, put out all your china, glassware, etc.

Some method should be found for displaying checks, for the donors of such a present have a right to be represented, but they should be arranged so the amount is not visible. Several checks might be laid overlapping one another, to conceal the amount of each, and a sheet of picture glass laid over all to hold them in place.

One word of caution: do not include in the display any cash that you receive, and do not endorse the checks before displaying them. Many brides have had such things "disappear" from a display of gifts. This is a shocking thing, but it is such a common experience that it must be mentioned. Apparently, many things besides want or need impel some poor creatures to thievery at such a time. Envy, self-pity, jealousy, or resentment for a fancied slight are sometimes at work in these cases.

Do not leave the donors' cards on the presents. This was formerly done so that friends could see from whom one's presents came, but it reduces the attractiveness of the picture and makes for invidious comparisons. The bride and her mother should try to remember who gave each of the presents so that they may tell callers from whom each came. This sounds difficult, but with a little effort it can usually be done. In the case of people in official life, it is, of course, impossible.

ACKNOWLEDGING WEDDING PRESENTS

All wedding presents are acknowledged by a hand-written note of thanks from the bride. There is no acceptable substitute for this. The notes should be written at the earliest date possible after receipt of the present. Friends understand that it is a busy time in the life of a bride, so that anything up to three months after the date of the wedding is considered reasonable. By that time all presents should have been acknowledged. Many brides write notes of thanks as soon as the gift is received or at least attempt to write many of them before the wedding, as time allows. Once the couple has returned from the wedding journey, some time each day should be spent in writing notes until all are finished. Acknowledge the gifts in the order in which they were received: the first one first, and the last one last. The obligation to respond to the receipt of wedding presents with a prompt, hand-written note is one of the most stringent which society imposes. The bride who is lax or indifferent about obeying it is, quite properly, considered ungrateful and ill-bred. For further discussion of this matter, see the chapter on "Wedding Correspondence and Printed Forms."

10

The Elaborate Wedding Ceremony

"Have you not read that the Creator, from the beginning, made them male and female, and said, 'For this cause a man shall leave his father and mother, and cleave to his wife, and the two shall become one flesh'?" (St. Matthew 19:4–6).

THE PLACE

Canon law declares that two Catholics should be married in the parish church of the bride, but permission may be obtained, for good cause, to be married in another church. Canon law also states that in an extraordinary case and for good cause one's bishop may consent to a marriage taking place in a private home. This is now *very* rare. Many bishops refuse to grant such permission.

The wedding of two Catholics consists of the marriage rite, followed by a Nuptial Mass and solemn nuptial blessing. The Nuptial Mass is a privilege reserved to two Catholics—it is not permitted in a mixed marriage. A wedding service properly performed by a priest is a valid ceremony in the eyes of the Church as well as the State, even though not accompanied by the Nuptial Mass and blessing. But the Mass and the blessing are such wonderful privileges that most Catholics wish to be married with a Nuptial Mass.

THE HOUR

A Catholic wedding with its Nuptial Mass may be scheduled for any hour before one o'clock, but not in the afternoon or evening. This restriction is due to the fact that a Mass may not be begun later than 12:59 o'clock in the afternoon, except under the special privileges for afternoon and evening Masses recently granted. But the new privilege is granted specifically "for the common good," so it cannot be extended to a Nuptial Mass, which would make it an individual benefit. Twelve o'clock, the traditional "high noon," is the most fashionable hour, but large weddings are held at any hour from ten-thirty on, with eleven o'clock highly favored in the East.

THE DATE

Catholics are not usually married during Advent and Lent because the solemn nuptial blessing may not be given in those periods except with special permission; and the penitential nature of the seasons does not accord with the pomp of a large wedding.

Catholics are not usually married on Sunday, although there is no Church law that forbids it. The day is avoided because a Sunday wedding unduly complicates the parish Masses scheduled for the day. This also applies to Christmas Day and the Feast of the Circumcision. June and September are the most popular marriage months, but this is merely a matter of fashion and custom.

INVITATIONS

Invitations are always issued to a large wedding. They are sent out three weeks before the date of the ceremony. For further discussion of invitations, see chapter on "Wedding Correspondence and Printed Forms."

DECORATIONS

The bride should engage a florist well in advance of the wedding date to plan the floral decorations for the church. If the florist has not hitherto decorated this particular church, he should visit it and examine the size and nature of the altar and sanctuary before plans are made.

Decorations usually consist of several altar bouquets—whatever the main altar will accommodate—and palms or other greenery to form a background for the wedding party at the altar. A bouquet may be placed on each side altar if desired. Bouquets and ribbon bows may also be tied to the pews to mark those reserved for the two families; or they may, for decorative purposes, be tied on the pews all the way down the main aisle—a bouquet on every fifth pew, for instance. The ribbons and flowers are always white.

It is not customary to rope off or enclose any pews with ribbons or silk ropes in a Catholic church. Any Mass, even a Nuptial Mass, is open to all who care to attend, so the roping off of the principal seats is avoided as a symbol of exclusiveness. In actual practice, anyone who comes to church for the purpose of hearing Mass and finds that he has come at an hour scheduled for a wedding should seat himself at the rear of the church on a side aisle as a matter of courtesy.

WEDDING FLOWERS

At this time the bride will also select the bouquets for her maid of honor and bridesmaids; usually the bridal bouquet and mothers' corsage bouquets, are ordered at this time, too. The bride's father pays for the attendants' bouquets. The bridegroom pays for the bride's bouquet and for the corsage of her mother, if she wishes to wear one. A romantic young man may wish to select these according to his taste, but usually the bridegroom lets the bride make her own choice and contents himself with paying for them. He also buys a corsage bouquet for his mother, if she wishes to wear one.

MUSIC

The bride arranges for her wedding music with the church organist. Most brides like to have a vocal soloist, either man or woman, in addition to the organ. Trios and quartets are sometimes used. Occasionally violin, cello, harp, or all three, may accompany the organ with beautiful results, but it is within the discretion of the pastor to forbid these additions if he wishes to.

Secular music may not be played in a Catholic church. There is no sensible reason for objecting to this, even though it means that one must forego the playing of the well-known Mendelssohn and Wagner wedding marches. Excessive familiarity long ago robbed these selections of any appeal they may have had. The church organist will explain what may properly be used. A list of selections acceptable to most dioceses is appended to this chapter.

CANOPY AND CARPET

It adds to the bride's peace of mind, as well as to the festive appearance of the church, to know that there will be a canopy to protect the wedding party from the weather on entering the church, but it is not essential and is often omitted. Permission to erect a canopy must be obtained from the church pastor, as some parishes do not permit it. A carpet from the curb to the church door is a protection for the gowns of the bride and her attendants, and is almost a necessity in bad weather.

Today it is customary for a white canvas to be laid down the main aisle of the church just after the bride's mother has been seated, and just before the bridal procession. It is unrolled from a spindle and is carried up the aisle to the gate of the altar rail by two of the ushers, who then return to the back of the church to take part in the procession.

CARS REQUIRED

A number of cars with drivers will be required on the wedding day. These may be hired, with uniformed drivers, but it is quite common for friends to offer the use of their cars and themselves to act as drivers or to furnish a driver. In this latter case, the cars should be freshly washed and polished. A car will be needed for: the bridegroom and his best man, the bridegroom's parents, the mother of the bride, the bride and her father, and the bride's attendants. Ushers may drive to the church in their own cars. The bridegroom's parents may do this also if they prefer. The bride's mother may be accompanied by any members of the immediate family (sisters or brothers of the bride) who are not in the wedding party and are not married.

PHOTOGRAPHS

A bride often has her formal wedding photograph taken some days before the wedding. She may either make a studio appointment and go with her bridal costume to have the picture taken, or she may have the photographer come to her house. It is taken well in advance of the wedding date if she wishes to have the picture appear in the newspapers directly following the wedding, when the account of the ceremony is published. This picture is of the bride only; it includes neither her future husband nor any of the wedding party.

Many brides also like to have a number of candid photographs (that is, pictures that are not retouched) taken on the wedding day to tell a picture story of the occasion. For these she engages a photographer who is a specialist in this line of work to be present on her wedding day and make a picture story of the event.

This photographer should be interviewed well in advance of the wedding date; he and the bride should determine in a general way what scenes she wants photographed. These pictures may include shots of: the bride surveying her wedding gifts at home, the bride and her attendants at home, the bride and her father entering the church, the processional, the bridegroom and best man approaching the sanctuary gates, the entrance of the bride's mother, the bridegroom's mother, an overall view of the ceremony and congregation taken from the choir loft, the ceremony, the recessional, the wedding breakfast, scenes in the receiving line, groups of friends and relatives at the reception, the couple and both sets of parents, the entire wedding party, the brides-maids, the ushers, throwing the bouquet, leaving for the wedding journey. This list may, of course, be enlarged to include the first toast at the breakfast, cutting the cake, and many other scenes, or it may be reduced, according to the bride's wishes and the amount she wants to spend.

The photographer should be cautioned to dress like a wedding guest so as to be inconspicuous and should be warned to perform his services at the church in an unobtrusive way, so as not to detract from the solemnity of the occasion.

NOTIFYING THE NEWSPAPERS

The account of the wedding which appears in local newspapers is the one detail of a wedding over which the bride and her family do not have complete control. Famous or very prominent people will find that the newspapers are determined to carry a news story of the wedding whether the participants wish it or not. People not so well-known may discover that the newspapers will not carry as complete a story of the ceremony as they would like.

Speaking very generally, one may say that in cities of more than one million population, it is standard newspaper policy to carry bridal photographs and a detailed account of the wedding only when the people concerned are comparatively well-known. In smaller communities, most newspapers will use a photograph and some kind of account of the wedding of any respectable couple but will reserve the right to decide upon what date the story will appear and what details it shall include.

But the bride can protect her interests by having her wedding photograph taken well in advance of the occasion and requesting the photographer to make up glossy prints of the picture she wishes to have published, one for each newspaper. She should write, or have written, a correct account of the wedding which includes the details she wishes to be published. The picture and story should be sent to the papers well in advance of the ceremony, marked "DO NOT RELEASE BEFORE—(the date of the day after the wedding)." The story of a wedding should never appear in a morning newspaper on the day of the wedding because the paper will be on the streets before the ceremony has actually occurred.

In preparing the wedding story, omit every unnecessary adjective. Avoid too detailed a description of the wedding costumes, for this sounds like a fashion show. This mistake is frequently made when the wedding story is prepared by a bridal consultant: her interest is mainly in the costumes. But wedding apparel is *not* the important part of the story and should be played down. Be sure all names are given in full, and correctly spelled. Grandparents of the bridal couple should not be referred to unless they are well-known locally. Following is an example of an account that might be written of a large wedding:

FOR RELEASE SUNDAY, OCTOBER 25, 1960, ONLY!

PHELAN-WAKEFIELD

The marriage of Miss Kathleen Marjorie Phelan, daughter of Mr. and Mrs. Charles Louis Phelan, 34 Van Vorst Street, to Stephen William Wakefield, eldest son of Mr. and Mrs. Francis Stephen Wakefield, 19 Meadow Road, was solemnized with a Nuptial Mass yesterday morning at eleven o'clock in the Cathedral of the Immaculate Conception. The Rev. F. Fay Murphy, S.J., a cousin of the bridegroom, performed the ceremony, assisted by the Rev. Lawrence Fahy, the pastor. Also present in the sanctuary were the Rt. Rev. Monsignor Edward Kerwin and the Rev. Beecher J. Sullivan, C.S.C.

The bride, who was escorted by her father, wore an ivory velvet gown with a court train and a veil of heirloom lace which had been worn by nine other family brides. She carried a bouquet of stephanotis and white orchids.

Miss Mildred Trombley of Buffalo was the bride's maid of honor. She wore copper-colored velvet and a coronet of ivy leaves, and carried a sheaf of copper-colored chrysanthemums. The bridesmaids were Miss Isabella Post, Miss Mary Rose Hunt, Miss Dorothy Crane, Miss Lois Panetta of Larchmont, and the bride's cousins, Miss Sheila and Miss Elizabeth McIntyre of Philadelphia, Pa. All wore dresses of dark green velvet and coronets of yellow daisies, and carried sheaves of yellow chrysanthemums.

Mr. Wakefield had his father for best man. The ushers were: Roger J. Maylone, George C. Rielley, Barrie S. Wood, the bride's brother, Dennis Phelan, and the bridegroom's brothers, Bruce and Brice Wakefield.

The bride's mother wore a gray satin suit, with blouse and hat of rose color, and a sable stole. Mrs. Wakefield wore a suit of blue Paisley silk with matching hat, and a jacket of fawn-dyed ermine.

Immediately following the ceremony a reception to several hundred guests was held at the Shaker Meadows Golf Club, after which Mr. and Mrs. Wakefield left for a Bermuda cruise.

Miss Phelan, who is a granddaughter of former state Senator Gerald Dwyer and Mrs. Dwyer and the late Dr. and Mrs. Ralph Phelan, was graduated from St. Monica's School for Girls and the College of St. Elizabeth. She has been a teacher of speech therapy at St. Vincent's Hospital Clinic.

Mr. Wakefield was graduated from St. Mark's School and Georgetown University, and from the School for Foreign Service of that institution. He is a member of the U. S. consular staff in London, where the couple will be at home after December 15th.

Among the wedding guests were Asst. Secretary of State Herman Estes and Mrs. Estes, former Gov. Norman Fowler and Mrs. Fowler, Senator Thomas Whelan, Judge and Mrs. Barr Weldon, and the Rev. Brother Walter, F.S.C., president of St. Peter's College.

The couple were granted the papal blessing.

Please note that in this account the color and fabric of the costumes of the bride, her attendants, and the two mothers are mentioned. Most newspapers allow this. But the style and trimmings are not mentioned. Foreign phrases such as the French names for lace (*duchesse, princesse,* etc.) or for styling (*robe de style a la reine,* etc.) should not be used, nor should words of praise, such as beautiful, striking, distinguished, etc. Addresses of attendants, ushers, etc. are not given if they are local residents. Out-of-town cities are given, with the state not mentioned if the city is in the same state as the one in which the wedding takes place, but are given if they are out of state. (See sample as given. The wedding is presumed to have taken place in New York State.) Note also that those mentioned in the guest list are persons of some prominence. Some smaller city newspapers will list all out-of-town guests, but all will not do so. It is proper to give information about the couple's education, employment, club membership, service in Armed Forces and any claim to prominence they may have, if desired. Example: "Miss Phelan was graduated from Our Lady of the Elms, where she was elected to 'Who's Who in American Colleges' and served as senior class president." Or: "Mr. Wakefield attended Manhattan College, where he was for two years captain of the golf team, and managed the debating team."

Some families feel that it shows a craving for publicity to offer a prepared account of the ceremony to the newspapers. Actually it does not; the more prominent the family, the more necessary that a prepared account be given. Some story of the wedding will certainly appear. It is better that it be one prepared by the family, with all the facts correct, and nothing included that might be in poor taste.

WEDDING COSTUMES

Bride

At a large wedding a bride wears white or pale ivory, very pale pink or very pale blue. White or ivory are the traditional colors, but the others are sometimes worn. Whether the dress is long or short is a matter of fashion. Currently, brides are wearing waltz length (mid-calf) or floor length gowns; but short skirts are once more becoming fashionable, and one may again see very short wedding dresses worn.

The material may be velvet, satin, brocade, tulle, net, lace or moire. For summer weddings, organdy, organza, peau de soie, nylon, dotted swiss, pique, linen and lawn are also worn.

She wears a veil the exact shade of her gown, of tulle, lace, nylon, or embroidered net. Usually it is attached to a small crown, tiara or headband. Caps and fresh flowers may again become fashionable to hold the veil on the head but they are not so at this time.

The bride's slippers are of satin or silk, to match her gown. The bride should remember to select slippers in which she can walk comfortably and gracefully. Unless her bridegroom is much taller than she, it might be well to choose low-heeled slippers, both for her own comfort and to make him appear taller. Ballet-type slippers, although fashionable, are a poor selection for either the bride or her attendants, for it is almost impossible to walk gracefully in them.

The bride carries a bouquet of white flowers or a white prayer book. One may have a small bouquet, such as a single large white orchid, attached to a white prayer book.

A Catholic bride always wears long or bracelet-length sleeves. She never wears a low-backed gown or one with an extreme décolletage.

Bridesmaids

Bridesmaids' gowns, head covering and slippers are always identical in style. Usually the gowns are the same length as the bride's, but they do not have to be so. Often all are the same color, but need not be. The dresses should not be low-backed or very low-necked, and they should have a sleeve of sorts. If the sleeve is a mere shoulder cap, they should wear opera-length gloves. Shoes match the dresses in color.

The head covering may be large or small hats, bands of ribbon or flowers, flower caps, tiaras, or small crowns. Sometimes the attendants wear short colored veils caught with a band or wreath of flowers. There is a wide choice in this area. They may carry a spray or bouquet of flowers, or small tulle or velvet muffs to which bouquets of flowers are attached.

Maid of Honor

The maid of honor usually wears a dress made exactly like the bridesmaids and it may be of the same color. In this latter case, her flowers and headdress are different from those of the other attendants. She may also wear a dress of a contrasting color, but it is always the same material and made in the same fashion as the bridesmaids'. She may wear a large hat, while the bridesmaids wear small ones; she may carry a large spray of flowers, while the bridesmaids carry small bouquets. The effect of her costume must resemble theirs, but with some differences to make her outstanding.

The bride makes all these choices to please her own taste. Her attendants agree to her selections without comment. Attendants pay for their bridal costumes, except for their flowers, which are bought by the bride's father.

Mothers of the Bridal Couple

The mothers of the bride and bridegroom wear costumes more elaborate and formal than are ever worn before luncheon on any other occasion. Save for the fact that they must have the "covered" look required for church wear at any time, they are as formal as cocktail dresses. The sleeves are long or bracelet length; the gloves are long enough to touch the ends of the sleeves. Floor-length gowns are not becoming to older women, but it is correct to wear them. Ankle or waltz-length gowns may also be worn. When short-skirts are fashionable for street wear, mothers of bridal couples may wear them.

The two mothers' dresses should be similar in length and degree of formality, but need not correspond in any other way. The colors of the two gowns should not match, nor should they match those of the bridal attendants, nor should they clash. White or black are not worn. Even though one parent may be a widow who has worn black for many years, she should choose a color for this occasion. Any shade of blue or gray is suitable, as are the lighter brown tones, such as beige, honey color or cocoa color, the purple tones of violet, lilac, or lavender, and the more delicate shades of green or rose color. For a winter wedding, the darker browns and greens as well as purple and wine color may be worn if the fabric is rich enough to give a formal effect.

The material may be silk, satin, chiffon, taffeta, velvet, velveteen, brocade, lace, or even lame or cloth-of-silver. A two-piece suit of velvet, a lace dress with long-sleeved jacket, or a dress of chiffon over taffeta, with taffeta jacket, are nice choices for older women.

Hats may be small or large, but should be formal style. Purses should be small and should match the dress, hat, or shoes. Flowers may be worn attached to the purse or at the shoulder or waist. Slippers should be of a delicate, dress type. To have the entire costume—dress, hat, shoes, purse, and gloves—of one color gives a rather monotonous effect. Hat and dress are usually of one shade, slippers, gloves and purse of another, but there is no rule about this. Some kind of ensemble in two shades should be worked out by each mother to give a finished effect.

Bridegroom

At a large Catholic wedding, the bridegroom wears formal morning attire, the only correct costume for the hours at which Catholic weddings are held. Dinner jackets or evening clothes are not proper, as is now generally understood. One mistake in men's wedding clothes is still quite common: at a summer wedding at which the bride and her attendants wear light summery gowns, the men in the party sometimes wear white dinner jackets and black evening trousers. This is wrong; such a costume may not properly be worn before six o'clock in the evening. If the young men want to wear something less heavy and winterish than formal morning dress, they might wear dark blue jackets and white trousers; but, strictly speaking, this is too informal for a large church wedding.

The traditional wear for men at a formal daytime wedding consists of: cutaway coat in black or oxford gray wool, waistcoat which matches cutaway or is made of pearl gray gabardine, trousers of gray and black or white and black stripe, without cuffs, starched white shirt with plain bosoms, stiff cuffs, and fold collar (not button-down), tie (ascot or four-in-hand, plain gray or striped gray and white or gray and black), plain black shoes and socks (the shoes would be delicate, with thin soles), and a boutonniere of white flowers, such as a carnation or a sprig of lilies of the valley. Winged collars, yellow waistcoats, and spats are proper but are not currently fashionable and are almost never seen. To and from the church, the groom should wear a silk hat or opera hat and carry a walking stick. But today many young men rebel at such formality. Black hombergs are often worn instead of top hats, and some go bareheaded. Few carry a stick. These deviations are permissible because these adjuncts to their costume are not seen during the ceremony itself. Any other deviation from the traditional costume is not correct.

Best Man

The best man wears exactly what the bridegroom wears.

Ushers

The ushers are dressed as are the bridegroom and best man, but the pattern of their ties and even of their trousers, may differ slightly from those worn by the two main figures. But all the ushers must be dressed exactly alike. For this reason their ties and gloves are a gift from the bridegroom, to make sure that they will be identical. Ushers must wear gray suede gloves.

Fathers of the Bridal Couple

Fathers of the bride and bridegroom dress as do the men in the bridal party, but their neckties may be different from those of anyone else; they may also wear differing waistcoats: gray instead of matching the coat or vice versa. Complete uniformity is to be avoided here.

Wedding Guests

Women guests at a large wedding dress as for a late afternoon party: street-length dresses or afternoon suits of silk, velvet, taffeta, crepe, brocade, etc. If a wool suit is worn, it should be dressed "up" with frilly blouse, lapel pin or fur scarf, and a dress hat should be worn. The shoes should be delicate afternoon style. Gloves are always worn. In cold weather, an afternoon coat, fur stole, or jacket may be worn. Any color costume is acceptable, but if black is worn, it should be festive enough so as not to be mistaken for mourning.

Men guests at a wedding seldom wear formal morning dress. Occasionally an older guest will appear in what was formerly the only correct costume for male wedding guests, but even he will usually prefer the short sack coat to the cutaway. With the short coat, a black homburg or derby should be worn. Most of the men guests will dress more simply in dark suits (either dark blue or oxford gray) with white shirt, black shoes and socks, and plain ties of blue or grey with a small figure.

Men guests should never wear shoes of any color but black, sports clothing such as unmatched jacket and trousers, colored shirts of any kind, or conspicuous ties.

SEATING ARRANGEMENTS

The family of the bride and her guests are always seated on the gospel (left) side of the main aisle of the church; the bridegroom's family and friends sit on the epistle side. The order of precedence in seating is no longer considered as important as formerly. The first gospel pew is occupied by the mother and father of the bride. Any unmarried sisters and brothers may also sit in this pew if there is room for them. Directly behind them are seated any married brothers and sisters, grandparents, aunts, uncles, etc. Friends are seated behind them, usually with no order of precedence attempted.

The family and friends of the bridegroom are seated on the epistle side, in the same order as above. Should the bride's mother wish to observe a strict order of precedence, she should furnish the head usher with a typewritten list showing the precise location for all guests. She should consult with the bridegroom's mother, and plan a similar exact list for the guests of the bridegroom. Ushers then ask the name of each guest they are escorting, and consult the list if in doubt as to where anyone should be seated. Today the list usually contains only the names of relatives, with friends seated behind them at random.

If distinguished government officials such as the President, members of the cabinet, ambassadors, or governors are expected to attend, their places are established by official protocol. In such a case the mother of the bride may consult with the social secretary of the most distinguished government official expected to attend, to learn the protocol for seating official guests. It is also a good plan to mail pew cards with the invitations to a wedding of this kind, although otherwise they are not much used today. (For further discussion of pew cards, see chapter on "Wedding Correspondence and Printed Forms.")

Priests who are personal friends of either family are invited by being sent the engraved invitation or by a personal note urging them to come. The latter is warmer and more complimentary, but either is correct. If the officiating priest is not the pastor of the bride's church or one of his assistants, the pastor should be sent an invitation, even though he may not be an intimate friend of either family. Any priests who accept the invitation will sit in the sanctuary. The bride's mother should make sure at the wedding rehearsal that there are seats provided there for all priests expected to attend. All priests attending the wedding are invited to any entertaining which follows the ceremony, no matter how simple it may be. Usually they will decline. If they do attend, it is a compliment to the bridal couple.

THE WEDDING PROCESSION

The order of the wedding procession will be determined at the wedding rehearsal. Priests of any city parish are well-versed in the correct procedure for large weddings, and, in addition to knowing what is proper, have usually determined the details which best suit the size of the sanctuary of the church which they serve. Their suggestions should be heeded. This does not mean that one should not feel free to express one's preferences and offer ideas.

Ideally, the sanctuary should be large enough to accommodate all the wedding party, priest—guests, officiating priest, altar boys, and the palms and greenery which form a background for the picture. There must also be enough individual prie-dieux for each member of the bridal party, which is not always the case. Where it is, the procedure is often as follows:

As the first notes of the processional sound, the congregation rises and remains standing throughout the marriage service. The priest enters the sanctuary accompanied by the altar boys and walks to a point in front of the main altar just behind the prie-dieu for the bride and bridegroom, and stands facing the congregation and awaiting the bridal couple. He is followed into the sanctuary by any attending priests, who go to the seats prepared for them and stand in front of them. At the same moment the bridegroom and his best man enter the body of the church from the epistle side and walk across the front of the church, outside the altar railing, to the altar gates, which are open. Bridegroom and best man stand at this point, facing the congregation, until the bride and her father reach them.

As the priest enters the sanctuary, the bridal procession starts up the aisle. The ushers come first, walking two by two, with about six feet of aisle between each pair. They are matched by size, with the shorter pair leading off. If there is an uneven number of ushers, the head usher or the shortest man, if there is no head usher, starts off first, walking alone, followed by the others in pairs. At the altar rail they separate, the man on the right side of the aisle going to prie-dieu placed near the right side wall of the sanctuary, the man on the left going to a similar position near the left sanctuary wall.

The bridesmaids follow about six feet behind the last ushers, also walking in matched pairs unless there is an uneven number, in which case the shortest leads, walking alone. The maid of honor follows the last bridesmaids, walking alone. If there are page boys or flower girls, they come next. The bride and her father conclude the procession unless she has train bearers; these are currently not fashionable.

The bridesmaids go to whatever altar prie-dieux were designated for them at the rehearsal.

The maid of honor does not follow the bridesmaids into the sanctuary. When she reaches the altar gates, she steps to the left of the aisle, makes a half-turn toward the congregation, and stands until the bride and bridegroom enter the sanctuary. At this point she and the best man turn and enter the sanctuary simultaneously, separating inside the rail. He goes directly to his prie-dieu next to the bridegroom's; she arranges the bride's train and veil if they require it, takes her bouquet from her, and goes to her prie-dieu beside the bride's. She returns the bouquet to the bride after the marriage service is completed.

The bride comes up the aisle on her father's right arm. At the gates of the altar, her father takes her right hand and places it gently on the left arm of her bridegroom. He then steps to his pew, genuflects, and joins his wife. The bridal couple enter the sanctuary together and stand before the priest for the ceremony.

In some parishes, the bride's father is permitted to kiss her and shake his future son-in-law's hand before laying his daughter's hand on the bridegroom's arm. Since the father of the bride otherwise takes no actual part in a Catholic ceremony, this is a pleasant way to signify his consent and approval of the match. But if one's parish does not allow it, consider it of no importance.

The recessional is usually an exact reverse of the processional, with the bride and bridegroom leading off, followed by the maid of honor, bridesmaids, and ushers. The best man is not a part of the recessional but leaves the church as he entered it. An acceptable alternate is for the newly married couple to be followed down the aisle by the maid of honor on the best man's arm, followed by the bridesmaids, each accompanied by an usher. If there are extra ushers, as frequently happens, two ushers make up the last pair down the aisle. This style is not quite as formal as the other one but is correct and is sometimes preferred because it gives the best man a place in the bridal recessional.

This method of pairing up bridesmaids and ushers is, as mentioned before, correct for the recessional of the most formal of weddings. But it may not be used for the processional except for a much simpler ceremony, and then only if the bride does not enter on her father's arm. When the bride has her father as escort, the correct processional is as just described. The processional may be altered in any number of small circumstances to suit the wedding and the church in which it is held. For churches with too small a sanctuary to accommodate the entire bridal party or those which lack sufficient prie-dieux, some modifications must be made. Palms and greenery may be dispensed with. If the sanctuary is still too small, the ushers may be seated in the first pew on the epistle side of the aisle directly in front of the bridegroom's parents, who, under these circumstances, occupy the second pew on the right. Only the best man and the women of the bridal party enter the sanctuary. If there is not room enough for this, the bridesmaids are seated in the first pew on the gospel side, in front of the bride's parents, and only the best man and maid of honor, who are the official witnesses, enter the sanctuary with the bridal pair. Priest-guests are always seated in the sanctuary, no matter how small it is.

THE WEEK OF THE WEDDING

For a large wedding to take place smoothly and happily, plans must be made well in advance so that events will mesh smoothly. Everyone must know what is expected of him and must do it properly and at the correct time. To demonstrate this, here is a résumé of what is expected of all concerned during the week of the wedding and on the day itself:

One week prior to the wedding, all the principals should have assembled their complete costumes and should make sure each detail is correct. The bridal trousseau should be ready to pack; reservations should have been made for the bridal journey. The wedding presents should be on display, a list of them carefully kept, and as many as possible acknowledged by a note from the bride as they are received. Reservations should be made for members of the bridal party coming from a distance and for out-of-town wedding guests who have accepted the invitation. The bachelor dinner is sometimes held during this week, but not on the eve of the wedding. Also the bridal luncheon, if one is to be held. The wedding license should be obtained and any other civil requirements be fulfilled. The wedding rehearsal is usually held early in the evening on the night prior to the wedding. Make sure that all participants understand their instructions. Run through the processional and recessional several times, so that it will go smoothly. The old superstition that the bride should not take part in the rehearsal is merely that—an old superstition—and should be ignored. The bride should take part.

After the rehearsal or on the afternoon prior to it, the bride and groom should go to confession so that they may receive Holy Communion at the Nuptial Mass. If all members of the bridal party are Catholic, it is well if they also go to confession and receive Holy Communion at the wedding. If there are some non-Catholics in the wedding party it may be better to omit this, as it looks awkward for some to receive and others to abstain. Bride and bridegroom always receive. The new rules of fasting make this a simple matter.

The rehearsal is followed by an informal dinner or supper served buffet style, or merely by drinks and substantial hors d'oeuvres. (See "Pre-Nuptial Entertaining.") This party is a simple one and ends at an early hour. The bridesmaids should take the responsibility for leaving early and helping to end it.

THE DAY OF THE WEDDING

At least one hour before the wedding, canopy and carpet should be in place at the church. If possible, the church decorations should be completed; but sometimes a prior wedding or funeral makes this impossible. The florist should be reminded of this when he is engaged, especially if he has not served a Catholic wedding party before. He may be obliged to perform his services very rapidly in a brief period of time, and may not be finished when the earliest guests begin to arrive. This is awkward but is sometimes unavoidable.

All the bridal bouquets and boutonnieres are delivered to the bride's home one hour before the wedding. An usher should be delegated to pick up the boutonnieres, take three of them to the bridegroom's home for the bridegroom, his father, and the best man, and the rest to the church to give to the other ushers. One half-hour before the ceremony, the maid of honor and bridesmaids arrive at the bride's house. One half-hour before the ceremony, the ushers are at the church. One half-hour before, the best man goes to the home of the bridegroom and escorts him to the church, which he should reach at least fifteen minutes before the ceremony.

Guests will begin coming to the church about twenty minutes before the wedding hour. The ushers will seat them in the proper places. The bridegroom's parents arrive and are seated just before the bride's mother. The mother of the bride arrives at the church accompanied by any unmarried children of the family or alone. If she is accompanied by children, they are seated first. The last to be seated is the mother of the bride. She is escorted by the head usher. For about fifteen minutes prior to the ceremony the organist has been softly playing appropriate music. As soon as the bride's mother is seated, two of the ushers unroll and carry down the aisle the white canvas on which the bridal party will walk.

The bride and her father leave for the church directly after her mother, followed by her attendants. All should be assembled in the vestibule before the bride's mother is seated. As soon as the canvas is laid and the ushers have returned to the back of the church, the organist begins to play the processional; all guests rise; the priest and altar boys come to the altar; the best man and the bridegroom enter the front of the church; the ushers begin the bridal march as outlined under "Wedding Processional." Efforts should be made so that the wedding may begin at *exactly* the hour named in the invitation. This courtesy is due to one's guests, to the officiating clergyman, and to anyone whose wedding may be scheduled to follow one's own. This is one occasion when there is no such thing as being "fashionably" late— it is a serious breach of etiquette for guests or bridal party to fail to be on time. The ceremony is followed by the Nuptial Mass. The recessional march of the bridal party concludes the ceremony. Following this, the head usher returns to the front pew and escorts the mother of the bride from the church, closely followed by the bridegroom's mother with another usher. Other guests are not escorted from the church.

French-Canadian Catholics conclude their wedding services with a charming custom which Americans would do well to emulate. At the conclusion of the recessional, the two mothers are not escorted down the aisle by ushers. Instead, the bridegroom's father and the bride's father rise and bow to each other. The bridegroom's father then crosses the aisle and offers his arm to the bride's mother, and escorts her to the vestibule. The bride's father does the same for the bridegroom's mother. This little gesture typifies the future unity and amity of the two newly-united families.

This custom should be attempted only when all four parents are living; it would be too awkward to have one mother escorted by an in-law, the other by an usher, etc.

It is good manners for those in the back of the church to allow the guests in the front of the church to precede them from the building, but one need not be punctilious about it. What is to be avoided is a rush into the aisle and out of the church. At the conclusion of a large wedding the bridal party and families drive away promptly to the scene of the reception, without lingering to receive congratulations or greet guests. Motor cars should be lined up to receive them as they come out: bridal couple's car, bridesmaids', ushers', bride's family's, bridegroom's family's.

WEDDING GUESTS

Wedding guests have three primary responsibilities: to acknowledge their invitations properly and promptly, to be on time for the ceremony and entertaining to follow, and to dress to suit the occasion.

A wedding announcement requires no acknowledgment. Neither does an invitation to the church ceremony. An invitation to the entertaining to follow the ceremony usually says "Please Respond," or "R.S.V.P." A response to these should be sent at the earliest possible date: as soon as one is sure that one will or will not be able to attend. Whether one is to accept or decline, failure to acknowledge the invitation in proper form and due time is very ill-bred. It also makes it more difficult for the bride's mother to plan the wedding breakfast. (The correct form for acknowledging wedding invitations is given in the chapter on "Wedding Correspondence and Printed Forms.")

One cannot be "fashionably late" for a wedding. All guests should plan to be in their seats at the church at least five minutes before the hour set for the ceremony. One should always arrive promptly to any nuptial entertaining that includes a seated meal. Otherwise one may arrive at any time during the hours given for the reception.

Correct attire for the large wedding is given elsewhere in this chapter. For weddings of any size, women wear clothing suitable for High Mass, but the smaller the wedding, the less elaborate the style of dress. Men should always wear dark blue or charcoal gray suits, white shirts, sober ties, and black shoes. Sports attire of any kind is unsuitable for a wedding.

There are certain mistakes which relatives and intimate friends frequently make in connection with a wedding, which lessen the bride's pleasure in the occasion and which should be avoided. Do not offer a bride advice on her wedding plans unless you are asked to give it. Never suggest changes after her arrangements have been completed; this can only upset her. Do not give advice, even when asked for it, unless you are sure that the information you are offering is correct for the size and style wedding the bride is planning. Never suggest that you, your child, or your spouse be included in the wedding party.

Never make any suggestions as to those to be invited either to the wedding or the entertaining to follow.

Unmarried men and women should not ask permission to bring their fiancés or beaus to the reception if the person in question is not a friend of the bridal couple and has not received an invitation.

Children old enough to behave properly in church may be brought to the church ceremony because, theoretically, a Catholic church service is always open to all. But one should not expect to bring children to a wedding reception (and one should never ask permission to bring them) if their names were not written on the inner envelope of the invitation which one has received. Even when they are so included, it is better not to bring children under fourteen to the nuptial entertaining. A reception or breakfast is entertaining planned for adults. The best-behaved children are apt to become bored and restless at such a party. If they are allowed to run about and annoy guests, they can ruin the occasion. Parents should not expect to take children with them to wedding entertaining and should not express surprise or injury if their children are not invited.

Guests should never feel offended if invited to the wedding ceremony but not to the entertaining which follows it. A Catholic can offer no greater proof of friendship than to desire one's presence at the religious ceremony which is the vital part of the occasion. Except at the very largest weddings, nuptial entertaining is limited by the father's purse, the number of relatives who must be invited, the health of the bride's mother, or any number of factors that have nothing to do with the degree of affection the bridal couple may feel for a friend. Fortunately, the number of guests bid to the church ceremony need be limited only by the size of the building; the couple may ask to the ceremony all the friends they long to have with them at this time.

Guests should understand this and regard an invitation to the ceremony as the compliment it is intended to be. Young friends of the bridal couple should remember also that a wedding is very much a family affair, that the actual hosts are the bride's parents, and that those who have first claim on their hospitality are the relatives of the two families. Usually this means that the couple themselves are not free to invite as many of their young friends as they would like to do. If, therefore, one is invited to the wedding but not to the nuptial entertaining of a young couple who are one's friends and contemporaries, one should understand that the omission is not meant as a slight. They were probably not free to invite all the friends they would have liked to have present.

Most important of all: it is a very un-Catholic attitude to regard any entertaining as more important, and more to be desired, than an invitation to be present at one of the great sacraments of the Church.

WEDDING PRESENTS

No rules of social behavior have ever been formulated to cover the giving of wedding presents and, theoretically at least, all relatives and friends of the bridal couple are free to give a present or not, just as they choose. This is all that most etiquette books venture to say about the matter. In actual practice, many people find this one of the thorniest of all the social questions they must solve and are eager for guidance. Therefore an attempt will be made to clear a path through this hitherto uncharted portion of the social map; common sense and loving kindness will be our guides in place of nonexistent social laws. The reader should remember that the following suggestions are offered solely as the opinions of the author, not as established social practice.

Let us begin by recalling the difference between a wedding invitation and a wedding announcement. The latter is exactly that: an announcement, sent to acquaint the recipient with the fact that the marriage has occurred and to enable him to put in his address book the new address of the bridal couple. Announcements are sent to a wider circle of acquaintances than invitations ever are, and great pains must be taken that no one entitled to receive one is overlooked, for this is a social slight and indicates that one does not wish to continue the acquaintance. (See chapter on "Wedding Correspondence . . ." for further discussion of this.)

Oddly enough, although to fail to send an announcement is a snub, to send one is no particular compliment; it is simply a courteous gesture. A wedding invitation is just the reverse: to receive one is a compliment, showing that the friendship is warm enough to make one's presence desired at the ceremony.

Some persons make a further distinction between an invitation to the wedding ceremony only and one that invites to the ceremony and any entertaining to follow. This is a distinction that should not be made: an invitation to a Catholic wedding service means that the people concerned want you to be present at a great moment in their life. They may be just as eager to include you in any entertaining that may follow but be prevented from doing so by a number of factors that have nothing to do with their affection for you. Therefore, although some people base their decision to send or not to send a present, on whether they receive an announcement, a church invitation, or an invitation to the nuptial entertaining, there is another measuring rod which is safer, kinder, and better-bred: it is, simply, the degree of friendship and affection one feels for the bridal couple and their families. Using these sentiments as a guide, it is surely safe to say that a wedding present should be sent by:

a) All blood kin of the bridal pair to whom either an invitation or an announcement has been sent. Relatives should realize that if they fail to do this they will hurt the feelings of the young couple and that family ties will be weakened or broken as a result. Even very straitened circumstances are scarcely an excuse for failure to send a gift. A relative so situated can always send a bit of old family china, linen, or bric-a-brac, which will be cherished because of its associations.

This suggestion does not apply to the in-laws of the bridal couple's married sisters and brothers. Such "connections" are not relatives; they need not be sent wedding invitations but must *always* be included if announcements are sent. But they need not acknowledge these announcements in any way unless they wish to.

b) Anyone who has received, or whose children have received wedding presents from the families of the bridal couple or from the bride or bridegroom. This is simple reciprocity; accepting a wedding present obligates the receiver to give one in turn when the occasion arises. The converse of this is also true: if one has previously sent an invitation or announcement of one's marriage or one's child's marriage to a friend, and that friend did not respond with a present, one need send no gift to that friend or that friend's child upon the occasion of his marriage.

c) Anyone who has previously given a wedding present to a sister or brother of either of the bridal couple, on the occasion of their wedding. This refers particularly to family friends. If the first child married in a family was married with a large reception which one attended and one sent a substantial present, one should do the same for the next child married, even though the second wedding may be a small one with only the families present. If one receives an announcement of this second wedding, one should send a present, unless one wishes it to be understood that one loves the first child more than the second.

The size of the ceremony should never be permitted to bear on whether one sends a gift, nor on its nature or value. These things should be determined solely by one's affection for the bridal couple.

An exception to this rule is: when a young person is "best friends" with one child in a family and has given her a generous gift, she is not expected to do likewise for another member of the family. Usually, however, she will receive no notice of the marriages of other children in the family.

d) Anyone who is invited to a wedding and any entertaining to follow. Such people should wish to send a present, *not* because of having been invited to a social gathering, but because the fact of having been invited shows the affection and esteem in which they are held by the bridal pair. The smaller the entertainment, the greater the compliment in being included. One should send a present whether one declines or accepts the invitation.

Beyond these four categories, there are no general rules that can be laid down. It is probably safe to say that anyone else who has received either an invitation to the church, or an announcement, may send a present or refrain from doing so as their affection dictates.

There is one set of circumstances in which one never need send a present: when one feels that those who sent the invitation have presumed on too slight an acquaintance or one which is wholly a business relationship. One must admit that there are greedy, ill-bred couples who will scatter invitations broadcast to business associates of the bridegroom or the fathers of the bridal pair in the hope that presents will be sent to maintain the business relationship. Such invitations should bring forth nothing but a formal refusal, although, sadly enough, people do submit to this social blackmail for business reasons.

Almost anything that one wishes to give is suitable as a wedding present. In selecting silver and china, one should find out what patterns the bride has selected and send what she has chosen. It is wise not to have silver monogrammed but to arrange with the jeweler to do so after the wedding, according to the bride's taste. This enables her to exchange the piece for another one if she has received duplicates. Jewelers say that the presents most frequently duplicated are clocks and trays. Before selecting either, it might be well to make sure that the bride has not already received several.

Relatives and very intimate friends of the couple may give money for a present—and very welcome it is—but others should avoid it.

A wall crucifix, a beautiful statue of the Madonna, or a large family Bible are nice religious presents particularly suitable for godparents or confirmation sponsors of either of the bridal couple to give as a wedding present.

Wedding guests should not bring their wedding presents to the bridal reception or to any entertaining that follows the wedding. In some localities this is a local custom. It is a very unfortunate one. One of the pleasures of the days just prior to the wedding is anticipating, receiving, and displaying one's wedding presents. If they are brought to the reception, these pleasures are lost. Also, the bride cannot spare the time from her guests to open and admire the presents at the reception. If she attempts to do so, the atmosphere becomes too much like that of a bridal shower. If the reception is not held at home, someone must be responsible for watching over the presents and seeing that they are carried to the bride's house after the party is over. All this is unnecessary and can be avoided if guests will send their presents to the bride's house prior to the ceremony, in the conventional way.

EXCHANGING WEDDING PRESENTS

A bride who has received duplicate wedding presents has the privilege of exchanging them if they were purchased locally and she knows the store from which they were bought. No one should feel offended if his present is exchanged. It was given to bring pleasure to the bridal pair. If they have received duplicate items, the extra ones are useless to them and their pleasure in them is destroyed. The couple should be—and are—free to exchange them. In most cases this can be done without the giver ever learning of it.

A bride should *not* ask the donor to exchange a present unless, when giving it, the donor says, "If this present is not what you need or want, please say so and I will exchange it." In such a case, one may "say so" but one should never say what one would like in place of it unless urged to do so. Otherwise, never, never, ask the giver to exchange a present. Let us be frank: wedding presents are sometimes purchased wholesale or at a sale or even obtained with trading stamps. This does not detract from their value, but the giver of such a gift is put in an unthinkably embarrassing position if asked to exchange them.

DAMAGED WEDDING PRESENTS

Sometimes a wedding present which is delivered by the shop at which it was bought or which is sent through the mail arrives damaged. If delivered from a store, the bride may call the store, explain the circumstances, and ask that a duplicate be sent. Since the store is responsible for safe delivery, no difficulty should arise in doing this. If it comes damaged through the mail, the bride should examine the outer wrapping paper to determine whether the package was insured. If it was, it is quite correct to write at once to the donor and explain the circumstances so that the giver may collect the insurance and replace the present. *This is the only circumstance in which it is permissible to ask a donor to replace a present.* If the present does not appear to be insured, the bride has no recourse but to write a grateful note of thanks to the giver without mentioning the fact that it was damaged.

SOME APPROVED NUPTIAL MUSICAL SELECTIONS

For use for processional or recessional:

Andante ....Abt
Entree ....Raffy
Finale ....Briggs
Processional ....Guilmant
Solemn March ....Bosi

For use as vocal selections:

Ave Maria ....Arcadelt
Ave Maria ....Bragers
Ave Maria ....Mauro-Cotton
Ave Maria ....Perosi
Ave Verum ....Mozart
Panis Angelicus ....Lambillote
Panis Angelicus ....Franck
Regina Coeli ....Mauro-Cotton

For other suitable selections, consult your church organist, or a book called "Approved Wedding Music," published by McLaughlin and Reilly Co., Boston, Mass.

11

Simpler Weddings

What, therefore, God has joined together, let no man put
asunder (Matthew 19:7).

THE LESS ELABORATE WEDDING

In the previous chapter the most elaborate type of wedding ceremony was discussed. Such weddings are not common. They are expensive in themselves and because such a wedding must be followed
by sumptuous entertaining. Many brides avoid such a wedding because
of the expense; many more eschew it because such lavishness is not in
accord with their ordinary style of living and they would feel pretentious in attempting it.

The bride who prefers the elaborate ceremony but wishes to avoid
some of the expense can achieve much the same effect with careful
planning. The changes she may make will not greatly reduce the cost
of the wedding ceremony but will permit her with propriety to follow
it with considerably less elaborate nuptial entertaining, always one of
the major expenses of a wedding.

For a less elaborate wedding, the canopy may be dispensed with,
the floral decorations limited to two altar bouquets and a few palms.
One soloist and the organ may furnish the music. In such a setting the
bride may still wear a white dress and veil and be attended by as many
as eight beautifully dressed bridesmaids. The men in the bridal party
wear morning costume. The processional and recessional are as
previously described, with the bride escorted by her father. A white
carpet may or may not be used. Seating arrangements, costumes for
guests, etc., are as for the larger wedding. To a ceremony of this sort
invitations are sent. The hour may be any time up to eleven o'clock.
Such a wedding may be followed by a large breakfast or reception,
but it is also permissible to follow it with a breakfast or other entertain-

ing to which only the immediate families are invited. No further description of this ceremony is required because all the details of it are included in the chapter on Elaborate Weddings.

SIMPLER WEDDINGS

Simpler weddings follow a slightly different pattern. Invitation is by word of mouth, telephone, or informal notes. Announcements are sent upon the day of the ceremony. The hour is earlier, usually nine or ten o'clock. The organ furnishes the music; the only decorations are two altar pieces; and these may be omitted.

The bride may wear a white dress and a veil; but she would not chose the more formal fabrics, such as velvet, brocade, lamé, or very precious lace. Starched lace is a nice choice for any season. In summer, organdy, tulle or dotted swiss are just right for such a wedding. The veil should be plain net or tulle, caught with flowers or shaped into a cap. A jewelled tiara or coronet is too elaborate. A wreath of flowers or a large garden-party hat may be substituted for the veil. A floor-length gown may be worn, especially if waltz-length is not currently fashionable. At the present time, waltz-length is usually worn at such a wedding.

This bride may or may not be escorted by her father. She may have as many as four attendants or as few as one. Like the bride's gown, those of the attendants must be slightly less elaborate than at a larger wedding and may properly be far simpler. The degree of simplicity is determined by that of the bride's costume. The costumes should be of a similar material, but colored. They always wear a hat if she does but may choose something else if the bride wears a veil.

The men in the bridal party wear oxford-gray or dark blue business suits, white shirts with starched turn-down collar (never oxford cloth or button-down), and black shoes. At a summer wedding they may prefer to wear dark blue jackets and white flannels, although such attire is not currently fashionable.

Mothers of the couple dress more simply than for a lavish wedding; they do not wear floor-length dresses, even though the bride may. Silk suits with small dainty hats are a good choice. Gloves are always worn; flowers may be. Fathers dress like the men in the bridal party.

If the bride is escorted by her father, the processional and recessional are the same as for elaborate weddings. If for any reason she is not to be escorted by her father, she may be preceded down the aisle by her ushers, bridesmaids, and maid of honor; and she may walk alone. At such a wedding there are usually only two ushers. The entertaining following such a wedding would not be more elaborate than a home reception for thirty guests or less and might be only breakfast for the immediate families. It might also be a family breakfast at home, followed by a small reception.

ANOTHER SIMPLE WEDDING

Still simpler is the wedding that takes place at eight or nine o'clock. Invitation is by word of mouth; announcements are sent on the day of the wedding. Canopy, carpet, and flower decorations are omitted; the organ furnishes the music. The wedding party consists of best man, two ushers, and a maid of honor. The bride may wear a white gown and veil but is more apt to wear a hat. She may prefer to wear her traveling suit with its accessories. In this latter case, she would not carry a bouquet but might wear a corsage bouquet. Her attendant is similarly dressed. Others at the wedding dress as described above.

At such a ceremony, the bride is not usually escorted by her father. Sometimes the ushers are not part of the processional and recessional. The bride is preceded only by her honor attendant. But the ushers may be part of the procession, even at such a small wedding, if desired.

The entertaining following the wedding is usually a breakfast for the bridal party and two families or a small and informal home reception for not more than twenty guests.

A VERY QUIET WEDDING

There is another even less ceremonious style of wedding. It is the one chosen if either of the families is just out of mourning or if a young couple are wholly orphaned or are newcomers to the city which is to be the scene of the marriage and have almost no friends there. This wedding too is held at eight or nine o'clock. Invitations are by word of mouth. In rare cases no guests at all are invited to be present. Announcements may be sent on the day of the wedding, but they need not be for such a quiet ceremony if the young couple do not wish to send any. There is no canopy, carpet, or flowers; the organ supplies the music. There need be no ushers, but there may be two, or even one. The ushers do not take part in the processional or recessional.

The bride may wear a white summer dress or a tailored–style white dress, with a hat or wreath of flowers, and may carry flowers. Or she may wear her traveling suit and hat and a corsage bouquet. Her attendant is similarly attired, either in a colored dress with hat or wreath, or in a suit and hat. Men dress as prescribed for other simple weddings.

The bride may go down the aisle alone, preceded only by her maid of honor. Or, for the very quiet wedding, with no guests, or almost no guests, the honor attendant may walk down the aisle with the best man, followed by the bride on the arm of her future husband. (In all the other simple weddings described, the best man and bridegroom meet the processional at the sanctuary steps.)

After such a wedding, the only celebration would be a breakfast for the parents and bridal party or merely the bridal party, if the parents are not present. It is never correct for the bridal party to go to a photographer's studio for group pictures after the ceremony because it makes an awkward lull for any guests invited to nuptial entertaining. Some young people who live informally choose to do so, but it is not correct.

For any of the simpler weddings just discussed, the bride may have a professional photographer to take photographs of the occasion. If expense is a factor, she may arrange with a friend who is competent to make a collection of snapshots or colored slides.

At the conclusion of all weddings save those followed by large receptions, the wedding party may, if the bride choses and the weather permits, assemble in the church entry or on the steps in an informal receiving line to receive the greetings and congratulations of the wedding guests. This moment of receiving is a brief one. But if there is another wedding scheduled to follow one's own immediately, one must omit this moment of greeting lest one infringe upon the time of the bride whose wedding is about to begin.

SECOND MARRIAGE

A second marriage in the Catholic Church is always that of a widow or widower. (Where an annulment has been granted, it is always because proof has been uncovered that the previous marriage service was in some vital detail invalid and, therefore, no marriage at all. A person who has had an invalid marriage properly annulled is not remarrying but is marrying validly for the first time.)

A widow does not receive a nuptial blessing at her second marriage because this blessing can only be received once.

A young woman marrying a widower may have as elaborate a wedding as her fancy dictates. The fact of her husband's previous marriage does not have to be considered, either in the style of announcing the engagement or in planning the ceremony.

A widow does not send an announcement of her engagement to the newspapers, nor does she announce it at a party. She does not have a large church wedding, although she may have a large reception if she chooses. A smaller one, however, is considered better taste. Widows do not wear a white or floor length dress or a veil. Very young widows may wear a dress of pale pink, blue, or yellow. Older women may wear gray, beige, rose color, brown, green, blue or wine color (but not black, purple, or any shade of violet, for these look too much like mourning). All widows wear hats. All but the very young choose the kind of dress or suit that is usually considered suitable for the mother of the bride at the ordinary large wedding. They may wear flowers but never carry them. One attendant is customary, dressed in the same general fashion as the bride.

One does not use canopy, carpet, floral decorations, or many musicians at a widow's wedding. One attendant and two ushers is customary.

In the newspaper account of a second marriage, reference to a widow's first marriage is made thus: "The marriage of Mrs. Archibald Crowe, daughter of Mr. and Mrs. Williard Nelson and widow of the late Archibald Crowe, to Mr. Donald Dunn, etc." In the case of a widower, the first marriage is not always referred to, but it may be. If one wishes to have a reference to the first marriage in the article, it is made at the end, when discussing the bridegroom's education, employment, etc. Thus: "Mr. Allen, whose late wife was Linda Latimer Allen, is head of the history department of Hamilton College." In both of these instances the reference, quite properly, is made in a subordinate phrase which tends to "play down" the fact of the former marriage, while not denying its existence. (For wedding invitations and announcements of widows, see chapter on "Wedding Correspondence and Printed Forms.")

OLDER BRIDES

Women who do not marry young sometimes feel that their age should be taken into account when making wedding plans. Up to the middle thirties, age may certainly be disregarded. Modern woman keeps her figure and her complexion; many a bride in her thirties could wear a white gown and a veil and look lovely in them; she could surround herself with a bevy of youthful bridesmaids and outshine them all. It would be well, however, for such a bride to chose

the more stately materials—brocade, velvet, or flattering chiffon—
rather than the more girlish fabrics, and a veil of mantilla-style lace
rather than tulle or net. This costume, of course, is suitable only for an
elaborate wedding.

An older bride usually feels that so much display is unsuitable.
She prefers a comparatively simple church ceremony at which she
wears a suit or a dress with a jacket, and a hat. The costume may be
beige, gray, rose color, any shade of blue except pale blue, light brown,
wine color or green. If she wears any type of dress, she might have
several junior bridesmaids—children under fourteen— dressed in similar material in a lighter shade: yellow if she wears beige, light green
if she wears dark green, etc. But it is more common for an older bride
to have only one attendant of her own age; usually both wear handsome suits, hats, and corsage bouquets. For a fall or winter wedding,
they may add fur scarves or stoles.

Even though the wedding is a quiet one, the older bride may have
nuptial entertaining as elaborate as she wishes.

As the older bride is frequently an orphan, the wedding invitations
or announcements are often made in her name. The correct form is
discussed in the chapter "Wedding Correspondence and Printed
Forms."

ALL ARE BEAUTIFUL

At these smaller weddings, the Catholic couple still is married with
a Nuptial Mass and blessing. None need be deprived of it, no matter
how simple the accoutrements. This is why all Catholic weddings are
formal—meaning "with due form and ceremony." The organ peals its
joyous tones over small weddings as for large ones; the profound and
moving words of the wedding service are the same. The ancient ritual
of the Nuptial Mass is quite as uplifting when heard by ten guests as
by five hundred. And always the blessing sanctifies the union and
strengthens the couple in their determination to preserve it. Thus all
are impressive, and all are beautiful.

Any reader who still feels that the ideal wedding is the large and
lavish one and that, given the means, any bride would choose it, may
be interested in the story of a bride the writer once knew. She was the
only daughter of very prosperous parents. She was a friendly and
lovable person, so much so that she had served as a bridal attendant at
six weddings prior to her own. She could have had as large and expensive a wedding as she chose. Her choice was: an eight o'clock wedding with no invitations and no announcements. She wore a white

chiffon dress and small white hat; her only attendant was a teen-age cousin as junior bridesmaid. Only the two families were guests, and only they went to her parent's house for a wedding breakfast.

The only other choice she could have made would have been an enormous wedding with innumerable attendants and a huge guest list for church and reception. She preferred the quiet one. On the day of her wedding, a large donation was received by the Sisters at an infants' home—the exact sum a large wedding would have cost. The couple thus wed have already celebrated the anniversary of thirty happy years of marriage.

12

The Mixed Marriage

Let each one of you also love his wife just as he loves
himself; and let the wife respect her husband (Ephesians
5:33).

ADVISABILITY

By the time a young couple of differing faiths has begun to discuss
wedding plans, they are too much in love to weigh dispassionately the
arguments against such a union. These are discussed in this book in
the chapter called "Guidance and Manners for Teen-Agers" and are
also very cogently expressed in two little pamphlets by Monsignor J.
D. Conway: *Marriage outside the Church* and *What They Ask about
Mixed Marriages*. Both are published by the Ave Maria Press, Notre
Dame, Indiana. Any young person trying to decide whether to marry
one of another faith would be helped by these two booklets.

A young couple of differing faiths determined to attempt a mixed
marriage should realize that the dangers of such a course are very
real. They threaten your future happiness, the permanence of your
union, and the welfare of your children. But they are not insurmounta-
ble. If you are emotionally mature, patient, and understanding, and
are willing to make the necessary concessions for your mutual happiness, your chances are good. Most important of all, both partners
should understand fully the premarital promises the Church requires
them to make before She can grant a dispensation and should make
them without reservations or hidden distaste. You *can* have a happy
marriage. The writer is the child of such a marriage, and it was beautiful; one sees evidence of thousands more on every side. One also sees
the many sad failures. Think long and hard before you decide. Are you
big enough to take such a risk?

189

SPIRITUAL REQUIREMENTS

The prospective partners in a mixed marriage should consult a pastor at least a month before the date planned for the marriage—earlier if possible. The matter is simpler when the girl is the Catholic. Her pastor is then consulted, and arrangements are made for the marriage to take place in her parish if the dispensation is granted. When the man is the Catholic, the matter is more complicated. They first consult his pastor. The marriage *may* take place in his parish, if both parties live in the same city; it might also take place in the parish in which the non-Catholic girl lives. If the man and girl live in different cities, they should consult his pastor, but the marriage will take place in the girl's home city, in the Catholic parish in which she resides. The man's pastor will apply for the dispensation and will then write to the pastor in the girl's city to help make arrangements for the marriage.

In such a case, the girl should have informed herself of the name and address of the pastor in her city. In any case, the non-Catholic party should bring proof of baptism, if he possesses it, because a special dispensation is required for the marriage of an unbaptized person to a Catholic.

The marriage of a baptized non-Catholic and a Catholic is a sacrament. That of an unbaptized non-Catholic and a Catholic is a valid and sacred contract, but it is not a sacrament.

Following is a general account of the regulations to be observed when a mixed marriage is to take place in the Catholic Church. There will be some sight variation from diocese to diocese, but this is the common practice, according to Monsignor Conway:

1. The parties should go to see their pastor a month before the date planned for the marriage.
2. The pastor will give a series of at least six instructions on Catholic teachings and practice in general and the nature and obligations of marriage in particular.
3. The prenuptial questionnaire will be answered under oath by both parties, and the necessary certificates will be furnished.
4. The prenuptial promises will be signed. Both parties promise that all children will be raised Catholic; and the non-Catholic promises, in addition, that he will not hinder in any way the Catholic party's religious belief or practice.
5. The pastor will apply to the bishop for the necessary dispensation, assuring him that he is certain these promises will be kept by both parties.

6. The bishop, if he find sufficient reason, will grant the dispensation. He has special faculties from the Holy See to do this.

7. The established fee for this dispensation is $5.00. The Catholic party will give this fee to the pastor when he (or she) signs the promises; the pastor has to send it to the bishop when he asks for the dispensation. If the Catholic party cannot afford the fee, it will be readily waived.

8. As a general rule the marriage will take place in the parish rectory. For sufficient reason the bishop will grant permission for the marriage to be celebrated in church. In this case the following rules will be observed:

   a) There shall be no Mass.

   b) The ceremony will not be after 6:00 p.m.

   c) No talking or visiting will be permitted in the church.

   d) Everyone participating in the ceremonies will observe Catholic practice in genuflecting and in general conduct in church.

   e) The priest will wear cassock and surplice, and follow the usual ceremonies for mixed marriages.

   f) Only music approved for use in church will be permitted.

The instructions referred to in section two above are intended to give the non-Catholic party a general knowledge of his future spouse's faith, so that the way in which that spouse practices her religion will not come as a surprise to him, and so that he will have some understanding of it. They will explain the church's law of fasting, the truth about confession and purgatory, attendance at Mass, the rosary, the saints, etc. But they will mainly be concerned with the Church's teaching on marriage, covering the following points: its holiness, indissolubility, unity, primary purpose (cooperating with God in creating new life), and other purposes.

A couple planning a mixed marriage should remember that a dispensation for such a marriage is granted only for good reason. Until they have applied for it and obtained it, they cannot be sure that it will be granted. Note also that these regulations apply only to applications from two hitherto-unmarried persons or widowed persons. "Unmarried persons" includes anyone who has obtained a Church annulment: the obtaining of a Church annulment is proof that the first ceremony was invalid and, hence, no marriage.

In circumstances where the marital status of either party is clouded, the two probably cannot marry. Certainly the Catholic party should never have permitted himself to become so emotionally involved as to wish to marry. Anyone who has allowed himself to drift into this unfortunate situation should consult his pastor; he should bring with him complete information about the possible impediment to the marriage. The pastor can then determine whether a marriage is possible. Usually it is not. The cases in which the impediment may be removed or be proven to be no impediment are so rare and so complicated that they cannot be discussed here.

No Catholic can be validly married in the eyes of the Church and of Her children except before a priest. A Catholic who turns his back on his Faith and marries before a justice of the peace, a minister, or a rabbi has contracted a valid civil marriage but is unmarried in the eyes of the Church. His family cannot condone or cooperate in any way in the matter. This creates a painful situation for the innocent parties. Catholic parents cannot give or attend such a wedding. Catholic relatives and friends cannot attend the ceremony, any entertaining to follow, or any prenuptial parties. They cannot send "wedding" or engagement presents. Of course they cannot take active part in the proceedings as one of the bridal party. Heart-rending though this may be for the family of the offending Catholic, they must remember that the offender is doing neither more nor less than publicly proclaiming his intention to live in sin, and the occasion must be so regarded. Any Catholic connected in any way with such a marriage must remember to pray for the offender, to hate the sin but love the sinner, to be just and charitable, and to strive to do or say nothing that adds to the scandal the marriage will cause.

A Catholic contracting an invalid marriage should remember that although his marriage is not recognized by the Church, the duties that result from it are. A Catholic who produces children in such an invalid union is quite as obligated to have them baptized, educated, and reared in the Church as if his marriage were a true one. This is equally true of children born out of wedlock with no ceremony of any kind having been performed. The sins of the fathers are not to be visited upon the children. They may not be denied their Catholic heritage.

FAMILY RESPONSIBILITIES

The duties and expenses of a mixed marriage are apportioned just as they are for any other wedding. The bride's parents are the hosts, and the bridegroom's are invited guests and passive observers. Like everything else about a mixed marriage, the *attitude* of the two families is harder to maintain. It is also more important than in the marriage of two Catholics.

The initial attitude of both families may well be disapproval or violent objection. But when the young people have finally reached the point of having applied for and obtained a dispensation to marry in the Church, it is "time for a change." The Catholic parents must realize the seriousness of their child's intentions and must approve and applaud the non-Catholic partner's willingness to accept and fulfill the requirements necessary for a dispensation. Now is the time for a display of affection, gentleness, helpfulness, and patience. The non-Catholic parents must face up to the choice they must make: total alienation from their child and possible future grandchildren, with all its accompanying heartache, or acceptance of the situation, however distasteful it may be to them. If this acceptance can be accompanied by a willingness to do whatever is expected of them, gracefully and ungrudgingly, their child will be spared much pain. Both sets of parents must make a real effort to welcome their new "in-laws" into their family circles with warmth and graciousness and to display affection for their new son or daughter-in-law.

Other relatives of the bridal pair should make the same attempt and refrain from all adverse comment as the best contribution they can make to family unity and the happiness of the young couple.

PLANNING THE CEREMONY

The ceremony selected for a mixed marriage is greatly influenced by the regulations governing such a marriage in the diocese in which it is to be held. As noted under the heading "Spiritual Requirements," the diocese may require that all such ceremonies be held in the parish rectory.

At such a ceremony, the limitations of space would be such that no one could be present except the two sets of parents, the best man, and the maid of honor. A couple of bridesmaids might be included, but since there would be no procession and no observers, there are usually no bridesmaids. There would also be no ushers. Since the wedding would not be performed in church, there would be no canopy, flowers, or music. No invitations could be issued. Usually announcements are sent, but if the small ceremony is to be followed by a large breakfast or reception, invitations to such entertaining could be sent out in the customary way, three weeks before the ceremony. Such invitations are discussed under "Wedding Correspondence and Printed Forms." The size and degree of formality of the entertaining to follow such a wedding may be whatever the bride's family chooses—elaborate or simple.

In some dioceses, as previously noted, a mixed marriage may be celebrated in church. There can be no Nuptial Mass, and the nuptial blessing is not given. The bridal pair are married either in the sanctuary or just outside it, according to diocesan regulations.

This difference in regulations among dioceses confuses many people. The explanation for it is given by Monsignor Conway in his pamphlet on mixed marriage as follows:

> The Church law, in Canon 1109, par. 3, prescribes that a marriage between a Catholic and a non-Catholic shall take place outside of church. The main purpose of this regulation is to show the Church's disapproval of these marriages and to discourage other people from entering into them.
>
> However, the same Canon provides that the Bishop can dispense from this law and permit a mixed marriage in the church when he prudently judges that greater harm would otherwise result.
>
> Many bishops in the U. S. have decided in recent years that the complete exclusion of mixed marriages from the church does result in "greater harm." It takes away all religious aspect and atmosphere, giving the marriage the appearance of a civil contract. It fails to impress the parties that they are receiving a sacrament (if both are baptized) and that they are entering into a solemn, sacred, life-long contract before Almighty God Himself. Since there is a widespread and growing tendency in America to belittle the sacred character of marriage and its perpetual obligations, these bishops have judged best to dispense, as Canon 1109 permits them to do. Usually this dispensation must be requested by the parties and recommended by the pastor before the bishop will grant it. Some parties may not ask it. In some cases the pastor may not recommend it. In some cases there may be no good reason for granting it.

When the diocese permits mixed marriages in the church, one may have as large or as small a wedding as taste dictates. One may have canopy, white carpet, lavish floral decorations, and music. One may have many attendants and ushers and wear an elaborate bridal gown and veil. One may also have one of the simpler weddings previously described.

In a mixed marriage, the question of non-Catholic attendants often arises. Frequently, in these cases, permission is granted for the non-

Catholic party to have a sister or brother or other Protestant as their honor attendant. If such permission is withheld, it is for good cause, and the decision should be accepted without rancor. Most Catholic priests regard the roles of bridesmaids and ushers as that of observers, not participants, in the ceremony; consequently one can usually have non-Catholic bridesmaids or ushers if one wishes. But permission to do so is not always given and therefore cannot be taken for granted.

The pastor in whose church the ceremony is to be performed should be consulted well in advance about all the details of it. He is the person best informed as to what is permitted and customary, and he will be able to answer all questions that may arise other than matters of simple etiquette. These latter are the same for a mixed marriage as for any Catholic wedding ceremony.

NUPTIAL ENTERTAINING

The wedding entertaining following a mixed marriage may be as simple or as elaborate as the bride desires. It need not differ in any way from that which follows the usual Catholic or non-Catholic wedding, except in one minor matter of etiquette, as follows:

The officiating priest at a mixed marriage is always invited to any entertaining which follows it. If the nuptial entertaining includes a seated family breakfast, followed by a reception, he is invited to both. For a seated breakfast, a problem arises in connection with seating him, due to the differing customs of Catholics and non-Catholics in this matter. At a Catholic wedding the priest is seated in the place of honor at the right of the bride's mother. At a non-Catholic wedding this position is reserved for the father of the bridegroom, and the officiating clergyman is seated, with his wife, in an honored position, but not *the* honored position.

In all the details of a wedding save those which are matters of faith and morals, everyone concerned takes great pains to accede to the preferences and wishes of the bride's parents, who are the hosts. Therefore the matter of where the officiating priest sits at the wedding breakfast following a mixed marriage may be resolved as follows: when the bride and her parents are the Catholics, the priest is seated in his customary place of honor on the right of the bride's mother. When the bride and her parents are the non-Catholics, the priest may be seated in his customary place of honor at the right of the bride's mother, if the bride's parents have no objection to seating him there. They might object, not through ill-will or reluctance to honor him, but because of their lack of experience in meeting a Catholic priest socially. In such a case, the priest might be seated on the right of the bridegroom's (Catholic) mother.

At the breakfast following a mixed marriage, it sometimes happens that the non-Catholic partner will have as guest a relative who is a minister in a Protestant sect. Like Catholic clerical relatives of the Catholic partner, such a man occupies a seat at the breakfast merely as a guest, not as a clergyman. That is, his clerical rank (and the clerical rank of any priest or brother present as a relative) does not entitle him to any particular seat of honor other than to be seated at the parents' table.

But the Protestant clerical relative may be honored by a graceful gesture, under certain specific circumstances: where the non-Catholic partner and his (her) parents have acceded, graciously and willingly, to all that a marriage in the Church requires of them, one of the Catholic parents, having consulted the officiating Catholic priest and obtained his permission, may suggest to the non-Catholic parents that their ministerial relative be invited to say grace at the breakfast. When this is done, the officiating priest may be asked to bless all present at the conclusion of the meal.

The reference here to "obtaining the consent of the priest" and "asking the minister to say grace" does not refer to the day of the wedding. All this must be done in advance, while other wedding preparations are being made, and be thoroughly understood, so that all concerned will know exactly what is to be expected of them at the breakfast. The gesture should never be attempted under any other circumstances than outlined here.

When permission for such a gesture is asked of the officiating priest and refused, the matter should be dropped. A refusal does not indicate narrow-mindedness on the part of the priest. He must consider whether the gesture would be misunderstood by some of those present. It is his further duty to be scrupulous about maintaining his priestly prerogatives. But where permission for such a gesture *is* obtained, the goodwill and amity thus displayed is usually the occasion for much favorable comment, and the non-Catholic parents are appreciative.

13

Making Your Wedding More Catholic

For we are the children of saints; and we must not be joined together like heathens who know not God (Tobias 8:5).

St. Paul said of marriage, "This is a great sacrament." All Catholics know this, but modern customs surround marriage with so much gift-giving, entertaining, and parade that the profound religious nature of the sacrament is sometimes obscured. To combat this trend, young Catholics, particularly those who have had the advantages of a Catholic college education or preparation for marriage at pre-Cana conferences, are making an effort to emphasize the sacramental nature of the ceremony by weaving into it various practices and symbolism of a religious nature. This is in line with the custom of canonical engagement, discussed in the chapter on "Engagement and Pre-Nuptial Entertaining."

To date this movement has had no official recognition from the Church herself; among Her members there are all shades of opinion as to its worth or permanence. The most that can be said at this time is that the Church neither requires nor forbids these practices. One can be truly and honorably married without them; but it is not forbidden to use any of them.

The most popular of the new customs appears in the wedding invitation. On these, the facing sheet, which ordinarily is inscribed with the invitation, bears instead a Church symbol. Some of these are: the Greek letters chi and rho (the first two letters of the name of Christ in Greek) superimposed with locked wedding rings; the True Vine and branches; jugs symbolical of the miracle of Cana; the Lamb of Christ; the symbol Chi Rho, two lighted candles, three wavy lines

below. The Chi Rho symbolizes Christ, the candles represent the man
and wife, and the waves below, which are the traditional symbols for
grace, represent the sacramental graces of marriage. The wedding
invitation is inscribed lengthwise on the inside of the paper, or horizontally on the sheet facing the reader when the fold is opened.

Ordinary social convention decrees that in all formal invitations
the message shall be inscribed on the first, or facing sheet. But this is
a custom which has no historical background or particular significance.
It may be ignored if one wishes to use a liturgical symbol on the
facing sheet.

Now we encounter a second new custom, which unfortunately must
be discouraged. The invitation sometimes reads:

"Mr. and Mrs. John Smith invite you to attend the Nuptial Mass at
which ——————— will be united in Christ in the Sacrament of Matrimony
to ———————." etc.

Convention decrees the wording of a wedding invitation, as given
in the chapter on "Wedding Correspondence and Printed Forms." This
too may be changed if one wishes. But the conventional form states the
facts briefly and correctly. The substitution quoted above does not. It
is wrong, not because it violates convention but because it contains a
serious misstatement of fact. The Nuptial Mass does not and cannot
"unite" anyone in anything. The young couple are united in marriage
by the sacrament of matrimony which precedes the Nuptial Mass; the
Nuptial Mass bestows the nuptial blessing and offers thanks for the
union; but the marriage itself has been accomplished before the
Nuptial Mass begins. The bride who chooses this form of invitation
does so in an attempt to make her invitation distinctly Catholic in form;
but this cannot be accomplished by using a wording which states an
untruth as a fact. This can only confuse Catholics and mislead non-
Catholics. This type of invitation, therefore, should not be used.

A variation of the form given above reads: "Mr. and Mrs. John
Smith invite your participation in the offering of the Nuptial Mass
following the ceremony at which their daughter, Joanne, will be united
in Christ in the Sacrament of Matrimony to Mr. James Ryan," etc.

This form states the facts correctly, but is so long that it is awkward to place properly on the paper, particularly if the reception invitation is included on the sheet instead of on an enclosure card. It also
may confuse some readers, since it specifically invites them only to
participate "in the Nuptial Mass," and may lead some to believe that
they are not invited to be present at the marriage ceremony itself.

This second form is far better than the first one, but neither is preferable to the classic, conventionally-worded invitation. The best choice might be to use a liturgical symbol on the facing sheet, with a conventionally worded invitation on the inner facing page.

RINGS

The couple may also have a liturgical symbol, as described, engraved inside or outside their wedding bands. Or they may prefer the olive, as a symbol of fertility. A charming choice is to inscribe the inner side of the man's ring with the word "Caput" (Head), symbolizing his duties as head of the home, and the woman's ring with "Cor" (Heart) for her position as the heart of the home.

FLOWERS

Church liturgy and art abound in symbols. Anyone interested enough to pursue the subject will find dozens that may be applied to all phases of a marriage. A bridal bouquet might include: roses to symbolize Mary, Rose of the World; lilies to symbolize the Resurection, or olive leaves for peace and fertility.

COMMUNION AT A NUPTIAL MASS

It has long been a practice for a bridal pair to receive Holy Communion at their Nuptial Mass. Frequently, members of the wedding party have received also, particularly when all are Catholics. Recently the custom has been extended: sometimes the parents of the bridal couple also receive. There can be no objection to this—it is indeed wholly laudable—but one should obtain the agreement of all four parents before planning it. If any are elderly, infirm, or even very self-conscious, they may be unwilling to receive so conspicuously. Their preferences in the matter should be respected. If one parent receives, all should. In the case of a convert's marriage, where one set of parents are not Catholics, it should not be attempted because it unpleasantly emphasizes the difference in belief.

Some recent brides have been anxious for their wedding guests to share in their joy by joining them in the reception of Communion at the Nuptial Mass. This is licit. In theory at least, anyone in the state of grace may receive the Eucharist at any Mass. Practically it poses several problems:

It is difficult for the Mass celebrant to serve Communion to a throng when the sanctuary is crowded with the wedding party, prie-dieux, and floral decorations.

It prolongs the time required to celebrate a wedding service—an important consideration in a busy city church which may, on any given day, have a full schedule of wedding Masses. This schedule is liable at any time to be complicated by funeral Masses, that, of course, cannot be planned in advance.

It may cause uncomfortable feelings among such of the congregation as come to the service unprepared to receive.

Any bride who wishes to invite her wedding guests to receive Communion at her wedding should first ask her pastor for permission to do so.

The invitation may take either of two forms. These are: A wedding invitation which reads: "Mr. and Mrs. John Smith invite your participation in the Nuptial Mass and reception of the Holy Eucharist following the ceremony at which their daughter, Joanne, will be united in Christ in the Sacrament of Holy Matrimony to Mr. James Ryan," etc.

Or a conventional wedding invitation may be sent, accompanied by an enclosure card about three by four inches in size, which reads: "The bride and bridegroom invite you to join with them in receiving Holy Communion." In the latter case, great care should be observed that such enclosure cards are not included with invitations sent to non-Catholic guests. In some Protestant denominations the Communion service is open to all, whether church members or not, and it is considered a compliment for non-members present to join in it. A member of such a denomination, receiving such an invitation from a Catholic, might innocently conclude that reception of the Eucharist was required of all present as a social gesture.

This danger cannot be avoided where the first form is used. Its use is therefore unwise. The second form is preferable.

WEDDING MISSAL

Another increasingly popular Catholic custom is to furnish the guests with printed copies of the ceremony and the Mass on the day of marriage. This enables all present to understand and appreciate exactly what is going on. They are made up in booklets, usually white and gold (wedding colors) and may be personalized by having the names of the bridal couple and the date of the ceremony printed on the cover; but this need not be done if one wishes to avoid the expense. The booklets are sufficient in themselves. The booklets can be ordered from the Liturgical Press, Collegeville, Minnesota; the Leaflet Missal, St. Paul, Minnesota; or the Catholic Truth Society, Portland, Oregon. They may usually be ordered also from any Catholic religious art shop.

ACOLYTES

One may have adult altar "boys" for a wedding ceremony if desired. If one has a relative or dear friend studying for the priesthood, this is the ideal way to include him in the wedding party. Of course if one acolyte is adult, the other must be also. Any man friend who has served on the altar may properly be asked.

BLESSING THE WINE

Religious customs may also be woven into the reception. One may ask the officiating priest to bless the wine before it is served for the first toast. This reminds all present of the miracle at Cana and also discourages immoderate drinking.

THE CAKE

The foolish bride-and-groom dolls or orange blossoms which usually decorate a wedding cake are symbols, although we seldom think of them as such because too-frequent use has rendered them almost meaningless. One might substitute for them one of the liturgical symbols previously discussed. In doing so, one must be sure that the maker of the cake thoroughly understands what you expect of him and that he will use artistry and taste in carrying out your ideas. In fact, any couple who wishes to weave symbolism into their wedding plans will need interested and expert help—from stationers, jewelers, florists, bakers, etc. One may have to search a bit to find this, but it is not impossible in any fairly large city. A good place to begin is a religious art shop; the proprietor can frequently refer you to people who have done similar work for other brides.

14

Nuptial Entertaining

Rejoice with me (Luke 15:9).

INTRODUCTION

Since Catholic weddings are celebrated not later than noon, any entertaining to follow is usually a breakfast, an afternoon reception, or some combination of the two. The family's choice in this matter depends upon their own preference; one takes into consideration the number to be invited, the size of place available, and the expense involved. Expense must be carefully weighed because, in all save the simplest and smallest home entertaining, the reception cost is the largest single wedding expense. Following is a detailed discussion of several types of nuptial entertaining.

LARGE AND LAVISH

A bride who does not have to count costs and enjoys elaborate entertaining may make her plans accordingly; but even such a one will discover that there are considerations to be weighed which may limit them. For instance, many people think that the ideal place for nuptial entertaining is the house of the bride's parents, and few will quarrel with this opinion as an ideal. But modern houses and apartments, even luxurious ones, are now built for everyday living, in which entertaining is intimate and informal. No allowance is made for the rare occasions when their occupants might wish to entertain a large group in the grand manner. Unless the bride's family is one of the few who still live in a town house with a ballroom and large drawing rooms or a fine old country house with plenty of space, our bride must choose between holding her reception outside her home or limiting her guest list to the number which her father's house will accommodate.

Arrangements

The bride who chooses the home reception enjoys the pleasure of receiving her guests for the last time amid the surroundings with which they have always associated her: her father's house. For the occasion, however, the reception rooms must be somewhat rearranged. Some large sofas and chairs may be stored away; if there is to be dancing the rugs must be taken up in that room. All rooms may be decorated with bouquets of flowers as the bride's mother chooses; some sort of background should be set up for the receiving line. This latter is usually held in the room where the guests will dance. The usual background is palms or a screen of vines, ferns, or flowers. The new screens of translucent materials or wood carving which are currently so popular would also make an attractive background, either flower-trimmed or plain.

A small orchestra is engaged for dancing; not more than three or four musicians; more would be overpowering in a private house. It plays softly while guests are being received, as well as for the dancing later.

A caterer is engaged also, who will furnish chairs, tables, china, glass, linen, and silver, as well as the food and wedding cake. He may also furnish the beverages, if desired, or the bride's father may obtain these from some other source.

There should be at least two rooms available for entertaining, one for the receiving line and dancing, the other for serving the breakfast. If more than two rooms are available, so much the better.

The Receiving Line

The correct position for those in a receiving line is always the same, whatever the size of the reception. Just inside the door of the room where guests are to be received, and to the guests' right as they enter, stands the bride's mother, with the bridegroom's mother on her right. She greets all arriving guests and introduces to the bridegroom's mother such of them as are not known to her. Some distance away stand the members of the receiving line, which consists of: bridesmaids, maid of honor, any flower girls, and the bride and bridegroom. They stand as follows: half the bridesmaids, whatever their number; on their left, the maid of honor; on her left, the bride, then the bridegroom, then the flower girl (if there is one), followed by the rest of the bridesmaids. The best man, ushers, and both fathers are not part of the receiving line. An exception to this rule is: if the bridegroom's parents live in another city and thus do not know many of the wedding guests, the bridegroom's father may stand with his wife to be introduced to the guests by the bride's mother.

An alternate arrangement, used when the number of bridesmaids is less than six, is: the bridegroom, the bride on his right, the maid of honor on her right, followed by all bridesmaids.

A modern innovation that is being accepted because it is sensible is for the bride's and the bridegroom's mothers to stand first in the actual receiving line as a part of it. In that case the order is: bride's mother, bridegroom's mother, the bride, the bridegroom, the maid of honor, all other female attendants. This is sensible because it means that every wedding guest can be greeted by someone with whom he is acquainted (either bride's mother or bridegroom's mother.) At all large weddings there are relatives and family connections present not hitherto-known to the bride and bridegroom or their attendants, who may, in this arrangement, be introduced to them by the one who knows them. Also, this arrangement seems simpler, more friendly, and more natural. But technically, the traditional arrangement is the correct one.

The Breakfast

Entertaining such as we are describing would always follow a very formal wedding, which, in the Catholic church, would be celebrated at noon. Consequently, it would be followed by a substantial wedding breakfast. The ideal seating arrangements would be: bride's table, parents' table, a number of smaller tables for guests, all served by waiters.

The Bride's Table

The bride's table is covered by a white damask cloth, with the wedding cake as the central decoration, and with arrangements of white flowers as additional decoration. Candles are not used for luncheon or breakfast. Otherwise the table is set as for a formal dinner.

The seating arrangement is as follows: bride and bridegroom together at one end of the table, or, as is now more popular, together at the middle of one side of the table. The best man at the bride's right, the maid of honor at the bridegroom's left, bridesmaids and ushers alternating around the table. Wives or husbands of attendants who are not themselves members of the bridal party are *not* seated at the bride's table.

The Parents' Table

At the parents' table, the bride's mother sits at one end, her husband at the other. On her right is the officiating priest (always the guest of honor at any gathering of Catholic laymen), at her left the bridegroom's father. (In this a Catholic breakfast differs from all others, at which the place of honor on the right of the bride's mother always goes to the bridegroom's father.) The bridegroom's mother sits at the right of the bride's father, on his left sits the next most important woman guest—a grandmother, or whomever he wishes to honor. If the bridegroom is an orphan, his closest male relative sits on the left of the bride's mother, his closest female relative on the right of the bride's father. Then follow the rest of the guests selected to sit at the parents' table, men and women alternating.

The officiating priest makes an "extra" man at the table, if all the others selected are couples. One may correct this difficulty by inviting a single woman to balance the table. Or if there is none such that one wishes to honor, the best solution is to put a man on the priest's right, and then alternate woman-man for the rest of the table.

The Guests' Tables

The rest of the guests are seated at tables for four or six, covered with white cloths and decorated with white flowers. There are no place cards; guests seat themselves in congenial groups. The tables are set as for luncheon. Ideally, the entire luncheon should be served, but even at very large home breakfasts guests often find the first course— melon or cold soup—on the table when they sit down after having selected their main course from a buffet table. But even with such an arrangement, there must be waiters to refill glasses, replenish butter, clear away and serve the dessert. If the entire meal is served, the first course may be a hot bouillon or consomme. (Menus are discussed in another section.) Whenever space permits, the bride's table, parents' table and guest tables are in the same room; but this is seldom possible at a home breakfast. Bride's and parents' tables usually occupy the dining room; guest tables are placed elsewhere. At some summer weddings, all tables are placed together under a marquee on the lawn. One of the principal drawbacks to a home reception is that the guests cannot usually be seated with the principals and thus cannot be present for the toasts and cutting the cake.

Menus

To serve more than four courses for a wedding breakfast is almost unheard of nowadays. Four is considered very elaborate; three is customary. For such a breakfast as we have been describing, four might be served, in which case a possible menu would be:

Consomme Madrilene

Lobster Newburg   Toast Points

Cold Ham in Aspic   Endive Salad

Pineapple Ice

The following three-course menus are also elaborate enough for a lavish breakfast:

Vichysoisse

Roast duck with oranges   Endive salad

Fruits *refraische au rhum*

Melon

Roast Squab with Wild Rice   Russian salad

Chocolate Ice Cream

Minted Fresh Pineapple

Chicken Eugenie   Asparagus, butter sauce

Strawberry Mousse

Simpler menus will be discussed with the reception at which they would be appropriate.

Beverages

The beverages served at any wedding depend, first of all, upon the drinking habits of the host family and their friends. Those who, as a matter of principle, do not serve or drink intoxicants, would not change their habits on this occasion. The beverages offered would be the coffee always served at such a breakfast and a non-alcoholic fruit punch for toasts.

For families who do ordinarily serve intoxicants, the choice is wider. Some families serve cocktails or sherry from trays in the room with the receiving line while guests are being received. This fills in the time for those first through the line, so that all may be seated simultaneously. But it is early in the day to take cocktails, and many people do not serve them at a wedding party.

The beverage served with the breakfast is almost always champagne, although this beverage would never be served so early in the day on a less festive occasion. Champagne or champagne punch is usually served from trays during the afternoon after the breakfast is over. Sometimes a choice of drinks—such as whiskey and soda, high-balls—is offered at this time. Socially this is a correct gesture, but it should be avoided. A wedding is certainly a time for gaiety and celebration, but it is also a sacramental occasion which should never be marred by over-indulgence. A generous host, eager to make a daughter's wedding a memorable event for all, may feel he must offer a choice of drinks to his guests. That is his privilege. Before taking advantage of it, however, he should consider that, in serving beverages stronger than wine, he greatly increases the possibility of over-indulgence by some of those present and should remember that more than a few otherwise beautiful wedding parties have been ruined by the tipsy behavior of some guests. When intoxicating beverages are served, one should always remember to serve a similar nonintoxicating drink for those present who do not care to take anything stronger.

Saying Grace

A seated breakfast or luncheon always begins with saying grace. If a priest is present, he is asked to say grace. If more than one priest is present, one may ask the Mass celebrant, the oldest man, or whomever one wishes to honor; but bear in mind that it is an honor, and in honoring one, be sure you are not slighting another. (See section on "Honoring Our Clergy.") If a bishop is present, he is always asked. If two clergymen are present, it is well to ask one to say grace, the other to offer a blessing on the assemblage at the end of the meal. If no clergyman is present, one may invite any religious brother to say grace. If no clergy or religious is present, the bride's father may say grace. If there is a child in the wedding party—flower girl or ring bearer—the child may be invited to say grace. If anyone save a priest or religious is to perform this duty, he or she should be forewarned, so as to be prepared.

Toasts

At all wedding receptions, it is the privilege of the best man to offer the first toast, and it is always "The Bride!" He should be fore-warned, so that he may be prepared with a graceful little speech. Other toasts may follow or not, as the host wishes, but this first one is never omitted. Other toasts might be: the bridegroom, toasting either his mother-in-law, his parents-in-law, or both sets of parents; the bride's father and the bridegroom's father, toasting the young couple; or a toast to the bridesmaids.

The Wedding Cake

The traditional wedding cake is a rich dark fruit cake with a white icing. In the South, a bride's cake which is all-white is served instead; this bride's cake is now becoming popular in all sections of the country because it is not so rich. Either cake is always heavily iced with white frosting. It may be several tiers high and be topped with a bridal bell, orange blossoms, or a pair of doves made of the icing. It stands in the middle of the bride's table, if there is one, or in the same position on the buffet table, if there is not.

Cutting the Cake

The wedding cake is cut when the dessert is served, and is a little ceremony. The bride cuts the first slice, with the bridegroom's hand resting on the knife handle also, and the bride offers the first piece to the bridegroom. He serves her the second piece. At large weddings, a waiter takes over at this point and continues to cut the cake, and the slices are carried to the guests by waiters. This latter should be done as rapidly and inconspicuously as possible, for it will be followed by the toasts.

Opening the Dance

The dancing following the breakfast is often opened with a little ceremony also. The bride and bridegroom take the floor alone and dance to a musical number that has some sentimental significance for them, or to a number such as "This Is My Lucky Day," or some other light piece suitable to the occasion. After they have danced for a few minutes, the bride's father may "cut in." The bridegroom then takes his mother-in-law for a partner. His father then 'cuts in' on this couple, and the bridegroom leads his mother into the dance. An involved ritual, including the men and women of the wedding party, may also be included in this ceremonial dance. Bridal consultants and some magazine articles on the subject sometimes go into great detail about the ritual of this dance, and discuss it as if there were some social law that requires it to be performed. This is not true. Except for the first few minutes in which the bridal couple dance alone, nothing further is required, unless one wishes to do it.

BRIDAL TRADITIONS

There are a few bridal traditions, wholly secular in their nature, which have been popular for many years. One is that the bride should wear "something old, something new, something borrowed, something blue." Her bridal outfit is new, her pearls might be borrowed from her mother and would also be old, the something blue is usually a knot of ribbon on her lingerie. A "penny in the shoe" is supposed to bring the bride luck. It may also be uncomfortable, so the bride may use her own judgment about observing this custom.

Throwing the bouquet is another old custom. Just before the bride dresses for her wedding journey, the unmarried women present assemble at the foot of a staircase or some similar spot. The bride then throws her bouquet from a landing above. The girl who catches it is supposed to be the next bride.

To the custom of throwing the bouquet another has recently been added. The bride wears one round satin garter. After she has thrown her bouquet, the bridegroom removes this garter and the bride throws it to a group of the unmarried men present. The man who catches it will be the next man married. This is a recent innovation, not rooted in tradition, and serving no useful purpose. For the bridegroom to remove the bride's garter at such a time and under such circumstances should be distasteful to a modest couple. It also gives rise to indelicate joking and is, in every respect, in extremely bad taste. No Catholic bride should consider following this custom.

GOING AWAY

Sometime during the afternoon, at whatever hour suits their plans, the bride and bridegroom slip away and change their wedding costumes for traveling clothes. While they are doing so, both sets of parents leave the guests for a short time, to say their private good-byes to their children. Usually first the mothers, then the fathers, slip away, so that hosts or hostesses are always with their guests.

The bridal couple usually "run the gauntlet" of their friends, to be pelted with rose leaves and confetti, and drive away. The rough horseplay that in former years was sometimes seen at this time is fortunately now completely outmoded. The bridegroom's car may wear a few old shoes, but the bridal luggage is never disturbed. Rice should not be thrown. It is hard enough to hurt, when thrown with force, and is slippery and dangerous underfoot. Rose leaves, confetti, and paper streamers take its place. The bridal couple should be allowed to drive away alone. The wild pursuit in other cars by wedding attendants— horns blaring, motors roaring—that one occasionally sees, is in very bad taste and, with modern traffic hazards as severe as they are, is actually dangerous both to the participants and to innocent bystanders.

GUESTS

Wedding guests invited to a breakfast or luncheon should arrive close to the hour named. Those invited to a reception may come at any time during the hours announced. To a wedding breakfast as just described, children under fourteen would not be invited, and frequently children under sixteen would not. Parents should not expect young children to be invited to such a party and of course should never bring them unless they have been specifically named in the invitation.

Out-of-town guests and relatives who come to a city solely to attend the wedding and its festivities show real consideration for the bride and her family if they avoid calling at the house on the day and evening just prior to the ceremony. This period is a hectic one for those most intimately involved with the ceremonies. They have not a minute to spare for casual callers, no matter how beloved. The evening is taken up with the rehearsal and rehearsal party, at which there should be no outsiders. Those who come from out of town should telephone the bride or bridegroom's home to announce their safe arrival, and offer congratulations on the coming event. They should reserve their house call, if any, for the "little reception." (See Section headed "The 'Little Reception.'")

OUT OF THE HOME

Modern brides planning a large and lavish breakfast or reception frequently decide to hold this entertaining in a public place rather than at home. Although the atmosphere is less intimate, it is far easier to entertain a large number of guests in rooms specifically planned for this type of entertaining than in our modern houses.

If the bride or her parents are members of a city club or a country club located at a convenient distance from the church, the club house is an ideal place for a wedding breakfast, since one's club is one's "home away from home" and will be spacious and comfortable. Lacking this, one may engage the public rooms of an hotel—ballrooms or private dining rooms. The ideal choice would be two rooms—one large enough for the receiving line and the dancing to follow the meal, the second large enough for bride's table, parents' table, and small tables for all other guests. If one very large room is engaged, the tables for dining might be set up around the dance floor, and the receiving line held just inside the entrance before an appropriately decorated background. Either of these choices is pleasant because it enables all guests to be present for the toasts and cutting the cake. If necessary of course, the bride's and parents' tables may be set up in a small room, the guests' tables in a larger one. All other details of a large and lavish wedding breakfast outside the home are the same as described for one at home.

SLIGHTLY LESS ELABORATE

The wedding breakfast just described is about as sumptuous—and expensive—as anyone would have and is comparatively rare. Far more frequent and popular is the one slightly less elaborate. This usually follows an eleven o'clock wedding (an hour quite as fashionable and popular as noon, but less formal) and is seldom held at home. The food service may be one of three types: a combined bride's and parents' table, served by waiters, with the other guests serving themselves from a buffet table, or a buffet for all, with only the bridal party seated, or a luncheon for parents and bridal party, followed by a reception at which a light menu is served buffet style. In the last case the invitation cards enclosed with the wedding invitations are an invitation to a reception, not a breakfast.

In the first two cases, the first order of business is the receiving line, which continues until all guests have been received. If small tables have been provided, the first guests through the line go to the buffet table and serve themselves and sit at the tables, or sit at the tables and are served by waiters. Because of the style of service the tables are not set with glass or silver and need not have a cloth if the table top is attractive. The menu selected must be one that can be gracefully served in this style.

When the receiving line is ended, the bridal party, parents, and priest seat themselves at a combined table which is set up and decorated as described for a lavish wedding, where they are served by waiters. Here the toasts are given, the bride cuts the cake, and then the dancing begins.

COMBINED TABLE

The seating arrangement at a combined table is as follows: bride and bridegroom are seated together on one side at the middle of the table. On the bride's right is seated the best man, on the bridegroom's left, the maid of honor. At one end of the table is seated the bride's mother, with the officiating priest on her right and the bridegroom's father on her left. At the other end of the table is the bride's father, with the bridegroom's mother on his right, a bridesmaid on his left. The other members of the wedding party are seated between these three groups. Wives or husbands of members of the wedding party who were not themselves in the party are not seated at such a table.

MENUS

Possible menus for such a meal are:

Lobster Mousse, Horseradish Dressing
Endive Salad
Orange Ice
Coffee

Cream Chicken in Pâté Shells
Asparagus
Raspberry Sherbet
Coffee

Cold Ham and Turkey
Cucumber in Tomato Aspic
Ice Cream Molds
Coffee

The only other beverage is champagne or champagne punch and nonalcoholic punch, and the wedding cake may be served with the dessert course. Champagne is served from trays, already poured, both during the meal and on through the afternoon.

For the second type of reception, a table is set up for the bridal party, with the wedding cake as its central decoration. The table is prettily trimmed, but is not laid as for dinner. Here the bridal party is served, toasts are drunk, and the cake is cut. Parents eat at small tables informally, as the other guests do.

The third type of entertaining falls into two parts. It has several advantages, and one possible drawback. Following an eleven o'clock wedding, the bridal party, priest, and parents go directly to the scene of the entertaining where, in a small dining room at a combined table seating all, a breakfast is served to them, and only them, which may be as elaborate as the bride wishes. The table is set as for dinner, but without candles. The wedding cake does not form the centerpiece for this table. Here the bridal party and immediate family can enjoy a substantial meal at leisure and in delightful privacy. The invitation card accompanying the wedding invitations has invited the guests to "a reception, from two until five o'clock." Therefore the guests will not arrive until the family breakfast is over, at which time the receiving line has been formed in the larger room in which the general entertaining will take place. The orchestra is in this room, and there is space for dancing. There are always plenty of chairs around the edge of the dance floor, and also small tables if there is room for them. The buffet table has the wedding cake for its central ornament. The food offered is small sandwiches of minced chicken, thinly sliced ham, or smoked turkey, cocktail type food, such as small open-faced sandwiches of caviar or mashed chicken liver, stuffed celery, and olives. Ices or ice cream are sometimes served, but they are frequently not eaten and are a little difficult to serve under the circumstances described. The beverages are coffee, nonalcoholic punch, and champagne or champagne punch.

Guests serve themselves from this buffet table or are assisted in doing so by waiters at any time they wish during the afternoon. Late in the afternoon the cake cutting ceremony is observed. The best man's toast to the bride is made at the private family table, along with any others desired. More toasts may be made in the main room following the cake cutting if the bride wishes it. Bride and bridegroom open the dancing in the ceremonious style previously described.

The only drawback to this style of entertaining is that, for the majority of the guests, there is a hiatus between the wedding ceremony and the reception to which they are invited. Some people consider this awkward; many do not.

To the three types of entertaining just described, children are seldom invited. Perhaps it should be pointed out that a bride may, if she wishes, invite the family children to *any* style of wedding entertaining, but she is never under any obligation to do so. When and if children of any age are invited to a wedding reception, parents should make it their primary obligation to see to it that their offspring behave properly and quietly and do not detract from the enjoyment of other guests.

PHOTOGRAPHS

At weddings where the bride is having a selection of informal pictures taken for a wedding album, a number are always taken at the reception. Some possible subjects include: the bridal table, the parents' table, the first toast, cutting the cake, opening the dance, the receiving line. In the case of the third type of entertaining with a private family breakfast, there is time and privacy before guests arrive to take a family picture of the bridal pair and parents and the wedding party. One usually has some "going away" scenes taken also, as well as throwing the bouquet.

NO DANCING

The entertaining just described can be made slightly simpler by providing no space for dancing, and no orchestra. Or, for a reception for fifty or less, the music for dancing might be provided by a record player.

SIMPLER TYPES OF ENTERTAINING

There are innumerable varieties of simpler nuptial entertaining. Usually a wedding at which the bridal party wears formal morning dress is followed by one of the types just described. But a bride who wishes to may have a strictly formal wedding service, followed only by a breakfast for the bridal party and immediate family, either at home or in a hotel. Such a choice is not currently fashionable, but it is correct, and only a few years ago was the universal choice of all but the very wealthy. Such a wedding as this would usually be held at ten o'clock in the morning.

Another choice, where the possible guest list would be fifty or less, is a private breakfast immediately following the ceremony, either catered at home or served in an hotel, followed by a small home reception late in the afternoon. The reception menu would be: small sandwiches, assorted cakes and cookies, coffee or tea or both, nonalcoholic punch, and champagne. All would be served from a buffet table. Guests would be greeted by a receiving line, there would be toasts and a cake cutting ceremony, but there would probably be no dancing.

For an afternoon reception, the buffet table is the central point of the entertaining and should be prettily arranged, with the wedding cake as a centerpeice, handsome urns or silver services at either end for serving coffee and tea; silver, napkins, and stacks of plates neatly grouped to make an attractive picture. The table may be set with candelabra for late afternoon. An aunt or sister of either of the bridal pair is asked to preside at the tea and coffee service. Let her be a woman of poise and some social experience, not a very young girl, as it requires some dexterity to serve gracefully a large group of people, particularly when using a service not one's own and to which one is not accustomed.

The champagne and punch are usually served from a separate table with a waitress to serve it and bring fresh bottles and glasses and keep the punch bowl filled. At a very small reception, the cold beverages

might be served from one end of the main buffet table, opposite to the
tea and coffee service.

Any one of these styles of entertaining or a combination of them
may be adapted to simpler and smaller weddings, according to the
taste of the bride. Large or small, let it be appropriate to the ceremony
being celebrated, beautiful, cordial, and correct. The one type of
entertaining to be avoided is the sort which, unfortunately, good-
hearted but socially inexperienced people often choose: a reception in
a garish public hall or cheap inn, with many people of all ages invited,
to be served a picnic menu of cold meats, potato salad, beer and
liquor. This is ugly, the atmosphere is all wrong, and it is simply not
suitable, whatever one's circumstances. Better to entertain for a dozen
of one's own family, gracefully and properly, than for a hundred in
inferior surroundings.

A WISE PRECAUTION

During the time of the wedding ceremony (and of the reception
also, when it is held outside the home) the house of the bride's parents
is empty of all its customary inmates. Even the servants, when one is
fortunate enough to employ them, wish to see the wedding of the
daughter of the house. As a result, this is the time when thieves often
break in, tempted by the wedding presents as well as family valuables.
It is, therefore, a wise precaution to see to it that someone remains in
the house at this time. A reliable man or woman may be hired to do
so, or a friend or relative may volunteer to stay. One can scarcely ask
anyone for this favor, as all whom one would know intimately enough
to ask to perform such a service would be invited to the wedding.
Whoever does remain to guard the house can also take telephone
messages and receive any packages or telegrams that may arrive.

THE "LITTLE RECEPTION"

During the last few years, in the eastern section of the country
with which the writer is most familiar, a new wedding custom has
become quite common. It may not be done in other sections of our
land, and may not occur at *your* wedding, but it is wise to be informed
of it, so that one may make the necessary preparations in case it should
occur.

Because Catholic weddings always are celebrated in the morning,
any entertaining to follow, even the most lavish, ends not later than
five o'clock. This is too early for dinner, too late for anything else. The
wedding guests are in a festive mood, reluctant to return to everyday

living. As a result, when the wedding entertaining has not been held at home, it frequently happens that the bride's relatives and her parents' intimate friends drop in informally at the parents' house immediately following the reception to admire the wedding presents, congratulate the parents on the happy occasion, and "talk over" the wedding in privacy.

This can be a highly enjoyable occasion for all if the hosts have prepared for it. It is a wise idea to hire an experienced waitress or barman, properly dressed, to stay in the house during the festivities and to remain to serve drinks during this "little reception." At this time one does not serve champagne or offer any food. But one should have nonalcoholic drinks on hand, as well as the ingredients for scotch and soda, rye, bourbon, etc., depending upon what one customarily serves. All guests usually have left by seven o'clock. This family time is particularly appreciated by one's relatives who have come to the wedding from other cities, for it provides a chance for a little private conversation together and gives them their only opportunity to see the wedding presents laid out for display.

Sometimes the bridegroom's parents, if they live in the city where the wedding has occurred, are similarly visited at this time by their relatives and friends. Of course either couple, if they wish to, can make these little parties an integral part of the wedding by planning for them in advance and quietly issuing verbal invitations at the wedding reception to such of their friends and relatives as they wish to call on them at home.

The point must be stressed that there is absolutely no social obligation requiring one to hold these "little receptions" if one does not wish to. But, since the possibility of many people making such an informal call at this time does exist, prospective hosts need be informed of it.

15

Duties of a Parishioner

What is most needed today in every parish is laymen who are virtuous, well-instructed, determined and apostolic (Pope Pius X).

INTRODUCTION

A generation ago, it was not uncommon for a couple to marry and begin housekeeping in the parish in which they were baptized and had grown up. Their pastor was the priest who had married them, and was well aware of the new home under his spiritual direction. The recent growth of the suburbs and the increasing mobility of the American people have changed this picture. Today a single family may make their home in several cities in as many years, changing parishes with each move. This creates some new parish obligations; the old ones continue to be in force.

WHEN YOU MOVE

When moving out of a parish, notify your pastor by letter that you will no longer be under his care. Ask the church office to remove your name from the parish mailing list and from the list of church contributors. This helps the pastor to estimate the school attendance each season, the amount of money he may count on to run the church plant, etc. Taking your name off the parish list saves unnecessary mailing and postage.

As soon as you have moved into your new home, notify your new pastor that you are joining his parish. This may be done by a personal call on him or by a note. A personal call makes you promptly acquainted with your new shepherd, but a letter is more business-like. Here is a sample of a letter which gives the necessary information.

17 Ridgewood Drive
Elmira, New York
July 22, 1960

The Rev. James A. Black
317 Chestnut Street
Elmira, New York

My dear Father Black:

Last week our family moved from our former home in
Dayton, Ohio, where we were members of St. James'
parish. We are now living in your parish, at the address
given above, and hope soon to become an integral part
of the parish life.

Our family consists of myself, my wife, and our two
children, boys aged seven and nine. We hope that in the
Fall we will be able to enroll them in the parish school,
Robert in the second grade, Edward in the fourth. Can
you tell me at this time whether there will be room for
them?

Please ask the parish office to send us four sets of
church envelopes, two for adults, made out in the name
of Mr. Robert Holdrich and Mrs. Robert Holdrich, and
two sets of junior envelopes, made out for Robert Holdrich, junior, and Edward Holdrich.

I hope that you will, at your convenience, call on us
and bless our new home. We are looking forward to
meeting you, and assure you that we will do our best to
be faithful and useful parish members.

Very sincerely yours,
ROBERT HOLDRICH

To receive a letter of this nature brings joy to the heart of any
pastor and opens the door to a happy parish life for you. It helps your
new pastor to keep up the parish census, estimate school attendance for
the coming year and the financial support the parish may count on.

YOU AND YOUR PASTOR

In all your dealings with your pastor, try to keep in mind the fact
that he is a very busy man. Make allowances for him if he does not do
all that you think he should, or when you think he should. If a letter
such as the one given above does not bring forth the response you
would like, remember that it probably lost out to a dozen more pressing
duties. Follow it up with a personal call at the rectory. Be friendly—
and brief!

Keep the rectory telephone number listed where anyone can easily find it, whether they know your family habits or not. Many families keep the number listed on a special sheet hung near a phone, along with the telephone number of the family doctor, a hospital and an ambulance service.

In an emergency, such as sudden serious illness or accident, do not hesitate to call the rectory at any time. Your pastor is anxious to give extreme unction whenever it is required. But in a case where a member of your family suffers an illness which puts him in proximate danger of death, it is thoughtless to wait until some late night crisis to call your pastor to administer extreme unction, rather than to call in the daylight hours.

Make all ordinary business calls to the rectory (for an appointment, information, etc.) during what are regarded as the business hours of the day. Try not to disturb the pastor during meals or in his evening hours.

Notify your pastor whenever a member of your family is in the hospital so that he may call on the invalid. If you do not tell him of the illness, your pastor has no way of knowing about it.

Notify your pastor if you have an invalid or aged person in your home, so that he may bring him Holy Communion regularly.

Avoid all idle criticism of the way your pastor performs his duties: the administration of church and school, intellectual content of his sermons, personal habits, mannerisms, and idiosyncrasies. Your pastor is a human being, prone to all the weaknesses and frailties of other human beings. Unlike many of us, he is trying to do his best at all times. If his best is in some respect not good enough (in your opinion), help him if you can. If you cannot help any other way, do so by failing to criticize.

This paragraph from the magazine *Once over Lightly* is worth thinking about.

> IF IF IF . . .
> the pastor preaches over ten minutes he's long winded;
> > his sermon is short he didn't prepare it.
> the parish funds are low he's a poor businessman;
> > he mentions money he's money-mad.
> he owns a car he's worldly;
> > he doesn't he's too late for sick calls.
> he visits his parishioners he's nosey;
> > he doesn't he's being snobbish.
> he has fairs and bazaars he's bleeding the people;

> he doesn't there isn't enough social life in the parish.
>
> he takes time in confession to help advise sinners, he's too long;
>> he doesn't he's not a good advisor.
>
> he starts Mass on the minute, his watch is fast;
>> he starts Mass late, he's holding up the congregation.
>
> he redecorates the church, he's spending too much money;
>> he doesn't he's letting it get run down.
>
> he's young, he's not experienced;
>> he's old, he should be retired.
>
> he dies, there's none who will ever replace him.

To this one might add: If he is business-like and capable, he is not humble. If he is pious and retiring, he is too unsophisticated.

"Not humble" seems to be the charge parishioners hurl about when they dislike their pastor but have no valid reason for doing so. Humility seems an odd virtue. Only priests are supposed to have it. One never hears a lawyer or doctor accused of lack of humility, yet both these groups have in their midst many practitioners who are as arrogant as they are successful.

Pray for your pastor at all times. This is help you can always give, and which he always needs. "Now I exhort you, brethren, through our Lord, Jesus Christ and through the charity of the Spirit, that you help me by your prayers to God for me" (Romans 15:30).

YOUR FINANCIAL CONTRIBUTION

Your church is the spiritual powerhouse of your parish. Just as a powerhouse generates electricity from coal or steam to light a city, your church generates moral and spiritual energy to vitalize the congregation. This moral and spiritual energy is generated from the prayers, good works, and church attendance of the pastor and people, and from the financial support the church receives from its members. All share; all should contribute.

At every stage of life there are sound reasons for scrimping your financial support of your parish.

The school child says, "My contribution is so small. What good does it do?"

The young adult says, "My salary is so small, and I have to buy so much with it; I'll wait until I am making a little more money."

The young married say, "We are just setting up our home. Our expenses are so heavy. We'll wait until we are better off."

Parents say, "My expenses for the children are so great; they are our first responsibility. We'll give more when they are older."

Older people say, "We have given faithfully all our life long. It is time to take care of ourselves. Let the young people take over."

Every excuse is a good one; but whom does it leave to support the Church? Let everyone of every age contribute regularly and faithfully according to his means. A burden thus shared is no burden to anyone.

Sensible people try to set up a yearly budget for all expenses, according to their income, and the expenses it must cover. Your church contribution should be estimated the same way: a yearly amount, contributed in weekly installments. Only you and your conscience know what that amount should be. One thing is sure: if the amount you contribute is less than the sum you spend for your barber, cigarettes, or golf lessons, you are living your spiritual life at someone else's expense!

A few years ago it was the writer's duty to close the home of an elderly friend who had died, a woman of straitened means. In her bureau drawer were her church envelopes, each containing her contribution for the remaining Sundays of that year. Apparently she filled them when she received them and so had them ready as each Sunday came round. Only God knows how much sacrifice this may have demanded. But He knows, and now she is enjoying her reward.

Americans in every walk of life and of all ages regard a car as a necessity, something they must have "for transportation." One could say that our parish church is the vehicle which we need "for transportation" to Heaven, a more important destination than any of our earthly errands. But if our contributions to our Church had to equal the yearly cost of our car, imagine the shrieks of protest that would rend the air!

No one can tell you the proper sum to contribute to your church, but it may certainly be said that, whether your income is large or small, you should give an amount large enough so that you feel it as a sacrifice. Anything less is not enough.

No one is obliged to attend his parish church. Some people feel such a fondness for a parish that they continue to go there when they have moved from its limits. Some choose to attend another parish because they have relatives serving there, etc. Sometimes a peculiarity in laying out parish boundaries results in another church being nearer to your home than your own parish church.

Whether you attend your parish church or not, you are obligated to support it. It is there to serve you, and whether or not you take advantage of its services, you have a moral obligation to contribute to its maintenance. You must also contribute to the church which you do attend, since you are using the services of that church with consequent expense to that parish.

PARISH SOCIETIES

In each parish there are a number of societies to foster the spiritual and social life of parishioners of both sexes and all ages. The most common ones are the Altar-Rosary Society, the Holy Name, the Confraternity of Christian Doctrine, the Society of St. Vincent de Paul, the Legion of Mary, and the Catholic Youth Organization. All have a noble purpose, spiritual or charitable. Membership in any of them redounds to one's spiritual good. If you take an active part, as an officer or committee member, it helps your pastor to enrich the spiritual life of the parish. Pope Pius XI defined Catholic Action as "the participation of the laity in the apostolate of the hierarchy."

16

Honoring Our Clergy

❖❖❖❖❖

With all thy soul fear the Lord, and reverence his priests (Ecclesiasticus 7:31).

Membership in the church is broadly divided into three groups: clergy, religious, and laity. The laity includes all Catholic laymen. "Religious" are all brothers and sisters. "Clerics" are all those who are in the priesthood; they become clerics from the time they take tonsure. Among our clerics there is a distinction in rank according to their position in the sacred hierarchy of the Church.

In social life one accords to any cleric or religious every possible mark of honor and respect.

Men, women and children rise and remain standing when speaking to such a one. Men and boys remove their hats and remain uncovered in the presence of a religious or cleric.

Those in religious life must be addressed by their correct title, both in writing and in direct address. One does not say, "Yes, Sir," to a priest, although men in military service sometimes do so because a chaplain is a commissioned officer. It is wrong, however, even under these circumstances. One correctly says, "Yes, Father," "Yes, Monsignor," "Yes, Sister," etc.

At any gathering of Catholics, such as a baptismal or wedding party or a meeting of a Catholic organization, any clergy present are the principal honor guests and, as such, always occupy a seat of honor. When only one member of the clergy is present, he is seated on the right of the hostess or chairman. When several are present, their position of honor is usually determined by their rank in the hierarchy of the church or, if all are equal in this respect, by the seniority of their elevation to the priesthood. Thus a cardinal outranks an archbishop not a cardinal; an archbishop outranks a bishop; all bishops outrank priests. A priest who is a prothonotary, domestic prelate, or papal chamberlain (monsignor) outranks priests who are not. A priest of thirty years' standing is honored above one ten years in the priesthood when there is no other distinction.

One exception to these rules: when the official speaker at a gathering is a priest, he usually occupies the honor seat, even though there are present other priests with more seniority. But he would not be so seated if a bishop were present: the honored place must be his. Similarly, at a baptismal party or nuptial entertaining, the officiating priest is usually given the place of honor at the right of the hostess even though there may be present as guests monsignors or priests who outrank him in seniority. This is done to honor him as the priest who has performed the ceremony being celebrated.

Clerics are honored above religious unless the religious is also a priest. (Many religious orders, such as the Jesuits, the Franciscans, and the Dominicans, include in their numbers both priests and brothers.) When the religious is also a priest, he is honored according to his rank or seniority in the priesthood.

A religious who is also a priest is honored above a religious who is not; that is, priests take precedence over brothers. Brothers take precedence over sisters. A brother or sister who is currently the head of the religious house at which he is stationed takes precedence over other members of the order. Sisters occupying such a position are sometimes (but not always) called "Mother." Some superiors are called "Mother Abbess," "Mother Prioress," "Mother Superior," or "Sister Servant." Some continue to be called merely "Sister." When possible, one should determine in advance what the correct title is and use it.

Anyone speaking before a gathering that includes clergy or religious opens his remarks by addressing them directly. He may say: "Your Excellency (or "Bishop Dunn,"), Monsignor Kirwin, Father Daly, Father Hughes, venerable Brothers and Sisters, ladies and gentlemen." If he is unsure of how to differentiate between the clerics present or does not wish to mention them specifically, he may say, "Honored clergy, venerable Brothers and Sisters, ladies and gentlemen:"

At a more intimate gathering, such as a wedding party or small parish meeting, the speaker would probably say, "Father Jamison (the pastor), Father Knowles (the assistant), Brother Barnabus, Brother Pierre, Sister Gertrude, Sister Angela, ladies and gentlemen."

If any sister or brother present is the head of his community, one should determine in advance what his or her correct title is and so address him.

HONORING A BISHOP

A bishop is a priest who has received the fullness of holy orders, that is, the power to administer confirmation and holy orders as well as all the other sacraments. Most bishops also have other administrative duties above those of a priest. Because of this, special distinction is shown a bishop by all other members of the Church.

A Catholic formally greets a bishop by kissing the ring which is one of his marks of office. When one is greeting a bishop within the diocese of which he is the head, one kneels to kiss his ring. Properly one should kneel upon the left knee (kneeling on the right knee as a mark of respect is reserved for the Blessed Sacrament); but many people find kneeling on the left knee awkward. If one kneels on the right knee, one need not be concerned; it is a minor lapse of no importance.

It is never wrong, either from a religious or social point of view, to greet a bishop by kissing his ring. It is done at weddings, funerals, ordinations, any entertaining at which the bishop is the host, or meetings of Catholic organizations.

The gesture is sometimes omitted at mixed gatherings, such as the dedication of a public building lest it be misunderstood by non-Catholics present; but it is proper to kiss the episcopal ring under these circumstances if one wishes.

If one has frequent dealings with a bishop because of the nature of one's work—when one meets him perhaps several times in a day—the usual practice is to kiss the ring at the first daily meeting and to omit the gesture for the remainder of the day.

No layman, religious, or cleric below the rank of bishop sits in the presence of a bishop until he requests one to do so. If seated, one rises when a bishop approaches to address one and remains standing until he invites one to be seated.

At a social gathering, the hostess or chairman says to the bishop, before any others present, "Please be seated, Your Excellency" and indicates a seat on her (his) right. If the bishop arrives after the other guests, all rise when he enters and remain standing until he is seated.

All these marks of respect (except kneeling and kissing the ring) should also be shown all clerics and religious by the laity.

17

Behavior At Mass

Remember, O Lord, thy servants . . . who offer up to
Thee this sacrifice of praise (The Mass).

DRESS

A few general rules cover proper dress for attendance at Mass,
novenas, and other church devotions.

For women:

Women must *always* dress modestly for any church service. *There
is no permissible exception to this rule.* The preferred costume is a
suit, coat, or dress with long sleeves and a modest neckline, hat, gloves,
stockings, and street shoes. Regardless of how warm the weather may
be, a low-cut dress or one without sleeves should not be worn. Any
dress must have, at the very least, a cap sleeve or a collar that covers
the shoulders.

Shorts may never be worn; neither should slacks, except under the
exception noted below.

A head covering, preferably a hat, is obligatory, but a scarf or veil
is permissible.

Exceptions for women: a woman planning to attend services while
on the way to or from work or school may wear the costume proper
for the activity in which she is about to engage. This means that a
woman whose work requires her to wear slacks may wear them to
Mass; a nurse may wear her uniform; a schoolgirl may wear head
scarf, socks, and school uniform. But this permission does not extend
to sports clothes such as a gymnasium suit, tennis dress, bathing suit;
and it is allowable only when the choice is between attending services
in working clothes or failing to attend.

For men:

Laymen never cover their heads in a Catholic church.

The ideal attire is a dark suit, white shirt, and sober tie. Slacks and a sports jacket are allowable. Some sort of suit coat or jacket is always worn. It is poor taste to come to Mass in a sports shirt or jersey without a coat, regardless of how warm the weather may be.

Men do not wear shorts to mass.

Exceptions for men: A man who goes to church while en route to work or school may wear school or work clothes. A laborer returning from work in soiled clothing who wishes to attend an evening Mass may do so, even though he would otherwise wish to appear neat and clean.

For girl children:

Girls and girl babies wear a bonnet or hat in church. If they are under twelve years old they may wear socks. If they are over twelve, they should wear stockings. Snowsuits are permissible in cold weather through the twelfth year. Play suits and shorts are not permissible at any age.

For boy children:

Boys of any age uncover their heads in church. Boys over the age of twelve should not wear shorts to church. Children should not come to church dressed sloppily in denims, jerseys, etc., unless they own no other clothing. Children should learn young to bathe and dress carefully for church and to present as neat and attractive an appearance as possible; this training will then carry over into adult life.

All these rules apply to attendance at church services at which others will be present. Anyone wishing to pay a private visit to the Blessed Sacrament may feel free to do so in any costume provided only that it is modest. Women and girls always wear a head covering; men and boys never do.

DEPORTMENT

Proper behavior at Mass and other church services begins outside the church door. If the church has a parking lot, a driver should take care to park properly, to obey all church rules on the subject, and to strive not to inconvenience any other parkers or take up more than his due share of space. If the church has no parking lot, one should not inconvenience the church's neighbors by parking in front of a driveway or a hydrant. One should never park double or disobey any of the laws of the road.

Other rules to observe are:

Come to Mass on time.

Dip the fingers of the right hand in holy water; make the sign of the cross upon entering and leaving.

Always be seated whenever there is space to permit it. Never stand in the back of the church unless you are sure that all seats are filled.

Genuflect before entering a pew: touch the right knee briefly to the floor as a sign of respect to the Presence on the altar.

Move into the pew as far as space permits; leave the entrance to the pew vacant so that others seeking a seat may easily find one. (The exception to this rule is a wedding; those who have the foresight to come early may step into the aisle to let others enter the pew, thus retaining their seat on the aisle, where they can better observe the ceremonies.)

Those intending to receive Holy Communion should remember to observe the ordinary social amenities as they do so; they should walk up the aisle at a pace that is fast enough to avoid holding others back and slow enough to keep from brushing past others. One should wait until one's turn arrives to approach the rail. If the church has adopted a special method of approaching the Communion rail—up the main aisle, down the side, etc.—all communicants should observe these rules exactly as requested.

Prepare your contribution before you come to Mass. If your church, like so many others, uses the envelope system for collecting, use the envelope proper to the day; mark on the face of it such information as your church has requested. If you have pledged yourself to contribute a set amount each week, keep your word unless some extraordinary change in your financial situation makes it impossible.

Children under four years of age are apt to become restless at Mass. It is not reasonable to expect such young children to behave properly throughout the service; therefore it is best, whenever possible, not to bring them. But of course they may be brought if there is no one to care for them at home. Every effort should be made to keep them from disturbing others. If they become irritable and noisy, they should be taken out.

Children over four can be taught to behave properly. They can understand the simple explanation that they are visiting in God's house and are in His Presence. Children between the ages of four and eight may bring a picture book "Life of Christ" or some similar book with which to occupy themselves and may be taught how to use their rosaries. Children eight years old and over should have a child's Mass Book, or simplified Missal in which they may follow the Mass service.

In some parishes the young women of the Children of Mary or a similar church group conduct nurseries in the school at which parents may leave young children during Mass. This is an excellent idea which all parishes should adopt whenever practical.

Mass is not over until the priest has left the altar; the congregation remains until he has done so. When there is an invalid or a baby at home, a man and wife may attend separate Masses. In such a case, one of them may need to leave the church a minute or so before services are ended so that the one waiting at home may be in time for the next Mass. When one has this excuse or some similar valid reason, it is allowable to leave the church before the final prayers have been said. But it is *not* allowable to leave merely because it is a warm day or in order to escape the crowd.

A Catholic who constantly remembers that his Father and Creator is present on our altars cannot fail to dress and behave properly whenever he is in the Presence and will be eager to go to Mass and loathe to leave.

HEARING MASS PROPERLY

One fulfills one's obligation to hear Mass on Sundays and holydays of obligation by one's presence at the principal parts of the Mass. One does not fulfill it by watching a Mass on television or hearing it on the radio.

But one's mere physical presence at Mass, although it satisfies one's obligation, does not otherwise redound to one's spiritual welfare. One must pray the Mass, in one form or another, with a full awareness of the profound mystery in which one is taking part and a real desire to share in its benefits and to win the spiritual rewards of the great Mass ceremony. This requirement may be fulfilled by: serious interior meditation and prayer, using a prayer book, or praying one's rosary. But the ideal method, and the one the Church urges and approves, is to pray the Mass with the priest by using a Missal.

The Missal is the official prayer book of the Church, in which are given, in Latin and in English translation, the ordinary prayers and the prayers for all the Feasts of the Church liturgical calendar. One who uses a Missal is following exactly all the prayers and actions of the Mass celebrant. With dialogue Masses becoming increasingly common, it is more and more important for all habitually to use a Missal for this service.

General rules for following the Mass, disregarding slight differences in custom in various localities, are these:

Low Mass

Stand when the priest enters the sanctuary at the beginning of Mass; remain standing until he begins the Prayers at the Foot of the Altar, then kneel. Kneel until the Epistle, then sit.

Stand for the reading of the Gospel, both in Latin and in English.

If announcements and a sermon follow the reading of the Gospel, sit for these.

Stand for the Creed, genuflecting at *Et incarnatus est.*

Sit during the offertory; remain seated until the bell is rung three times before the Sanctus.

Kneel for the Sanctus; remain kneeling until all have received Holy Communion. (If one is receiving, one approaches the Communion rail at this time). This means that one remains kneeling throughout the Sanctus, the prayers before Consecration, the Commemoration of the Living, the Commemoration of the Saints, the Consecration of the Host, the Consecration of the Wine, the Continuation of the Canon, the Commemoration of the Dead, the Communion, and the Thanksgiving.

Sit following the purification of the chalice; remain seated until the *Ite Missa Est* is said; then kneel for the blessing.

Stand for the Last Gospel; genuflect at the words *Et verbum cara factum est.*

Kneel for the Prayers after Mass. Respond to the prayers.

Stand until the priest has left the altar.

Genuflect before leaving the pew.

High Mass

If the Asperges is given before the High Mass (permissible only at the principal Mass on Sundays), stand until the celebrant passes the pew one is occupying; kneel as one receives the Asperges; then stand until the Asperges is concluded.

Stand when priest enters the sanctuary at the beginning of Mass. Remain standing until the priest begins the Prayers at the Foot of the Altar. Then kneel.

Remain kneeling until the Gloria. Stand as the celebrant sings the Gloria; sit while the choir sings.

Stand for the singing of the Collects.

Sit for the Epistle.

Stand for the Gospel when it is read in Latin and when it is read in English.

Sit during the sermon and any announcements.

Stand while the priest says the Credo; sit for the part sung by the choir except for the *Et Incarnatus Est,* which one hears while kneeling.

Then stand when the priest returns to the altar; remain standing until he sings the Oremus.

Sit until the prayer which begins the Preface. Stand for the singing of the Preface.

Kneel through the principal parts of the Mass as outlined for Low Mass; remain kneeling until the sanctuary door is closed.

Stand for the singing of the Postcommunion.

Kneel for the final blessing.

Stand for the Last Gospel; genuflect as outlined for Low Mass.

Stand until the priest and acolytes have left the altar.

18

Educating Our Children

And you, fathers, do not provoke your children to anger,
but rear them in the discipline and admonition of the
Lord (Ephesians 6:4).

A PRIMARY RESPONSIBILITY

The education of children is a responsibility given by God to
parents. This is recognized by Church and the State, both of which
can and do stand ready to assist but who cannot supplant the parents
in this matter.

Education of children—for what? For making a living, for citizen-
ship, for fellowship in the community, for appreciation and practice
of the arts, for physical well-being? All of these are good, even vital,
but there is something more important than all these: parents are
bound by a grave obligation to provide to the best of their ability for
the religious and moral education of their children.

Religious and moral training begins in the home. What is taught
there can seldom be eradicated or changed by any other influence,
however good—or bad. A frivolous mother and a wicked father could
force their children to memorize the Catechism from cover to cover;
but what they would learn from so doing would weigh little against
the bad example constantly before their eyes in the persons of their
parents. Conversely, children who observe from their infancy their
parents' pious and informed practice of their Faith in every act of their
daily life are armed forever against the seductions and temptations of
the world.

If all parents were equipped to teach their children what they need
to know about morality and religion, no other source would be required for this training. In actuality, few parents are so equipped: as
few perhaps, as the number who can teach their children to play a
flute, or to read ancient Greek.

A good Catholic continues to study his Faith and to enlarge his knowledge of religion and morals to the day of his death. To do so, he turns to the source of this information: his Church, the pastors, teachers, and others empowered so to inform him, and to the newspapers, magazines and literature produced under their auspices.

It is to the Church also that the Catholic turns for aid in teaching these matters to his children. American Catholics are peculiarly fortunate in this respect. Across the length and breadth of our land spreads a great network of Catholic parochial schools and colleges devoted to teaching our children the truths of their Faith; these meet all the standards required by the various states for an excellent secular education.

This body of schools was not a gift from heaven. As early as 1884 the Third Plenary Council of Baltimore declared

> Near every Church where there is no parochial school one shall be established within two years after the promulgation of this Council and shall be perpetually maintained, unless the bishop for serious reasons sees fit to allow delay.

Energetic building of schools began forthwith; but in many parishes a "serious reason for delay" existed: the financial inability of the parishioners to build and maintain such a school at their expense. But as the years passed, thousands and thousands of such schools were built and are being built, a tribute to the parishioners whose donations have made them possible. There are still some areas in which parochial schools do not exist, but they are becoming steadily fewer.

The Third Plenary Council further declared

> all parents shall be bound to send their children to a parochial school unless it be evident that such children obtain a sufficient Christian education at home, or unless they attend another Catholic school, or unless, for sufficient cause approved by the bishop, with proper cautions and remedies duly applied, they attend another school.

This means that a Catholic should send his children to a parochial school, if his parish has such a school, unless he sends them to another (private) Catholic school or unless the mother or a governess is qualified to teach them at home. If they attend a public school, it should be for due cause, with the permission of one's pastor. In this latter case the "proper cautions and remedies duly applied" are faithful attendance at the religious education classes conducted by the parish for children not attending Catholic schools.

Permission to attend other than a parochial school is given for good reason. Some examples: no parochial school within a reasonable distance and no means of transportation; special educational problems such as arise with crippled, spastic, or retarded children; children peculiarly gifted as musicians, actors, etc., who might wish training at an early age in a special school; children who are slow learners or who have a reading block, who need special schools. A parent who does not send his child to the parochial school should obtain permission to educate him elsewhere and should see to it that he is instructed in his religion.

Today parochial schools have a new problem. Our post-war population of school-age children is so large that the problem lies not so much in convincing the parents of the desirability of Catholic education as in finding room for all the children in the parish who wish to attend. The situation is acute in suburban areas, where new families are moving in so rapidly that schools are overcrowded almost as soon as they are built.

A Catholic parent who wishes his children to attend the parish school may find that there is no room in the school for them. What then is the parent's duty? He should accept the fact of his children's exclusion without resentment, and understand that there are physical limits to the number any one school can educate. He should, if his finances permit, send the children to a private Catholic school if such is available. If they go to public school, he should arrange for their regular attendance at religious education classes provided by the parish.

He should continue his financial support of the parish school, for this is the duty of all parishioners, whether they have children in the school or not. He should, when a drive is instituted to enlarge the school, work for it energetically for the sake of his own children and others. He should never criticize the exclusion of his children or accuse pastor or principal of "favoritism" in the admission of children to the school. He should strive to live a truly Christian life that will edify his children and inspire them to emulation.

WHY CATHOLIC SCHOOLS?

The American public school system was founded to provide every child enrolled in it with a basic education at the taxpayers' expense. Its founders understood that because we are a pluralistic society it would be impossible for the public schools to provide each child with instruction in his particular faith; neither would it be proper to teach one or several and ignore all others. The solution was to empower the state to provide a wholly secular education. In so providing, the founders did not—indeed they could not—deprive citizens of their right to provide for the religious instruction of their children at their own expense and as they saw fit. Anything else would have been an abridgement of their right to free practice of their faith.

American Catholics have always understood the peculiar circumstances which require our public education to be wholly secular and have never suggested that it should be otherwise. Recognizing also their solemn personal obligation to provide their children with a knowledge of their Faith and the morals and ethics which it requires of them, Catholics have, at untold expense to themselves, built and maintained the parochial school system. It provides a secular education equal or superior to that of the public school system, is supervised by the same authorities in any given state, and offers a thorough grounding in religion and morality.

The essence of Catholicity—its basic beliefs—can be understood and practiced by the simplest and most unlettered among us. The fullness of Catholic belief—its philosophy, mysticism, history, etc.— have provided a lifetime study for some of our most brilliant minds. Catholic schools provide the means for this study from the kindergarten, where the child learns that God made him "to love Him and serve Him in this world and to be happy with Him forever in the next," to the logic, philosophy and ethics taught in Catholic colleges.

It is a curious paradox that the most fanatic supporters of the principle of "separation of church and state," those who interpret it to mean a total exclusion of any recognition of the Fatherhood of God and the Brotherhood of Man from our schools and from public life, are usually violently opposed to Catholic schools. Yet the parochial school is an outgrowth of this principle. The state may, properly, furnish a child only a secular education. A parent who exercises his right to educate his child as he thinks best and chooses to give him a God-centered education may surely do so. If one grants that public education is, and must be, secular, why should these critics deny the right of parents to turn elsewhere for a God-centered education, if they wish?

From the beginning of the Christian era, education was a function of the church, and of the church only. For two hundred years prior to the establishment of the public school system, American education was church-sponsored, little of it under Catholic auspices. Other faiths in our nation have shown in many ways their recognition that the teaching of the word of God is a primary duty. The Sunday school is the backbone of Protestantism. Some Lutheran and Episcopalian congregations have church schools similar to ours; the Hebrew school is an integral part of the synagogue. Most American private schools and many colleges were founded by one denomination or another and include in their curricula, as a matter of course, the teaching of the word of God.

But it should be noted that most non-Catholic Christian and Jewish believers have felt that it is possible to give children a secular education in the public schools and relegate the teaching of religion and morals to a few hours a week. There are some current indications, however, that a number of the more thoughtful of them are beginning to doubt the validity of this position. In proof of this, here are portions of an article that appeared in the Albany, N. Y., *Knickerbocker News* of August 11, 1960, written by Howard Lewis. Loudonville, the community referred to, is a suburb of Albany.

> "Education in the public schools is in danger of becoming 'neutral to God,' a Loudonville minister said yesterday.
>
> "Naturally, religion should never be regarded as a cure-all," said the Rev. Dennis Kinlaw. "But an education that is neutral to God is like teaching physics and ignoring the sun."
>
> Mr. Kinlaw, pastor of the Loudonville Community Church, declared himself on the eve of the opening of a Christian Day School at his church.
>
> Plans call for instruction of boys and girls from kindergarten through grade four. The new private school will stress morality through religion on an inter-denominational basis.
>
> "I don't believe one can teach moral values without God," the minister said. "And the teaching of morality must be the prime educational objective."
>
> In a discussion with this reporter and Dr. D. A. Berberian, a member of the church school's planning committee, Mr. Kinlaw charged:
>
> "We seem to have no philosophy to give to people—just food and dollars."
>
> Dr. Berberian, a native of the Middle East, noted that in many states teachers are discouraged, even forbidden, to read the Bible . . .
>
> Explaining the reason for the formation of the new

day school, which will open next month, Dr. Berberian reiterated that public education does not place as much emphasis on religious and moral precepts as he believes it should.

"Christian parents are alarmed because the faith of their children is being undermined in many public schools," he asserted. "We believe that moral rearmament is the greatest need of our country." . . .

The new school will be subject to the same general supervision as other schools and will meet State Education Department requirements.

Each day will begin with prayer and a general devotional period in following the course of study recommended by the National Association of Christian Schools.

This article is interesting, not only because of the trend the foundation of this school may indicate but also because it is a correct statement, from the lips of a non-Catholic, of Catholic views on education which have resulted in the parochial school system.

Parents of parochial school children pay the same taxes as their neighbors whose children attend public schools. For this they deserve no applause. The same taxes are also borne by childless citizens and are the civic duty of all. Catholics also pay all the costs of building and maintaining their own schools. In maintaining these schools, Catholics relieve the state of the cost of educating the children who attend them —no small burden. In a city of more than one hundred thousand near which the writer lives, fifty-one per cent of all the children from kindergarten through high school are attending Catholic or other private schools (1959 figures). Imagine the added burden to the taxpayers if these schools should close their doors! Yet there are still some communities in which the construction of parochial schools is criticized and even resisted.

19

The Home Life of Catholics

He is happiest, be he king or peasant, who finds peace
in his home (Goethe).

A PATTERN FOR YOUR LIFE

The first days of a marriage are exciting and full of surprises. The
couple are learning their roles as marriage partners, learning by doing.
The wife is practicing housekeeping and cooking and adjusting both
to her husband's taste. The husband is struggling with a budget for
two, and marveling at the strange and wonderful ways of woman. Each
is finding the other full of hitherto-undreamed-of idiosyncrasies, with
habits and attitudes unlike his own. Both are taking the first steps—
often very difficult—to mutual sex compatibility.

In addition to this intense private life, they are learning to be a pair
—making friends, entertaining and being entertained, discovering
those sports, hobbies and tastes they can share, and those in which
they must walk alone.

All this should be enough, one might think, to fill every waking
hour. But there is one other consideration, so important it cannot be
neglected. In the early days of marriage, one should give earnest
thought to the kind of life pattern which one wishes to establish. It is
astonishing how quickly the casual act of yesterday becomes the fixed
habit of tomorrow. Try to remember this and, in the earliest days of
marriage, form habits that will make your married life more rewarding,
more loving and more Christian. Many people live out their life
without setting themselves a purpose or a goal. They go along in a
rut, vaguely dreaming of the interesting things they will do in the
future, but doing nothing constructive *now* to make that future
possible. Today follows today, each like the other, and suddenly most
of the future has become the past and there is nothing to look forward
to but a dull old age.

One method to avoid such aimlessness is to review regularly all one's daily actions, to check on their value, and to judge one's progress toward one's goals.

But first the goals themselves must be established. A newly-married couple should discuss their life ambitions to make sure that they coincide, and then determine how they will set about to attempt to fulfill them. Having determined this, they should try to live so that each day they take one step nearer the distant goal. It helps to remember: Today is all we have. Yesterday is gone; tomorrow never comes. Only *now* is meaningful. It is now you must study, grow spiritually, save for the future, spend your leisure enjoyably. You can never do it tomorrow. How dreadful to talk about "wasting" an afternoon, or "passing" an evening. They are all we have, or ever will have; in God's name, let us use them purposefully!

Another self-help is a review, yearly and even quarterly, to determine one's progress to richer living. First, a spiritual inventory:

Am I so living that I have a better chance of earning heaven than I did a year ago?

Am I practicing my religion faithfully and meaningfully?

Am I dealing honorably, charitably, with my fellow-men?

Am I deepening the love which my marriage partner and I feel for one another by my devotion, patience and understanding?

Am I aware of his/her virtues, tolerant of his/her shortcomings?

Am I helping him/her to get to heaven?

Am I doing my duty by my family joyfully, unremittingly?

Do I deal generously with my employer or employees?

Do I ever strive to help the poor or oppressed?

If you are a parent, examine your children's development:

Am I helping my children's spiritual growth by personal example, inculcating habits of daily prayer, Mass attendance, rosary devotions, etc.?

Are they learning to control their emotions and their desires?

Are they happy and adjusted to life?

Are they truthful, honorable, self-reliant?

Do they share joys, belongings, and duties cheerfully?

Are their manners improving?

What of your family life?

Do you talk to one another of anything save the mechanics of living?

Do you confide in one another?

Are you loyal?

Do you present a united front to the world?

Do you enjoy each other's company?

Do you read, sing, play games, go on outings together?

Do you respect one another's confidences, take pride in accomplishments, sympathize with troubles?

What of your life as a couple?

Has your concern for children or job pushed your wife/husband into the background of your life?

Do you confide in one another?

Do you listen when your mate talks of his/her problems, ambitions, worries and accomplishments?

Do you speak of him/her to others, in and out of his/her presence, with pride and admiration?

Do you respect one another's opinions?

Do you express your love in words and deeds?

Do you have time for each other?

Do you happily spend some of your leisure hours together, without children or others?

Do you try as hard to please each other as you did during your courting days?

Who is your husband's sports hero?

What color is your wife's winter coat?

If you cannot answer these last two questions, you are losing interest in each other.

What of your personal life? Ask yourself:

Do I enjoy the work that fills my days? What can I do to make it pleasanter?

Is my leisure spent in ways that truly please me, with people I really like, or does sheer inertia keep me glued to a television screen or gossiping with bores?

How long is it since I have: learned a new skill, craft, art, or game? Read material that challenged my intellect, enlarged my horizons, deepened my understanding of life?

Am I keeping abreast of world affairs and scientific advances?

Have I made new friends? Kept in touch with old ones?

Am I becoming narrow-minded, opinionated, boresome?

What can I do for me to make next year happier?

FINANCES

Take a regular financial inventory. Few people understand that a man can begin work at the age of twenty, work forty hours a week for two dollars an hour until he is sixty-five without improving himself or earning any overtime, and will, in so doing, earn $187,200! Where does it all go? Most of it is spent in keeping himself and his family clothed, fed, sheltered, clean, and in good health. But surely, of this immense sum, a part should have remained for the realization of some of his earthly dreams. Sadly enough it is seldom so, even for those wage earners in a higher income bracket than our hypothetical man. Misfortune, mistakes, and plain bad luck account for some of it, but much of it dribbles away in unwise, unplanned spending!

The way to control your income is not a glamorous one, but there is no other: you must budget your income realistically, in relation to your needs, and stick to it. Do not spend to inflate your ego or impress your neighbor. Save for future security and also for short or long-time goals that will bring you pleasure. It is easier to save ten dollars a week so that you will be able to make a downpayment on a house in four years than to save "some" money to buy a house "sometime." Save and buy to please your own tastes. If your brother urges you to go on a fishing trip with him, and you would rather save the money to buy a hi-fi, do it. And do not try to do both merely because you do not want to say, "No, I can't afford it." If you are willing to wear last year's coat to pay for violin lessons, take them! It's your life. But do not do it if you are so self-conscious that you are going to feel apologetic about your shabby coat.

In spending the household money, remember that you can buy time with money, just as you can spend time to save money. You can buy chicken already roasted. It costs more this way, but it may be a wise purchase if you are currently so busy that the time saved is worth more to you than the extra money spent. Conversely, a pie made at home is cheaper than one bought at the bakery; a pie made of its various ingredients is also cheaper than one made of prepared mixtures. Every full-time homemaker should know how to bake pies and cakes, make dressing, jelly, etc., without using the preparations now on the market to cut the work in half. She may not always use the long method, but she should know how to do so; when using the quick way, she should realize that the prepared products cost more than the basic ingredients. The point here is to weigh convenience against cost to decide whether in this case time is worth more than money or is not, and buy accordingly.

The same yardstick should be used in purchasing household appliances. A freezer is a wise buy for a large family if the homemaker has the time and training to keep it filled with home-prepared soups, stews, casseroles, cakes, pies, vegetables, fruits and meats. But a home freezer containing six packages of frozen peas and the haunch of the deer Dad shot last fall should be a reproach to the homemaker and is a proof of money poorly spent.

Similarly, a young mother of three who lives in a house without any indoor drying space may regard a clothes dryer as a wonderful help. But an older woman, with her family raised, plenty of leisure to "do" her small laundry in one session, and an airy spot to dry it in, wastes money with such a purchase. So please remember to ask yourself: which is more necessary for me: to spend money to buy time, or to save money by spending time? Only you know the answer.

Divide the spending of your money fairly between family members. A mother who "sacrifices everything" for her children turns into a spiritless drudge, overlooked and unappreciated. A father who works night and day to furnish his family with the luxuries owned by their wealthier friends may suddenly find he counts for very little in the family circle.

Americans are devoted parents. Their commonest mistake is to give children too much of material things, too little of their time and attention. It is natural to want one's children to have everything their associates have, natural too to want to give them anything which one craved, and did not have, as a child. Natural, but not wise. A child who knows he is beloved and valued, who knows he is treated as generously as his sisters and brothers, and whose parents give him some of their time and attention, will cheerfully do without many material things.

In spending your income, then, do not sacrifice parents for children, or vice versa. Do not lavish the bulk of your money on the most brilliant child or the prettiest girl. Fair shares for all makes for happy family life and well-adjusted children. And in this sharing, let the children share in the sacrifices, too. Children can understand that it is fun to give up something so that Mommy can go to the P.T.A. convention, or Daddy can be given a new watch for his birthday.

When children reach their teen years and their active social life begins, it is really true that Mother will gladly wear last year's suit to buy Susie the evening dress of her dreams, and often it is the wise thing to do. This is the time to pamper them a *little* if you can, particularly if they are timid about their first steps into society. But do not go to extremes. Remember that at this age children are sensitive about everything, including the way Mother and Father dress. Do not neglect yourself to the point that they may be ashamed of you.

FIND TIME FOR GOD

Many couples feel that half an hour at Sunday Mass and occasional reception of the Holy Eucharist is all the help they need to live a Catholic life. They are like children who own a treasure chest of inexhaustible wealth but draw on it for only a penny a week! The primary ingredients for a happy marriage are: good humor, a loving heart, patience and forbearance. Put God first in your home through faithful daily practice of your Faith, and He will renew these virtues for you daily and give you the grace to bear every sorrow and multiply every joy.

There are so many beautiful religious observances by which family life can be enriched that one can hardly list them all. Few of us can find the time for all of them, but please give serious consideration to the ones discussed here. They can be the key to your future happiness.

Daily Prayer

A young Catholic couple marry and go off on their honeymoon. From infancy, each has been accustomed to close each day by kneeling at his bedside and saying his nightly prayers. But each has been used to doing this alone or in the bosom of his family. On this, their first night together, embarrassment overcomes them and each resolves to slip into bed and then say his prayers. Thus begins the establishment of a bad habit. Better far to get down on one's knees as one has always done; better still to ask one's new life partner to join one in asking God's blessing on the marriage.

The same is true of morning prayers. What better way to start the day than to ask God's help in making it a good one? Take the minute or two required for this observance, for each day brings us closer to our last; the acts of a single day may, in the final accounting, earn us heaven or hell.

First Friday and Saturday

Reception of Holy Communion on the First Friday of nine consecutive months is one means of demonstrating devotion to the Sacred Heart of Jesus and brings with it many spiritual rewards and benefits. Accompanied by some prayers in reparation for the injuries offered to the Sacred Heart, reception of the Sacrament on First Friday earns one a plenary indulgence. It is also an easy way to see to it that one goes to confession and Communion regularly. The mere effort involved in remembering to go to Confession and in rising early to go to Mass and Communion before setting forth on one's daily tasks is a good spiritual exercise. It is a way for a couple to share their religious life. In a mixed marriage, the sight of the Catholic partner quietly performing this observance sets a fine example and demonstrates perhaps as well as any single effort can how precious and meaningful is the inner spiritual life of the Catholic partner.

A beautiful devotion to the Blessed Mother and to her Divine Son is the reception of the Holy Eucharist on the First Saturday of the month. At Fatima she promised the graces necessary to salvation to those who would, on the First Saturday of five consecutive months, confess their sins, receive Communion, recite five decades of the rosary and spend fifteen minutes' meditation on the mysteries of the rosary.

Blessing the Home

As soon as you are settled in your new house, invite your pastor to come and bless it. This is a ceremony which places your home and those who dwell in it under our Lord's protection. When you ask your pastor to come, let him select a time and date convenient to him. If possible, let it be in the evening when the man of the house is at home. Your pastor may have time to follow the ceremony with a brief social call. This helps you all to become better acquainted.

Grace at Meals

Dinner is often the one meal which the family can eat together. Begin it by asking God's blessing on the food and those who eat it. The blessing offered by Catholics consists of the sign of the cross and this prayer: "Bless us, O Lord, and these, Thy gifts, which we are about to receive from Thy bounty, through Christ our Lord. Amen." The sign of the cross concludes the prayer.

A meal thus begun should be peaceful, happy and gracious. When there are children in the family, let one of them say it. In some families the eldest or youngest child always says the blessing; in others, the children take turns.

Celebrating One's Saint's Day

A Catholic should feel special affection for, and devotion to, the saint for whom he is named. This can be fostered by celebrating the saint's "birthday" on the date chosen by the Church to honor him. Just as a child's birthday is celebrated by the giving of gifts and special attention, the saint's day can be observed by giving the saint the "gift" of special prayers and attendance at Mass. The story of his life should be retold, and one can tell the child why one gave him the name of this particular saint.

Blessing After Childbirth

The blessing after childbirth, sometimes called the "churching" of women, is an act of thanksgiving for the safe delivery of a child. It is a simple and beautiful act of thanks and blessing. It is not required to be done; it is merely one of the many sacramentals of the Church by which one's spiritual life may be enriched.

Other Catholic Practices

There are many other Catholic devotions by which a Catholic couple may choose to inspire their personal and family life. These include: family rosary, Forty Hours Devotion, Stations of the Cross, novenas, spiritual retreats, mission services, the wearing of scapulars and medals, blessings for children, sick people, and religious objects. Use them to weave the blessing and glory of your Faith into the tapestry of your daily life, the golden thread to brighten and sanctify the darkest days.

THE CHRISTIAN OBSERVANCE OF CHRISTMAS AND EASTER

It does not take a very thoughtful person to notice how secularized the observance of Christmas and Easter has become. Many persons who are, by their own admission, complete unbelievers, "celebrate" Christmas with a lavish exchange of gifts, feasting and parties, send Easter lilies to their mothers, and welcome the coming of "Santa Claus" and the "Easter Bunny." From all this, such persons derive the earthly pleasure which is all they can hope for, now or ever.

But for the believing Christian these are the two great feasts which embody the major tenets of our Faith: Christmas, the miraculous Birth of our Savior; Easter, the glorious proof of His power to redeem us! All Catholics *know* these facts because they have been taught them as facets of their belief. Whether they feel them in the depths of their soul, whether they perceive, even dimly, the wonder and joy of these mysteries, depends in large part upon how they have been taught to keep these feasts.

A Catholic couple starting their life together should plan to celebrate Christmas and Easter in a manner that will emphasize, for themselves and their children, the beautiful spiritual import of these holidays.

The celebration of Christmas properly begins with the season of Advent. Although the Church no longer requires the laity to observe this period with fast and abstinence, She does recommend that the faithful, of their own accord, practice some abstinence and self-denial at this time. This is an ideal preparation for the Great Gift of Christmas. As the holiday approaches, the Christmas story should be told and retold to the children, in the simplest terms when they are very young, in more detail when they are older. A beautiful Christmas Eve observance is to read together the story of the birth of Christ as told in the Gospels of St. Luke and St. Matthew. Children may be taken to Christmas Mass and for a visit to the Crib, even when very tiny. All who have made their First Communion should regard the reception of Holy Communion on Christmas Day as a most wonderful privilege.

Does this mean that all the dear old Christmas customs—the tree, the holly, Santa Claus, the stockings, the Christmas tree—are unworthy, and should be discarded? Of course not. All are charming, enjoyable, and harmless. Each has its place. Remember only: the heart of Christmas is the manger, not the tree. Santa Claus is really a remembrance of St. Nicholas, friend of children, Catholic bishop and saint.

Christmas gift-giving can be a happy way of teaching little ones many valuable lessons: the joy of giving, of sacrificing self to bring pleasure to another, of expressing love for parents, sisters, and brothers in a tangible way. Help them young to earn money for gifts or to make them, to ponder, plan and strive to please one another. Help them to understand that all of this is but a pale reflection of the greatest Gift: the Babe of Bethlehem.

Easter should be similarly God-centered. A proper observance of Lent and the great ceremonies of Holy Week are the preparation. Easter is the Resurrection, Jesus' triumph over death, the indisputable proof of His divinity and our redemption. ". . . to as many as received him he gave the power of becoming sons of God" (John 1:12). New clothes are fun, and one may even be said to wear them for the honor of God and His Son; the Easter Bunny is a charming and harmless whimsy; but both must be put in their proper perspective.

LENT

The most ignorant Catholic knows the purpose of Lent as a penitential season in preparation for Easter and knows, too, what the Church expects of him in the way of fasting and abstinence. The more thoughtful Catholic adds to this frequent attendance at church services: daily Mass, Stations of the Cross, rosary, and Benediction, as well as private acts of self-denial and charity. Our thoughts are more frequently centered on heaven and our daily life is not cluttered with social events.

THREADS IN THE PATTERN

A pattern of living does not just happen—or, if it does, it is haphazard. Someone in the family must devote thought and effort to making it smooth and handsome. One does so by the establishment of family habits that help make home life happy and united. Here are some suggestions one Catholic mother found helpful:

Dinner Time Is Family Time

In many homes, dinner is the only meal in which all can share. As the children grow up, it is sometimes the *only time* in which the whole family is together. Thus this meal can have a real influence in shaping family life.

First of all, let the dinner scene be attractive. As soon as children are old enough to sit at the table, insist that they wash their hands and face and comb their hair before dinner. (Make sure also, that *your* nose is powdered, and hair smooth!) Boys ten and over should be encouraged to wear a jacket to the table. It is a fine habit to acquire.

Set the table attractively. The ideal way is with a dinner cloth, flower centerpiece, sparkling glass and china. But this is not always possible. What *is* always possible, if you will take the mere seconds required to obtain it, is a table neatly set, with clean mats, place settings properly aligned, serving dishes arranged in some sort of pattern, and a centerpiece. A pot of ivy or a bowl of apples is not very original, but it is better than no centerpiece at all. A few seeds from a grapefruit, planted in a bowl, will grow into pretty green plants that make an attractive centerpiece.

Remember that a half-soiled damask cloth, crumpled dinner napkins, unpolished silverware and unmatched china are far less attractive than clean mats, fresh paper napkins, inexpensive matching pottery, and stainless steel flatware. "Tawdry elegance" is always to be avoided.

Young mothers of large families may moan at the thought of the extra effort involved in all this, but it is really not much trouble— indeed, it is largely a matter of habit—and the rewards are well worth it.

Never watch television during dinner. Watching at such a time is death to conversation, good manners, and family life. If your husband is a television addict or one of your children has a favorite program that falls in the dinner hour, talk to him privately and explain what you are trying to accomplish by banishing television at dinner.

As soon as children are old enough to sit up to the table comfortably, they should share in family dinner. High chair babies usually eat better and are happier if they are fed alone before the main meal. Certainly dinner is more peaceful that way. Not much in the way of table manners should be expected of children under four. As they grow older, their manners should steadily improve. (This is discussed at length under "Manners for Small Children" and "Manners for Teen-Agers.")

Begin the meal with all standing quietly behind their chairs while grace is said. Then the eldest boy should pull out his mother's chair for her. Brothers should be taught to pull out their sisters' chairs for them; sisters should be taught to expect this service and receive it gracefully.

The dinner table is not an ideal place to teach table manners—at least it does not make for a happy meal to sprinkle the conversation with interjections like "Jane! Sit up straight!" "Paul! Elbows off the table!" When children are still small enough to need these constant reminders, get them out of the way at the beginning of the meal by saying cheerfully, "Now, tonight we are all going to remember to sit up straight, keep elbows off the table, eat with our mouths closed, wipe our lips before drinking, and not interrupt the conversation!"

The meal begins with Father carving the roast, while Mother serves the vegetables. If your husband does not know how to carve, urge him to learn early in your married life and encourage him by your admiration of his skill. Teach the children to pass bread and condiments, offering them to others before they serve themselves. If there are six or more in your family, set the table with two bread trays and three sets of salt and pepper shakers to avoid excessive passing.

A few rules of conversation should be strictly enforced. Never permit your family to comment unfavorably about any food served. A child who dislikes certain foods should not be compelled to eat them. Neither should he be permitted to say "Ugh! Asparagus *again?* I hate it!"

Of course one may comment favorably. To say, "Gee Mom! I sure love your muffins!" or "May I have more of these *good* creamed potatoes?" is a compliment to the cook. But in general, frequent comments on the food should be avoided.

Teach your children not to interrupt when anyone else is speaking, particularly at the table. This can be done by allowing them an opportunity to speak freely in their turn.

Try to keep the subject matter of your conversation agreeable. Do not discuss your worries, problems, or quarrels. Such subjects should be talked about, for, as the old Irish proverb says, "Troubles shared are troubles halved," and home is the place where one should be able to talk openly and freely. But don't do so at dinner.

When your children are young, most of the conversation at dinner should be geared to their level. Let them discuss their interests and little triumphs. "Today in school we drawed bunnies and chickens." "Teacher wants me to learn a poem for Thanksgiving exercises." "Daddy, today I made a big tower and used *all* my blocks." This is good dinner table talk from young children.

Children can be helped to understand what is expected of them in the way of table talk by urging them to save a bit of their day's news to tell at dinner. If they have no news to share, suggest that they have a riddle, pun, or joke to tell, or even a new word whose meaning they have just learned. Mother and Father should have similar contributions to make. Children usually think their fathers are very witty men. Father can enhance this reputation by recalling the riddles and puns he enjoyed as a small boy and repeating them to his children.

Family plans make good table talk: next summer's vacation, a trip to the zoo, a picnic, a visit to Grandmother's. Children over ten can talk intelligently about sports events, television programs, books they are reading, a school science experiment.

When children are twelve or over, the range of topics for table talk is unlimited. Let them express themselves freely. Don't appear bored, angry, or shocked at anything they have to say. A child has profound respect for his parents' judgment—far more so than parents realize, or the child would admit. Don't squelch him by labeling his ideas as foolish, impractical, or confused. Don't offer your opinions as the last word on the subject. To do so can have three unfortunate results: it may give the child an abiding distrust of his own judgment; it may cause him to stop talking freely to you; it fails to teach him the give-and-take of polite discourse.

Weigh his ideas as if each were valuable. Agree and applaud when you can. Disagree calmly and reasonably, giving reasons and quoting authorities for your point of view. *Never* say, "When I was your age . . . !" Remember that a discussion is not an argument. When it degenerates into one, insist on dropping the conversation at that time. You may pursue it later if you feel it important to do so, but try always to keep your temper. The object of a discussion is to throw light on a subject. When, instead, heat is generated, you have an argument on your hands. Most important of all, never be afraid to say, "I don't know." This little sentence, perhaps more than any other you can utter, can impress your child with your honesty and sense of fair play. Followed by the suggestion, "Let's look it up," it can do much to enlarge your child's mind. And when you do express yourself with authority, he will be convinced that you do know what you are talking about.

When children are under the age of ten, it is unreasonable to expect them to remain at table until all have finished the meal. Some young children eat steadily and heartily and are eager to be off to play. Others prefer to dream and dawdle over their food. It is best to serve them their dessert when they have finished the main course. Then, when they have asked, "May I be excused, please?" let them leave the table when they are through. While lingering alone over dessert and coffee, Mother and Father can talk peacefully together.

By the time the youngest child is ten, another pattern should be established. Put the dessert and serving dishes on a side table. Let those who finish their main course first wait patiently until all are finished. Then let the children carry the dishes from the main course into the kitchen. (The table must be cleared some time; why not do it now and set the stage for a pretty dessert?) Then let Mother serve the dessert from her place at table. All must remain until it is finished and grace after the meal is said; the boys pull out the chairs for Mother and the girls; all leave the table together.

Good Habits

Hurry, confusion, nagging and whining are all foes to peaceful family life. The establishment of good habits does away with many of them. Determine the hour at which the family must rise to dress, eat a calm breakfast, and set out on their daily duties, and stick to it. Habit soon makes all easy and natural. The frantic scramble with which many families begin their day is not conducive to comfort or happiness, yet the cause for it is often merely the wish for an extra fifteen minutes' sleep. The simple remedy is a reasonable rising hour for all.

Bedtime habits are similarly important. Each child should have a set hour for going to bed, suitable to his years, and should be held to it firmly. This does away with whining and teasing for "just five more minutes." Allow half an hour, or whatever amount of time is required, for preparing for bed. This time is used in putting away toys and books, undressing, bathing, brushing hair and teeth, putting away one's day clothes, saying prayers. For school children, it should include laying out the clothes for the next day, including wraps, rubbers, etc., assembling school books and homework where they can be easily found (also anything else they must take to school, such as small sums of money for milk). All this puts a "period" to the day and prepares one for the night's sleep; it also avoids confusion in the morning.

Parents, too, should try to observe a reasonable retiring hour; the best preparation for a day's work is a good night's rest. What do we see on the "Late, Late Show" that is worth the sleep we sacrifice?

Families should have a regular time for children to do homework. In establishing this, the children themselves should be consulted and given their preference when possible. In some homes, all do their homework at the same time; in others, the children choose individual times. Once having determined how this problem should be solved, the children should be required to do their work at the time agreed upon without reminders from Mother or protests on their part.

Health authorities urge that children be sent to play outdoors after their day in school. They need to use their large muscles in running and jumping and the psychological release of noisy play. The hour just before or just after dinner is therefore a good time for homework.

Family Manners

Home is the place where one can be completely relaxed, natural and at ease. Pursuing this goal, some people feel that home is the place where one wears one's oldest clothes, says exactly what one pleases, does as one likes, and leaves one's manners outside the front door. If such behavior made for a happy and comfortable home, it might be allowable. Too often the result is exactly the reverse. A sloppily dressed person may feel comfortable, but he is a painful sight to see. To say exactly what one pleases is frequently to say what wounds, angers, or belittles. To do as one likes is often to do what others very much dislike. To be unmannerly is to forget the purpose of good manners: they are the lubricant which oils the wheels of daily living and makes it smooth and easy for all. A happy home is one in which each member is granted the right of:

PRIVACY. Husbands and wives, do not open one another's mail, listen to telephone conversations, pry into the contents of pockets, desk, or bureau. If there is some area of life in which you feel your partner is not being frank, ask about it openly and in a friendly manner. Accept any reasonable explanation as true. Trust each other as you wish to be trusted. Grant the same right of privacy to your children. If you are worried about a child's behavior and feel you need to know more about what he is doing, tell him so. Respect his confidences. Do not discuss his affairs outside the home or make them the subject of jokes.

COURTESY. The smallest child knows the difference between a request and a command, a harsh tone and a pleasant one, sympathy and indifference. Like little mirrors, they reflect what they observe. So, in large part, do their elders. Outside the home, few of us attempt to command or dominate. We do not belittle the actions and opinions of our associates. We attempt to appear interested even when bored. How few of us make the same effort at home with those who are dearest to us! Every member of a family should be free to tell the news of his day, confident that it will be heard with interest and sympathy; everyone should be able to express his opinions and know that they will get a respectful and unbiased hearing.

In ordinary intercourse, how helpful is courtesy! To say, "Edna, please hang up your sweater," is just as effective as *"How many times have I told you to hang up your sweater?"* and takes even less time! Reproof and corrections administered with patience and sympathy are twice as valuable as when done in anger. To say to a small child, "I'm sorry, I didn't hear you. What did you say?" reminds him, as no other method can, that it is impolite to say "What?"

LOYALTY. This is the keystone of the home. A wife should constantly hold up her husband before her children's eyes as the pattern of all that is good. She should remind them of all he sacrifices for them, all he does to give them protection and pleasure. Her accolade for any childish triumph should be "Wait until we tell Daddy! How pleased he will be!" A husband's success in business, sports, even in gardening and family repair jobs, should be a matter for admiration and rejoicing. Help your children to understand that everything their father does, he does for them. His only reward is their affection and appreciation.

Husbands, remember that your wife's sole reward for her hard-working days is the comfort and well-being of her family, and the words of praise that she so rarely hears. Let your unfailing courtesy and consideration for her set a constant example to your children. A wife who knows she is admired and treasured by spouse and children can bear hardship, toil, sorrow and privation. An honest compliment can be as warming as a mink coat!

Let your family present a united front to the world. Don't repeat to outsiders anything your husband tells you about his business affairs. And remember, "outsiders" includes your mother, sister, and very best friend! If you want your husband to talk freely about his business pursuits, let him discover that what he says to you will be kept an inviolable confidence.

Discuss your sex life only with a doctor or priest. To mention it to anyone else is an unpardonable betrayal of your life partner.

Don't discuss family problems with others. Don't criticize your husband, wife, or children to outsiders. Always present them in the very best light possible. Teach your children similar behavior. Explain to them that you are happy to talk things over freely with them at home, but if they repeat what they hear outside, they prove they are unworthy of your trust and it will be withdrawn. Don't repeat your children's confidences to others, no matter how amusing or touching they may be. To do so proves that *you* are untrustworthy.

If an outsider comes to you with a complaint about your child, hear his story fully and weigh it calmly. Do nothing about the matter until you have given your child a chance to tell his side of the story. Do not scold or punish him until you are sure that he was in the wrong. Uphold him and defend him whenever you can, so that he will learn that he can always depend upon getting fair treatment at home.

Teach your children to be loyal to each other: not to carry tales, to defend one another against outsiders, to rejoice wholeheartedly in the honors brothers or sisters may attain, to sympathize with troubles. Encourage the boys to cherish and protect their sisters and the girls to look up to their brothers as their champions. Teach the older children to help the younger and the little ones to obey and respect the older ones.

APPRECIATION. How different is our awareness of the emotional needs of our own dear selves and of the identical ones of others! If a little daughter says, "Oh Mom! All the girls just loved my new pinafore! When I told them you made it for me, they couldn't believe it," the little compliment repays Mother for all her efforts. When Dad says, "Honey, you typed up those reports for me beautifully! Where did you find the time to do them?" the simple remark puts a rainbow around Mother's day and fully repays her for her tedious job.

Our own gratification at a word of thanks or praise should remind us that everyone loves to be appreciated, yet this is a fact that we often forget in dealing with our family. We become so concerned with correcting our children's faults and urging them to better behavior that we often forget to recognize and compliment them upon an improvement. Yet a word of praise is often a more powerful spur to continued good behavior than a dozen scoldings. "See my good boy, picking up his toys!" is encouragement a four-year-old needs when trying to behave as you want him to. "Tommy, your table manners are improving wonderfully. I know you are trying hard to eat like a gentleman. We will have to go to the club for luncheon soon, as a little treat," will make Tommy try harder to eat nicely than would a dozen reproofs.

Between husband and wife, appreciation expressed in words and deeds is vital. Here a difference between the sexes appears. Women treasure words above deeds. A man who devotes his life to supporting and caring for his family feels that this is sufficient expression of his devotion to them. A wife craves to be told that she is admired and loved. In this she is sometimes unfair. She may take for granted her husband's effort to support his family in comfort, the fact that he is honorable, faithful and home-loving, and secretly pity herself because her spouse forgets anniversaries, fails to notice a new dress, or goes fishing with "the boys."

While she is pitying herself for her husband's lack of appreciation, she may be guilty of the same fault toward him: she is taking his good qualities for granted and failing to say the little word of gratitude which would warm his heart.

Wives should strive constantly to remain aware of the burdens a husband carries in the business world. If his job is a lowly one, it is probably monotonous and unrewarding, carrying with it no sense of worth or dignity, done only to earn the means to support his family. If his position is a prominent one, he is under constant tension, aware of the many employees whose jobs may depend on how well his is done —aware, too, of many brilliant and energetic men who are eager to oust him from his niche.

A man's home is his haven of rest—from the pressures of the outside world, from unreasonable demands, carping criticism and disparagement. If it is not this, it is nothing. It is to establish such a haven that a man marries and assumes the burdens of a head of a family. A wife should bear in mind that the husband's basic job—as breadwinner —is no trifle, and should show her gratitude for his faithful performance of it by making home a happy, peaceful place and by expressing her thanks for the comforts and conveniences bought through his efforts.

Set your husband a good example. Let him learn for himself how pleasant it is to be verbally appreciated. "That touch of gray in your hair looks *so* distinguished—and I'm so glad you're not getting bald." "I heard you discussing inflation with Mr. Hefferin last night—you expressed yourself so well." "Mrs. Dallas says we have the finest

garden on the block. I told her it was all your doing." "Ask Dad to
help you with your pitching, Brian. Dad was the star of our high
school team." These are a few of the million ways it is possible to say,
"I love you still; I am proud of you. I *appreciate* all you do for us." It
is so easy and so rewarding.

A wife needs similar assurances. Homemaking, satisfying though it
may be, is monotonous, repetitious, and lonely work. A man coming
home from the noise, pressures and conflict of his work day may crave
only solitude and understanding. A woman at the end of her toilsome
day may be frantic for conversation, stimulus, and change. The needs
of both should be recognized and met.

When Dad is worn out, he should be able to rest and relax, undis-
turbed. When he is not, he should endeavor to contribute to the conversation, listen with interest to family news, go out for an evening of
pleasure without undue protest. And if he can understand that the
remark will be remembered and treasured long after it is made, it is
not so hard to say, "Hilda, that shade of blue is lovely on you. It brings
out the color of your eyes." "Dear, haven't you lost some weight? That
dress fits beautifully." "Thanks for sending my suit to the cleaners.
What would I do without my girl!"

"I love you. I am proud of you. I appreciate you." This is what we
want our loved ones to feel about us. This, in one form or another,
is what we all need to hear.

Sharing Responsibilities

"It takes a heap o' livin' to make a house a home," said a minor
American writer. It also takes a lot of work on somebody's part.
Domestic help is almost a vanished race; the housewife who has the
services of a weekly cleaning woman considers herself lucky. Despite
our vaunted household appliances, the work load in a family with
several small children is a heavy one. The major responsibility is the
housewife's, of course, but she is entitled to help from every member
of the family, in proportion to their other duties. No husband should
be expected to devote all his leisure hours to helping at home. He is
entitled to rest and recreation. But the head of the house usually takes
it as a matter of course that he will do the yard work, take care of
cleaning walks, put up screens and storm windows, care for the family
car, and make minor repairs to the home and home equipment. A
thoughtful husband usually prefers to help with washing the dishes
so that his wife can have an evening of leisure, rather than to rest
while his wife does this job alone. Occasionally to care for the children

on a Saturday afternoon to give his wife some "time off" pays dividends in the form of a refreshed and grateful mate.

Most men loathe doing errands, and a wise wife does not burden her husband with them every time he leaves the house. Neither does she call him at the office every time a minor domestic crisis occurs.

Each child in a family should have regular, definite household duties which he performs as his share toward a happy home. Very small children usually love to "help Mommy." I have seen a little girl fifteen months old delighted to toddle from dining table to kitchen carrying a fork or cup, "helping" to clear the table. At this stage, any help the child can give is more bother than it is worth, but the mother who has the time and patience to encourage a child at this time will have her reward later in a child who is a real helper.

Some mothers feel that it demeans a boy to be expected to help in the house. The traditional work for boys—caring for the furnace, taking out ashes, shoveling walks, mowing lawns—has either vanished or been taken over by professionals. Should the boys, therefore, have no responsibilities while the girls continue to do their share of home tasks? Surely this is both unwise and unfair. Boys ten and older can dispose of garbage and waste, help to clean the family car, weed the flower beds, polish shoes, help in cleaning attic and cellar, sweep porches, wash windows, polish floors.

Even very small children can be taught to pick up their toys and clothes, hang up outer garments, empty wastebaskets, run small errands from room to room. ("Andy! Please bring me the dustcloth from the mop cupboard.")

All children over eight can be taught to keep their own room picked up, to clean the tub and tidy the bathroom after their bath, to put their outdoor clothing away where they can find it when next they need it. At this age they can, with supervision, both lay the dinner table and clear it. Add some attractive jobs to their work list: fixing a bouquet for the dinner table, making a gelatin dessert, cutting cookies, helping to pack the picnic lunch.

Much more can be expected of teen-agers, but care should be taken at this age not to impose, especially when the family is a large one. A fifteen-year-old girl should not be expected to be a full-time nurse to the new baby just because she is conscientious and capable and Mother is busy. Divide the jobs fairly, in proportion to age and other duties, and insist that each do his part. Praise heartily whenever you can; encourage the inept, punish the slacker. Help them to understand that their reward for their efforts is a clean and attractive home in which all have leisure to share together. For this is the reason for helping, so that the household tasks can be accomplished without exhausting Mother, with time to spare for shared fun. And Mother, when tasks pile up, remember this: better a dusty house filled with happy people, than a spotless one occupied by tiptoeing robots.

Family Fun

A genuine zest for daily living, which is the ability to extract pleasure from the simple things of life, is perhaps the most valuable attribute a homemaker can have. You want an orderly home and a healthy, well-fed family, of course, but don't be grim and tense about attaining them. Look for the means that lie all about you to add laughter and shared fun to family living.

"Surprises" are wonderful to children, and can consist of such little things. An eight-year-old trudges home from school in the autumn rain. He opens the door—and smells woodsmoke. Mother has a fire in the fireplace! Or there is an odor of warm butter. She's popping corn! A wonderful chocolatey smell—oh, JOY! She's making fudge! These are trifles, which take only a little time, but what a wonderful atmosphere they produce.

Mary comes home and finds a sheet strung up between foyer and living room. What's going on here? "We're going to make up a play," says Mother. "We're all going to be in it. We'll practice now, and after dinner, we'll do it for Daddy!" What fun! What an opportunity to stretch little minds, exercise the imagination, and laugh and play together.

Teen-agers like surprises too. At dinner, Mother says mysteriously to her sixteen-year-old, "Cindy, when you go to your room, look under your pillow." Cindy does, and finds the awful rock 'n roll record she has been longing for. Later she asks, "Mother, how did you happen to buy it for me?" Mother says, "Mothers aren't blind, dear. I've noticed how kind you have been to the little ones lately, how hard you are working in school, and how well you are controlling that flaming temper of yours. So I bought you the little present to say, 'Good Girl! Keep it up, I'm proud of you!'"

The minor holidays are a grand excuse to cheer up family life. A few table decorations or something seasonal in the menu make dinner a party for children. The great feasts—Christmas, Easter and Thanksgiving (birthdays, too, if you can manage it)—should call forth your handsomest tablecloth and dinner napkins, silver, china, and crystal, plus a centerpiece of fruit, flowers, and candles. Never mind if one of your "best" goblets is broken by an excited child: consider it a worthy sacrifice to your goal of happy family life.

Once a gay-hearted mother brought to the dinner table a dessert consisting of a magnificent cake, elaborately iced. The family eyed one another. "What day is it? Whose birthday? What anniversary?" They read the message on the icing, and were further mystified. "Happy Tuesday to All," it said.

"It isn't any special occasion," said Mother. "I was just happy to be *me,* and felt like celebrating. So I did."

Father likes surprises, too. How grand for a tense and worried man to come home to a fresh and smiling wife and a meal of all his favorite dishes. Dessert over, Mother nods to six-year-old Bobby, who runs out of the room and comes back, bursting with pride, bearing a large silver platter on which repose—two golf balls. Or two fine cigars. Or a paper-back copy of a good mystery story or *Seven Years in Tibet,* depending on Daddy's tastes. The prime requisites for these little surprises are that they are something you know will be received with pleasure, and are spontaneous, with no reason for them except to display affection and appreciation of one another.

If you will think for a moment about your happiest childhood memories, you will find that they usually concern family fun. A trip to Grandmother's, a picnic, a boating trip, breakfast on the patio— some pleasant break in the daily routine that the family shared. Build these memories for your children with such outings: a trip to the zoo, museum, library, or art gallery, to the river to see the boats, or even to the station to watch the trains. Let them share in your garden, teach them to skate, swim, or hunt. If you take pleasure in reading, sewing, music or art, try to pass it on to your children; it is the best gift you can make them. Reading aloud to a group is great fun, so are simple games. Some youngsters love to cook; others long to work in Dad's workshop. Teach, help, and share.

This applies to man and wife also; any interest that you can share draws you closer together. A wife who plays golf can listen intelligently when her husband tells her about the thrilling second shot he made on the fifteenth hole; a husband who knows something of music will rejoice when his pianist wife conquers the tricky arpeggio in the sonata she is studying.

IT'S NOT ALL "TOGETHERNESS"

In planning all these shared activities, it is well to remember that all the pleasure in life does not, and should not, spring solely from the things the family does together. Each member will and should have interests which are his alone. Mother and Father will have an adult social life in which the children do not take part. Don't expect to drag your children wherever you go; it is bad for them, it does not give you the change which you need, and it is unfair to your hostess. Never bring your children to any ceremonial entertaining, such as a wedding or anniversary party, unless they have been specifically invited, and do not feel hurt if they are not included. Such entertaining is not meant for children. This also applies to dinner invitations, patio parties, theater parties, etc. And of course children should never be included in cocktail parties or evening entertaining. Parents should also have an occasional vacation or weekend trip without their offspring, if it can be arranged.

Children, too, will have their own social life, according to their age, and parents should not obtrude on this unduly. Of course Mother should be present for school plays and entertainments, and the whole family should root for Dan when he plays Little League ball or makes the basketball team. Children are proud when their parents act as den mother, scout leader, sport coach or school party hostess. But it is unwise always to be the parent who does these things; your children should enter into some activities without the assurance which your presence gives them.

Never allow children of any age to entertain at home without an adult present; don't let them go to homes where it is permitted. All children need the restraint and the support which an adult presence imposes. To ask them to do without it burdens them with too much responsibility for their own actions and those of others. It is a responsibility which they do not have enough authority to manage successfully. To expect them to attempt it is asking for trouble. *Never* deviate from this rule.

Members of a family will have individual interests, too. John may adore reading; Ned may love to skate and ski; Father may be a weekend painter, Doris a jazz buff. Each may be indifferent to the other's favorite pastimes. This does not matter; an intelligent display of interest is all that is required. If you can interest your child in one activity which he can pursue happily *alone,* you will have done him an enormous favor.

COMMUNICATION

Extroverts are naturally communicative; it is no effort for them to confide in those they love. Introverts are born reserved; they tend to keep both joys and sorrows bottled up within them. Because these tendencies are inborn, it will always be true that some can share their life's experience with others through conversation easily, while some cannot. People concerned with learning what makes for a happy marriage—such as psychologists and marriage counselors—now lay stress upon the ability to communicate, regarding it as a vital part of married happiness.

The line of communication should be kept open between husbands and wives, parents and children. The ability to talk freely with a loved one contributes to the mental health of the speaker and strengthens the fabric of family life. Silent sulking, cherishing an unexplained grievance, refusing to quarrel, are practices by which the offender cuts himself off from others and leaves them no method of resolving the difficulty. At the same time he is admitting the weakness of his own position by refusing to defend his side of the argument or state his complaints.

Everyone who keeps his affairs to himself is not necessarily introverted; he may have discovered from experience that his confidences will not be received as he would like. Married couples should create a climate of family living that encourages shared confidences in the following ways:

a) Listen, really listen, when talked to; try to understand the emotions behind the words; and strive to enter completely into the shared experience. An ideal confidant must never be bored by what he hears. One must listen with *sympathy*. This is not easy. A five-year-old telling what he saw on Miss Millie's Kiddy Hour will scarcely make an absorbing story of it. But he should be heard with a display of interest. It helps if one remembers that by listening sympathetically one is helping him to verbalize his experiences and teaching him that Mother and Daddy will always share his world. When children get into their teens, Mother is thrilled to hear "what happened at the Prom," and Dad loves to hear an account of what Bob did in the big game. They will not be told, unless they have previously listened for hours and hours, with sympathy and attention, to long stories of why Eunice broke up with Phil, and big doings at Cub Scout meeting.

b) Believe what you hear. This is particularly necessary in dealing with children. Children are capable of profound emotional reactions before they have a vocabulary adequate to express them. Remember that what they say about anything, meager though it may be, represents how that happening affected them. They should be heard with attention and sympathy. Be very careful about accusing a small child of an untruth. If you catch him in a downright lie, try to determine what caused him to lie. It may not be mere fear of the consequences; sometimes he does not see the incident as you do; sometimes he is striving for another good, such as the protection of a friend by a lie.

c) Respect the confidences of your marriage partner and your children. Do not share them with *anyone*. This has been mentioned before, but bears repeating. This applies particularly to a man's business experiences. If you want to hear about your husband's triumphs, failures, worries, and fears in the world of commerce, you must show him that you hold his confidences inviolate. It also holds true for the confidences your children offer you.

d) Respect the opinions of others. Discuss them calmly, as if all were valuable. Differ courteously, without heat. Praise and approve whenever you can.

e) Don't worry in silence. If you have a problem, either in or out of the home, confide in your spouse. Looking at the problem from another's point of view may help you to find a solution. Even if it does not, merely talking it over will relieve your mind and help your mate to share your inner feelings.

f) Don't hoard confessions of failure, wrong-doing or omission to hurl at the offender when you are angry. This is the quickest way to lose your family's confidence.

g) Don't let your account of the day's happenings turn into a continual dreary recital of the small annoyances we each must meet. Sharing one's experiences means sharing all—the pleasant as well as the unpleasant. If you had a flat tire or got caught in a subway tie-up, you want to tell about it. Well and good, but don't turn it into a tragedy. And did nothing pleasant happen on this day—lunch with a friend, a funny story, a big order sold? "What happened today" depends, to a surprising extent, upon one's point of view. If the dryer broke down, Tommy tore the slide fastener from his new snowsuit, and the cake fell, a harassed housewife feels like crying a bit on her husband's shoulder. But if, on the same day she got an interesting letter from Cousin Jane and found two daffodils blooming in the garden, these incidents are worth mentioning, too, and may lead to a peaceful discussion of Cousin Jane's affairs or summer garden plans.

THE WORKING WIFE

Much of the previous discussion of the home life of Catholics has been based on the assumption that the wife will be a full-time housewife. But thousands of wives work outside the home. Many are the sole support of their famlies, many others make a financial contribution to income that is vital to family welfare. Some work because doing so makes them happier, better-adjusted persons.

To work or not to work is a personal decision, depending upon one's own circumstances and preferences. Where the mother is the family's sole support, she has little choice. She must work that her family may live, and, whether she likes it or not, she must struggle with the double job of breadwinner and homemaker. In other cases, marriage experts generally agree that in homes with children of preschool age or even older, it is better in most cases if the mother does not work outside the home. Mother may be working to help buy a home, a car, a summer camp, a boat, or some other advantage for the whole family. To do so she must carry an extra-heavy work load, and Father and the older children must take over some of her family responsibilities, thus increasing their work load. Regardless of how conscientious she may be, she cannot find the time to give her children the attention and careful supervision that she could if she were home all day. And she must expend so much physical and nervous energy in coping with her two jobs that only a woman with superb health should attempt it.

Before deciding that it is to the best interests of all to work outside the home, a mother should carefully analyze exactly how much she is adding to the family income: she must spend money that otherwise would not be spent for working clothes, luncheons, transportation, and personal grooming. To replace her services in the home, or to supplement them, she may need to purchase added household equipment, laundry service, expensive precooked foods, or the services of cleaning woman and nursery school. Add to this the increased amount of income tax the family must pay and one often ends up with the family income very little augmented by the mother's efforts. If she attempts to work without the assistances just referred to, she will be working too hard and attempting too much. Most important of all, working outside does cut down on one's time with one's children—particularly the lazy, intimate, apparently unimportant hours when one does not appear to be doing anything vital but during which one is forging the ties of confidence and understanding that are so valuable.

To work or not to work is a decision that one rightfully makes for oneself. A Catholic mother, in making it, must remember: one's children are priceless immortal souls, entrusted to one's care by God, to Whom one must one day render an accounting as to how one fulfilled that trust. In rendering that final accounting, it will weigh little to point to the home, car, camp, educational advantages or other worldly blessings one obtained for those children by working if in so doing one has left them to blunder, unprotected, down the road to ruin.

Many young couples today begin their married life with the wife planning to work until the first baby arrives. This is much easier to do than to work after there are children, but even at this time there is much to be said for a young wife using the early months of married life learning to be a wife, a housewife, and half of a married pair. If she does work, the husband must remember that she is carrying two jobs, one of them new to her, and should make a special effort to help with the shopping and household tasks.

Such a young couple should not set up their household budget on the sum of their combined earnings. If they do, they will find themselves in financial difficulties when the first baby arrives: the family income will be greatly reduced just as their expenses are increasing. They should set up a budget in which all ordinary expenses—rent, car upkeep, heat, light, telephone, food, clothing, insurance and charity—are geared solely to the husband's income. The wife's earning may be used to pay for the furnishings of the home (not a permanent expense), substantial savings, part of their taxes, entertainment, and miscellaneous expenses, such as presents. She should pay her own business expenses: extra clothing, grooming, transportation, luncheons, etc. They should save the greater portion of her earnings. When she can no longer work, her contribution will not be seriously missed and they will have savings to meet the extra expense of the new life.

READING MATERIALS

The reading matter that is available in your home is very important in the development of reading habits on the part of your children. The most glaring mistake in many American homes is the failure to furnish any reading materials, good or bad. Gordon Dupee, in an article in the *Saturday Review* of June 2, 1956, reports that twenty-five per cent of college graduates queried say that they have not read one book the past year! Only seventeen per cent of adults, at any time, are reading a book; only twelve per cent of the houses being constructed will have built-in book cases; forty-two per cent of American homes have no bookcases at all; only thirteen per cent of Americans borrow books from libraries; according to the judgment of librarians, only five per cent of these are good reading, seven per cent are of fair quality and eighty-eight per cent are of poor quality.

These last figures are open to question on two counts: few librarians pay attention to the books that are drawn. Assuming that they do pay attention, the quality of the book is only a matter of their personal judgment. And why are so many books of poor quality in our libraries? One thing is sure, poor though they may be, they are at least not pornographic or absolute trash. But Mr. Dupee rightly says, "We are asking the next generation to exhibit a virtue of mind which we ourselves have debased through indifference and disuse."

Worse, perhaps, than no reading matter at all is the presence in your home of the very cheapest quality magazines and books—those devoted to crime, violence, lurid and immoral romance, photographic "art studies," etc. Like certain medicine bottles, these should bear large labels reading "POISON!" for that is what they are: a poison as subtle, deadly, and habit-forming as narcotics.

Those addicted to such material sometimes defend their choice by saying it is "relaxing" or "easy to read" and of course they maintain that they are not personally affected by it. Granting the truth of this assertion, doubtful though it is, no thoughtful person would argue that the unformed minds and strong passions of youth will be unaffected. Any individual, parent or not, who makes such matter available to young people is contributing to their corruption.

Any parent who has been in the habit of reading such trash should make a strong effort to reject it and to improve his reading habits, at least to the point of reading the large circulation magazines intended for the whole family. They are relatively harmless.

The Catholic press has improved enormously in the last thirty years. Today most of the material it produces can be read with interest and pleasure by anyone. Every Catholic home should contain the diocesan newspaper. In it you will find extended accounts of Catholic news—the activities of the Vatican and Curia, missionary work, episcopal pronouncements, popular features by Catholic writers, local happenings in your diocese and parishes, etc. Many families would enjoy some of the following Catholic magazines:

America: Erudite magazine of opinion. Readers will not always agree with views expressed, but will never fail to find them stimulating.

The Catholic Digest: Condensed reprints from Catholic and secular magazines.

Columbia: The official magazine of the Knights of Columbus.

The Commonweal: By and for the literate Catholic layman.

The Critic: A Catholic review of books and the arts.

Friar: Profound and witty, in the Franciscan tradition.

Information: News and factual articles, sprightly and easy-to-read.

Jubilee: A fine Catholic picture magazine.

Marriage: Short, readable articles on marrying and marriage.

The Sign: Fiction, factual articles, book and television reviews.

Every Catholic home should contain:

A Bible. Not a showy, expensive one, but one that can be handled and used, with print large enough to be read by old and young.

A catechism, for quick reference on matters of faith.

A dictionary, modern and complete.

A reference work. Preferably a set of good encyclopedia, but if this is too expensive, the *World Almanac* is often helpful. This is issued annually and costs less than two dollars.

An up-to-date atlas. This can settle arguments and help to give children a sense of the size and variety of the world.

PRAYERS

A Prayer for Home and Family

O eternal Spirit of Love, Bond of unity in the Holy Trinity, preserve love, unity and peace in our home. Make of it a faithful reproduction of the Holy House of Nazareth, upon which Thou didst look with such kindness. Bind us all together, not merely by worldly ties, but by the golden bonds of charity, prayer, and mutual service. By the gift of piety, help us to forgive and forget the little grievances which the events of life and diversity of character may foster among us. Whatsoever duty may call us, let us never bring dishonor upon our home and family. Ward off from our home the spirit of pride, irreligion and worldliness. Allow not the lax principles and perverse maxims of the world to take root among us. Teach us to love and respect that Christian modesty which reigned supreme in the Holy Family. As by Thy help we live in unity here below, give us, we

beseech Thee, the grace of final perseverance, that
together we may praise Thee and love Thee through a
happy eternity. Amen.

Consecration of the Family to the Sacred Heart of Jesus

We consecrate to thee, O Jesus of love,

The trials and joys, the sorrows and happiness of our
family life.

We beseech Thee to pour out Thy best blessings on all
its members, absent or present, living or dead.

And when one after another we shall have fallen asleep
in Thy blessed bosom,

O Jesus, may all of us in Paradise find again our family
united in Thy Sacred Heart. Amen.

20

Guidance and Manners for Children

Train a boy up in the way he should go; even when he is
old he will not swerve from it (Proverbs 22:6).

AUTHORITY

Parents are responsible to God for the welfare of the souls of all
children born to them, and will one day be called to give an account of
their stewardship before the Throne of Judgment. This responsibility
endows them with the authority to teach, guide, counsel, advise, and
command their children so that their offspring may earn Heaven by
leading Christian lives. The Fourth Commandment enjoins children
to obey their parents in all things until they reach maturity and assume
responsibility for their own actions, and to reverence and cherish their
parents as long as they live.

This divinely ordained authority does not permit parents to be
irresponsible tyrants; rather it requires them to exercise their powers
with all the love, wisdom, and justice which their individual capabili-
ties permit.

IT TAKES TWO

Parental responsibility and authority is bestowed equally on both
parents. In exercising it, they should strive constantly to act as one.
Before the birth of their first child, it is good for a couple to have long
thoughtful talks to learn one another's views on childrearing, to find
out where they differ and where they agree, and to study the opinions
of experts to make sure their methods will be sound. Such discussions
will not prepare them for all the problems that will arise later, but it
will make them aware of each other's attitudes and help them to find a

common ground from which to work. They should then agree to present a united front to their children; that is, when either parent has taken a position on some matter, the other parent should uphold him *in the child's presence,* even though he may not actually agree with the stand taken. This is for the good of the child. He regards his parents as the fount of all wisdom and justice; to see them disagree frightens and confuses him and makes him insecure. Better to be wrong together in one single matter than to argue over it in his presence. The disagreeing parent should certainly discuss the matter with his mate later, in private, so that they may not so err again, but the vital consideration is to appear united. If parents frequently differ in the child's presence, he will learn, all too quickly, that he can elude the authority of one by appealing to the other.

Parents should determine their mutual position and take a united stand on all matters of discipline, permissiveness, health habits, and manners. Often, in seeking mutual ground, a couple discovers that the father leans toward strictness, the mother toward permissiveness, although of course this is not always so. A father may say, "My Dad was always quick to use the strap on me. Kids shouldn't be coddled." A mother may find her energy drained and her nerves frazzled by the demands her children make upon her and may be over-permissive through sheer fatigue. These are natural attitudes, but not wise. Does the young father who was frequently whipped consider himself so perfect a person that the methods used in his up-bringing should not be questioned? And the too-permissive young mother will quickly learn that over-permissiveness does not solve her problems, rather it increases them. So the young pair should seek for a reasonable middle ground.

Decisions about child-rearing should be given to the child as the combined opinions of both parents. "Your father and I have decided"; "Your mother and I have agreed" is the way to begin talking to children about these matters as soon as the child can understand you.

Children need the weight of the parental opinions of both parents. A boy more than eight years old who says to his friends "My mother won't let me do so-and-so" will be jeered at by his companions. But "My Dad won't let me" is an honorable excuse which will be acceptable to the group.

Because Mother spends more time with the children than Father, her authority will be more frequently exercised. Most decisions about young children must be made at once, as the occasion arises. The deferring of punishment is particularly unfortunate. It is hard for a child to have something unpleasant hanging over his head; and in the case of a very young child, if the punishment does not immediately follow the misdeed, he will not understand that the misdeed brought on the punishment. Many young wives, seeking to bolster their authority and to bring Daddy into the picture, will say "Wait until Daddy comes home. He will punish you for that." This is wrong. Father should not be made the ogre, the punishment-dispenser. He may take over the job when he is on the scene when the misdeed occurs; decisions may be made subject to his approval; but he should not be the Lord High Executioner.

Children never really resent firm but gentle guidance. A child reared to know what he may or may not do, what is expected of him, and what is forbidden, is secure and at ease in his little world. The limits set to his behavior are like the sheltering walls of a house, that protect him from the dangers of the world outside. He will, by his behavior, constantly test these limits, as much to make sure that they are still there as to attempt to enlarge them. The child of too-permissive parents, who do not exert their authority, will frequently misbehave recklessly in an unconscious but desperate attempt to force them to define the lengths beyond which he may not go.

BEGIN WITH LOVE

George Sokolsky, the columnist, once made this profound observation: "Wealth, of course, is only for adults. Children do not wear diamonds or minks; they crave to be clothed in love. When love is absent, the child lives in fear and hopelessness."

Love, then, is the vital ingredient in child-rearing. A child can actually die of lovelessness, as he would smother from lack of air or starve from want of food. Love is not riches, nor comfort, nor indulgence, nor overprotectiveness. Love is the power to comprehend the fact that each child born into this world is an immortal soul, unique, individual, to grant him the right to be himself, and to cherish and value him for *what he is.*

Love expresses itself in wise and tender physical care, in patience, understanding, interest, guidance, and discipline. It flowers in hours and confidences happily shared, in mutual loyalty, dependence and trust. Love is demonstrated by caresses and words of affection and praise, and all this is good, and good for a child. But one must be sincere. Let the caress spring naturally from your feeling of love; let the praise be truly earned.

Acceptance is the most perfect expression of love. Love your child, not for his beauty or brains or resemblance to you or your husband or for his ability to fulfill your ambitions for him, but completely and wholly for what he is. A small child, hurt and bewildered over a school discipline which he did not comprehend, said to the writer, "Mother, when you do the best you can, why isn't it good enough?" This is a profound question, embodying one of life's deepest tragedies. In school, in sports, in one's life work, it is only too true that one's best is frequently not good enough to meet the world's standards for these activities. Teachers, coaches, or employers may set goals that are too high for us. If we can honestly tell ourselves that our failure was due to laziness, boredom, or inattention, the failure is bearable. But if we *know* that we were doing our very best and still failed, we can only conclude that we cannot measure up to certain standards that others seem to reach easily. The resulting psychic wound is deep and hard to bear. For young children, it is almost intolerable.

Educators, employers, and their supervisory personnel should therefore try to find out whether an individual is failing to measure up because of momentary inattention, home problems, plain "goofing off," or actual incapacity. Otherwise their conclusions may be very unfair.

Parents' obligations in this field are even greater. One must study one's child from infancy, trying to learn his native capacity, natural bent, work habits, attention span, study skills, etc., and one should strive to judge all these things objectively. Once one has done so, one has a fair idea as to what one's child is capable of, and when he is doing his best. In the home circle, a child's best should *always* be good enough to satisfy his parents, even when he is failing by outside standards, and he should often be assured that this is so.

LOVE AND HATE

One of the problems a parent must solve is how to teach a child to understand and accept his own feeling about himself, the world, and the people in it. This question has great scope. In the list of books at the end of this chapter are several that will help you with this problem. It is too extensive to cover here, but one phase is so vital it must be touched on.

The Church says that a child who has not reached the age of reason cannot sin, since he is incapable of distinguishing right from wrong. The age of reason for normal children is considered to be about seven years, but for some it may be a little older. Until that age, therefore, he is not personally responsible for his thoughts, feelings or deeds.

Keep this firmly in mind. Never tell a very young child that anything he has said or done is "a sin." That is not true, and to use such a statement as a method of discipline will result in setting up guilt feelings which the child is too young to handle.

Almost from the instant of birth, a baby is aware that he is totally helpless. For comfort, food, health, and happiness, he must depend on you; hence you are everything to him. A baby cannot distinguish between temporary absence and total abandonment and proves it by wailing miserably when Mother first leaves him for a little while with someone else. The possibility of being bereft of his caretakers is a child's first great fear. Because of his need of you, a child loves you—and hates you, for he senses that you have the power to do him irreparable injury.

A small child wants what he wants when he wants it, which is right now, immediately, at once! He has no sense of time save the present. He cannot understand that it takes time to warm a bottle before feeding him. When food is not forthcoming the instant that he wails for it, it is *you* who are withholding it, as well as you who finally satisfies him.

Thus he learns early of your power to withhold some good from him. As he grows older, he develops a time sense and gradually learns to put up with a delay in satisfying his needs. Now another problem arises. He craves total approval from you. He also wants to do as he likes, and only as he likes. He discovers that some of the things he wants to do you will prevent him from doing by physical restraint, by punishment, or by withholding your approval. He wants his own way; he wants your approval. Sometimes he cannot have both. Result: a frustrated baby, full of love and hate feelings for you.

These ambivalent feelings of child toward parent never cease. The power of a parent is absolute. It is too frequently his duty to curb, restrain, or withhold some fancied good from his offspring. The child needs parental approval too intensely, even when, as an adult, he is beyond the power of the parent to control, save by disapproval. Understand, and try to accept calmly, the fact that your child will often feel anger, resentment, even hate, for you.

How does one handle this problem? Not by trying slavishly to satisfy his every whim the instant it is expressed. This is impossible and not even desirable. A child so reared is sent maimed and unprepared into a world that will constantly curb, restrain, disappoint, and frustrate him.

There are two things that one can do. As early as you can, by whatever means seem wise to you, teach your child that your love for him is permanent, unchanging, and can be relied upon as long as you live. Help him to understand that you can disapprove of what he does, and even punish him for doing it, while yet approving of him. Let him know that you love the whole child—his frailties and his weaknesses, as well as his good qualities, and that this whole, complete love will cause you to stand by him and help him through any troubles he may encounter. Help him and sustain him, and punish him too, if punishment is required, once the trouble has been resolved. But before you will punish, you will help—always.

A child convinced that his parents love him and will always love him, despite his faults, is able to like himself and accept himself: the vital ingredient for a fruitful, well-adjusted life. Self-distrust and self-hatred are almost always engendered by parental disapproval, real or fancied. They can make life a torment. Assurance of permanent parental love and acceptance also helps a child to understand and endure discipline and punishment, and to adjust to his native frailties and frequent failure.

The second thing that one can do is to help the child find acceptable ways of expressing and relieving his "bad" emotions. A baby quickly learns that it is "bad" to hate his dear, good, *powerful* mother. This knowledge creates two new emotions: fear, lest his wicked feelings permanently alienate her; guilt, that he can so feel toward the giver of all good. These are violent emotions, and Baby needs help in handling them. Fear and guilt can be avoided if you teach the child that he is not an unnatural person if he occasionally hates his best-beloved, and that everyone sometimes feels so. Allow him some physical means of relieving his feelings. Any attempt at complete suppression of such intense emotion is bad for the child—or for anyone. An acceptable release must be found. Let an angry baby cry—cry hard—for a while. It is an outlet. After a bit, soothe him, pet him, sympathize with him. "Poor Baby, I know you feel bad. The stove is so pretty and shiny. But it is *hot;* Baby must not touch, it will burn him. Now let's look at the bunny book." Baby has had his cry out; Mother still loves him; he feels better. But Mother has still not given in about letting him touch the stove.

As babies grow older they are frustrated by material objects and by their inability to cope with the world physically. Chairs and beds are too high, lovely things are tucked away on shelves they cannot reach, the door will *not* open, the block tower *will* fall over. The result is frustration and anger. Be sympathetic; do not laugh. Let him grumble or cry a bit, then find release in physical action. "Let's turn somersaults." "Let me see how quickly you can run to the lilac bush and back." "Let's play ball." Any strenuous physical action helps.

Some mothers give their children a kind of whipping boy on which to vent their feelings. One mother had a soft old rag doll. When her four-year-old was angry or frustrated, she would say, "Quick! Where's the bad old doll?" Then she would hold up the unoffending object and say, "Slap it! Slap it hard!" Sometimes she would make grotesque faces and imitate the attitudes of the pommelled toy. Thus her boy learned that people do get angry; indeed they cannot help it, but that there are ways of relieving anger that are socially acceptable and others that are not. Taking it out on the rag doll was an acceptable way.

It must be noted that to suppress, ignore, or deny the existence of the feeling of anger is most unwise. "Control yourself! Stop that crying instantly, or I will give you something to cry for!" is bad advice. A few tears of rage are often a blessed relief.

The first time a baby has a temper tantrum is merely an extra-violent reaction to some frustration that has deeply wounded him. He is seeking relief in the only way he knows of. His reaction may be so intense that his mother is frightened or startled into giving him his way. So Baby discovers a wonderful new method to control adults: a temper tantrum will do it. Once such a pattern has been set, the parent has only one recourse. The screaming baby must be totally ignored. He must cry it out, painful as it may be for all concerned. He must *not* get his own way. Whining and sulking are similarly treated. Do not give in on the point at issue, but divert the child's attention to something else as soon as he is ready to listen to you.

When a child is about seven, he will be preparing to receive the sacrament of penance and will learn about sin. He will realize that some wrongdoing is wrong not merely because it offends humans, but because it offends God. In discussing the sin of anger, the point might be made that it is beyond the power of human beings never to feel anger. Our human nature is such that injury to or frustration of our beloved self *will* cause us to *feel* angry. This is not the sin of anger, although we should nevertheless try to control ourselves and not get into a rage over a small injury or fancied slight. The sin of anger, says the Baltimore Catechism, is "the inordinate seeking of revenge, or an unreasonable opposition to a person or thing." The sin is in the way we seek to relieve our anger—quarreling, slapping, damaging another's property, person or reputation, etc. Make this clear to your child, so that he will not be unduly disturbed over the simple fact of having felt angry.

Encourage older children too, to relieve anger feelings by hard exercise: punching a bag, racing around the block, skipping rope, etc. It all helps. One mother sets her children an amusing example of how to relieve frustration. If she goes into the back yard with a small rug and an old-fashioned carpet beater and commences to pound the rug violently, the children will giggle and say, "Oh-oh! Run for the hills! Mommy's beating rugs again!" When she returns to the house, they will inquire innocently, "Feeling better, Mommy?" The answer from Mommy is a sheepish smile, and a brisk, "Lucky for you that I am; there was a storm brewing!"

Help your children to understand their ambivalent feelings for you and others without feeling guilty; help them to live with anger and frustration by talking it out, working it off, learning to accept it.

A child's need for complete acceptance should impel a parent never to compare one child unfavorably with another, never to set unrealistic goals for him, never to expect him to be a carbon copy of oneself, or to swerve him from his natural bent. A father who shone at athletics should not be disappointed if his son is indifferent to them; a mother whose social life was a series of triumphs should not urge her daughter to repeat them. A marigold plant cannot produce violets and should not be expected to. But one can so nurture, feed, and tend one's marigold plant that it can produce fine healthy marigolds. Do the same with your child; raise him in a climate of love and understanding to do and be "the best he can."

THE POWER OF EXAMPLE

A child born to two highly intelligent and exquisitely civilized parents comes into this world quite as ignorant of what is expected of him as does the offspring of African pygmies. All that we mean by Christianity and Western culture, all that his forbears, through thousands of years of trial and struggle, have learned to recognize as good or evil, he must learn for himself. Such of this as he masters in later life will rest, firmly or shakily, upon the foundation of what he has absorbed during his first six years on earth. During that time he acquires an ineradicable impression of what the world is like and of his place in it. He learns habits, attitudes, emotional responses, values. Even his physical development is conditioned by what he sees about him at this time. His gait, tone of voice, speech habits, gestures, and manners will be patterned upon those of his family.

The powers of observation of a small child are awesome. He cannot be fooled. Long before he understands what you say, he knows very well what you mean from your tone of voice, expression, gestures —even from your touch. Every waking hour, a child is unconsciously observing and imitating his parents' actions and reactions. For the child, they constitute perfect behavior, for they are the only example constantly before him. This begins long before he can understand what is said and continues long afterward. *What you do will always have more weight than what you say.*

This brings us to the inescapable conclusion that a well-mannered child is the product of a home in which courtesy is practiced naturally, habitually, unconsciously. No rules of behavior, talks on good conduct, or just plain nagging will ever convince a child that the behavior you recommend is superior to that which you practice. It therefore is good for new parents to take a long hard look at their daily habits, manners, and attitudes, to make sure that they are such as they will want their child to emulate. A boy whose father is unfailingly courteous and considerate of his wife knows instinctively that women are to be cared for and protected; his daughter understands that father and brothers are her champions. A husband who is habitually rude, sarcastic, and contemptuous of his wife's opinions should not be surprised to learn that his son bullies his little sister.

The writer knows a two-year-old girl who has a vocabulary of about twelve words. These include "Please" and "Thank-you." This did not happen by accident. Long before Janie could talk, her mother was saying to her, "*Please* come here, darling. Please pick up your blocks. Please give me a kiss." Every time the baby held out a toy for her inspection, the mother took it and said, "Thank you." As a result, the two-year-old now says, "Cookie, *please*, Mommy?" When she gets it, she smiles broadly and says "Thank you!" This is the only really effective way to teach acceptable behavior.

If you accidentally knock over a small child's blocks, bump against him, or interrupt when he is speaking, say, "Excuse me," just as you would to an adult. If you pull his hair or scratch his cheek while dressing him, say, "Oh, I'm sorry! Did I hurt you?" Do this faithfully, and you will soon get the same response from the child in similar situations.

PREPARE THE WAY

You will increase your child's natural poise and lessen his doubts in an unfamiliar situation if you prepare him for it in advance by telling him, as well as you can, what to expect. Thus a child going to his first children's party should be told that you are going to make a visit to help Tommy celebrate his birthday. You are going to Tommy's house; you are wearing your best clothes and bringing him a present to honor his day. There will be other children there to play with. One must greet Tommy's mother nicely, wish Tommy "Happy Birthday," and greet the other children. Food will be served and one must remember to eat neatly.

A child should be thus prepared for a visit to the doctor, dentist, or hospital, for a ride on a bus, a trip to the city, a picnic, a restaurant meal, or even a call on friends. Children are eager to please. If they know what is expected of them, they will try to live up to your expectations.

PLAY LESSONS

A child four years old or over can learn a good deal about how to behave in unfamiliar situations by acting them out. Children have vivid imaginations; to act usually comes as naturally to them as breathing. All of the occasions discussed in the previous paragraph can be acted out, with mother playing first one role, then another, and the child doing the same thing. This makes the whole matter more real and vivid to them than just hearing you tell about it. Thus in "acting out" a bus ride, the child can play himself, Mommy, the passengers, the bus driver and even the bus, and he will love it.

Despite this preparation for an unfamiliar situation, a child will never be wholly prepared for it and will certainly not view it with your eyes, as the following charming true story will illustrate: Four-year-old Melissa, who did not usually go to Mass, was taken there by her mother one summer Sunday, after having been told that they were going to make a visit to God's house, that there would be many other people there, and that she must be quiet and not disturb others. She behaved very well. When she returned home, her father said, "Well, Melissa, did you and Mommy go to God's house?"

"Yes we did, Daddy," said the youngster seriously. "But, you know, I don't think He was home. I heard His doorbell ringing, but nobody answered!"

GOALS

Teaching a small child courteous behavior requires patience and realism on the parent's part. Do not expect too much too soon. Allow for the effect of tension, fear, excitement, illness, embarassment, shyness, over-stimulation, and fatigue. Do not expect a steady rate of progress; there are bound to be lapses and retrogessions. The arrival of a new baby in the home, for instance, may cause the older child to lapse into babyish behavior. This is a bid for attention and reassurance. It is natural, and should be responded to with an increased display of affection from you.

Under three, little or nothing should be expected of a child in the way of manners. A three-year-old can be expected to say "Please," "Thank-you," and "Excuse me" when the occasion requires. He should go to bed willingly and should feed himself. How he feeds himself is not yet important. Most children are toilet-trained, at least in the day-time, at this age. He should know that one washes one's hands before meals, but will need help in doing so. He should be encouraged to pick up his toys when playtime is over, but will seldom do so without help.

Between five and seven, a child should learn to greet people grace-fully, saying, "How-do-you-do, Mrs. Smith?" and offering his hand. Please do not let your children say, "Hi!" as a greeting. This has become all too common in all walks of life, even among adults. It is dreadful; there is no excuse for this lapse into crude speech.

A five-year-old boy should, theoretically at least, have learned to touch or tip his cap when greeting people. Today we have a problem here. Most small boys go hatless, or wear a head covering that fastens beneath the chin, such as a snowsuit cap, which cannot be tipped. They should, however, be taught to tip their caps whenever they can be easily removed, and also to take off *any* head covering as soon as they enter a room.

For generations, five-year-old girls have been taught to make a little bobbing curtsey when offering their hand, particularly to ladies. Many modern parents no longer approve of this, condemning it as artificial and unnatural. But is naturalness always to be the criterion? One shudders to think of the deterioration in adult behavior that would occur if we insisted on always behaving naturally!

Five-year-olds should rise when guests enter a room, and should not interrupt when adults are speaking. They should be allowed an opportunity to take some part in the conversation and should not be expected to sit quietly for very long; rather they should be excused to play elsewhere.

They should say, "No, Grandmother" or "Yes sir" or "Yes, Mrs. Smith" when answering a question. If they are attending kindergarten they will learn this quickly from hearing older children say, "Yes, Sister," "No, Father." They also learn to take off, put on, and hang up their outer clothing, to go to the lavatory unattended, and to wash their hands before meals.

A child this age should know that a closed door means that the person behind it wishes privacy. He should knock and wait to be invited in before he opens a closed door. Remember to do the same thing yourself, when his door is closed.

Eight-year-olds can dress and undress themselves, and, with occasional supervision, take their own baths. They should be urged to keep nails clean and hair brushed, pick up after themselves, have regular hours for study and play. They should be learning to be tolerant and kind to younger children.

A child this age should be able to answer the door. To strangers at the door he says, "Please wait here. I will get my mother." To friends he says, "Please come in." He then ushers them into the living room, offers them a chair, and says, "Excuse me. I will tell Mother you are here."

An eight-year-old boy allows adults and girl children to precede him through a door and holds it open for them. But he will not do this if you continue the habit, so natural when he was younger, of shooing him through a door ahead of you.

At eight, a child should be able to take leave gracefully, saying "Please excuse me" if he leaves a room. When leaving a gathering he should say, "I must go home now, Mrs. Smith. Thank you for inviting me to the party. I had a fine time." He should offer his hand in greeting automatically.

At ten, the manners expected of a child do not differ greatly from what is expected of younger children, but the things the younger ones are struggling to learn he should have mastered. A ten-year-old boy helps adults and young children to put on and remove their wraps. He offers his chair to adults. ("Would you like to sit here, Mr. Johnson?") He attempts to introduce a subject if conversation lags. He should be able to sit quietly, not lounging, squirming, or wriggling. He should appear attentive to any conversation addressed to him by adults, even if it does not interest him. He should have conquered any unpleasant mannerisms, such as tugging at a lock of hair, biting nails, pulling his ear, scratching, or sniffing.

Children this age should begin to have genuine responsibilities around the home and should be living up to them without too much adult supervision. Both girls and boys should help younger children by taking off and putting on wraps, getting ready for bed, playing with them just to amuse the younger ones, and learning to be tolerant and kind. They can clear the table and wash and wipe dishes, make their own beds, run rather complicated errands, etc. Girls usually do more than boys; they can now learn simple cookery and sewing, dust and polish furniture, arrange flowers, etc.

A ten-year-old boy should be urged to be manly—indeed, if it is not too old-fashioned a word, to be gentlemanly. This means to accept responsibility for his own acts, to take deserved punishment without whimpering, to confess to misdeeds, never to try to shift the blame for wrong-doing, never to tell tales, not to take unfair advantage, to "play the game." It is the age to begin to encourage the Spartan virtues, the ones that we hold too lightly in America, and which are so well and truly taught in the English public schools.

Similarly, a girl of ten should learn about the womanly virtues. Our daughters must learn that the forbearance imposed upon boys when they are taught to protect and cherish women must not be abused. If you expect your son to call for his sister and "walk her home" when she has been dining at a friend's house, you should teach your daughter to offer grateful thanks to him for so doing, and to prove that she means it by doing him a favor—sewing on a button, hunting for lost homework, or just listening with appreciation when he talks of his triumphs in the Little League.

Siblings often quarrel. It is too, too natural, and cannot be wholly eliminated. But, given the right home climate, brothers and sisters can and do enjoy one another's company, share confidences, stand up for one another, and are even, in their secret hearts, proud of one another, although they will seldom admit it.

TELEPHONE MANNERS

When a child is learning to talk, it gives his doting relatives much pleasure to hear him speak on the telephone. Because of this, many a young child grows up thinking of the telephone as a toy with which he may play as he likes. Avoid this. Do not let your child use the telephone before he is eight, unless the call is supervised. Do not ever let him dial the phone aimlessly or use it as a plaything. Under eight, do not let him answer incoming calls except in cases of emergency. Teach him how to answer the phone properly. This is the way: "Hello. This is Mr. Smith's house. This is Bobby Smith speaking. Whom do you want to talk with, please?"

He should be taught that, as soon as he understands with whom the caller wishes to speak, he should promptly call that person to the phone, and that, if he cannot understand who is wanted, he should at once call an adult to the phone to complete the call. Until a child is old enough to do this, he should not be allowed to answer the telephone. These habits may be taught through play lessons, with a toy telephone. A child of eight or over may be allowed to make calls to his friends and relatives. This is the age to begin to teach him to put a time limit on his calls. A child so taught is less apt, when he reaches the teen years, to expect to be permitted to hang on the phone interminably.

Children ten or older should be able to take and write down simple telephone messages, Example: "My Father is not at home now. Do you want to speak with my mother, or do you want to leave a message?" He should be able to write on the telephone pad. "Dad: Mr. March called. His number is UN 9-2520." Teach him not to be ashamed to ask the caller to spell out his name, letter by letter, as he writes it down. But impress upon him that if, for any reason, he cannot understand what the caller says, he should say, "Wait one moment, please, I will get my mother (or older brother, etc.)" so that the message will be correctly taken. If no adult is at home, he should say, "I'm very sorry, but I do not understand you. My father will be home after six o'clock. Please call back then." Children like to assume this kind of responsibility; it makes them feel important and reliable.

TABLE MANNERS

Table manners are discussed in a separate category because, while they are important and must be learned at an early age, they are secondary to another vital consideration: before a child is taught to eat nicely, he must learn to feed himself. The method is unimportant; first he must learn to eat, unassisted, enough food to nourish him. Adults forget that this is really a complicated process, involving the use of the hands and implements, plus the acts of conveying food to mouth, drinking, chewing, swallowing, etc. A child's attention span is short. He frequently tires of this laborious activity before he has actually had enough to eat.

Watch a fifteen-months-old baby attempt to eat cereal. First he has trouble getting any on the spoon. When he does, he is apt to spill it long before it reaches his chin. And oh, what a hard job it is to find his mouth! The first time he actually manages to convey food from a dish into his mouth should be celebrated. It is truly a major accomplishment!

From the first morsel awkwardly dumped into his lap to complete control of his knife and fork and the muscles that govern them is a long, long road, and until the end is reached, table manners should be subordinated to the greater good of allowing the child to learn to feed himself adequately. A two-year-old or younger does best when fed at hours other than family mealtimes. There is a two-fold purpose in this: Baby does better when not distracted by the presence of the family, and the family meal is more peaceful without the distraction of the baby happily dumping a bowl of soup over his head.

The young child should have a comfortable high chair with a tray firmly attached at a convenient level. His first tableware should be light-weight and unbreakable, his spoon should have a wide bowl and a short handle. Protect his clothing with a *large* bib, place plenty of newspaper or a plastic sheet beneath and round his chair to catch flying debris, and let him go to it! Much food will land on the floor, in his hair, and over his shoulder, but this apparently aimless activity is all teaching him muscle control. Help him when he appears to tire.

At age three, many children have learned to feed themselves well enough so that they may join the family meal in a chair raised to a comfortable height or in a high chair. They still have a lot to learn. Pediatricians urge that children this age be fed much food that can be eaten with the fingers—carrot sticks, small sandwiches, fruit, cookies—and food that does not require a great deal of chewing—chopped beef, lamb patties, croquettes. Roasts, chops and chicken should be cut into small pieces before being served to them. Creamed foods or anything thin or runny are hard for children to manage. They may be permitted to use a spoon to eat this type of food, in defiance of correct table manners, until they can manage a fork well. Small children are apt to wash solid food down with gulps of milk to avoid the effort of chewing. Therefore many parents serve a young child a very small amount of any beverage with his meal; some eschew it entirely until the main part is over. His milk is then served him with or after his dessert.

Do not force your child to "clean his plate" or to eat food that is distasteful to him. Parents do this because they feel a child eats too little. The purpose is good; the method is useless, often actually harmful to the development of good eating habits. Be relaxed and try to feel or at least to show little concern over how much or how many things a child eats. Here, as elsewhere, example is the best teacher.

Let small children leave the table when they have had enough to eat. It is unrealistic to expect a child under eight, to sit quietly at the table when he has finished eating. Up to this age a child may wear a bib or a napkin tucked under the chin. At age eight, a child should eat neatly enough so that his napkin is laid across the lap. Occasional accidents will occur, but the rule should be maintained from this age onward.

At age five, begin to teach a child to:

> Sit erect, leaning ever so slightly forward.
>
> Wipe lips, and have no food in the mouth when drinking.
>
> Take all food on fork or spoon into the mouth in one bite or sip.
>
> Avoid overloading fork or spoon.
>
> Keep hands and elbows off table.
>
> Avoid interrupting the conversation. Wait for one's turn to speak.
>
> Break bread into quarter slices before buttering.
>
> Eat anything put into the mouth that can be eaten. What cannot be eaten (olive pits, cherry stones, fish bones, etc.) is cleansed of food in the mouth, removed with the hand and placed on side of the plate. While this is not in all cases correct for an adult, it is enough to expect of young children.
>
> Make no adverse comments on any food served, such as "Ugh, squash! I *hate* it!"
>
> Never put one's own table implements into a common serving dish: one's knife into the butter, spoon into the jam, etc.
>
> Fold napkin when finished.
>
> Ask to be excused before leaving the table.

These are the forms on which one should concentrate from five to ten. Parents eager to teach their child attractive table manners tend to make each meal a lesson in manners. Avoid this; it makes for a tense, disagreeable atmosphere. Ignore table manners frequently, especially minor lapses, to teach the more important lesson that meal time should be a relaxed and pleasant occasion for all present. Devote only an occasional meal to a lesson in correct eating.

Table manners can be taught well through play lessons, using a child's toy equipment (small tables and dishes). One plays "Going to a party," "Helping Mommy serve tea," "Company for dinner," and simply, "How we behave at meals." Explain the true purpose of table manners, which is to eat neatly and attractively, so as not to disgust others or detract from their pleasure in eating a meal. It is more effective to say gently, "It does not look pretty to butter a whole slice of bread" than to say, "Little ladies do not butter a whole slice of bread."

One must remember that what one does is always more effective than what one says. Father and Mother must be alert to correct any careless habits into which they have fallen and to strive to set the children an example of proper behavior at all meals.

By the time a child is ten, he should have mastered the rules previously given, although one must make reasonable allowance for occasional lapses and omissions. At this age, one can enlarge these rules to include:

Boys wear jackets to the dinner table and pull out chair for the mother or sister.

Soup is spooned away from the diner, not toward him.

Never leave the spoon in soup dish or teacup.

Anything served in a dish or cup with a handle is drunk, not spooned.

Food is cut up one bite at a time.

Never crook the little finger.

Try not to push food around the plate when transferring it to the fork.

Salad is eaten entirely with the fork. The only exception to this is a quarter of iceberg lettuce which must sometimes be cut because it is so solid.

Children now must learn to eat creamed foods, aspics, etc. with a fork.

Ask to have food passed; don't reach.

Dunking is a sport to be indulged in only when one is eating by oneself.

Children may now be allowed to rest the left arm against the edge of the table occasionally, when not using the left hand for eating, instead of being required to keep the unused hand in the lap, and may be permitted to rest an elbow on the table once in a while between courses. This makes for ease and an appearance of naturalness. Strict etiquette requires that no one shall eat until all are served, and children should be taught that in some homes which they visit this will be expected of them, even though you may in your house follow the more modern practice of starting to eat after two or three have been served.

For food which is taken into the mouth but cannot be eaten, the rule should now be: what goes in on a spoon comes out on a spoon. (The pits of cooked plums, cherries) What goes in in the hand comes out the same way. (Olive pits, grape seeds) Fish bones, any bit of nutshell or meat bone which one has accidentally put into the mouth, are all removed with the fingers.

When one has finished eating, the knife and fork should be laid quietly across the middle of the plate, with the handles on the right. The tines of the forks are up, the sharp edge of the knife is turned toward the diner. The fork is on the inside, nearer the diner. The butter knife is laid on the butter plate in the same fashion; spoons are placed on the side of the serving saucer or dish. All these implements should be placed squarely, so that they will not slide off the plate when it is being removed.

Remain at the table until all have finished.

ENTERTAINING GUESTS

There are many occasions on which one entertains from which one's children should be excluded—cocktail parties, all-adult dinner parties, after-dinner entertaining. At such times children should take it as a matter of course that they will eat privately and may not necessarily put in any appearance at all. The most that they should be permitted is to come into the living room, meet the guests, exchange a few remarks, and leave. With children under the age of five, even this may be omitted.

When you are entertaining relatives, intimate friends, or friends who are bringing their own children with them, your children will be expected to be present and, if they have been properly taught, can add to the pleasure of the occasion. Children should not be taught a set of "company" manners, different from those they habitually use, but the point can be made that the reason for inviting guests into one's home is to give them pleasure, that one therefore strives to behave in a manner that will be pleasing to them, and that this sometimes requires one to act in a fashion somewhat different from one's normal routine. Thus, before the coming of guests, children can be reminded not to interrupt or dominate the conversation, not to romp noisily in the presence of adult guests, to offer food to others before serving themselves, etc. They should also be cautioned against making any comment on the behavior of the guests. It is extremely embarassing to have an observant child remark innocently, "Daddy, see how queerly Aunt Betty holds her fork," or, "Mommy, Cousin Timmy is talking with his mouth full!"

LETTERS OF THANKS

Acknowledging presents with a prompt and graceful note of thanks is an obligation which no well-bred person can delegate to another. The younger a child is taught to perform this duty for himself, the easier and more automatic it will be for him to do so in adult life. A normal seven-year-old can write *Dear Grandma, Thank you for my Christmas fire engine. I love you. Timmy.*

It will be an effort, and perhaps it will take a long time, but Grandma will treasure such a letter fondly; and the writer will learn much from attempting it. In these first little notes, which usually go to relatives, do not worry too much about correct spelling—the recipients find the mistakes endearing; and it is more valuable to teach the importance of writing the note of thanks than to teach correct spelling at this time. Here is a sample of an actual note of thanks from a seven-year-old girl to a far-away grand-uncle:

> Dear Uncle Ray,
>   Thank you for the dollar bells you sent my brother and me. I wish we were akwainted. If you would come to visit us we could get akwainted. We love you anyhow. Love, Tracey.

This is a good letter for a child of that age. It acknowledges the present and expresses thanks and loving feelings.

Ten-year-olds should be required to write letters of thanks for all presents and also to write acceptances (or regrets) for all written invitations. At ten, the spelling should be correct, as should the spacing, punctuation, etc., but do not make the child rewrite because of a single misspelled word. See to it that the letters are written promptly.

MORAL PRINCIPLES AND RELIGIOUS PRACTICE

Like everything else a child learns, his concepts of right and wrong behavior are based far more on what he observes others doing in everyday life than upon what one says. Consider the following situations:

Mother keeps Angela home from school to take her into town for a day's shopping. The next day she writes the school a note of excuse: *Dear Sister, Please excuse Angela's absence of yesterday. She had an upset stomach.*

Dad comes home from the office and says "Here kids. Here are some school supplies I picked up for you at the office." Then he gives them a handful of pencils, erasers, or rulers.

Or he says to Mother, "Boy, I had a narrow escape this morning! I was late for work, and I was doing sixty in that forty-mile zone on the Boulevard, when I heard a cop coming! I cut into Grand Avenue and lost him. If I hadn't, I would surely have gotten a ticket."

Or: "I see by the papers that the mayor has ordered an investigation of the building commissioner's office. That bunch are feathering their own nest, but I don't suppose anything will come of it. They're a bunch of crooks. All politicians are."

Big brother Dick says, "Dad, Coach Brown says I can't play in the game Saturday because I missed practice twice. That's not the real reason, though. He is always picking on me, and besides he plays favorites."

Mother says, "How long-winded Father Quinn was at Mass this morning! I thought he would never stop talking! Besides, I have heard that sermon of his about the evils of criticism a dozen times!"

All of these incidents are concerned with minor lapses from the moral code. But what impression do they make upon a child who has been taught always to tell the truth, never to steal the smallest thing, to obey the law, to respect those in authority, to take responsibility for his own misdeeds, and to reverence the clergy? He will, inevitably, do, think, and speak as you do rather than as you tell him to do. And while these are minor lapses, apparently unimportant, they are concrete things which he sees and understands, and it is from such things that he learns most.

It is a painful conclusion, perhaps the hardest a parent must face, but it is irrefutable: a child grows up to be honest, honorable, reverent, and law-abiding because his parents were so in the simple dealings of common living. The only exception to this rule occurs when the parents set the child such a horrible example of bad living (dipsomania, open adultery, convicted theft, etc.) that the child is revolted and strives to become all that his parents were not. Who among us wants his children to become good adults through this method! Parents, therefore, have a double reason to do and be "the best they can." They should do so not only for their own soul's sake but because the power of their example is the vital ingredient in rearing their children properly. If this means greatly improving your own behavior and attitudes when you become a parent, ask God's help, and strive to do so.

The power of example is equally forceful in the practice of one's faith. What a child can learn from attendance at religious instruction or at a Catholic school, or from observing the lives of Sisters and priests, is valuable, but never outweighs the religious practices of his parents. Children easily comprehend that the lessons taught them in morals and religion are ideal conduct to which they may aspire but which they never wholly attain; and that priests and Sisters are holy and dedicated people, serving God more perfectly than most laymen can ever do. The practices of their parents, lax or fervent, are what form their ideas as to what is expected of the Catholic laity.

It is good to send your children regularly to confession and Holy Eucharist, good to urge them to make the First Fridays, or a novena, or Stations of the Cross; but it is far better to make these devotions with them, to show and tell them the joys and consolations, rewards and satisfactions of a generous, varied, and meaningful practice of the many religious observances by which our faith is strengthened.

MOVING PICTURES, TELEVISION, AND READING

The censorship of entertainment media has always been a subject of argument, with those on both sides of the question holding strong views. Recently the advocates of censorship have received a number of setbacks due to adverse court decisions about postal regulations, moving picture licensing, and similar matters. The rights and wrongs of the question are not a suitable subject for discussion in this book.

Even the most ardent up-holders of the no-censorship position agree that it is the right and duty of parents to examine the entertainment offered through the various media and to determine what is suitable for their children to see. This responsibility must be taken seriously; since the recent removal of some legal barriers to unsuitable material, it is more vital than ever. The things that a child reads, sees, and hears for entertainment have great weight in forming his ideas of right and wrong.

Parents should attempt to check all entertainment media for its moral content. A play or book that approves euthanasia, abortion, contraception, divorce, taking the law into one's own hands, doing evil that good may come of it, etc., is not suitable for a Catholic child. Moral values are the important consideration, but conscientious parents will also try to determine how any given entertainment will affect a child's aesthetic tastes, manners, and speech habits.

Moving pictures are not now as much of a problem as they were before the advent of television. Small children are not as eager to

attend and do not make so much of an issue of it. No child under the
age of ten should go to a moving picture theater unless accompanied
by an adult. The precaution is for his safety. Young children should
only attend occasionally, and the picture should be intended specifically for a child audience; "The Wizard of Oz" or "Toby Tyler," for
example.

Any picture that has received an A-1 rating from The National
Legion of Decency is morally suitable for a child to see. This classification certifies that the picture is morally unobjectionable for general
patronage. But note that word *moral*. If your child is nervous, timid,
or easily affected by what he sees, a picture receiving this classification
may still be too exciting or too emotional for him to see without adverse
affect upon his nervous system. Otherwise you are on safe grounds with
any A-1 picture.

Legion of Decency ratings for all current moving pictures are
published weekly in Catholic newspapers and are frequently posted
in the lobbies of churches and Catholic schools. You are personally
responsible for determining the rating of a picture before you permit
your child to see it.

Television is a more difficult problem. It is always with us. A busy
mother is often tempted to use it as a built-in baby sitter; while her
youngsters are watching they are kept out of other mischief. Try to
avoid too great a reliance on this entertainment medium. Decide how
much time each day you will let your child watch, and stick to it. The
younger the child, the less viewing he should do. Do not let it become
a substitute for outdoor play, play with friends, or constructive indoor
play such as building with blocks, or coloring. If the program is suitable, watching before dinner or at bedtime is good entertainment and
relaxes the children before eating or sleeping.

When a child reaches school age, one should see to it that his viewing does not interfere with sleep, homework, play outdoors, or learning
some worthwhile activity such as skating, riding a bike, or learning a
musical instrument. Staying up beyond the usual bedtime to see a
program should be rarely permitted, and then only for a program
intended for children, such as "Peter Pan" or "Peter and the Wolf."

The difficulty with screening television programs lies in determining in advance what they will be like. About all one can do is to check
on the programs one's children sees while they are watching and
screen them out if they are unsuitable. Encourage your youngsters to
watch opera, symphonic music, and classical ballet; it is through
familiarity with these arts that one learns to enjoy them. It is unfor-

tunate that the art of the dance, so beautiful, so enjoyable, and so easily appreciated by children, is, on television, frequently debased by half-nude or skin-tight costuming and highly sensual routines.

Remember that nervous children can be adversely affected by a production which is moral and in good taste, if it is too exciting or too stimulating.

You can develop your child's taste for reading by reading to him before he can read to himself. Small children like simple stories about lives similar to their own; they also enjoy fantasy and nonsense tales. They love rhythm and verse; if one does not check this natural taste by suggesting that poetry is difficult or dull they will not lose their taste for it as they grow older but will enjoy increasingly abstruse poetry.

Few hard-cover books for children are morally unsuitable. Responsible publishers take every precaution to see that they do not offend and that the illustrations are tasteful and the print suitable for childish eyes. A parent's main responsibility is to see that books are made available to children. If you cannot afford to buy many books, begin when your children are small to take them to the public library and help them with their first selections. Most schools now have their own libraries; you should urge your children to draw books from them for their own pleasure as well as for help in their school work. If you do not feel qualified to select reading material for your child, a librarian or his teacher will give you a list of books suitable to his age.

The cheap paper-cover books known as "comic" books are the real reading problem. Children enjoy looking at the pictures in these books before they have learned to read and, by so doing, develop a desire to learn. This is good. Unfortunately the format and subject matter of most comic books is undesirable. The paper is cheap, the colors used are harsh and garish, and the drawing is poor. As to subject matter: the animal cartoon comics are comparatively harmless. Some others are devoted to fairy tales and condensed versions of famous children's stories, but even these have their drawbacks. Fairy tales are best when read, with the child's imagination picturing the scenes; the fine children's stories are better read in their original form than in the chopped-up comic book versions. It is by reading good writing that one learns to appreciate literary style and enlarge one's vocabulary. Excessive simplification of reading material prevents this.

The worst of the comic books are very bad, full of scenes of bloodshed, crime, violence, and lurid fantasy. Keep a close watch over the books your children see. They love to "swap" comic books; check on the ones your child gets this way. It is better to buy a child one good hard-cover book than five comic books, and the single book will bring more pleasure in the long run because it will last longer.

Anyone who truly loves to read need never be lonely or bored. You can do your child no greater kindness than to help him develop a taste for reading.

DARE TO BE DIFFERENT

Many influences in modern living unite to induce the general public to accept a universal standard of morals, behavior, opinion, manners, and dress. To some extent this has always been so; our ideas in these areas have ever been heavily influenced by those of our fellows. Universal literacy, the availability of inexpensive books and magazines, and our public school system have encouraged the spread of common standards. To these we add today television, radio, and moving pictures, and, most important of all, the development of certain psychological theories as to how man can best function in a modern world.

Some of these influences are good; none of them are deliberately wicked; at least, none are the result of a planned conspiracy of evil. The educators engaged in teaching children how to "function in the group," to accept the "will of the majority" as the standard of what constitutes right behavior, are, from their own point of view, merely assisting children to live happily with their fellows. All of this would be intensely valuable, if the ideas and standards upheld were *the noblest possible.* Unfortunately, setting such a universal uniform standard always means levelling *down.* One can never level "up." The standards acceptable to humanity at large will always be inferior to those possible to the brightest and best. If these inferior standards are held up to the superior members of society as ideal, such members are robbed of all incentive to struggle to the heights which may be possible to them.

This results in an incalculable loss to mankind. Our great philosophers, saints, radicals, inventors—those whom A. W. E. O'Shaughnessy called "the movers and shakers of the world"—have always been "different" from the common run of man, and have been rightfully proud of their difference. Such people are the yeast which leavens the loaf of mankind; if they fail to rise, the loaf will become a pancake.

For society at large, the acceptance of a low dead level of conformity, the spread of a common fear to differ from one's fellows, is a tragedy. For Catholics, it is impossible. We are, and will continue to be (for how long, only God knows, but He knoweth) a minority group.

Socially and governmentally, this is unimportant. In the realm of ideas and moral standards, it is important, and it is just in these realms that we are far more of a minority than we were a hundred years ago.

In the nineteenth century, Catholic beliefs as to Who made us, and why, the need to earn Heaven, the binding force of the Ten Commandments and the moral law, were generally acceptable, not only to non-Catholic Christians and Jews, but to many who formally subscribed to no religious belief. These ideas were accepted as norms. Today this is no longer so. Thousands—millions—live out their lives acknowledging no influences save secular ones and accepting no moral standards as fundamental.

In March of 1863, in a presidential proclamation, President Abraham Lincoln wrote:

> Whereas it is the duty of nations as well as of men to owe their dependence upon the overruling power of God, to confess their sins and transgressions in humble sorrow, yet with assured hope that genuine repentance will lead to mercy and pardon, and to recognize the sublime truth, announced in Holy Scriptures, and proven by all history, that those nations only are blessed whose God is the Lord.
> And insomuch as we know that by His divine law nations, like individuals, are subjected to punishments and chastisements in this world, may we not justly fear that the awful calamity of Civil War which now desolates the land may be but a punishment inflicted upon us for our presumptuous sins, to the needful end of our national reformation as a whole people?

These statements were accepted without comment by the general public of 1863. They were regarded by Catholics of that day as basic concepts, and are still so regarded by us. But if an American president were to issue such a proclamation today, a storm of protest would arise. Thousands would deny the power of God over nations, the reality of sin, the need for atonement, and the recognition of war as a chastisement of nations, visited upon them by God. This is a striking illustration of how far away from us, in moral concepts, many of our fellow citizens have moved in the last hundred years.

This means that present-day Catholics must learn and must teach their children to differ from the majority of their fellows in many basic moral principles, to love and cherish those with whom they differ, while refusing to accept, as their moral guides, standards with which they do not agree. To do this, neither doubting one's own position nor rejecting all who differ from it, one must constantly bear in mind that the *number* of persons who hold any set of opinions has nothing to do with their correctness. To agree with the majority is not in itself any proof of the rightness of one's position; to differ, and to be in the minority while differing, has no bearing on whether one is right or wrong.

Granting that it is valuable to dare to be different, how does one go about teaching one's children independence of thought and action? One first examines one's own attitudes and opinions to see whether they are based on independent conclusions, or unconscious acceptance of what one sees and hears. Would you accept the following statements as true?

"X toothpaste cleans and polishes better."

"Y toilet soap is milder and purer."

"Z cigarettes filter out forty-six per cent more impurities."

What do these remarks mean? Nothing. No assertion expressed in the comparative degree means anything unless the comparison is completed. Whenever you hear or read such an assertion, ask yourself "Better—than what?" "Purer, milder—than what?" "46% more—than what?" Such unfinished comparisons are meaningless and should convince no thoughtful person. "Independent laboratory tests prove" is another advertising claim that is worthless unless you personally know how reliable the laboratory quoted really is.

All of these examples of sleazy argument are from the advertising world and are in themselves of little significance. If you unthinkingly accept such claims, it will have little influence on your life. What is important is the fact that we are all constantly subjected to a barrage of such meaningless gobbledegook about matters of consequence. Politicians, educators, labor leaders, and others in the public eye frequently make similar remarks about important affairs and consider them logical. They are nothing of the kind, and intelligent people should be alert to recognize and reject this kind of reasoning.

If one is to think independently, how does one form one's conclusions?

　　a) Weigh the truth or falsity of what you hear against what you know to be true from personal experience or your own studies.

　　b) Examine the motives of the speaker. If he has something to gain from convincing you, he is bound to be biased toward the side of the question that favors him. His opinions are therefore worth less than those of an expert with no personal involvement in the question at issue.

c) Examine the qualifications of the speaker to pose as an expert on the subject—his education, experience, number of years in the job. Take care lest the prominence of a speaker in one field induce you to believe that he is an expert on a subject other than the one in which he has gained fame. A famous architect is not necessarily qualified to speak with authority on the subject of literature. One frequently hears actors who are well-known because of their ability to entertain use their entertainment medium to express their opinions on politics, morals, and world affairs. They have a right to their opinions in such matters; but these opinions are no more valuable than those of a postman, garage mechanic or any other private citizen. The entertainers are cheating the public when they employ the time supposed to be used for entertainment to express their views. The weight that children and thoughtless people give to the opinions of actors on morals, manners, and dress is particularly unfortunate, since a famous and brilliant actor may also be undereducated, ill-bred, and amoral.

d) Evaluate the reputation of the speaker for honesty, morality, and fair play. Listen respectfully and with an open mind to an honorable and informed man with no ax to grind, speaking in the field in which he has made himself an expert.

e) Do not let the good habit of questioning and weighing the truth or falsity of what you hear lead you into cynicism, so that you adopt the attitude, "All politicians are liars"; "All social workers are bleeding hearts"; "College professors are egg-heads." Judge each man as an individual; remember that there are thousands of people in the world who are striving to live up to the highest Christian ideals and who find their deepest joy in striving to make our life on earth a little more like that we hope to lead in heaven.

f) Have the courage of your convictions. Cling to, live up to, what you think is right, regardless of how many disagree with you.

g) Keep an open mind. Do not be afraid to admit to a change of opinion when convinced that you have been in the wrong.

h) Occasionally read or listen to speeches which express views counter to the ones you hold. An industrialist should listen to labor leaders, working men should listen to executives, Republicans to Democrats. Test your opinions against what you hear. See if you can successfully defend them against the arguments you have heard. If you cannot, seek to find material on your side of the question which refutes what you have heard. If you cannot refute it, it is time to consider changing your opinions. Such activity teaches you to keep an open mind, and to know why you believe as you do.

i) Keep trying to increase your own knowledge through study, reading, and observation.

Until a child goes to school, you will find him easy to convince; that is, he will accept the validity of what you say or do, as ideals, although he will not always live up to them. Once he steps into the wider world of school, you will begin to hear remarks like these: "Tommy doesn't have to go to bed at seven-thirty. Sometimes he stays up until ten o'clock." "Hilda's mother lets her watch television all she wants to, and whatever shows she likes." "Mrs. Jennings didn't make Edna and me pick up her toys." "Willy can have a soft drink any time, and he eats *lots* between meals." "Fred talked with his mouth full, and slobbered up his glass, and his Mommy didn't say nuffin."

The standards and values of the rest of the world are beginning to be observed by your child; and he is comparing them to yours. When your small child first does this, it is enough to listen agreeably to what he has to say and then dismiss it lightly with such remarks as, "Tommy must be awfully sleepy in school." "Mrs. Jennings and Hilda's Mommy must decide what is best for their little girls, and I do the same with mine." "Willy must have a better appetite than you do." "It's too bad Fred is not learning better manners. I see you noticed that he was not eating nicely." Such simple comments will take care of the matter, especially if you show no sign of wavering in your own standards of what you expect from your children.

As they grow older you will have to go into the matter a little more. Explain that different people often have different ideas as to what is right. Often the ideas are not better or worse—just different. But sometimes they *are* better or worse. Those who have had the advantage of being gently reared or have had more educational opportunities will have higher standards than those who have not. Children who are taught from infancy about morals and ethics will try harder to be good than those who never hear the subject mentioned. Explain that you are trying to teach them what you consider to be the very best behavior: the most honorable, the most courteous, the kindest. Admit that there may be people with higher standards than yours, and many with standards that are lower. But your standards are the ones that you are convinced are best for you and your family. You therefore expect your children to learn to live up to them, even though in so doing their lives will often differ in many ways from those of their friends. They should consider themselves fortunate that they have parents so devoted and so idealistic, and they *will* so consider themselves when they are older and know enough to evaluate such matters. They should never be afraid to differ from their comrades in doing that which they know, from their home training, is right.

Caution your children, also, not to criticize the behavior of others. Explain that those fortunate enough to be taught at home to strive for the highest standards have an obligation to be kind and forbearing to those who have not had such advantages. If you are convinced of the truth of all this, your children will sense the weight of your conviction and will abide by your opinions.

It is true that, from earliest childhood, children long to be "like everybody else." This desire for conformity is very strong and is often an influence for good. Accede to it wherever you can in minor matters. If all Tommy's friends wear blue jeans to school, don't make him wear shorts. If "all the girls" wear rain hats and coats, don't buy your little girl an umbrella, no matter how attractive you think it is. Let your children go "with the group" when you can. If "everybody" has money to buy milk at recess, let your child do so. If the class has a day for banking, try to give your children banking money, if you can without hardship. But when you really think that what "everybody" does is not good practice or is something you really cannot afford, explain the facts to your child and require him to differ from the others in this matter. It may be painful to him so to differ, but it is a valuable lesson. He may learn, among other things, that it is not as difficult as he had fancied.

Parents who would like further reading material to aid them in rearing small children may find the following books and pamphlets helpful:

De Lourdes, Sister Mary, R.S.M., *Baby Grows In Age and Grace.* (Through the seventy-second month of life.) A Guide and Record for Catholic Mothers. C. R. Gibson & Co. Norwalk, Conn.
Foster, Constance J., *Developing Responsibility in Children.* Chicago, Ill.: Science Research Associates, Inc.

Gesell, A., and Ilg, F. L., *The Child From Five to Ten*. New York, N. Y.: Harper Bros.

Grant, Eva H., *Parents and Teachers as Partners*. Science Research Associates, Inc.

Gruenberg, Sidonie, *The Wonderful Story of How You Were Born*. Garden City, N. Y.: Doubleday.

Lord, S.J., Daniel A., *Some Notes for the Guidance of Parents*. St. Louis 18, Mo.: Queen's Work.

Rosenheim, Lucile. *Let's Give a Party*. Science Research Associates, Inc.

Sattler, C.Ss.R. Henry V., *Parents, Children and the Facts of Life*. Garden City, N. Y.: Image Books, Doubleday.

Schmiedler, O.S.B., Edward J., ed. *The Child and Problems of Today*. St. Meinrad, Indiana: A Grail Publication.

Spock, M.D., Benjamin, *The Complete Book of Baby and Child Care*. New York 15, N. Y.: Duell, Sloan and Pearce. The soft-cover edition of this book is: *Baby and Child Care*. New York, N. Y.: Pocket Books.

Allen, Patricia H., editor. *Best Books for Children, Including Adult Books for Young People*. New York, N. Y.: R. R. Bowker Co. A list of 3300 currently available books for children, arranged by grade and subject.

21

Guidance and Manners for Sub-Teens

He that spareth the rod hateth his son; but he that
loveth him correcteth him betimes (Proverbs 13:24).

AIMS

Many parents devote twenty years of their life to a devoted, prayer-
ful effort to raise a child properly without once asking themselves,
"What are we trying to accomplish? What is our goal for our child?"
Of course we all want our children to become good Catholics, to be
self-supporting, courteous, and happy in the state of life to which God
calls them. But there is another goal at which you should aim that is
secondary to nothing save the attempt to make them good Catholics,
and yet is one that parents frequently overlook: when the child
becomes an adult he should be mentally, spiritually, socially, and
emotionally mature, and wholly independent—of you. Parents often
complain that their adult children never ask for their advice or views,
they feel that their independence of thought and action is a rejection
of their elders. In rare cases this may be true, but in most it should be
regarded as a heart-warming proof that they have successfully completed their most important job: rearing their children to maturity and
independence. The adult who cherishes parent above mate, who seeks
parental approval for every act and idea, who is constantly fearful of
being on his own, is one whose parents failed in their responsibility
toward him. Somewhere in his childhood—probably through excessive
caution and unwillingness to let him assume responsibility or to extend
him freedom of action—his parents have crippled him emotionally, so
that he doubts the value of his own opinions and fears to act on his
own judgment. A person so hampered can never mature. Thoughtful

parents will strive, during his childhood and adolescence, to give a child increasing responsibility and freedom of thought and action, so that he will learn to exercise these valuable qualities while still under their care.

WHAT IS A TEEN-AGER?

The current habit of substituting the phrase "teen-ager" for the more correct term "adolescent," is in some respects unfortunate. People employing this term usually mean young people between the ages of sixteen and nineteen—the years of adolescence. But children themselves, always literal-minded, interpret it to mean all the teen years. This results in children thirteen to fifteen demanding to be treated as 'teen-agers," pressing for the freedom, responsibilities, and privileges of the older group.

The attitude is intensified by the unconscious eagerness of some parents to hurry their children out of childhood. Up to the age of eight or nine, if left to themselves, boys and girls will frequently play happily together without regard to sex. From eight to twelve, the natural attitude is to regard the opposite sex as "the enemy." Boys hate girls; girls hate boys. Today, if four-year-old Janie plays contentedly with her contemporary Jimmie, her parents quickly label Jimmie "Janie's boy-friend," thus filling both children with foolish ideas that would otherwise not have occurred to them. Please don't do this. Childhood at best is all too brief. Let your children *be* children; let the sexes play together without any differentiation unnatural to their age, reminding your daughters only that some boyish play is too rough and dangerous for them, and your sons that girls must be treated gently and courteously merely because they are girls. Do not joke about courtship, love, or marriage; it is in childhood that one begins to impress upon one's children that these are beautiful and sacred subjects.

Present-day educational theories approve dividing children into three age-groups: kindergarten through sixth grade, seventh grade through ninth grade (junior high), and senior high.

Whether this is a desirable division educationally the writer is not qualified to discuss; certainly it is not ideal socially. It means that sixth-graders, as the top of their group, press for privileges not suitable to their age. In junior high, the freshmen and sophomores, as the top of their school divisions, are hurried too young into school responsibilities; the period of senior high is too brief. Under the old two-division system, seventh- and eighth-graders are associating, as they should, with younger children; freshman and sophomores in high school are lowly creatures, slowly learning the responsibilities that they will not assume until they become juniors and seniors. This system takes pressure off children and parents.

Regardless of whether your children are being educated under the two-division or three-division system, don't let yourself be coerced into granting them too young the privileges of older adolescence. Through the twelfth year, children are children and should be treated as such. They may go to properly supervised mixed parties occasionally, but there should be no question of pairing off or dating. Through the twelfth year, children should be occupied with school, sports, scouting, and other clubs, learning skills such as music, painting, or sewing, and with reading, swimming, picnics, and family outings. They will be happier and better-adjusted if confined to these.

Between twelve and fifteen, children begin to develop a romantic interest in the opposite sex. Girls mature in this respect earlier and more easily than boys. Fourteen and fifteen-year-olds may be permitted to pair off for parties, hayrides, picnics, and school activities limited to their own age group. All these should be group activities; single dating of any kind should not be permitted; and the children should be discouraged from pairing off with one partner or anything that resembles "going steady." All of their social life should be supervised by a responsible adult.

Are these goals unrealistic? Many parents will claim that they are, and will assert, with considerable justice, that other parents and school authorities will not help in restraining the social life of children of this age. But it may well be that these persons are quite as eager as you to keep their children living like children but feel pressured into consenting to activities of which they do not approve. Take it upon yourself to make the first gesture. Seek out other parents and school heads; find out how they really feel about these matters. You may find allies in many unexpected places and learn that you are not alone in your ideas as to what is proper for this age.

Since the privileges granted to children under fifteen differ so much from those permitted the older teens, let us refer to the twelve- to fifteen-year-olds as the "sub-teens," reserving the expression "teen-agers" for the older group who are beginning an active social life.

THE SUB-TEENS

These are difficult years for a child. Many of his impulses and tastes are still wholly childish; certainly he has as yet nothing but the experiences of childhood to guide him. But stirring within him are powerful urges to step into the joys and dangers of adult life—urges physical, mental and emotional. He very much needs his parents' supervision, and their loving, sympathetic, untiring interest in his ideas and his doings. A child who has always enjoyed a happy open relationship with his parents will still wish to confide in them and, if not discouraged, will do so—interminably. Girls, especially, tend to talk and talk and *talk* about their small doings at this age.

Listen; listen with patience, sympathy and understanding, always remembering that the speaker is still a child. Don't belittle his ideas, no matter how foolish. Appear to give them respectful consideration. Do not be shocked by anything you hear. This does not mean that you should not express disapproval of impropriety or wrong-doing. It does mean that you should not be shocked because your child *tells* you about such things. When he does so, it is a proof that, up to this time, you have taught him that he can safely confide in you without being misunderstood. Keep the line of communication open. Discuss what he tells you honestly. If you disapprove of what you have been told, say so; point out why you feel as you do and just what is wrong with what he has told you. But stress the point that he was right, not wrong, in telling it to you, and that you are honored by his confidence. If your child thinks some line of action is right which you consider wrong, listen to his arguments and opinions as though they were worthy of being heard (as they are), then state your ideas calmly and reasonably to support your position. This is far more effective than shouting, scolding, and laying down the law.

The sub-teen years are frequently a period of beautiful idealism. At this age many young people feel a desire to draw closer to God, which manifests itself in an increased ardor in their religious practices. They want to serve their fellow man as missionaries, priests, sisters, nurses, social workers. They yearn to make a better world than the one into which they were born. All this is intensely valuable and should be encouraged and treated seriously. Some of mankind's noblest yearnings first manifest themselves at this age. With some, it is a temporary enthusiasm that flares up briefly and dies away; with others, it is the beginning of a life of dedicated service. More often than we may think, the end result depends on how we, as parents, react to these first aspirations.

Take care that you do not think your children worse than they are. "The heart that knows no evil thinks no evil" says an old Irish proverb. Often gently-reared sub-teens indulge in or approve of behavior which is improper because they have not lived long enough and do not know enough of wrong-doing to recognize it as such. Be *very* careful not to accuse them of deliberate wrong-doing unless you are positive of your facts; *never* accuse them of doing an act with motives lower or meaner than the ones to which they have admitted. A sub-teen wrongfully accused by a parent or teacher of lying or cheating will be revolted and deeply hurt. You will lose his confidence instantly and forever.

There will be another unfortunate result which is best illustrated by a true story. A high school girl talking to her mother was complaining about a new Sister Superior who had come to her school to replace a wise and beloved principal. The girl had many complaints about the new principal. The mother heard her out, then reminded the girl that it was not easy for the new nun to step into the shoes of one who had been so popular and successful. She suggested that the school girls withhold judgment for a few months and give the newcomer a chance to adjust to her position. She concluded by asking, "Just what is it that Sister Josephine does that is so different from Sister Christine, and that you resent so much?"

The daughter thought for a moment and then said, "If anyone brought a complaint to Sister Christine about something we were supposed to have done, she always said, 'Oh, I feel there must be some mistake. No St. Catherine's girl would ever behave like that. I will investigate thoroughly, but I must have concrete evidence before I can believe such a story.' She *would* investigate, and if the story was true, the offender would be punished. But if the offense could not be proven, she would accuse no one. In other words, Mother," the girl concluded thoughtfully, "Sister Christine always *expected the best* of us, and we leaned over backwards to deserve her trust. Sister Josephine seems to expect the worst, and, if she keeps it up, *that's what she's going to get.*"

This school girl was intuitively aware of a psychological reality: children are eager to do what is expected of them. If you happily, confidently, trustfully expect their best, you are very apt to get it. If you constantly expect the worst and accuse them of it without full proof, they despair of winning your approval and confidence and devote their energies to "getting away with" as much as they can.

STEPPING OUT OF CHILDHOOD

Although sub-teens should not be permitted to ape the social life of teen-agers, there are many ways in which their life will begin to differ from that of younger children. Their retiring hour is later. They should be permitted greater freedom of choice of television programs, reading material, and other entertainment media. They should be allowed greater freedom of action outside the home. This may include attending the early show at the moving pictures, if it is within walking distance of home and the streets are safe at night. If they go in a car, it should be driven by an adult.

This is the age for dancing school. Properly conducted classes teach a lot about the social amenities. Many CYO clubs have parties and dances planned for sub-teens. These are well-supervised; children can safely attend them, but parents should see to it that they have a safe means of getting to and from these parties.

If you belong to a country club, your sub-teens may use its facilities for swimming, golf, and tennis. You may also give an all-girl luncheon or a mixed dinner party at your club for your child and her friends, but she may not otherwise use the club dining room unless accompanied by an adult member.

Sub-teens may also go in groups to properly supervised public swimming pools, tennis courts, and other recreation areas. In rural communities and small cities they may also go to town baseball and football games, but in very large cities girls should not do this without an adult. Of course they may go to sports programs sponsored by their school and to church-sponsored parties.

Encourage your sub-teens to bring their friends home. If the atmosphere is relaxed and friendly, they will be eager to do so. Tell your son or daughter your home is open to their friends whenever there is an adult present. Do not allow them to entertain at home at any time if no older person is there. You should make this a standing rule to which there is no exception, not because you distrust your child or his companions, but because to do otherwise is to burden a child with too much responsibility. Without an adult to fall back on, the sub-teen may find situations arising which he is too young and inexperienced to cope with. To protect his safety and spare him embarassment, you should not allow such a circumstance to develop. *Never allow a child to entertain at home without an adult present.*

Let them bring friends home from school to study, chat, and play records. Let them have chums in for dinner or an overnight stay. Let them feel free to say, "The committee can meet at my house." Keep your supervision light and inconspicuous, but feel free to exercise it to put down loud, rude, boisterous, or improper behavior.

Home parties for mixed groups need preparation and supervision. Plan a program to keep the youngsters occupied—games, dancing, etc. Keep the group small enough so that it will not overcrowd your house and may be kept under control. The refreshments should be plentiful and hearty. If they are attractively served, it will help curb the native boisterousness of boys this age. Several adults should help with the service. Do not let the youngsters wander about the house with plates of food and soft drinks. After all have been served, clear the food away. Do not admit any guest who has not been duly invited. (This will be discussed at length in connection with teen-agers.)

RESPONSIBILITIES

Children are always eager for the privileges of adult life but find it hard to understand that every privilege carries with it a responsibility. If one is allowed to stay out until eleven o'clock, one is responsible for being home by eleven o'clock. If allowed to wear "a little" lipstick, one should refrain from slathering on a lot. If one is allowed to go in a group to places in the city, one is responsible for behaving properly and sensibly without adult supervision. All this should be explained. The point should be made that failure to accept the responsibility with the privilege is proof that one is still too immature to have been granted the privilege. This point should be enforced: continued failure to accept the responsibility should mean withdrawal of the privilege.

Sub-teens should also be expected to assume increased responsibility for their own life. They should do homework, keep appointments, bathe and dress properly, keep promises, answer letters, write notes of thanks and acceptance, all without parental urging or reminders.

Sub-teens should also be given increased responsibility in the home. This is sometimes resented. A child who has always been comfortably housed, fed, clothed, entertained, and given presents is apt to take it all for granted, giving little thought to the effort, expense, and sacrifice this may have demanded of his parents. All this, he feels, is his by divine right; he rejects with indignation and self-pity the idea that his age and his increased privileges now require him to take a larger share in the duties of family life. This is particularly common if his parents did not, in childhood, give him duties suitable to his age or discuss with him some of the problems of financing a family. But even if one has been conscientious about this, most sub-teens are quick to feel abused.

Take the trouble to explain this to your sub-teen, emphasizing the fact that growing up entails increased responsibilities and should bring a desire to repay parents for past care. Also that you give him these increased responsibilities to teach him how to handle those he must assume in adult life.

Sub-teen girls should baby-sit with younger children for their parents, care for their own rooms, and do a reasonable number of household tasks agreed to by mother and child.

Sub-teen boys should shovel the home sidewalks and mow the lawn, care for their own rooms, run errands, and do a reasonable number of household tasks agreed to by mother and child.

Children should not be paid for these simple tasks; these should be their contribution to family living. If you want help from your children in some major job, such as cleaning attic, cellar, or garage, washing the car, or painting a room, the children may be paid for their services, but *they need not be if you do not feel that they should.* Children are a part of a family unit, to which, for the common good, all should contribute services commensurate to their age.

Take care that you treat all your children fairly in this respect. Watch out lest you impose upon the more willing and reliable of your children by letting them perform the jobs which the less responsible have left undone. Parents of large families are prone to make this mistake. It is so much easier to depend upon the helpful ones than to require all to do their share. Let all have their assigned tasks according to their age and ability; insist that each perform them.

THEY ARE ALL DIFFERENT

One responsibility that should never be laid on a child is the social life of a sister or brother. Some siblings are intimate friends all their life and prefer one another's company to that of any outsider. Others seem to have nothing in common save their parentage and the mechanics of daily living. In the latter instance, please do not force them on one another. Let each find his own friends outside the home; let each discover and enjoy his own interests.

When one child is friendly and outgoing and another is timid and self-contained, a parent is very apt to make this mistake. It is so natural to say, "Why don't you take your sister to the basketball game with you? You know she will enjoy it once she gets there, and I am sure the other girls in your crowd won't mind."

Neither child will tell you that the timid one may not enjoy it at all, and that, regardless of whether or not the other girls "won't mind," both will be unhappy and ill at ease because they will feel that the others do "mind." This applies especially to brother and sister. There are almost no occasions to which a brother can take a sister without both of them feeling miserable. And to require him to "get a date for Sally with one of your friends" puts both sub-teens in an impossible position. These situations arise only from parental anxiety to help a shy child into social life. It does not help. In social life as in so many fields, one must stand on one's own feet. Even when these attempts appear successful, they are not. The child so helped knows that she is not being accepted or sought after for her own sake; the knowledge makes her more timid and self-distrustful than before.

Parents find this hard to accept. Some go to such lengths they require one sub-teen to bring her sub-teen sister to a party to which she was not invited. The invited child is then miserable, the uninvited one is in agony, and their hostess is embarrassed, resentful, and angry. The pleasure of the party has been ruined for all three, and nothing has been accomplished. Please avoid this. "I must do it for myself" is one of the hard facts of life that must be learned in childhood.

MONEY RESPONSIBILITIES

Sub-teens must begin to learn to handle money. They are prone to think of an allowance as intended to be spent only for pleasure and recreation. They learn little from this. A sub-teen's allowance should be large enough to cover carfare, toiletries, school lunches, and school supplies, as well as entertainment tickets, soda fountain treats, and occasional record purchases. It is by struggling to allot a given sum to cover both necessities and pleasures that he learns the evils of extravagance and impulse buying. He will not learn this unless you let him suffer the consequences of unwise spending. A boy who has been obliged to stay home from the big basketball game because he bought sodas with his ticket money will learn a valuable lesson. A girl who impulsively spent carefully-saved lipstick money for a new record will likewise profit from the experience.

They are still too young to manage a clothes allowance or select their clothing without guidance, but their taste and choice should have much weight when you choose their clothes. The decision as to whether an article of clothing is modest or suitable is yours, and yours alone. In these days of skin-tight jeans and shorts, this applies to boys as well as to girls. Assuming that the garment is modest and suitable, let them exercise their taste as to color, style and material. It is useless to buy any clothing for which they have expressed a dislike; it will simply hang in their closet, unworn. Express your opinion and try to guide them, but do not go directly counter to their taste.

WALLFLOWER WOES

As a sub-teen, your daughter may taste the bitter experience of being a wallflower. Treat this with tact and sympathy. Let her agonize over it. Don't minimize it, and *don't* permit any member of the family to laugh over it. Tell her about some similar experience of your own; no woman ever lived who has not tasted this loathsome fruit! Tell her, too, about a friend who suffered in the same way but in later years became a belle. Explain that the boys whom she regards as the lords of the earth are quite as fearful and unsure of themselves as she is, that their tastes are undeveloped, which causes them to follow the crowd and to bolster their own uncertainty by seeking out the girls who appear most sure of themselves. You can say, too, that the girls they now like are seldom the ones they admire in later life. This will help—but not much! For children from twelve to twenty, now is the only reality. They cannot believe that the pain—or joy—they feel today will not endure forever. This is why they so much need our sympathy and understanding.

You can help your daughter further by not appearing unduly concerned about her social ineptitude. While sympathizing with her present pain and embarrassment, make it clear that you are not concerned about her lack of social success but are confident that it is temporary and will be quickly corrected. The woes of many a sub-teen girl spring partly from the fact that her mother is overly-concerned with her social life. If time proves that your child lacks the gift for social pre-eminence, try to shift her goals to something else: her studies, the arts, or sports.

Practically, you can help by seeing to it that she is attractively dressed and dressed like the others in her group, if their standards are acceptable. See that her hair is becomingly arranged; teach her to be exquisitely clean and well-groomed. At parties, let her wear a light floral perfume, a dusting of face powder, even a bit of light lipstick, if it is customary in her group. All this will increase her confidence in her power to please.

THE ART OF PLEASING

Assure your child that, aside from the indefinable quality called charm, which seems to be a gift from Heaven, the art of pleasing can be learned. It consists largely of:

a) Interest, genuine or cultivated, in the interests of others.

b) Honest admiration of others, generously expressed.

c) Loyalty to one's friends and one's group.

d) Willingness to share in the work necessary to make group action successful. This refers to school, club, and sodality doings.

e) Simple friendliness: the power to make the first gesture of friendship or to respond to one gracefully, without seeming to pursue one girl or boy.

f) Skills. Encourage your child to develop a reasonable competence in the things which interest her group—dancing, skating, swimming.

g) Independent judgment. Sub-teens accept the opinions of their group on the worth of their fellows as the last word. Suppose a boy whom her friends have labeled an "oddball" because of his intense interest in mathematics seeks out your daughter. Urge her to give herself a chance to know him and to judge for herself whether she enjoys his company. If she enjoys the friendship, encourage her to continue it, regardless of the opinion of others.

h) A guarded tongue. Criticism is never winning. When a girl criticizes another in a boy's hearing, he invariably attributes it to envy and jealousy. A girl who works hard to make a project a success is always happier than one who stands aside and criticizes, no matter how valid the comment may be. It even applies to criticisms of another's morals. One may quite properly refuse to accept moral standards lower than one's own and avoid unsuitable companionship, but to express disapproval is dangerous. One may be guilty of slander or of pushing a fellow creature further down the road to ruin. Certainly, expressing one's disapprobation is useless.

i) Realism. Too often a youngster feels herself a pariah merely because she is not the crashing success she expected to be. Few of us score a triumph when taking our first steps into social life; none of us are universally admired on every occasion; but a subteen unconsciously assumes that she will be the center of attention wherever she goes. Another common mistake is to hope to captivate the boy most admired and sought after by her group, and to count herself a failure if she does not succeed. Teach your daughter to receive gracefully the attentions of any respectable boy, because:

It is the courteous thing to do.

She may find she enjoys his company.

This is the age to enlarge one's acquaintances as much as possible.

His interest in her shows he is a boy of taste!

Boys are followers; if one seems to enjoy her company, others will seek her out.

STICK TO YOUR GUNS!

Failure to achieve the degree of popularity to which one feels entitled often creates a grave problem. Hurt and angered by un-popularity, adolescents always attribute it to the fact that their stand-ards of conduct are too high. The sub-teen says, "I know what is wrong—I am too prim, proper and quiet. If I were rough and noisy and boisterous like the other girls, I know the boys would like me."

The teen-age girl says, "My moral code is too strict. There are no more "nice" boys, such as Mother talks about. They *all* expect you to allow familiarities. How am I going to get married if I can't get a date?"

Because this excuse relieves them of the effort of trying to please and because it attributes their unpopularity to a quality of which they are proud, it is difficult to argue against. One must tell and tell and *tell* one's adolescents: anything—*anything*—which one obtains by denying one's own standards of ethics and morals is not worth the winning, and this is true in every stage of our life. A game of tiddly-winks won by cheating is something to be ashamed of, not rejoiced over. A business promotion earned by sharp practice or lying about one's associates is not worth the having. The companionship or the love of a boy who asks you to lower your standards for his selfish pleasure will never content you. This matter is discussed further in the section on "teen-agers," but it is mentioned here because it is to sub-teens that you must first stress this point.

PAVING THE WAY

It may seem odd advice in connection with this age group, but it is still true: sub-teens are helped to prepare for an unfamiliar situation by telling them, insofar as you can, what to expect and acting out possible occurences. Of course one does not call it that at this age. Begin by saying, "You know how to introduce people, don't you?" Regardless of whether they say "yes" or "no," you say, "Let's practice a bit to make sure." From this one can go on to practice going down a receiving line, greeting and taking leave of a hostess, getting in and out of a car, accepting or refusing an invitation to dance, etc. This help is quite as useful to a boy as to a girl, and for him one may add: helping a girl with her wraps, serving her at a buffet supper, meeting her parents, entering and leaving a bus, theater, or dance floor.

The more you know about the occasion for which they are plan-ning, the more helpful you can be. Thus, if your child is to attend a Junior dance at your country club, make sure he or she knows all the rules of conduct peculiar to it; many clubs have house rules which are not encountered elsewhere.

OUTSIDE JOBS

Unless a family desperately needs to have its income augmented in every available way, children in the sub-teen group should not be encouraged to take jobs which require them to work every day or to keep regular working hours. Some few may do so without injury, but for most the schedule is too demanding. Odd jobs are different. A strong boy can, for pay, shovel walks, mow lawns, deliver papers, or wash cars and be more self-reliant for doing so. Remind him that he is expected to do a thorough job and to finish it at the specified time.

BABY SITTING

Today baby sitting is the favorite odd job for sub-teen girls. Girls of teen-age are probably better qualified for this work, but often when they reach the teen years their social engagements are such that they are not free to sit. So the sub-teens are the ones who get the jobs. If you are confident that your sub-teen daughter is mature and reliable enough to assume this very real responsibility, let her attempt it, under the following conditions.

For the Parents of the Sitter:

a) Let the girl take engagements only for weekend evenings unless her employers are returning home early (from a PTA meeting, restaurant meal, etc.). Never allow her to sit more than one week night per week.

b) Know where your child is going, the telephone number, the hour at which she is to be home, the respectability of the family for whom she is working.

c) Do not permit a sub-teen to sit for a family in which there are more than three children; the responsibility is too great. Evening dates, when the children will go to bed early, are better than day engagements. The day care of a couple of lively youngsters may be too much for a sub-teen to attempt.

d) Urge your sub-teen to telephone home at once if any emergency or unusual situation arises.

e) Forbid her to have any boy callers while she is sitting. Permit her to have not more than one girl companion, and then only with the permission of her employer.

f) Make sure she understands the duties and responsibilities of her work.

Employers' Responsibilities

a) Know your sitter; make sure she is qualified.

b) Tell her exactly what you expect of her.

c) Tell her what she may and may not do. This applies to raiding the ice-box, talking on the phone, using the hi-fi, having company, etc.

d) Tell her where you will be, how you may be reached, what hour you expect to be home. Give her the telephone number of your doctor, local fire and police station, and any nearby adult who will help in an emergency.

e) Respect your agreement with her. If you are to be detained beyond the hour agreed upon, telephone to learn whether it is agreeable to her, and tell her the new hour at which you will return.

f) Pay her fairly at a rate agreed upon before the engagement. If you want extra service, such as dishwashing, pay extra for it— a sum agreed upon before she undertakes the work.

g) Telephone home at least once to make sure all is well.

h) Take her home in your car. If this is impossible, send her home in a taxi for which you have paid, and ask her to phone you when she has arrived home, to insure her safety.

i) Treat her as you would want your child to be treated in a similar situation.

For the Sitter

a) Realize your responsibility. During the hours of your work, you are a substitute mother, responsible for the safety and welfare of the children in your care. Put this first—ahead of homework, reading, watching TV, or telephoning.

b) Know your job. To care for infants properly, one must know how to diaper them, give a bottle feeding, burp them, and soothe them. If you do not know how, ask your employer to teach you. With older children, you should know how to win their confidence and affection, get them to obey you (go to bed, stay in bed) supervise their going to bed (bathe, go to toilet, brush teeth) and how to reassure them if they are frightened at their parents' absence. Find out if they have any special sleep habits—a favorite toy or blanket or pillow without which they cannot sleep. Remember that on any sitting job, no matter how routine it appears, a serious emergency may arise, with no one to meet it but you. Try to anticipate what such emergencies might be and how you would handle them.

c) Do not attempt to care for a sick child unless you are an experienced sitter and have cared for your own sisters and brothers when ill. Even if you are so qualified, don't try it unless you know the illness from which the child is suffering, the treatment or medication the child will require from you, your own ability to administer such treatment (inducing the child to take medicine, for example), and the symptoms which indicate that he has taken a turn for the worse.

d) Never take unfair advantage of your employers' absence. Don't pry into drawers, desks, or cupboards, do not take food or drink or entertain your friends without permission. Don't sample your employers' perfumes or toiletries. Treat your employers' possessions with respect. Don't leave rings on tables, soil books, tear magazines, or put your feet on furniture.

e) Accidents will happen. If you are unfortunate enough to break a record or a glass, spill something on a rug, or damage a book, admit it as soon as your employers return home and offer to pay for the damage. Usually your offer will be refused, but your honesty will be appreciated. If your offer *is* accepted, do not feel injured. You are now old enough so that you must expect to pay, in one way or another, for your mistakes, even though they were wholly accidental.

f) Write down accurately any messages your employer receives in his absence. But, for your own safety, be careful how you answer a telephone call from a stranger while you are alone. Don't say, "The Smiths are out for the evening. This is the baby sitter speaking." This tells an unknown that you are alone and unprotected. Say rather, "Mr. and Mrs. Smith have stepped out for a minute. May I take a message?" If the caller continues to phone, be more and more wary. Give as little information as possible. If after a call of this kind the doorbell rings, *don't open the door* unless you are positive that you recognize the voice of the person on the other side. If the visitor claims he wants to deliver a telegram, tell him to leave it in the mailbox or slip it under the door. If he says the telegram, or a package, must be signed for, tell him to come back another time. Report this to your employers upon their return. If it was a bonafide telegram, they can call the office, and it will be read to them. If the person at the door claims to be the apartment house porter or elevator man, don't open the door. Make him talk through it. If anything in the situation frightens you, do not hesitate to telephone your parents, the police, or a near neighbor on whom you know that you can rely. Never attempt to cope with a situation which may be beyond you. Turn to the nearest adult help. In so doing you will be proving your maturity.

g) When babysitting, always make sure that all entrances to the house or apartment are securely locked, and that you can unlock them quickly and easily in case of emergency.

h) Try always to behave as you would wish someone to behave to whom you had entrusted your children and your possessions.

Baby sitting is a serious matter, not to be undertaken unless all concerned understand and accept their mutual responsibility. Because of this, it must be said, without wishing to alarm that the writer has of her own personal knowledge known cases in which sitters have: prowled through the contents of everything in the house, including correspondence; stolen a bank containing twenty-five dollars; dropped and broken a stack of ten records without admitting it; entertained twelve couples without permission; and frightened their little charges by unkind behavior or weird stories. All this in addition to the serious cases of molestation and physical injury that get into the newspapers! Sitters are sinned against, too, by: failure to pay fully and promptly; improper advances from their employers; too heavy a work load; failure to see that they get home safely. Sitting is no lark; no one should regard it as such.

A sub-teen boy may also earn money as a baby sitter if he does not find the idea distasteful. Boys of this age are often better able than girls to manage a couple of lively six- to eight-year-old boys. Such youngsters are sometimes more willing to obey a boy than a girl, and a boy may be more resourceful in entertaining them.

WHOSE MONEY?

Parents who are habitually pressed for funds to meet family expenses need not hesitate to require their children of any age to contribute all or a portion of any money they may earn to the family funds. When they do so, it is usually to ask the child to spend his earnings for clothing, school supplies or similar personal expenses. The child cannot be expected to feel happy about it, but if the parents explain fully the family income and the concomitant expenses, so that the child understands the necessity for his contribution, he will seldom rebel.

Unless the need for augmenting family funds is pressing, a sub-teen should be permitted to keep for himself money that he has earned and to spend it as he likes. The power to spend money to gratify an idle whim or momentary impulse is one of the delights to which a wage-earner is entitled; to experience it gives a sub-teen a taste of the rewards of working and earning.

Suppose sub-teen Barbara longs for a twelve-dollar sweater, but you do not feel that you can spend more than eight. To suggest that she contribute four dollars of money she has earned to the purchase is not to require her to contribute to the family income. It is to permit her to spend her money as she likes—that is, to buy something that she could not otherwise have had.

Permitting children to spend money they have earned "as they like" does not mean permission to spend it for something you do not want them to have—an immoral book, a vulgar record, liquor, an immodest dress, or anything of which you disapprove of on moral grounds.

GROUP PRESSURE

The sub-teen years are the ones in which a child becomes aware of himself as a part of a unit other than his family. This unit is, of course, his friends and contemporaries. Hitherto he has submitted to the opinions and standards of the family, both because he accepted them and because he, alone and unsupported, lacked the strength to resist them. Suddenly he discovers that his fellows are one with him in chafing at restrictions imposed by parents and energetic in upholding conduct and opinions which may differ markedly from those which he has been taught to uphold.

This is exhilarating. A sub-teen knows instinctively that the time is not far distant when he must assume responsibility for his own acts, set his own standards, and rise or fall thereby. He is right. A man who has not learned to do this will be an adult in age, but he will be a child in his dependency. In the first stages of learning self guidance, the sub-teen will lean heavily upon the support of contemporary opinion.

This can be valuable. A child fortunate enough to fall in with a group of keen-minded, idealistic companions can rise to heights to which he has never before aspired. It can be fatal. A youth lacking proper home training can become a cop-hater, thief, mugger, or sadist against his secret inclinations, merely for the support and sense of assurance he derives from acceptance as one of a strong unit.

In either case, one of the first signs will be the adoption of a number of silly fads in dress and jewelry. The group will speak a semi-secret *patois* that can be trying to adult ears. The youngsters will admire music, actors, and entertainers offensive to your aesthetic taste.

Much of this is just froth—foam on a brew which may be good or bad—and in itself proves nothing. Allow it wherever you can do so without a lowering of your basic standards of morality and propriety. Don't condemn hastily, just because the matter under discussion is not what you did when you were young. Think, think hard, and try to remember how you behaved and thought at that age. Try to recall the heroes of your youth, the silly fads you cherished, the conduct you admired. You will end up smiling—though perhaps sadly. Other times, other manners. You have improved, so will your child. Be as permissive as you safely can.

You are still the man in authority. Exert it when you must. Your son cannot stop shaving, wear one pair of socks a week, use vulgar or indecent language, read filth, roam at will. Your daughter cannot disguise herself under a mask of make-up, stop bathing, flaunt her budding charms, stay out all night. For both, the home moral standards must be upheld.

This is easier if you began, in childhood, to teach them to "dare to be different." But it will still be a problem. The desire to be an "insider" is so intense that the thought of being an "outsider" is almost intolerable. Consider how painful it would be for you yourself to be rejected by your associates, even with your maturity and self-assurance. How much the harder for these sub-teens who are barely half-adult!

But somehow, the point must be made. It may help to explain to your sub-teens that, at their age, it is wholly natural to display their increasing maturity by rebelling at parental and school authority, to test its limits and find out how far they may go. It is also natural to regard rebellion, in itself, as proof of maturity. But the real proof lies in how willingly and how successfully the sub-teen accepts the responsibilities that go with the privileges of growing up.

You may also seek outside help. If you are not wholly opposed to the group with which your sub-teen is associating, seek out the parents and get their points of view. You may be able to exert group parental pressure even more effective than group sub-teen pressure. Seek help from church and school. The church is always willing to help, the school usually is. Try to shift the group interest to Sodality activities, sports programs, senior scouting, the Police Athletic League, the CYO, or Junior Red Cross. Try to establish reasonable limits to the hours and pursuits of the group, which will be supported by all the parents.

If you feel the group is wholly unacceptable, help your child to escape from it by seeking new contacts and a new group through the agencies mentioned above.

WHERE ARE THEY?

You can save your child from the danger of bad associations outside the home if you investigate thoroughly the character of the places where he spends his leisure hours. This duty is too frequently neglected. Go, alone and unannounced, to the corner store where your boy meets his friends. Observe the general atmosphere of the place—who frequents it, what is offered for sale. Examine any comic books and paperbacks for vulgarity, pornography and indecency. Look for gambling, sales of policy slips, marijuana, liquor. Go to the theater, athletic hall, canteen or dance hall that he attends. Check for proper lighting, observance of fire laws, and firm supervision of patrons. Investigate rest rooms. If you find improper conditions in any of these latter places you can appeal to local authorities; they are probably in violation of municipal ordinances. In the case of any retail store, it is best to appeal to school authorities to ask them to place it off-limits for students. This will usually result in a prompt clean-up by the owner: he is losing business. You have a right to do all these things; you have a duty to do them. Exercise both.

ENTERTAINMENT MEDIA

The entertainment media of sub-teens must be supervised, like that of younger children, but they should be given more latitude, as follows:

Any motion picture that carries the A-I rating of the Legion of Decency is permissible. The next classification A-II is "Morally unobjectionable for adults and adolescents." Twelve and thirteen-year-olds should not be allowed to see pictures in this classification as they are still really children. Fourteen to fifteen-year-olds may be allowed to go to them, but if, in your opinion, any given picture in this category is not suitable for your sub-teen, you may refuse permission. No sub-teen should see a picture in any category except A-I and A-II.

Supervising television for sub-teens is particularly difficult. The younger half of the group should be treated as children in this matter. The older half should be urged to keep all viewing at a minimum. There are so many things a child thirteen to sixteen can do besides watch television, so many new fields and new interests are opening to him, if he can be induced to pursue them, that it is really sad to see a sub-teen whose primary source of entertainment is television. Encourage your sub-teens to join school clubs and teams, learn to play tennis, golf, swim, sew, cook, garden, ski, play cards. This is the Learning Age. The interests they develop now will determine how full—or how empty—their adult life will be. Selection of what programs they may see now becomes almost impossible. One can urge them to watch symphony, opera, science programs, or good plays, but it is hopeless to try to screen out all the junk.

Reading choices are now very important. Withhold all indecencies —the trash magazines, pornography, the crime "comics," such paperbacks as dwell on lewdness, immorality, violence and filthy dialogue. If any member of your family other than your sub-teen is in the habit of bringing such reading material into the home, now is the time to stop! Forbid these completely. To do so requires no explanation or defense. Children cannot eat poison, or read it.

There is another reading area that still needs supervision but is harder to define and to oversee. This includes works intended for adult readers and written with taste and literary skill, which you may still wish to withhold from your sub-teen because:

a) They probe too deeply and too frankly into problems of adult life which you do not yet wish him to explore.

b) They resolve the difficulties of their characters with wholly secular solutions of their problems, ignoring the laws of God and man's duty to obey them.

c) They discuss flagrant immorality and indecent behavior as if it were both universal and attractive and do so with such literary skill and charm as profoundly to influence the unsophisticated reader.

In the first category, one might put Francois Mauriac's *Therese*, a literary masterpiece, which probes too deeply and too subtly into the problems of lovelessness for immature minds to grapple with. In the second category, one places works such as those of D. H. Lawrence, in which the philosophy is wholly amoral. In the third are found such works as the writings of Ronald Firbank—witty, irreverent, charming— and scandalous. This is literary absinthe, to be sipped, very occasionally, by the adult sophisticate, but requiring the label "not for children."

Try to know what your sub-teen is reading and pass judgment on it if you have the ability. Anything you read which you think not yet suitable for him may be withheld. Seek help from teachers and librarians in choosing material adult enough to hold his interest without turning his world upside down.

GOING STEADY

Going steady in the sense of two young people pairing off regularly and frequently and centering their romantic dreams on one another should never be permitted in the sub-teen years. Yet, pairing off at this age is becoming increasingly common, particularly in the South and the Midwest, and the secular influences that formerly helped restrain it are giving up the fight. This is one area in which the Catholic parent must "dare to be different" in guiding his children.

What are the advantages of such dating; what are the arguments advanced for it? "Everybody does it"—children want to be like their fellows. "We want to be popular"—a "steady" will take the child to all the activities of their group. "It isn't serious"—this is the modern way sub-teens have fun, and it is harmless.

The arguments against: sub-teens are still children in their judgment, their opinions, and their knowledge of what the world is really like. They improve in all these fields and in their knowledge of character by meeting and knowing as many people as possible. Popularity is not achieved, nor is the knowledge of how to be popular learned, by settling down with the first social partner who offers himself, just for the sake of a dependable escort. Most important of all: while sub-teens are children in so many important ways, they are fully adult in the strength and drive of their physical urges. If allowed to center their social life around one partner, to indulge in the intimacies and privacy which may be extended to older teens who are properly seeking a life partner, the danger is real and fearful.

Speaking on the "terrifying multiplication of child marriages," Archbishop William O. Brady of St. Paul recently said, "It is the duty of our parish priests to speak bluntly to old and young about this matter, at a time when both must listen." Among causes for child marriage the archbishop cited

> too many teen-agers keeping steady company, excessive freedom of dress and conduct among us, and amusements without check, which all disturb a budding concupiscence and lead to tragedy more often than a sound Christian society can sustain.
>
> Somebody should say "NO" strongly and often to these children, before a mother starts weeping for her

baby's lost innocence, and a father, suddenly righteous-
minded, rises up in his wrath to demand that his
daughter "be done right by" and his wholly-unexpected
grandchild be given a name other than Tom, Dick, or
Harry.

The Church cannot and will not give approval to
wedding ceremonies that are to be only ceremonies.
Parents can weep—and should—until their throats are
sore. Signing a marriage paper does not solve the problem. Christian marriage is not a formula for the moment,
to regularize yesterday's mistakes. It is for life. It is a
contract. It is a sacrament. It is a permanent and holy
thing. It demands responsibility which the too-young
have not yet attained. Unless there be a certainty of a
solid and lasting union, the *Church cannot witness nor
bless what it expects to fail.*

The archbishop's solution is: "Put off the marriages of the young.
Let them stop keeping company."

Early marriage is not a problem for Catholics only; all thoughtful
Americans are concerned about it. Here are the causes of too-early
marriage given by Dr. Paul Popenoe, director of the American Institute
of Family Relations, and his opinions on the matter:

Going steady too early and through this propinquity
supposing that they are falling in love.

Tremendous sex stimulation from all the "mass
media" of public education such as the movies, TV,
music, advertising, and popular fiction.

Escape from discipline at home, from dissatisfaction
with school, from unpleasant situations at home, of all
kinds. Increased divorce and remarriage has vastly increased the number of children living with a stepfather
or stepmother. There is often conflict which leads a girl,
for instance, to think the way to escape from it is to
marry some man who will have her.

Chain reaction. When one high school girl marries,
others immediately begin to think that they could do
likewise. High school principals are continually complaining that these marriages become a fad, like wearing
blue jeans or bobby sox.

City living. Youngsters in cities have more freedom
and much less supervision than they did when they lived
on the farms and in small towns.

High employment, which makes it easy for young people to get jobs of some sort and support themselves to some extent in marriage. However, surveys show that most of the high school marriages depend largely on relatives to support them.

War crisis atmosphere. Many a girl hurries a marriage in order to become a wife before her boy friend goes into the armed services. Still more seem to feel that, with everything so uncertain, they might as well take advantage of the opportunity and get all out of life that they can while there is still time.

Those and similar influences are the main ones, but let me say that they are not producing satisfactory marriages. One study found that when both partners are under twenty there are just twice as many divorces as there are when they marry somewhere between the ages of 20 and 25. It's high time for every parent and every citizen to take this question as a personal one and insist that home, school, church, and community organizations concentrate on giving young people better preparation for marriage. All studies indicate that the more they know about it, the less they are likely to rush into premature matrimony.

This matter is discussed in the section devoted to the sub-teens because, in many instances, the roots of teen-age tragedy, or too-early marriage, are implanted by permitting too much liberty to the sub-teens.

Stick to your guns. The children are wrong; you are right. Going steady is, for sub-teens, always wrong.

LIMITS FOR SUB-TEENS

For those in the lower half of this age group—the twelve-to-thirteen-year olds—there should be almost no occasions on which they stay out later than ten-thirty without an adult. For the older half, eleven-thirty should be the limit, and they should seldom stay out this late. You may, however, when you consider it suitable, grant them a slight extension of this time-limit.

The younger ones should be discouraged from pairing off, but they may do so for a matinee or early movie date of several couples, or to be escorted home from a party.

No week-night social life should be permitted during the school year. They may, on week-nights, attend a club meeting, rehearsal, or orchestra practice if necessary, but usually these are not scheduled for the evening hours, but take place after school.

Sub-teen children should not be permitted to travel anywhere in a car without an adult—in most states it is illegal to drive at this age.

The older half will pair off a little more—for school functions, picnics, house parties, club dances—but should go with other couples.

Anything like settling down to one partner should be energetically discouraged.

They must abide by your opinion as to what is modest and suitable clothing, but should otherwise be permitted considerable freedom of choice.

Any pronounced drop in school grades should result in curtailment of social or athletic life until grades are brought back to their customary level. This is not punishment; it is done to give them the extra time they obviously need to maintain their usual standard. A drop in grades may also indicate that the child needs a physical examination to make sure it is not caused by an unrecognized ailment. It may also mean that the sub-teen is attempting too much. Perhaps he has an outside job: it should be resigned. Or he may have to give up music lessons or some other outside activity. Throughout the school years, a child's primary responsibility is to earn the best grades of which he is capable. Throughout these years it is vital that the parents place this responsibility ahead of everything but moral guidance.

Sub-teens should not be allowed to go to outdoor moving picture theaters without an adult—these are dangerous places.

In vacation time, sub-teens can be permitted week-night social life but should not be out later than nine-thirty on these nights without permission. Always know where your child is, and with whom. Encourage him to bring his friends home and make it pleasant for them there when he does. Try to know what the life is like in the homes of his friends, and whether you may safely allow him to go there.

No friends should be invited into the home unless an adult is present. No visits to the home of a friend should be made unless an adult is present. Never violate this rule.

Parents, make every reasonable effort to know your children's friends, their background, and their parents. Make it a solemn duty to investigate their places of amusement—theaters, soda bars, swimming pools, canteens, dance halls—to make sure they are respectable and properly supervised. If these places are substandard, consult the proper authorities and see to it that they are improved.

22

Guidance and Manners for Teen-Agers

When I was a child, I spoke as a child, I felt as a child,
I thought as a child. Now that I have become a man, I
have put away the things of a child (1 Corinthians
13:11).

AIMS

By the time a child reaches his sixteenth year, parents must face up
to a realization that some find difficult: their task is almost done. In a
few years, five at the very most, their child will be an adult, responsible
for his acts, free to make his own choices. How well prepared he will
be for this liberty of action, how successfully he will cope with it, will
depend largely on how he was reared.

Ever since infancy your child's ideas of right conduct have been
developing, based on your ideas and opinions. As mentioned so often
before, how you have behaved has made far more impression than
anything you have said. Basically, his opinions are now fixed. His own
experiences of later life may modify some of them; others may sometimes sway him but, in essentials, the outlook of the average adult is
much conditioned by his childhood experiences.

When he is sixteen, one must begin to allow the teen-ager more
liberty of thought and action and be confident that his behavior when
beyond reach of our supervision will be governed by what we have
taught him. There are two reasons for this:

a) He must begin to use these freedoms while still under our guidance and supervision, to enable him to manage them successfully
   in adult life.
b) This is the age when we can no longer keep our teen-agers

completely under our control. One must now trust them to behave, out of our presence, by the standards we have taught them at home.

Some will say that sixteen is too young for this, and there is validity to their objections. But we must face facts: in modern American society, sixteen is the age—the very latest age—at which they will begin to clamor for these freedoms, and it is unrealistic to attempt to defer them. Better to decide how to cope with them.

BEGIN WITH TRUST

Begin with trust. If your child has always been honest, devout, and reliable, do not fear that he will overnight turn into a monster of deceit. The teen-ager suffers from a "bad press." So much is written about the instability, indecency, and violence of a minority of our teen-agers that many parents fear lest the mere attainment of the late teen years will turn their loving, obedient child into a criminal. Don't do this. Look about you. You will see teen-agers devoting their time to Red Cross and other community services, developing their budding talents for writing or music, taking prizes in 4–H and at county fairs for their homemaking skills, absorbed in athletics, auto mechanics, and a dozen other rewarding interests. Look at the many young married people whom you know who are devoting themselves to their families and a happy home life. Only a few years ago they, too, were teen-agers. *Most of them don't go bad.*

Do you feel that you have mismanaged the rearing of your child up to this time? If true, this is very, very unfortunate. "Too late." Dreadful words, but sometimes true. If this is your position, there is little that you can do about it. One can try—one must try, as hard as one can, to make up for the mistakes and neglect of earlier years, but the effort will be trebly difficult—and may fail. For readers who are worried about this problem, a word of consolation: if you are concerned enough about your child's welfare to say, "I am afraid I have failed to do my duty by him," it usually means you have *not* failed—you are only unduly concerned. The mere fact that you have obtained and read this book shows how genuine is your interest in your child, and that you are trying to live up to your responsibility. Keep trying. You have probably "builded better than you know."

Until and unless he proves unworthy, therefore, trust your child:

a) To tell you the truth.
b) To keep the rules you lay down.
c) To behave properly away from home.
d) To choose proper companions and places of amusement.

If you "catch" him in an untruth, be very, very sure of your facts. Be slow to accuse him until you *are* sure. Do not upbraid him and brand him a liar. Ask for an explanation—there may be an excellent one. Your communication lines may be crossed. If it is an untruth, try to find out why he lied—whether in fear of what you would say to the truth, to conceal the breaking of a rule or some misdeed, or to cover up for a friend. Try to discuss it calmly and seriously, urge him never to fear to tell you the truth, but warn him that habitual lying will result in curtailment of his liberties.

A teen-ager must abide by the rules you lay down, just as a sub-teen must. The rules will be more liberal, but they must be observed. Failure to live up to them is a proof of immaturity and will result in less freedom of action.

Trust your child to behave properly away from home—because you must. You cannot go with him wherever he goes; it would be very bad for him if you could. Once more, he must "do it for himself." Be positive in your attitude. Take the position, "You are a fine boy and have always made your family proud of you. I *know* you will always do so. I *know* you have the courage to "dare to be different," and that you will, when necessary, set your less fortunate friends an example of how a Catholic gentleman behaves." Expect the best, and you are very apt to get it. If someone brings you a tale of misbehavior or if you stumble upon your child misbehaving (entertaining with no adults in the house, sneaking a date while baby sitting, drinking to excess), suppress your fear and anger. Express your disapproval of the misconduct (although he is no doubt well aware of this) and express, too, tenderly and seriously, the love and interest which makes you, and will always make you, far more concerned than anyone else with his welfare and well-being.

Continue to try to know your teen-ager's friends, as you did when he was a sub-teen. Welcome them to your home, try (unobtrusively of course) to observe them, as your youngster still cannot do, with the reasoned judgment of an adult. Then, be slow to form your judgment and slow to criticize. Many a teen-ager who is basically a decent, indeed, an admirable person, appears otherwise because of crude manners or speech, addiction to sloppy dress, or unfortunate mannerisms. These are surface things. Try to know the whole boy or girl. In so weighing your teen-ager's friends, remember that your child, if carefully reared, is probably aware of these flaws in his companion, and may be sensitive about them, but has chosen his friend in spite of them.

None of this means that you should hesitate to speak out if you feel the companionship is a dangerous one. One should condemn improper or immoral behavior, apparent lack of a true moral code, recklessness or defiance of the law, undue familiarity—any character flaw that might endanger your teen-ager in pursuing the association. Discuss the matter with your child—ask him for his opinions. State your objections and reasons for feeling as you do. If you are still not convinced that the association is harmless, it must be forbidden. To do otherwise is unfair to your child, and less than your duty.

If it is the companion's manners or dress that you object to, some criticism may be expressed, but try to be tactful about it. Take the attitude that it is unfortunate that a youngser who is basically an attractive person is handicapped in some manner through his parents' failure to teach him better, contrasting this with your child's good fortune in not being so handicapped.

Thus if you have entertained at dinner a teen-ager whose table manners are atrocious, you might say mildly, "I am sure you noticed, as we all did, how very bad Terry's table manners are. It's a shame his parents did not teach him better; it will handicap him all his life. People will judge him by something that is really not his fault. When you were a child and I was nagging you to 'sit up straight, break your bread, hold your fork right,' I sometimes wondered if the result would be worth the trouble, but now I know it is. Thank goodness, you could, as your Irish grandmother used to say, 'dine with kings' and be relaxed and at ease, because you know how to behave."

KEEP CLOSE TO GOD

A teen-ager should be supervising his own spiritual life. If your teen-ager receives the sacraments regularly and attends voluntarily devotions such as novenas or Stations of the Cross, you can feel confident that he is on the right road. A young person who endeavors to keep close to God seldom fails to do so. If your youngster is not pursuing his devotions as you feel he should, it is still your responsibility to remind him of his duties and to see that he fulfills them. This is the one Resource on which we can always depend, and which never fails us.

TALKING IT OVER

Now, more than ever, it is vital that your child should feel free to talk to you about his interests, confident that he will not be misunderstood or his confidence be betrayed. Always take time to listen when your teen-ager voluntarily confides in you. Listen with sympathy,

remembering how you thought and felt at his age. Listen with understanding of how trifles may be tragedies. Listen with patience to what
"He said" and "I said." If you really want your child's confidence, you
must convince him that your ear is always a willing one, and that the
story of his simplest activities is never boring to you. In this, as in so
many other matters, his willingness to confide in these years will
depend to a great extent on how you received his confidences in the
past.

Many teen-agers who have formerly confided in and listened to the
opinions of their parents now become much more reserved. The teen-
ager suddenly feels a great gap between his generation and yours.
"Father and Mother are too old, and too hopelessly old-fashioned to
understand modern life and modern young people. There is just no use
talking to them." How does one combat this? Admittedly, it is very
hard.

It helps to review your present attitudes and opinions. Does
your child have grounds for feeling as he does? Do you constantly
belittle the music, entertainers, moving pictures, books, clothing styles,
and fads of his age group? Have you ever tried to find out about these
things and judge them for yourself, on their merits, or do you condemn
them out of hand merely because they are different from the things you
admired when young? Do you belittle his friends because of your own
prejudices against various racial stocks, Negroes, Jews? If you are
guilty of this, be *proud* that your child is not. Get acquainted with the
Mexican boy your son likes, the Jewish girl in your daughter's dancing
class. Judge them as *people*—just people—to decide whether or not
they are suitable companions. Admit that in this area this generation
may be better than ours; learn from them.

When your child tries seriously to discuss world events and problems, listen respectfully. If his ideas differ in some areas from your
own, he is not necessarily wrong; it may be you. Listen to his opinions
on politics, labor problems, votes for eighteen-year-olds, military service, and similar matters. When you express your opinions, be prepared
to defend them with reason and sensible argument. Don't be angry
and try to cram your views down his throat.

When you are laying out rules for him—the hours he may keep,
whether he may work after school, when he may drive a car—let him
advance his ideas, and thresh the matter out between you. If he has
any points to make, other than that "everybody" does as he prefers,
weigh them, and at least appear to give them consideration.

Keep constantly in mind, when talking things over with him, that you want to generate light, not heat. An attitude of sweet reasonableness can go a long way toward retaining your teen-ager's respect for your opinions. You will be better able to do this if you remember that, in everything that is really important—his moral code, his choice of companions, the hours he keeps—final word is yours. Be permissive wherever you can, especially in minor matters. But in the important things, do not hesitate to express your opinions and to exert your authority with assurance and conviction. If it finally comes down to the point where you must say, "As long as you are under my roof and under my care you must do so-and-so, because I say so"—say so, and let the matter rest there. But do not use this method except as a last resort.

"Tell me how you feel about this matter, and why. I am always interested in your ideas, and will do my best to understand them" gets better results than, "What a lot of tomfoolery! Where you kids pick up these crazy notions beats me! Don't they teach you anything at that fancy school you go to?"

Even though you do your best to keep abreast of the younger generation, and to treat your teen-ager with consideration, there will still be a gap between you. He cannot believe that you ever felt as he does now, and telling him you once did will do no good. He cannot believe that you are really conversant with the modern world. If he continues to feel that, despite these failings, you can be depended upon to help him in trouble or emergency, to stand by him and promote his interests and welfare, that is the best you can hope for. "This, too, will pass." Remember what Mark Twain said about his father: When he was seventeen he was ashamed of the old man's ignorance, but at twenty-one, he was surprised at how much his father had learned in four years!

FAMILY SOLIDARITY

When small children get in trouble, they know instinctively that they can turn to their parents to help them out of it. Whether the difficulty is a broken window, a bike stolen, or a neighborhood fight, Mommy and Daddy will stand up for their children and protect them. In the teen years they sometimes lose this confidence. When in difficulty a teen-ager will fear to turn to his parents, lest they scold and punish, rather than help.

It is, therefore, a good idea to discuss this matter with your teen-ager, to assure him that he still has, and will always have, your unfailing support. Something along these lines covers the matter: "Laura and Don, you are no longer children, as you very well realize. You are not adults, either, though you soon will be. This in-between stage is hard on you, and hard on me. Your mother and I are eager to give you all the privileges and all the responsibility for your own acts that you can cope with. But in assuming them, I want you to remember one thing: situations are bound to arise in the teen years which you cannot manage; you will require adult help. Whether these circumstances are caused by your own mistakes or those of your companions, please, remember *always*, if you are in any kind of trouble, come to us at once for help. *You will always get it.* Whether it is difficulty with your school work, an automobile accident, a prank that got out of hand, trouble with the opposite sex, tell us, and tell us as soon as possible. We will do everything in our power to correct the situation. To do this, we must be sure that you tell us the truth—all the truth—about what happened. No matter how bad it is, give us the actual facts. Otherwise our hands are tied in helping. Remember, too, that the more serious the difficulty is, the more you need our help.

"After we have helped you, you will, if you have done wrong, be punished. But if you do wrong and lie about it, you will have cut yourself off from our help and will be punished more severely than you would have been if you had not lied. Don't plan on lying and covering up the matter. It won't work. The more serious the difficulty, the less chances of it working. Please rely on us. We are never farther away from you than the nearest telephone. Use it!"

Parents who give their children such assurances as these must be prepared to fulfill them when the occasion arises. It may not be easy. Lean over backward to be fair to your child. Whenever possible, give him the benefit of the doubt: if one's parents are not slightly prejudiced in one's favor, who will be? This does not mean that you should help him throw the blame for a misdeed on someone else or that you should brush off really bad behavior as "a boyish prank" merely because the boy involved is yours. It does mean that your child's word should have weight with you. If he tells one story and a companion tells another, and the facts fit both, it is right that you should accept your child's version. But you cannot do so if his story does not fit the facts or if the word of several others is against him.

Help to repair any damage done: reimburse injured parties, repair damaged property, settle matters with the proper authorities, etc. Where possible, require the child himself to reimburse or repair—the lesson learned thus is invaluable. Then see to it that the child is punished if at fault. Don't punish for mere accident.

When you have learned the facts, settled the difficulty, made such reparations as are required, punished as indicated, and discussed the matter thoroughly, drop it. Don't talk and talk and *talk* about it. Don't bring it up every time he asks for a favor or a privilege. Don't let it destroy your basic confidence in your teen-ager. All of us have done wrong sometimes. All of us have required forgiveness. Judge him in the future by his future behavior. Don't assume he will misbehave again, until and unless he does.

STANDARDS OF CONDUCT

Throughout the life of any child, his parents have been setting up for him, consciously or otherwise, standards of ideal conduct based on parental ideas of what constitutes correct behavior. These standards cannot be higher than the parents' own. If you have not previously raised this point with your child, it should now be made: whether his personal standards are, in the world's eyes, high or low, idealistic or down-to-earth, he will never be happy unless trying to live up to them.

Nothing obtained by denying one's own standards is ever worth having. "To thine own self be true" is a psychological truth. Whenever one deviates from it to obtain some desired goal, the attainment of it brings no happiness. The inner self rejects it as worthless because of the way in which it was achieved; the person hates himself because of the methods to which he has stooped. This is misery.

One frequently sees people who have passed examinations by cheating, advanced in business by stabbing associates in the back, made fortunes by bilking the public, who seem thoroughly satisfied with the resulting gains. Their satisfaction may be quite genuine, if their personal standards are low enough to enable them, by a little "intelligent" rationalization, to convince themselves of the propriety of their behavior.

Might it not be wise, therefore, not to set one's standards too high? To keep them low enough and flexible enough to adjust to the world "as it is," to be "practical" and "realistic"? There are many who declare that this is a sensible attitude—including some psychologists and educators.

The true Christian must reject this solution. Admittedly, Jesus Christ set "impossibly" high standards for us. Few of us can live up to them, even when striving to do the best we can. The grace to live the life of perfection is given by God only to those rare souls whom we call saints. For the rest of us, "the best we can" means only the highest to which we, with all our individual human limitations, can strive. No more is required of us.

The struggle for perfection is precisely that: a struggle. We are precluded, by the fallibility of human nature, from reaching our goal. One must try—and fail; try again—and fail again. It is in the struggle to succeed that we fight the good fight. It is in the struggle to do and be "the best we can," within the limits of our human nature and native frailties, that we earn heaven.

To lower our standards so that we can successfully accomplish the little we attempt is to evade the issue. The brave Christian keeps his standards as high as he can. The happy Christian strives, unceasingly, to be true to them.

Warn your child that worldly influences will constantly tempt him to lower his standards or reject them, to obtain some fancied good. Warn him that any good so obtained will never satisfy. "Stolen sweets" do *not* "taste best."

RULES OF CONDUCT

For the purposes of this book, we are defining a teen-ager as a child between the ages of sixteen and nineteen. But in the late teen years, many have finished high school and are working or are away at college, or even married. The problems of this group must be separated from the younger ones, and will be discussed elsewhere.

Even for the younger teen-agers, those still in high school, it becomes difficult to lay down general rules of conduct. So much depends on where one lives, one's income group, and the maturity and the dependability of the individual boy or girl. Speaking very generally one may say:

> The teen-ager's primary responsibility is still to do the very best of which he is capable in school.
>
> No week-night social life is allowed during the school year.
>
> Know where your child is going, with whom, and when he or she expects to get home, on all evening engagements.
>
> No entertaining is done at home without an adult present. No permission is given to visit in a friend's house without an adult present.
>
> Discourage steady dating before the last half of junior year, at the very earliest.
>
> Try to know your child's friends. You still have the right

to forbid him to associate with one whose general reputation is bad or one whose behavior, on some occasion
upon which you were present, was objectionable. Girls
should be discouraged from going out with boys more
than four years older than themselves. Their attitudes,
interests and privileges will be too different from their
own, and it will cut them off from their own age group.

The reader will note that in the rules given above, no attempt has
been made to suggest the hours which a teen-ager should keep. This
is because circumstances so alter cases that any general suggestions
that might be made are valueless.

Some parents handle this matter by saying to a sixteen-year-old
daughter, "Janet, you are now old enough so that it is impractical and
perhaps unreasonable to lay down set hours for you. All your life we
have been teaching you how to behave. If you do not yet know how,
we have failed in our duty to you. But I do not think we have failed. I
think you are mature for your years, sensible and responsible. So,
henceforward, when you are going out for the evening, tell us where
you are going, with whom, and the hour at which you expect to be
home. If you come home at the time agreed upon, well and good.

"Thus, if you tell me that you are going to the movies with Don, Jill
and Ned, that after the movies you are going to get a soda at Jackson's,
and that you will be home at half-past twelve, and then come home at
that time, all will be well. If you tell me, "Tonight is the big Prom, the
dance lasts until three, and afterwards we are all invited to Dodie's
house for scrambled eggs. I may not be home until half-past four," and
come home at that hour, that too is all right.

"But if you say you are going to the movies and will be home at
eleven, and do not come home until two, you will be in trouble. If
something happens to delay you or change your plans, I expect you to
telephone and tell us so. Don't worry about waking us—we will never
reproach you for that. We think these rules are fair and reasonable. If
you abide by them, all will be well. If you do not, we will have to
change the rules.

"One more thing. When you tell us where you are going, or if you
telephone to report a change of plans, I assume that you will tell the
truth. We will continue to assume this until something happens to
prove otherwise. If and when this should happen, the results will be
very unfortunate—for you."

A parent can lay down similar rules for a boy, keeping in mind
the fact that he must take his date home before he comes home him-

self, which will require that he be allowed to keep slightly later hours than would a girl. These flexible rules work well with a truthful and fairly responsible youngster. If not lived up to, more strict supervision should be imposed. An occasional infringement should be punished with curtailment of activity for a given period—a week, two weeks.

Flexible rules help a teen-ager to learn to manage his affairs. But if, under this system, your child habitually fails to live up to the rules laid down, or takes advantage of them to do things of which you do not approve, you will have to employ a more rigid schedule and see to it that he lives up to it. Explain the reason for the change: he has proved to be too immature and unreliable to live up to the responsibility laid upon him by the freedom given. Hold out the hope that better behavior and more dependability on his part will induce you to give back the privileges you have had to withdraw.

MANNERS

The manners of a teen-ager should, when the occasion requires it, be those of a well-bred adult, plus the little extra deference to their elders that so becomes this age. This does not mean that a teen-ager will always so behave, nor be expected to do so. In the bosom of his family, or with his contemporaries, he will frequently be boisterous, uncouth and silly—a natural outlet for the high spirits common to this age. It does mean that teen-agers should instinctively employ the good manners you have taught them at school, in business, or on social occasions when conventional behavior is expected of them.

Both boys and girls should rise when an older person enters the room. They should be particularly careful to do this for clergymen and religious, teachers, parents other than their own. They should rise for their own parents at a social gathering, in their own home or away from it, but need not observe such ceremony as a part of daily life. At a large party they rise, not when an older person enters the room, but when he approaches the group they are in, or when he speaks to them. Boys address men over forty as "Sir." Both sexes should take care to add, "Mrs. Smith," "Miss Wilson," to their remarks to women of all ages.

If teen-agers have not been taught how to introduce people or how to behave at a formal dinner, in a restaurant or nightclub, at the theater, while traveling, they should now learn. They should also learn how to be part of, or "go down" a receiving line.

This is the age at which they will be introduced to uncommon foods which may not be served at the family table—oysters and clams, lobster, exotic cheeses, artichokes, caviar, pâté de fois gras, table wines, poultry under glass, food on skewers, or foreign dishes. If you do not wish to serve these at home, discuss them with your teen-agers; their nature, when they are usually served, and the serving implements which accompany them (oyster forks, lobster crackers, various wine glasses, grape shearers). Young people are often concerned about correct usage when obliged to use a serving implement which is un-familiar to them. They have merely to observe how it is employed by a guest served before them. Because of his youth, the teen-ager is almost never the guest of honor at any gathering, and may therefore depend upon others being served before him. However, to help him to feel confident and at ease, it is good to teach him, insofar as one is able, the type of service he may expect at various parties, from the simplest to the most formal.

Girls

Teen-age girls act as hostess for luncheons, teas, and dinners for their own age group, and should master the duties involved in doing so. They should also learn how to preside at a tea table and serve after-dinner coffee.

How to receive a compliment gracefully worries some teen girls. The first requirement is to take it at its face value as genuine, even though one suspects that one is being teased. Even if one fears that the remark is sarcastic, the best rejoinder is always to reply as if the com-pliment were a sincere one—with a glance of surprise and pleasure and a bright, "Thank you! That's nice to hear," or "It is kind of you to think so." If the compliment was a genuine one, it has then been duly acknowledged; if it was offered in sarcasm, the intended unkindness has glanced off its mark.

Embarrassment, or fear of appearing conceited, makes young girls reject a compliment with a remark like, "Oh, you can't think that! Ann's hair is far prettier than mine!" or "This old rag! I've had it for ages. Silly boy, you've seen it lots of times." Such a response makes the giver of the compliment, who intended to please by his remark, feel awkward and silly. It is always to be avoided.

Declining invitations is another of a teen-age girl's problems. A conscientious girl does not want to lie about having a previous engage-ment. You can always refuse and still tell the truth, by saying, "Next Tuesday? Oh, I'm sorry I am going to be busy that night." Or, "I have other plans for Tuesday." If you do not say what they are, it can always be true that next Tuesday you will be busy doing something or other.

Suppose a boy asks you well in advance to a dance you want to go to—but not with him. If you refuse him, must you stay home from the dance even though someone else asks you? Not if you are tactful. Just say, "I'm so sorry. I am busy that night." If he says "Are you going to the dance?" giggle and say, "I didn't say. But I'll tell you what I'll do. I'll save you a dance. O.K.?"

If you do get another bid and go to the dance, he will think the date was made before he asked you. If you do not, the subject will probably not come up again between you. If it does, say, "I was just teasing you. I never said I had a date for the dance."

Once you have made a date, or accepted a bid for anything, you must keep it. The only way out is to plead illness and *stay home.* You cannot withdraw from one date because a more attractive one is later offered to you. If you try such tactics, you will regret it. Boys gossip quite as much as girls. The boy you rejected will find out, and hate you for it. Other boys, when you refuse them a date, will wonder if you had a "better offer."

Suppose a boy you like asks you for a first date, and you really do have a previous engagement. How can you encourage him to try again? Say, with real regret, "Oh, what a shame! That's the night of the Yacht Club dance. I made a date for it ages ago. Call me again soon, please? I would have so liked to go to the open house *with you.*"

Boys

Teen-age boys should know how to escort a girl or woman into and out of theaters and restaurants, up and down a staircase, on and off a bus, into and out of a car. They should rise when any woman joins a group at table or anywhere else. They should be briefed on tipping and paying checks. At a dance, they should always dance at least once with the hostess and once with their dinner partner, if a dinner preceded the dance. When several couples go to a dance together or sit at table together around the dance floor, courtesy requires that he dance at least once with each girl in the group. Modern young people, however, are so addicted to dancing only with the partner with whom they go to the dance that they often ignore this simple courtesy. It is still the right thing to do.

Some prep schools and colleges still have program dances—the "big" prom of the year is apt to be a program dance. In such cases, take pains to make out your program several days before the dance. Otherwise you may find that you and your partner are dancing drearily round and round, all evening, while all others change partners. The night of the dance is too late to make out a program—others will have their program filled.

RULES FOR DATING

For Boys

a) Call for a girl at her house. Ask her to meet you elsewhere only in special circumstances. If you live in one suburb and she in another, you might ask a girl with whom you have a theater date to meet you at a respectable place in town, to avoid being late for the performance. But you take her to her door when going home, regardless of how far it is. You may not ask a girl to meet you anywhere, even under these circumstances, unless you have previously called at her home, and met one of her parents.

b) Go to her door and ring the bell. Go in, if invited, and meet her parents.

c) Do not use her car, even though she has one and you do not. To use hers makes you seem less the man and the escort—it puts you in a false position.

d) Plan your dates in advance whenever possible—and plan to *do* something. It is more fun and less moral risk to go dancing, see a show, or play cards than it is to drive aimlessly about the countryside or lounge in a tavern.

e) When asking a girl for a date, tell her what you have planned, or give her her choice of several amusements, thus: "Ralph Saunders, Dave Thorpe and I thought it would be fun if you and Betty Gregory and Janet Giarve went to the square dance at Lakeside. Ralph will have his car. We will leave at eight and be home around half-past-one. Can you make it?" This kind of invitation tells a girl how to dress, leaves her an opening to refuse gracefully, and provides her with the information most parents require of a daughter. (Where are you going, with whom, who is driving, what time will you be home?)

If you have nothing planned for your date, say, "If you are not busy Saturday I thought you might like to go to the antique car show, or dancing at the Crillon. Which would you prefer?" She can then make a choice, and know that her selection is within the limits of what you had planned.

f) Assume all expenses for any date unless it was previously agreed to be some kind of a Dutch treat party (agreed by a group, never by the two of you) or unless your date is hostess at a party, at home or elsewhere. In the latter case, and in the case of all entertaining where you are guest, not host, a man must be prepared to take care of small expenses that may arise—taxi fare, tipping a parking lot attendant, purchasing cigarettes, or buying a round of drinks. Do not find this advice discouraging. A girl who likes her escort is happy to ride a bus, take a walk, play records or go to church with him—prefers it to an elaborate date with one in whom she is not interested.

g) The rules of our society give the man the power of choice as to whom he will date—that is, to be the aggressor. The girl, except in some special cases such as home parties or proms at girls' schools, has only the right of refusal. This power of choice obligates you to behave in a certain way: having made and kept a date, always behave as if you were enjoying yourself. You need never go out with the girl again (the power of choice), but you did seek this date. Even though the girl is not as attractive as you had fancied—too serious, too silly, too dull —you must not pain and embarrass her by showing your disappointment. Even if the girl's behavior is pointedly disagreeable, you must act the gentleman. Do not do or say anything you will later regret. It is particularly important to show no displeasure or chagrin if a "blind date" is not all you hoped she would be. Remember please, the girl ran quite as much risk as you did—and may be equally disappointed! For the space of an evening, pretend to be pleased with one another, and enjoy yourselves as best you can.

When a girl asks you to a party, you may of course refuse if the girl or the date does not appeal to you. But, once you have accepted *you must keep the engagement* and must try to appear as if you were enjoying the party and the girl's company. If you do not intend to ask her for further dates, you need not imply that you will. Just make this one evening a happy occasion for her. The fact that she asked you to this party, one of the rare occasions on which *she* had the power of choice, shows that she is attracted to you and looked forward to spending an evening with you. Don't disappoint her.

h) Don't put a price on your date's favors. A kiss is an expression of liking. It cannot be bought with a dinner or theater ticket, but must be earned by winning her affection.

i) Don't take her anyplace where you are not proud to be seen.

j) Don't urge her to go anyplace or do anything of which she seems to disapprove. She has the right to live up to her own standards of conduct, even though you may think them unduly strict.

k) Help her to keep the rules and hours her parents have laid out for her. Do this cheerfully and without grousing. For you to act otherwise puts her in an uncomfortable position: she must either displease you or disobey her parents.

l) Promise yourself that *you* will never be the one to introduce any girl to a person, place or situation which may be a source of harm to her.

m) Always remember: an escort is, in one sense, a guardian. For the space of an evening, a girl's immortal soul is in your care. Cherish it!

For Girls

a) Never date a boy you do not know. You may be said to "know" a boy who is in your classes at school or lives neighbor to you, with whom you have a speaking acquaintance, even though no one has actually introduced you. You could safely date such a boy if he asks you. Otherwise, never date a boy who has not been introduced to you by someone who knows him and knows you. This is not merely a social rule. It is physically and morally dangerous to date a stranger, no matter how attractive he seems or how romantic the circumstances under which you first saw him.

b) Always require an escort to call for you at home. Don't meet him elsewhere except in special circumstances (as outlined under Dating for Boys) and then very rarely. If he calls for you by lounging in his car and blowing the horn, go out, greet him pleasantly and say, "Please come in for a minute and meet my family." If he refuses, break the date. If he does as you ask, he will probably understand what you are getting at and will come to your door the next time he calls. If he does not, say, "Will you please ring my bell when you call for me? The neighbors are awfully stuffy about kids honking their horns." If he still does not get the idea—he's hopeless.

c) Going on a date with a boy puts you under no obligation to him. He has the power to choose whom he will ask for a date and to determine what the evening's entertainment will be. You have the power to refuse or accept. When you accept, you are doing him a favor. His return for the money he expends on a date is the pleasure of your company for the evening—nothing more. Kisses are not doled out to "pay" for a pleasant evening; they are a proof of liking or affection. Any boy who thinks otherwise is a boor.

d) When a boy first calls you for a date, don't be ashamed to say, "I'll find out if I may go." Well-bred boys understand that a girl must have parental permission to go out with a "new" boy, or to some place where she has never gone before. It is proof that she is cherished and *looked after* by her family, and quickly puts the relationship on the right plane, as being something open and above-board.

e) You may also ask a boy where you are going, who with, who is driving, and what time you will leave and arrive home. Your parents have a right to ask these questions and get answers. They also have a right to restrict your hours and the places to which you may go. Whenever you can, tell a boy, when making the date, the hour at which you must be home. Give him a chance to "back out" gracefully, if your hours do not suit him. If he agrees to your parents' restrictions, he should be prepared to live up to them without complaining. If he actually calls off the date because of them, do not regret it. He is proving himself selfish, self-centered, socially inept—and not much attracted to you.

f) It is the girl who sets the "tone" for the relationship between herself and her escort. It is really true that people usually treat one as one expects to be treated. If a girl is friendly, amiable, and well-bred, she will be treated like the lady she is. If she is boisterous, overly-familiar and vulgar in speech, her escort will still treat her as she seems to expect to be treated. It is up to you.

Of course there are exceptions. Every girl will sometimes have the experience of finding herself on a first date with a boy who is simply not her sort. Disregarding all her signs of displeasure, he is familiar, crude, tells off-color stories. What to do? If possible: be sick, have a sudden headache, and insist on going home immediately. If circumstances make this impossible, be steadily colder and more reserved. Don't laugh at his stories, do not try to ignore his behavior or cajole him into behaving properly. If he is still impossible, say, "I think we have both made a mistake. Apparently I am not the sort of girl you thought I was when you asked me to go out. If this behavior of yours is any sample, *you* are not the kind of boy I thought you were when I accepted the date. I am ready to go home whenever you are willing to take me."

g) Never lower your own standards of conduct to conform with those of your escort or the group you are in. You will never be happy in so doing, and at the worst may involve yourself in a situation which you may regret for the rest of your life. Don't do things you know are wrong. Don't go places where you should not be. Don't associate with bad companions.

h) Help make dates successful. Try to enjoy—and show you enjoy —the entertainment offered you, no matter how elaborate or simple. Don't constantly apologize if you are a poor swimmer or golfer—ask your partner for tips and admire *his* skill. Don't criticize food or service anyplace or infer that you are used to much finer places. Don't hang back or fail to take part in any games or amusements as best you can, unless they are improper. Don't monopolize the conversation. Draw your escort out if you can. Don't strive to appear sophisticated if you are not. Don't talk about imaginary trips and engagements. Don't tell a Manhattan man what a divine time you had at Holy Cross last winter!

i) Don't break dates for a whim. Emergencies do arise; we are all ill occasionally, so sometimes a date must be broken and, if for a legitimate reason, it should create no ill-feeling. But never make a date you do not intend to keep or break one without cause.

j) Don't telephone a boy without a reason, unless you date frequently and he has asked you to do so. Otherwise, call only to invite him to something: a dance at your school, a party you or a friend are giving, or a club party.

k) Avoid the appearance of being the aggressor in any dealings with boys. The pursued always has the advantage over the pursuer. You may ask a boy who has never taken you out to a party or dance—once. If he does not return the compliment, don't ask him again, no matter how much fun the first date was.

One special situation should be discussed here: in co-educational high schools, it is usually the rule that any member of the junior class may ask someone to the junior Prom. This means that both girls and boys will be inviting. If a junior girl does not care to wait for a junior boy to ask her, she may properly ask a boy who is *not* a member of the junior class to go to the dance —one from another class or another school. She should not ask a classmate. If a classmate wants to go with her, he can invite her.

l) Be realistic in deciding whether or not a boy likes you. Suppose he accepts an invitation from you when you ask him, talks pleasantly with you whenever he sees you, but never asks you for a date. Face the facts. He is not really interested. When corresponding with a boy, write once. Never write again unless he answers your letter. Boys do not neglect to write because they are "too busy." They are just not interested. Don't center your affections and your dreams around someone who is not attracted to you. Look about you for a new interest.

m) Promise yourself that no boy will ever be injured by association with you. Never intentionally dress or behave so as to inflame his passions. Never permit intimacies such as to impose too great a strain upon his self-control. The better you like a boy, the greater your responsibility in this matter.

PARTIES AT HOME

From fifteen years of age upward, young people enjoy giving and attending parties held in one another's homes. Wise parents will encourage their children to entertain but, in permitting them to do so, will be aware of their own responsibilities in the matter. An impromptu get-together occasionally is fun, especially if the group is small—two or three couples. For such a group, record playing, dancing to the radio, singing on the porch, or cooking weenies on the terrace is entertainment enough, and supervision can be kept to a minimum.

For larger parties, much more planning and supervision is required. The number of guests expected and their names should be known to you. A definite program should be planned to keep the young people occupied and amused; and it should be carried out. Otherwise the party will degenerate into a smooching match, boredom, or boisterousness. Do not invite more than you can comfortably accommodate. Serve the food nicely; this encourages nice behavior in eating it. Serve at a definite time and clear all away after allowing a reasonable time to eat it. Enlist the aid of some of the guests in carrying out the program and making the party a success. The help of the most admired boy is invaluable.

Require your child—the one who is host or hostess for the party—to help in preparing the home and the refreshments for the party. Expect him or her also to help in cleaning up afterwards. This is the price of social life!

In some communities, young people like to entertain at home before or after a school prom. Pre-prom parties are called cocktail parties, but only punch or other soft drinks should be served. Serve them in pretty glasses, accompanied by cocktail type snack food; the young people will enjoy it.

Parents, one word of advice: please, never, *never*, permit your child to drink anything from a bottle, once he is weaned! It is very bad manners, always and under all circumstances. Even in advertisements for soft drinks, one never sees anyone actually drinking from a bottle —only holding it. This is because the act of drinking from a bottle is one of the most ungraceful and unattractive sights imaginable. There is no way to do it acceptably. Use a glass always. And remember, the prettier the glass, the better will be the manners of the user. But even a paper cup is better than drinking from a bottle.

After-prom parties may be called supper or breakfast. To hold one at home is better than to allow the young people to go on to a restaurant or tavern for an after-prom party. Scrambled eggs, sausages, and bacon are the type of food usually served. Encourage group singing and story-telling. Do not let it last until dawn. Do not serve intoxicants.

Party Crashing

The most popular seasons for home parties are the Christmas and Easter holidays and graduation week. Often these are large parties which include almost all a child's classmates. A problem has arisen in recent years in connection with such parties: uninvited classmates or teen-agers from other schools—especially boys—may attempt to "crash" them. Boys may do so in groups, acting on the not-unreasonable assumption that, as extra men, they will be an asset and will be gladly welcomed. Girls sometimes crash such a party by coming as the "guest" of a boy who has been invited.

The parents of the host child should never permit party-crashing, for the good of the party and for the good of the youngsters attempting to crash. A dignified but definite rebuff of a crasher will teach him not to attempt it again. A party where crashing is permitted quickly turns into a rout. This is a job for a parent. A child cannot be expected to turn away a crasher. A parent has the age and the authority to do so.

Parties for Girls

Girls can learn a great deal about the duties of a hostess by giving adult-style parties for members of their own sex. Coke parties at which one lounges about in blue jeans are permissible occasionally. But from age sixteen upward, one should encourage a daughter to give luncheons, card parties, and teas at which she and her guests dress in their very best and behave as adults. Teen-agers have enough of the child in them so that the first parties of this kind which they attend have a "dressing-up-and-playing-lady" quality about them which they secretly find highly enjoyable. As they continue to attend them, their manners steadily become smoother, more natural, and more graceful. It is a valuable preparation for later years. Entertaining for an out-of-town houseguest provides an ideal opportunity to begin this style of entertaining. The local girls fancy that this is what the stranger is accustomed to, and will follow your daughter's lead in pretending that they, too, habitually entertain this way. The visiting girl will want to give exactly the same impression!

Let your daughter help in preparing the house for the party, in selecting and preparing the menu, and in setting the table. It is an ideal time to discuss various types of service with her, stressing what is or is not correct for a given occasion. It teaches her how to introduce people gracefully, how to keep conversation flowing, and how to preside at a tea-table. And it is *fun*—fun for you, and your daughter.

BLIND DATES

A blind date is one on which a boy and girl hitherto unacquainted are introduced by a third party known to both of them, after which they, the person who introduced them, and his dating partner go out together as a four-some. Under the terms just laid down, there is nothing improper about a blind date; it is, in fact, a valuable way of enlarging one's acquaintances. The points to observe are: *both* young people must be intimately known to the person performing the introduction. If either is not, the introducer is taking too great a responsibility upon himself. The first date should always be a foursome. This eliminates awkwardness and any risk. If a boy you barely know introduces you to a boy he scarcely knows in the neighborhood coke parlor, and you then agree to go out alone with the stranger that night, *don't* consider it a blind date. It is a blind-deaf-and-dumb, locked-in-a-strait-jacket-date, and you are asking for trouble which you will probably get! Stick to the definition laid down at the beginning of this section, and blind dates will be safe, can be fun, and can even be highly romantic. Settle for anything less, and you may regret it.

DRESS

One way in which a teen-ager shows his awareness of growing up is in his dress. It used to be that mothers had a hard time persuading their sixteen-year-old girls not to dress like movie vampires or international spies. They longed to wear black evening gowns, veils, long earrings—very grown-up clothes of all kinds. With today's youngsters, the problem seems to be reversed. Too many of them, both teens and sub-teens, think that the correct clothing for all occasions save formal parties is blue jeans, short shorts, sweat shirts, ponytails tied with string, sneakers, dirty socks—a generally unkempt and sloppy appearance. This is apparently an off-shoot of the beatnik influence. Whatever it is, it is very unfortunate.

Nothing is more attractive than cleanliness—glowing skin, shining hair, gleaming teeth, clothing clean, pressed, and appropriate. If one is returning from working at a dirty job or playing an active game, one may be excused for not appearing perfectly neat. One is not excused under any other circumstances. To be unshaven, dirty, or ill-groomed in public is an affront to all who see one. It is also proof that, secretly, one does not like oneself very much. Very poor people may own no clothes save those that are shabby and worn. None of us have as many as we would like. But all of us can, if we make the effort, see to it that those that we wear are clean and well-pressed.

Teen-agers who feel that they are old enough to claim adult privileges in other fields should be willing to assume adult responsibility in their way of dressing. This means neat, clean and appropriate clothing for school, sports, work, and dating. There is something effeminate about the current fad for elaborate hair styles and pink and purple slacks for boys. At best, they are *kid stuff*. Girls, wherever you can, wear skirts instead of slacks. This is one way of proving you are a girl!

No decent boy or girl should need to be urged to dress modestly. A girl who wears short shorts, bikinis, revealing necklines, insufficient underwear, or too-transparent clothing is inviting men to take liberties with her and has no cause to be insulted if they accept the invitation. A boy who wears slacks that are three sizes too small and skin-tight jerseys may feel he is treating the public to a beautiful display of muscle. If he has no other means of asserting his masculinity, he is a sad case!

Display always defeats its purpose. Surely you are now old enough to have noticed how much more inviting the Christmas gifts look when all are still hidden under their holiday wrappings, regardless of how wonderful the presents inside them prove to be? It is the mystery, the uncertainty, the *concealment* of the gifts which allows us to exercise our imagination and sharpens our interest. It is precisely the same with displaying, or veiling, our personal charms.

It is a subtle compliment to your date when you dress nicely for the occasion. It is really an insult, though usually not intended as such, when you are ill-groomed and not properly dressed. It also makes a bad impression on older people, who may misjudge you as a result of it.

To be nicely dressed affects our behavior. Unconsciously, we all try to live up to our appearance. It is easy to be courteous and to enjoy oneself in an adult way when "dressed for the part." It is equally easy, when dressed like a rowdy, to behave like one.

Teen-agers, it is time to grow up. Leave the kid stuff to the kids. Model your dress on the smoothest, trimmest, most attractive adult you know. The result will delight you. It does not take money. It does take time, patience, forethought, and taste. They are all free.

JOBS

Many sixteen-year-olds are eager for part-time work of some kind. Most of them do well with vacation jobs, either for the summer or for the shorter vacations. The money they can earn is an inducement. From the parental point of view, jobs are good for the youngsters because they teach them how hard it is to earn money, how much more a stranger may require of them than their parents do, and the discipline needed to keep regular working hours. Quick-tempered lads learn the necessity of holding their tongue; slackers discover there is no place for them in the working world. Assuming that the place of employment is respectable and the work not too demanding, parents should encourage children to attempt vacation jobs.

A job-and-school schedule is something else. As long as a child is in school, his primary responsibility should be to do the best he can in his school work. He should have all the time he needs to do so. Bright children or exceptionally energetic and ambitious ones may manage both school and job and be successful at both. But generally speaking, unless the need for the extra money is very great, jobs during the school term should not be attempted.

BABY SITTING

The rules for baby sitting are thoroughly covered in the chapter on sub-teens. These rules apply with equal force to teen-age sitters, with these exceptions: teen-agers may take occasional week-night jobs. They may take daytime sitting jobs, despite the increased responsibility. They may care for a family of four or five children, if qualified to do so. Sitting for a weekend, which means that no adult will be at home during the night and the entire responsibility for the family welfare is on the sitter, should still not be attempted except by very mature and experienced girls. Even they should not try it unless their own parents or a responsible adult relative of the children will be within easy call. Weekend sitting is really a job for adults.

MANAGING MONEY

Teen-agers should, if family finances permit, be given more leeway in managing money. An allowance intended to cover all their weekly spending is a good thing; it teaches them the folly of impulse spending. When you grant them an adequate allowance, insist that they live on it, regardless of the embarassments and disappointments that may result. Otherwise they learn nothing from having their "own" money to spend.

A quarterly dress allowance is also good when possible. This should be spent when and as the teenager sees fit, with Mother reserving only the right to check on the propriety of clothes purchased and to veto the selections if they are not modest. The result may be some absurd or highly unsuitable purchases, or all the allowance spent in one mad splurge, with no money for stockings or haircut at the end of the quarter. This will be valuable, if the parent sticks to his guns and does not hand over extra money to meet the emergency. If he doles out extra funds when needed, the experiment is worthless.

Unless a family is desperately pressed for money, any that a teen-ager earns should be his—to save for higher education, to spend on clothes and entertainment. When a family is pressed, a teen-ager may be expected to use his earned money in place of an allowance from Dad. Explain the reasons—he has a right to know. When a family is truly pressed, a teen-ager may be required to contribute some of his income to family expenses as his contribution to happy family life. When this happens, the contributing teen-ager should, where possible, be excused from performing some of the work around the house that has been his responsibility.

Another money responsibility first begins in the teen years. This is the responsibility for handling other people's money honestly and reliably as a club or class treasurer or dance or dinner chairman. This is excellent experience. Most teen-agers rise to these occasions beautifully, and perform the tasks with credit. Don't discourage your teen-ager from attempting them unless you have very good cause for thinking that he will fail. Even when you are somewhat doubtful, it is better to let him do it and try to maintain, gently and unobtrusively, a steady supervision of how he does the job. We all learn by doing.

HOME RESPONSIBILITIES

A teen-ager should continue to have home responsibilities similar to those of his sub-teen years. He may not be able to do much more than he did as a sub-teen because his activities outside the home are steadily increasing. The bright and energetic ones are taking enrichment courses, making teams, running school and church clubs, increasing social skills. The butterflies are happily whirling through a dizzy social pace. The slow learners are working harder than ever to keep up.

Home duties should still be expected of them, with due allowance made for their outside schedule. What work they do at home should be done more efficiently, because they should be becoming more capable. In a time of emergency, such as the homemaker falling ill or being called out of town, teen-agers should be able to keep the home running smoothly until Mother is back at her post; they should rise to the challenge and do it cheerfully and well. Most of them will do so.

PERSONAL RESPONSIBILITIES

One test of a teen-ager's maturity is the degree to which he manages his personal affairs without adult supervision. Both sexes should take charge of their wardrobes and personal grooming, make and keep appointments, write and answer letters and invitations, remember the tiresome little personal chores: making dental appointments, getting hair cut and shoes repaired, sending garments to cleaners. Mother should now be relieved of these jobs. They should likewise be managing their school life without help, as well as their spiritual life. If they appear to be failing in any of these things, a parent always has the duty to remind them of their lapses; but when this is necessary, it should be regarded as proof that they are not living up to what can properly be expected of them at this age.

TEEN-AGE DRIVING

One of the worrisome problems of modern life is the physical and moral risk involved in permitting teen-agers to drive automobiles. It would be simple to solve it by forbidding all teen-agers to drive, but this is not practical. In many situations, an automobile is the only available means of transportation and a teen-ager the only available driver. Our social customs and the laws of many states grant teen-agers the privilege of driving.

The point to be emphasized is that driving *is* a privilege, not a right. It is a privilege to be awarded after the prospective driver has learned the rules of driving and traffic control and how to operate the vehicle properly and has given some proof of good judgment and emotional maturity such as to minimize the risk of placing in his hands a terrible potential instrument of destruction. Mere attainment of the legal driving age proves none of these things.

A teen-age boy will say—correctly—that one his age has keen sight and hearing, quick reflexes, and, quite often, a better knowledge of the mechanics of a car than many older drivers. Theoretically then, all teen-agers should be fine drivers. Cold insurance statistics prove exactly the reverse. Unmarried male drivers between the ages of eighteen and twenty-five have the highest accident rate of any driving group, and the highest number of accidents which result in fatalities. These figures are the same throughout our country. As a result, the insurance rate for this group is higher than for any other. The figures do not apply to teen-age girls. Their accident rate is about the same as that of adult drivers. The number of accidents resulting in fatalities in which teen-age girls are the drivers is markedly lower than that of boys. Recklessness, immaturity, childish showing off, and disregard for the rights of others make teen-age boys our worst drivers, rather than our best. Therefore parents should think long and hard before granting their sons the right to drive and should curtail their driving sharply until they give real proof of their ability to handle a car.

When your son or daughter wants to drive, there are a number of things that you should do for their protection. They are:

a) Set them a constant example of safe driving and strict observance of all traffic laws. If you do not do this, they will not.

b) Learn the laws of your state about teen-age driving. If it imposes any restrictions on such drivers, insist that they be lived up to. Most state codes (but not all) are similar to those of

Iowa, which says, "No persons, except hereinafter expressly exempted shall drive any motor vehicle upon a highway in this state unless such person has a valid license as an operator or chauffeur issued by the department of public safety. . . . A restricted license may be issued to any person between the ages of fourteen and sixteen years, to be valid only in going to and from school over the most direct and accessible route, or at any other time when accompanied by a parent or guardian who is a holder of a valid operator or chauffeur's license, and who is actually occupying a seat beside the driver." If your teen-ager is to have a restricted license, insist that he live up to the restrictions.

c) Before you permit your child to operate a car, teach him, or have him properly taught, the state and city traffic laws and how to operate the vehicle.

d) If you are not buying your teen-ager a car, it is presumably the family car he will be driving. The family car is a car for the use of the family. If any member of the family unit is to have a monopoly on the use of it, it should be Dad. Others must take their turn. The teen-age son or daughter should be reminded that his use of the car is a privilege, not a right. It is a privilege to be granted only if the teen-ager:

Obeys the traffic laws.

Uses it for the purpose for which he requested it.

Keeps the hours laid down for him.

Does not overload the car or drive aimlessly for long distances.

Does not injure or abuse the vehicle.

Does not drive while drinking.

Does not race or drive recklessly.

Helps keep the car clean and in good condition.

It is not only as the driver of a car that your teen-ager may be in danger. As a passenger with a reckless driver the risk will be great, and as a passenger he is a helpless bystander with no control over the operation of the machine. This is a common problem for girls. Often they are not the driver—neither is their escort—they are guests in the car of another. If that other drives dangerously or drunkenly, there is little that they can do about it. They hesitate even to protest, because they are, after all, guests of the foolish driver.

There is no ready solution to this problem. Sometimes all one can do at the moment is pray to live through it. One such experience should be enough to warn the teen-ager not to drive with that operator again. If he does he is courting unnecessary risk.

If your son is a sane, responsible driver, he may be safer at the wheel of your car than while riding with a friend. But any real evidence of reckless driving by your teen-ager is grounds for forbidding him to use the car.

Try to keep your children constantly alert to the car as a vehicle of destruction. Tell them of the weight, mass, and impact of a moving vehicle. Read the statistics of death by automobile. Help them to realize that the reckless driver, playing "chicken," speeding, driving while drinking, forcing other cars off the road, is neither brave, daring, or skillful. He is a motor moron, risking his life and the life and property of innocent people for a momentary thrill and sense of power, too stupid to comprehend the possible consequences. Hundreds of this kind are paying with years of their life for their thrill-seeking; thousands of their helpless victims are dead or maimed.

The moral dangers attendant on the use of a car are hard for a teen-ager to recognize and accept. The mobility a car provides enables them to range beyond parental or police supervision, to attain a privacy not otherwise possible. To warn them of the dangers of parking and love-making does little good. One must so warn them, but whether they heed the warnings will depend on how well they have been taught moral principles to govern all their activities, and how faithfully they live up to them.

OWNING A CAR

It is very unwise of parents to permit teen-agers to own a car. It weakens parental control more than any other single thing that one can do because it places in the young person's hands the means to go oftener and farther beyond the reach of parental care and authority than they could otherwise do. Almost invariably it has an adverse effect upon study habits and school grades. These conclusions are not mere adult opinion. Several serious and extensive sociological surveys have all shown the same results: there is a higher percentage of school failures among students owning cars than among non-car owners. There are fewer car-owners, proportionately, in the top ten percent of any given class than in any other segment. As one goes downward in the class ranks, the number of car owners rises: fewer (proportionately) among the B students than among the C's; fewer among the C's than the D's. Astonishingly enough, these figures hold good for *both high school and college students!* Thoughtful people must conclude that, in general, owning a car reduces a student's interest in his work and the amount of time he devotes to it.

Some parents feel it is good to let a boy buy a car with money he has earned and to maintain it at his own expense because it teaches him the expense of operating such a vehicle and the effort required to earn the money to maintain it. This is good in theory. Too often, it means that the boy will neglect his school and other duties to earn the money to support his car.

One possible exception to the no-car rule might be made: some boys love cars as machinery. They long to own one so that they can tear it down, build it up, make it over. With such a boy, the car need seldom be regarded as a means of transportation—most of the time it will be standing, torn down, in the garage! For such a boy, tinkering with a car is a good hobby from which he will learn much. But if he keeps it in good running order and uses it to roam far and wide, it will be a danger to him.

Teach your children to make the following petition to Our Lady for protection on the highway whenever they set out on a trip in a car, however brief:

> Our Lady of the highways,
> Be thou our aid in setting out,
> Our comfort on the way,
> Our support in weariness,
> Our refuge in danger. . . .
> So that under thy guidance
> We may in safety reach our destination
> And return unharmed to our homes.

SMOKING

Smoking is not a sin or an occasion of sin. It cannot be condemned on moral grounds. Even the social conventions which formerly frowned upon women smoking have vanished in all save the most puritanical communities.

This does not mean that smoking is desirable—only that the objections to it are not based on moral grounds. The most inveterate smoker will usually admit, if questioned on the subject, that he wishes he had never acquired the habit. It is expensive, useless, and hard to overcome. It creates a fire hazard that has resulted in a shocking loss of life and property.

Medical research is currently engaged in a number of studies to determine the possible connection between lung cancer and the use of tobacco. Results thus far seem to indicate a connection. Since lung cancer is far more common in men than in women, it would appear that the smoking habit is actually more dangerous for men than for women.

Smoking is particularly bad for young people because it is a deterrent to the attainment of maximum growth and health. Athletes willingly eschew the habit because they know its bad effect on their speed, wind, and endurance.

Taking all these factors into consideration, one might think that the wise course would be to forbid smoking among teen-agers. Unfortunately, in this as in other areas of modern life, "it is a condition, not a theory, that confronts us."

Innumerable adults smoke; many young people are allowed to do so. The custom of smoking is a part of most social occasions. It relieves tension, gives one something to do with one's hands, helps one share in the give and take of social life, and may prove helpful in the avoidance of another worse habit: drinking.

Teen-agers are very self-conscious, desperately eager to behave as their contemporaries do. One who neither smokes nor drinks often feels gauche and ill at ease in a group where the others do these things. Granted, he should not feel so; rather, he should be proud that he "dares to be different." Nevertheless, his desire to conform will put much pressure on him. One might, therefore, permit a teen-ager seventeen or older to smoke, rather than to drink. If he (and particularly *she*) may carry and use the paraphernalia of smoking—cigarette cases, holders, lighters—he feels it proves he is "not a kid," and may help him to refrain from attempting to prove it by drinking. There is one other possible advantage to smoking that must be mentioned here, although some may be shocked by it: an inexperienced young girl endeavoring to cope with a too-persistent and too-ardent swain will find a lighted cigarette of help in fending him off. It serves the same purpose that a long sharp hatpin did for her grandmother!

If you feel that your older teen-ager is determined to smoke, let him do so at home with his family; it takes much of the thrill out of it. Warn him of the fire hazard and do not let him smoke to excess. One way to avoid this is to time your smoking: do not smoke until after dinner, do not smoke alone. Never permit a young person to smoke before breakfast. It is bad to smoke before any meal, as it cuts the appetite.

DRINKING

The use of alcohol is not a sin. The Church rightfully recognizes alcoholic beverages as one of the good things of life, put here for our enjoyment. The abuse, or excessive use of alcohol, *is* sinful; even the moderate use of it may be an occasion of sin.

The first duty of parents in this matter is to set their children a constant example of moderation and restraint. Here as elsewhere they will do as you do, not as you tell them to do. Parents should discuss at length with their children the dangers inherent in even a moderate use of alcohol. The evils of excessive use lie all about us and are apparent to any observant person.

What teen-agers will find hard to understand is the fact that individual tolerance to alcohol differs greatly. What is moderation for one person may be excess to another; for some, even one drink is too much.

Hard it is, too, to appreciate that alcohol, which appears to stimulate, is really a depressant which acts on the central nervous system to still the voice of conscience and diminish self-restraint and the sense of right and wrong. And it so acts *before* its effect causes one to speak and act irrationally.

Nevertheless, many parents feel it is unrealistic to forbid their older teen-age children to drink because an absolute prohibition may lead them to drink on the sly. Admittedly, the point is a difficult one in sophisticated circles. If one feels that permission to drink moderately should be extended to sons and daughters in their late teens, the matter may be handled as follows:

a) Do not make a mystery of drinking. If you serve alcoholic beverages in your home, and a child wishes to taste them, let him. The average youngster will find the taste unpleasant and wonder how anyone can like it. The taste for alcohol is an acquired one; very few like it when first tasting it.

b) Set him an unfailing example of moderation and restraint. On any occasion where you transgress and indulge to excess, express to him your disgust with yourself and your regret at having so done. Unfortunate though the incident may be, it yet provides an excellent opportunity for making a point that is hard to explain: the effect of alcohol upon the nervous system is so insidious that the most well-meaning person, intending to drink only moderately, may find his judgment so affected by a *moderate* consumption of alcohol that he goes on to drink to excess without being at the time able to understand that his consumption *is* excessive. Hardly anyone drinks with the intention of getting drunk; one loses one's sense of what is moderate and what excessive while drinking *moderately*.

c) Learn, and discuss with your children, the bad physical and psychological effects of the use of alcohol.

d) Know the laws of your state regarding the sale of alcohol to and the use of alcohol by minors. In some states it is against the law to sell or serve alcohol to anyone under twenty-one; in others the age limit is eighteen. Check on the restaurants and taverns to which your children go to make sure they are observing the law. Do not hesitate to report to the proper authority any establishment which is not doing so.

e) Absolutely prohibit your children to drink when they are to operate a car. The dangers of any other course are too terrible to think of. Driving is a privilege; it cannot be extended to a teen-ager at any time when he is to drink.

f) Do not serve alcoholic beverages in your home at any teen-age party; do not permit it to be done at any party where your opinion carries any weight, as at a club dance.

g) If your teen-ager persists in drinking too much or too often, you can help control him by cutting down on the money he has to spend and on the hours he may keep.

h) When feasible, get the help of the parents of your teen-ager's friends to present a united front as to what is permissible and to discourage drinking at parties in their homes.

i) PRAY!

How to be Moderate

A parent may warn his children repeatedly to be "moderate" in their drinking without really making himself understood. Some people think it suitable to be "moderately" drunk—that is, sufficiently in control of one's behavior and tongue to avoid being boisterous, rude, or vulgar, although one has imbibed considerable alcohol. This is the wrong goal. Make it plain to your children that moderation really means drinking only in small enough amounts to *remain sober:* that is, in full control of one's faculties, behavior and senses.

How does one do this, especially on festive occasions when one is offered frequent opportunities to drink? Here are a few general rules:

a) Avoid drinking cocktails. These drinks are a heavy concentration of alcohol and, because they are "short," are quickly drunk. Young people should make it a rule never to drink more than two cocktails on any occasion. Better still, substitute when possible a milder drink, such as sherry, claret, dubonnet, or vermouth, "on the rocks."

b) When drinking a mixed drink—rye, scotch or bourbon, with a mixer—ask for a long drink that is, one made with plenty of mixer, and sip it slowly. A milder drink that serves the same purpose is rhine wine and seltzer. One must learn to pace oneself and drink slowly; a clever person can carry the same glass about for hours and appear to take part in the festivities while remaining sober.

c) At dinner, where a different wine is served with each course, it is proper to leave several of them untouched at one's place. It is equally proper just to take a sip of each.

d) Avoid drinking heavy liqueurs at the end of a meal. Brandy has a higher alcoholic content than creme de menthe, though both are proper after-dinner drinks. When given a choice, specify the milder drink. It is also proper to refuse entirely.

e) Keep account of the number of drinks you have been served. Know your own limits and stay within them. Never be ashamed to refuse a drink when you know you have had enough.

f) Never be ashamed not to drink; it is your privilege. To refuse a drink you do not want or cannot handle is proof of your maturity and *savoir faire*.

g) Alcohol has less immediate effect upon the system when taken with food. Be careful to eat whenever food is served with beverages—even cocktail snacks. When drinks are served without food, reduce your consumption of the beverage.

h) Try always to take one less drink than you feel you can safely imbibe.

i) Remember that no one ever awakened the morning after a party and said "Oh dear Heaven! How I wish I had had *more* to drink last night!" Pray that you will never suffer the embarrassments, fears, and regrets that assail those who wake to remember that they had far too much.

A Word to Girls

It is only in the last thirty years that our social code has considered drinking, in any amount, as acceptable behavior for unmarried young women. Even now the world expects young women to exercise more judgment and restraint than it requires of their brothers. A man may occasionally overstep his limits without suffering social ostracism, but

a girl may not. Immoderate drinking adversely affects a girl's social
life, reputation, and chances for married happiness. It may also induce
her to behave as she would never dream of doing if she were in poses-
sion of her faculties.

Because of this, it is the writer's personal conviction (but only that)
that a girl should not drink *at all* until she is over twenty-one or a
married woman with a husband to protect her. This is really the easy
way out—a protection against a host of dangers that may assail her
even when drinking moderately. No sensible person disapproves of a
girl's abstaining from drinking. Many do disapprove of a girl's drinking, no matter how moderately. A glass of ginger ale is just as refresh-
ing as a highball (it even looks the same) and contains no hidden
dangers. Why not stick with it?

If an older teen-age girl still feels she *must* drink:

a) Do not take more than three drinks an evening, of any kind.
b) Choose light drinks (wine, beer, punch) over the heavier ones.
c) Never drink unless you know your escort, and know him to be
   a gentleman.

ENLARGING SOCIAL GRACES

A thoughtful person feels regret when he sees young people full of
health, energy, and intelligence, lounging in a tavern, dawdling for
hours before a television screen, or racing about recklessly in cars. The
malicious mischief and senseless destruction to which some resort for
"fun" terrifies us all. Too few of us stop to think that teen-agers may
resort to such amusements because they have not been taught how
otherwise to enjoy themselves. Young people are eager to excel, or at
least to be as good as their contemporaries, in all that they do. They
are reluctant to attempt any activity at which they, as beginners,
appear awkward and inexpert, and this may be why they fall back on
the behavior just described, which requires no practice or preparation.

Hence it is more important than one may think to help our teen-
agers learn how to do well the wholesome and pleasurable pastimes
which can be substituted for less innocent ones. See to it that your
children learn how to dance really well, to play bridge, canasta, and
other card games, to swim, skate, ski, bowl, play golf or tennis—whatever sports their friends enjoy. Bright teeners will also enjoy astronomy,
chemical experimentation, photography, painting, wood-working, sewing, or cooking. Be alert to signs of these interests and encourage them.
The more they are immersed in worthwhile interests, the less attraction
the dangerous ones will have. The more interests you can create for

them at this age, the fuller and richer their adult life will be. Many a man's lifetime career has sprung from a childhood hobby. In any event, reasonable adequacy in the social skills of his group increases a teen-ager's confidence in himself and his ability to move gracefully in the social sphere.

STEADY DATING

Much of the difficulty a parent faces concerning his children's dating activities springs from a fact seldom recognized: in our modern American culture, dating has a four-fold purpose.

a) To increase acquaintance among members of the opposite sex.

b) To test the ability to know, understand, and evaluate the worth of members of the opposite sex.

c) To provide each with a partner for the social life of his group, in which all, like the animals in the ark, must go two by two on every occasion.

d) To find the ideal marriage partner.

These purposes tend to overlap. One flows naturally into another. This has long been so, but has caused little difficulty because young people themselves seemed aware of these different purposes and the differing importance of each. Since World War II, another concept has arisen among them. Teen-agers seem to ignore the first two purposes and to regard three and four as synonymous; that is, the first dating partner with whom he can pleasurably socialize, he clings to and regards, very quickly, as an ideal marriage mate. This he does without giving himself opportunity to know and compare other possible partners or to allow himself sufficient time to acquire any maturity of judgment. This is the crux of the modern dating problem.

This attitude, which results so frequently in early and unsuitable marriages, is disturbing to all thoughtful people. The resultant high divorce rate, with its concomitant of broken homes and parentless children, is a social and economic waste no society can afford, to say nothing of the personal disillusionment and heartache involved. For Catholics the matter is especially disturbing, for these unfortunate child marriages among us cannot be "solved" by divorce. The Church cannot and will not put its sanction on marriages which have no real hope of permanence. She cannot and will not permit a couple to marry merely to regularize past improprieties.

But when two Catholic teen-agers come with parental approval to make marriage arrangements, it is very difficult for their pastor to refuse them. When such a marriage fails, the two contracting parties must drag out a life of misery together or separately live out their lives without a helpmeet. All teen-age marriages do not fail, but such a high proportion of them do that the risk is grave. In the case of such a Catholic marriage failing, there is the chance of worse harm resulting; one of the partners, wearying of his lonely life, may turn his back on his Faith and "remarry" outside the Church. Adults know all this. Young people will not and cannot believe it. The fact that they cannot is one proof of their immaturity.

Help your child to develop good dating habits by pointing out to him the fourfold purpose of dating. Sub-teen dating should concern itself exclusively with meeting and knowing as many of the opposite sex as possible. The goal should be to find partners with whom one can enjoy a happy social life. In these years a girl may enjoy going out with a boy because he is a wonderful dancer or plays a fine game of tennis or is the school sports hero; in the sub-teens, this is reason enough. This is youth's playtime. Pairing off should be happy, casual, and of brief duration. But too often, a sub-teen, having selected a dating partner for one of these reasons and finding himself feeling for her the physical attraction that springs into being so easily between two healthy and attractive young people who are much together, quickly mistakes liking for love and is sure he has found his life's partner. No questions as to her real character or disposition or her fitness as a wife disturb his dreams. She is fun, she is pretty, she moves him— it is enough.

There is no quick and easy formula for solving this problem. The following suggestions help to avoid creating it. They are intended to apply, like all the material in this chapter, to young people sixteen and older.

a) Limit the amount of time spent dating. During the school year, dating should be limited to the weekends: one or two evening dates per weekend, plus occasional daytime activity, such as picnics. Encourage group activity in preference to single dating. Discourage after-school "twosing": playing records at home in the afternoon, driving about together. There is nothing wrong with such behavior, except that it throws the young people involved too frequently together, makes them too dependent upon one another, too absorbed in each other.

b) Encourage your teen-ager to spend time with friends of his own sex. In addition to its other benefits, pursuing such friendships prevents him from relying on dating for all his pleasures.

c) Do what you can to help your teen-ager make new friends and enlarge his acquaintance with the opposite sex. If you spend your summers out of the city, do not permit him to have friends from town visit him all summer; rather let him become acquainted with new young people at the resort you frequent. If you spend your vacation on a motor trip, he should not expect to bring a friend with him, particularly of the opposite sex. He (or she) should be expected, as a matter of course, occasionally to do things as part of the family unit and to enjoy them as such. If he does not enjoy them, he should yet take part in them cheerfully and not spoil the pleasure of the others. Anything else is childish behavior.

d) Treat his infatuations lightly, particularly his first ones, and the early stages of all of them. Assume that one of the pleasures of his youth, of which he will not wish to be deprived, is to test his power to attract many dating partners. Remind him that the girls he admired at fourteen are not now the ones that please him. Suggest that, although his judgment at sixteen is, of course, much better, even the girls he now likes may not be the ones whose company he will enjoy when he is twenty-one.

Sensible parents may regard the advice just given as superfluous; of course one will treat "kid romance" lightly. But mothers of daughters do not always do so. Unconsciously, they tend to relive their own girl-hood in their daughter's romances, thus giving these an importance in her eyes that they might otherwise not have. They may admire exces-sively an attractive, manly boy whom she is dating and so encourage her to magnify her own feeling for him. This parental attitude is not as silly as one might think. A parent may be so relieved that his child likes and has been chosen by a sensible decent boy rather than an undesirable one, that he becomes too approving, too permissive. This is a natural feeling, but there are many dangers inherent in it. *The right boy is the wrong boy, if your daughter becomes emotionally involved with him too young.*

e) Encourage your teen-ager's interests which do not depend upon dating: sports, music, dramatics, social work, civic activity, a part-time job.

f) Boys and girls planning to attend college should be repeatedly urged to avoid any serious interest in their high school friends. To become so involved often results in a decision not to attend college, or it sends them away to school only half a person, unable to concentrate on their studies or to enjoy the new friends and new experiences they will encounter.

g) Boys and girls who do not go to college often find their life partners among those they begin to date in their last high school years. Parents of such teen-agers should make a special effort to know their children's dating partners, particularly when they date one exclusively, and to weigh their apparent merits as a life mate. They should also discuss with their children the qualities one should seek in a helpmate. When a young couple decide that they are serious about marrying, at least at some future date, they should be urged to attend pre-Cana conferences if any are held in the area. They are of great help in inducing a serious attitude and in setting up standards of evaluation.

h) Remind your sons that one of the proofs of "real" love is the feeling of protectiveness it engenders toward the loved one. It is this desire to protect the loved one that enables a decent man never to demean or injure his beloved.

i) Tell your daughters that the essence of feminine love is the desire to give—anything the loved one wants. But when the loved one desires what would injure him by causing him to sin, the greatest proof of *her* love is the power to withhold from him the gratification which would deface his immortal soul.

WHAT IS LOVE?

How many mistakes—how many tragedies—could be avoided if one could discover an infallible method to distinguish between violent infatuation and true love! Unfortunately, these emotions have so much in common and are so intensely personal that the wisest among us frequently mistake one for another. Because they are so personal, we are apt to reject (perhaps rightly) the opinions of a third person as to their nature; we feel that no one can truly understand how we feel and that no opinion, no matter how thoughtful and well-intentioned, can have any bearing upon the matter save our own. In this field, as in no other, we distrust the judgment of our well-wishers and cling to our own.

This is a natural attitude, but one should nevertheless recognize that over the centuries man has discovered some guideposts which, if honestly followed, can help us to distinguish the true nature of our feelings.

All degrees of physical attraction between the sexes have three things in common: the desire to possess, the desire to give, the desire to be united—to be as one. These desires are profound and urgent; they crave immediate satisfaction. The wish to possess is personal and self-centered. The wish to give is other-centered, unselfish, concerned with gratifying the beloved. The desire for union—mental, spiritual, and physical—is mystical, a human counterpart of the soul's longing for union with its Creator, and, like this other nobler yearning, can never be wholly satisfied. We seldom feel these three desires with equal intensity, and in the strength of these various emotions lie some indication of the true nature of our feelings.

The desire to possess is selfish; it is concerned with the gratification of our own desires. One feels this emotion whether infatuated or truly in love. In the first case, it is paramount, unconcerned with the wishes or desires of the love object. In the second, it is subservient to the good of the beloved, because true love is, above everything else, unselfish. True love glories in self-denial—derives from it an exquisite and subtle joy—if by self-denial one is cherishing, protecting, and promoting the welfare of the beloved. This self-denial extends to *unselfishly* denying the loved one some gratification if this denial is for his spiritual or temporal well-being. Thus a boy violently infatuated might persuade his date to stay out very late because of the intense pleasure he derives from her company. A boy in love would feel an equally strong desire to prolong the hours with his beloved, but would bring her home at a reasonable hour because of his unselfish wish to protect her good name, and to help her observe the limits set by her parents.

The desire to give is, in the main, unselfish, concerned with giving joy to the beloved. On this concomitant of love are based some of the noblest and happiest of marriages. But this is a peculiar and involved emotion, and sometimes wears a false face. An infatuated young girl might grant the object of her infatuation sinful sexual gratification and fancy that in so doing she is "proving" her love and her wish to please him in every way. True love understands the limits of the desire to give: one truly in love shrinks back in horror from the giving of anything that would tend to injure, degrade, or sully the soul of the loved one. A girl who thus gives herself sinfully misunderstands the nature of the desire to give: one truly in love does not wish to give the loved one a momentary sensual gratification which panders only to his animalistic nature; rather she strives always to help him to live up to all that is best and highest in his soul.

The desire for union is also shared by those infatuated and those truly in love. The most noticeable characteristic of "calf love" is the desire to be always together and always alone. Calf lovers do not wish to share their time, their thoughts, their amusements with anyone else. This is also characteristic of true lovers, but these latter, secure in the mutuality of their feelings and ability to share experiences, can also work and play happily in a group, endure separation, and share the beloved's company with a third person without jealousy or fear of competition. The desire for union among the infatuated is unrealistic. It demands whole and entire satisfaction at once, is fearful of the effects of delay, time, or distance upon the feelings of the love partner. True love is realistic, willing to accept separation, delay, or deferrment of its hopes, if these hardships promote the welfare of the beloved or aid in laying the foundations of a future of permanent union. Here is what Monsignor J. D. Conway says about love and infatuation in his booklet, "Love and Dating":

> Our love is human. So it is an expression of our complete human nature, both body and soul. True love is not of the body alone; nor is it exclusively a thing of the soul. Man loves not as the animal or the angel, but as man. And man is not a composite of two natures in conflict, but the only creature God ever made by union of matter and spirit in one nature and one personality. So man's love, if true, has its roots in the soul while it expresses itself through the senses and emotions. If it is not really a thing of the soul, it is not real human love; if it is only in the soul, it is not the love of a real man.
>
> The union engendered by true love is a joining of soul and body to soul and body. It is a union of two minds and two free wills expressed in physical embrace.
>
> True love is not romantic love. True love loves truth—reality. Romantic love creates the object of its love, in dreams. It is blind —to facts; drugged by false expectations.
>
> Love grows and growth takes time. It has to sink its roots firmly into the deep soil of the soul. It is a perennial plant, and these grow slowly. You fall into infatuation. Falling is fast, with acceleration. Falling is uncontrollable, seldom lasts long, and is often disastrous; but it does provide a whooshing, engulfing thrill.
>
> In other words, if you have fallen head over heels, you are probably infatuated. If the thing has crept up on you quietly but thrillingly, you may well be in love.
>
> True love is based on knowledge. It knows well the one it loves, and knows why it loves. It observes. It appraises. It is held firmly by many ties. It can enumerate in detail the points of beauty of the loved one, the flights of spirit, the qualities of soul; the walk, voice, words, interests, and mannerisms. The time of its growth has provided it with varied experiences and memories to enrich its thrill. Infatuation is apt to be swept up in the strong attraction of a few compelling traits. It sees blonde hair, fine face, or fancy figure and forgets all the rest.
>
> Love embraces the whole personality, aware of shortcomings

and defects, evaluating them. Infatuation ignores them—as though intensity of feeling should burn them up.

True love is realistic. Its thrill comes from facts. Even its dreams are reasonable and realizable. Infatuation thrives on fancy and fantasy.

True love is honest. It does not express what it does not feel and believe. Having fixed its roots in the soul, it lets tendrils grow out through the senses and emotions, where they become words and actions to entwine the lovers into union—in both soul and body. Expressions of love come slowly, sincerely, naturally. They are never forced or faked. Physical expressions, when they do come, have real deep meaning. Infatuation reverses the process. It is born of expression, thrives on it for hasty growth, and may as quickly wither. The meaning is lacking; it is just fun, thrilling.

Love is constant, enduring, even patient when it must be. Infatuation is as changeable as it was hasty.

Love tends to be faithful. Infatuation is apt to flitter.

Love gives calmness, security, peace, trust, and happiness. Infatuation gives thrills, joys, sorrows, jealousies, and uncertainties.

Love gives ambition, inspires work, and leads to honest planning. Infatuation destroys application, appetite, and disposition; and leads to rosy dreams.

Love has ideals, but doesn't over-idealize. Unconsciously its dreams of an ideal partner are revamped to fit the person loved. Infatuation believes that the person fits its highest ideals. It believes that true love was made in heaven and descended like a ton of electrified dynamite on the predestined mates, chosen inevitably for each other by benign fate.

The physical element is present in true love, strongly present; but it does not dominate good sense and right spirit. Infatuation stresses the sensual.

True love makes no apologies for the loved one; it does not feel ashamed. Infatuation is apt to be embarrassed—before parents, pals, and priests.

True love makes sacrifices; it seeks the happiness of the loved one, and finds its own happiness therein.

True love is based on realities of family, background, education, social position, religion, moral standards, financial situation, friends, interests, and experiences. Infatuation ignores such basic concerns.

You may not know his love, for sure, when he tells you, or when he touches you. But you may know it from his faithful devotion to you, his consideration of you, his thoughtfulness towards you, his concern and his sacrifice, his compliance with your wishes, his honest planning of your future, his sharing of self and experiences with you, his pride and his joy in you, and his peace and happiness with you. He likes very much being with you, even when he is not making love to you.

DATING NON-CATHOLICS

Should parents forbid their children to date non-Catholics? Do they have the right to do so? Let us examine the arguments on both sides of the question. Going back to the four purposes of steady dating, we can find no objection to dating non-Catholics under the first three headings. It is when we come to the fourth—"to find the ideal marriage partner"—that the difficulties arise, so it is from this viewpoint that we will discuss the matter.

Dating a non-Catholic may lead to falling in love and wishing to marry. The Church forbids marriage to non-Catholics. Every time a Catholic marries a non-Catholic in the Church, it is because a dispensation has been granted in this individual case, based upon a number of considerations including the probable permanence of the union. No Catholic can safely assume that he will be granted a similar dispensation until he has applied for it and it has been granted. The Church forbids marriage to non-Catholics because:

a) Such marriages sometimes result in the Catholic partner falling away from the Church.

b) Many children of such marriages have *no* religion when they are adults (because of the conflicts and mixed loyalties they have experienced.) A greater percentage of the children of these marriages have no adult faith than the children of a marriage wholly Catholic or wholly non-Catholic.

c) When such marriages fail, the non-Catholic partner may resort to divorce to escape from it. The Catholic party, bound for life to a mate who has deserted him, will go through life in a state half-celibate, half-married, suffering the disabilities of both conditions and the advantages of neither.

d) Even when such marriages do not terminate in divorce, the peace and happiness of both partners may be lessened by arguments about birth control, Catholic education, religious principles, or financial support of one's church. A large and vitally important area of potential friction exists which is not present in a marriage of co-religionists, whatever their faith.

Today, informed secular opinion agrees with the position of the Church, that mixed marriages have less chance of success than those of co-religionists. "Opposites attract" say romanticists and, as far as it goes, this may be true. We may be drawn to an individual because he is so different from ourselves; the difference makes him seem exotic and interesting. But it is *not* true that opposites live happily together in the bonds of marriage. We see the truth of this on every side, and it has recently been attested to by sociological surveys: the more ways in which you and your marriage partner match, or agree, the better your chances of marital happiness. This means that two young people of the same age group, racial stock, social background, education, financial status, and religious belief have a better chance for a happy marriage than two who differ in any of these respects. Please note that word *"chance"*—such similarity does not guarantee marital happiness; it merely reduces the number of subjects about which the two marriage partners may disagree. And two who differ in some of these areas may still have a successful marriage if they are generous enough and mature enough to work to make it so.

There is also one exception to the above statement, in regard to age group. It is true as to marriage partners twenty-one or over. It is not true as to teen-agers. Teen-age marriages of every variety have a higher record of failure than do marriages of young adults. The highest record of teen-age marriage failure is among those in which neither partner professes any religious belief at all. The next highest in the teen-age group is a mixed marriage in which the girl is the non-Catholic. But what should be born in mind is that *any* marriage of teen-agers is dangerous and has considerably less chance for success than marriages contracted in adult life. Two Catholic teen-agers have a slightly better chance for a successful marriage than any other combination in the teen-age group, but they too have less chance for a permanent marriage than do two adult Catholics.

What are the arguments in favor of dating non-Catholics? First of all, we live in a society that is mixed, with non-Catholics out-numbering Catholics. In the course of growing up, each Catholic child will meet and like dozens of non-Catholic youngsters. When the dating age is reached, many of them will be drawn to date the non-Catholic children. To do so certainly fulfills the first three purposes of dating: to increase acquaintance among the opposite sex, to test ability to know, understand and evaluate the worth of members of the opposite sex, and to provide a partner in social life. It has the added value of teaching both youngsters how to live happily in a society that is religiously diversified and to respect the religious convictions of others while remaining true to his own.

But, says the anxious Catholic parent, *all* first dating is casual and not seriously intended. Few youngsters are thinking of marriage on their first dates; it is only when they know one another better that they wish to marry. That is when the problem arises. Could it not be best avoided by forbidding any dates with non-Catholics?

No. Such a blanket prohibition is unfair and unrealistic. It overlooks some very important considerations, which are:

a) Much dating is casual and brief, and does not lead to marriage, just to fun and learning about other people.

b) A blanket prohibition denies your child the right to mature by exercising his *own* judgment as to the worth of those he meets. It keeps him in mental swaddling clothes by depending on your opinions, not his, to decide with whom he will associate and where he will look for a mate.

c) A blanket prohibition on dating non-Catholics immediately surrounds such dating with a glamorous aura merely because it is forbidden. This would cause many a rebellious teen-ager to regard dating non-Catholics as especially attractive, and to seek out non-Catholic dating partners merely because they are non-Catholic. The possible end result might be that such a youngster would contract a religiously invalid marriage outside the Church to assert his independence.

d) It is unfair to non-Catholics. Thousands of them are mature enough, reasonable, fair-minded, honorable enough, to make and keep the promises required of them if they wish to marry in the Church. When they do so, the chances for marital happiness are good. For many of them it is a means of learning about our Faith, which they would not otherwise have encountered; often it leads to understanding and respect—even to conversion.

e) Many, many mixed marriages *are* successful, enormously so. The Church herself recognizes this, by providing for the possibility of mixed marriages with dispensations, and granting them so frequently. At the present time, almost one-third of the marriages performed in the Catholic Church in the United States are between Catholics and non-Catholics.

None of the foregoing means that parents do not have the *right* to forbid their children to date non-Catholics. All parents have the right to lay down such rules and such prohibitions for their children as they are convinced are for that child's good. Until their child is an adult, the ultimate control of his actions and the ultimate responsibility for them rests with the parents. In fulfilling this responsibility, they may use such means as their consciences dictate. Parents who choose to resort to such a blanket prohibition should realize, however, that in employing it they are turning their backs on the opinions of the wisest among us as to how to handle this problem.

It is not a sin to date a non-Catholic. In some cases, it may prove to be an *occasion* of sin. If the relationship deepens into love, the Catholic party may be induced to leave his Church and marry outside it. Or, he may marry the non-Catholic in the Church, and she, faithless to her pre-marital promises, may deny their children the heritage of their faith or cause her husband to be faithless to it. Under any of these circumstances, the original relationship was certainly an occasion of sin, since continuance of it did lead to grave sin.

These possibilities cause responsible Catholic parents to question the wisdom of dating non-Catholics. But it must be pointed out that there are thousands of cases of Catholics and non-Catholics dating and marrying which do not end thus tragically—quite the reverse. The suitability of a non-Catholic dating partner must be judged on the merits of the individual. In the early days of dating one can determine whether the non-Catholic is ignorant or well-informed about the Church, hostile or interested, prejudiced or open-minded. These attitudes should determine whether the association should be tolerated or discouraged. Attractive and suitable though the non-Catholic may be in all other ways, if he hates or scorns the Church, the relationship should be terminated. If he is generous and open-minded and is in all other ways desirable mate-material, the companionship may be pursued without undue risk.

Long before your child becomes interested in dating, the point should be made that, everything else being equal, the chances of happiness in a mixed marriage are not as high as in a marriage of co-religionists. Such a marriage always demands more of both partners in maturity, generosity, patience, and mutual respect. The risk of marriage with a partner who feels free to dissolve it with divorce at will, while the Catholic partner remains permanently bound, should also be pointed out.

When your child begins to date a non-Catholic, he should not "play down" the fact of his Catholicity. He should behave just as he would with a fellow-Catholic, discussing church services, nuns, priests, Catholic dogma, fast and abstinence, and sacraments. This in fairness to the non-Catholic, so that he may understand how the faith of a Catholic permeates all phases of his life. Because Catholicity is so all-pervasive it will be easy and natural to do this; indeed, to do otherwise would be artificial. If the non-Catholic reacts with incredulity, contempt, or antagonism, the chances for a happy future as a married pair are slight. Fortunately, if this information is exchanged and thus reacted to early in the association, one or the other of the pair will usually terminate it before either has become seriously interested. But if the non-Catholic shows interest, respect, and an open mind upon the subject of Catholicity, the association is not dangerous at this point.

When a young Catholic feels the dawning of a genuine romantic interest in a non-Catholic dating partner—an interest such that he is beginning to consider her as a possible mate—he should take a further step immediately, and this before there is any question of an engagement: he should tell the non-Catholic, fully and accurately, what is required of a non-Catholic partner in a mixed marriage. Before doing so, he should make sure he knows exactly what is required and tell it all: premarital commitments, permanence of the union, laws about birth control, education of children, freedom to practice one's religion.

There need be no awkwardness and no pointedness about this. Young people love to talk about marriage in general, long before they are seriously considering it. In such a discussion, it would be natural to say one had never thought seriously about marrying outside one's Faith because of the problems created; that indeed it would be impossible to do so unless the non-Catholic would agree to—etc. If the non-Catholic reacts unfavorably to this information, this is the time to terminate the association. One has had due warning of breakers ahead.

Even though the non-Catholic dating partner shows a complete willingness to perform any obligations required of him or her, one further step should be taken before a formal engagement is entered into. The pair should visit the Catholic's parish priest and ask him to tell the non-Catholic exactly what will be required of him in all respects; great pains should be taken that the non-Catholic understands and is perfectly willing to accede to what is required of him. This is far better than leaving this visit until marriage plans are in prospect. Many Catholics are not themselves thoroughly conversant with the matter. Expert advice is needed; the earlier it is obtained, the better.

If the non-Catholic displays a willingness to do all required of him without inward hostility or mental reservations, a dispensation for the marriage can probably be obtained and, assuming that the Catholic partner is determined to go through with the marriage, the Catholic parents should no longer object to it. They should demonstrate affection for and confidence in the non-Catholic, and prayerfully resign the future welfare of the pair to their Heavenly Father.

ENTERTAINMENT MEDIA

In the area of entertainment, as in all others, the teen-ager must be granted more freedom of choice than he has had formerly. This means that one must feel free to let him exercise his own judgment and taste in the selection of his entertainment because he has proved himself capable of wise choice. Any teen-ager who has demonstrated that he is markedly immature or unstable requires continued parental supervision, exercised without hesitation.

A teen-ager may attend any moving picture which has received the A-I or A-II rating of the Legion of Decency. A teen-ager might occasionally attend a picture in the A-III category—"morally unobjectionable for adults only," but only if he is intelligent and mature enough to be considered adult in his thinking. A teen-ager considering going to a picture in this category should discuss the matter with his parents. It is thus he proves that he may be mature enough safely to attend it.

It is almost impossible to supervise the television viewing of teen-agers. They should be urged to keep their viewing at a minimum and never be permitted to let it interfere with school assignments or home tasks. Try to interest them in watching good drama, news, and cultural programs—better still, watch and discuss such programs with them. Make sure they see the televised showings of great historical or news events, such as the Coronation of Queen Elizabeth II, national political conventions, or presidential inaugurations. News programs which discuss special subjects in depth and give historical background, current opinions pro and con are very good, and are one field in which television can do a job superior to that done in the newspapers.

By the time your child is a teen-ager, one facet of his nature will be apparent: he loves to read, or he does not. The child who does not love the printed word will do such reading as is required for his school work and will occasionally read the newspapers, magazines, or very light fiction, but only if he can find no other means of amusing himself. The teen-ager who is an ardent reader will by this age have developed broad and deep reading tastes, but the true proof of his addiction to the written word is the fact that he will read anything available, regardless of its subject or worth, rather than not read at all.

With teen-agers, as with sub-teens and, indeed, readers of all ages, the trash magazines, pornography, books that dwell on lewdness and immorality are out of bounds. This material has been discussed in the chapters on "The Home Life of Catholics" and "Manners for Teen-agers," but the subject is so important that it must be referred to once more: such reading is poison. No decent person should indulge in it. It should never be allowed to enter your home. If you discover a teen-ager in your family who displays a genuine fondness for such printed filth, you should discuss the matter with him with the greatest serious-ness, point out its unhealthfulness and dangers; urge him to make it a matter for confession. One should not overlook the fact that a fondness for such reading matter is sometimes one of the first symptoms of serious personality problems which may need psychiatric help.

It is nonsense to say, as opponents of any kind of censorship so often do, that "no one was ever seduced by a book." This statement is true only in its literal sense. Otherwise it denies the power which the printed word most certainly has to change the minds of men. Sociolo-gists declare that "Uncle Tom's Cabin" helped bring on the Civil War. Historians agree that the writings of Tom Paine unified the American colonists in their determination to be free. The Bible, the Koran, and the Bhagavad-Gita changed the religious and ethical concepts of mil-lions. Admitting this, one cannot deny to the printed word its equal power to harm, to convince the unsophisticated that wrong is right, and evil good.

Considering all this, how much supervision does teen-age reading require? Expert opinion differs widely here, but this much may be safely said: the child of parents who themselves are inveterate readers whose choices range widely through the whole field of literature can be granted considerable freedom, because his parents are capable of discussing his reading material with him and pointing out its merits and its flaws, its point of view, its aims. Parents not so qualified, who have a child who loves to read serious literature, may, by the time he is sixteen, depend to a large extent on the child's own taste and judgment but should, if in doubt about his choices, consult teachers or librarians for their opinions as to its suitability.

Save for exercising this degree of supervision, one must depend, in this as in other fields, upon the efficacy of the spiritual, moral, and ethical teachings one has endeavored to impart to one's child through-out his life to resist the evil and recognize the good in everything that he reads.

One mistake frequently made by parents and educators is the failure to realize the intellectual capability and high purpose of many of our teen-agers. Here are some excerpts from letters written by teen-agers to J. Donald Adams, who writes the "Speaking of Books" column in the Sunday Book Review Section of the New York Times. They were recently published in his column. Let the teen-agers speak for themselves.

> Says Karen Mitnick: "Our minds are capable of attacking serious problems, and if we seem held back our only blockade remains the elders who do not give us the mental nourishment so important at this period in our life. . . . We are a searching generation, looking for guidance along that long road towards growing up."

> Michael Solarz: "Our parents don't bother to teach us, not even the things a parent should teach. Our teachers today (with few exceptions) already accept the teen-ager's debased taste. . . . We are seldom asked to stretch our minds and imagination, and when we do, we must stay within the teacher's limit."

> "I believe," writes Elaine Kasdan, "that teen-agers, for the most part, are not reading literature worthy of their true intelligence and in so doing are weakening their capacity for thinking and reasoning."

Commenting on these intelligent letters, Mr. Adams says:

> To me the most racking conundrum of education is why so many bookish people seek to communicate the drudgery of scholarship instead of the delights which surely must have seduced them to a life of study.
> What is desperately needed today are more teachers able to communicate the joy to be found in reading good literature, and fewer death-dealing analysts who are unable to connect literature with life. Such teachers have killed the literary taste-buds of countless American young. And one of the saddest aspects of recent American life has been the gradual abandonment in too many homes of the practice of family-shared reading aloud.

To this one need only add: with youngsters of such intelligence and judgment a parent's primary responsibility is to see that they are provided with reading matter worthy of them—in the home library, if possible, certainly by access to good public and school libraries.

AFTER HIGH SCHOOL

Whatever the age at which a child graduates from high school, he can no longer be considered a member of the teen-age group. Henceforward, whatever his activity, he must be regarded as a young adult. The graduates will take one of three paths: they will enter religious life, they will go to college, or they will begin their business career.

For the parents of those who attempt the religious life, the problems of child rearing are almost over. Henceforward, with joyous thanks to their Creator for the honor bestowed upon them, they can consign the welfare of their child to the hands of his religious superiors, their sole remaining duty being to encourage the child to persevere in the path he has chosen. They will suffer pangs of loneliness for the child who has forever left their roof just as they do for a child who marries and leaves them, but he who enters religious life leaves with them this consolation: wherever his future path may lead, his parents remain *first* in his earthly affections forever.

Parents of a child who goes away to college must relax their supervision of him simply because they will not be with him to continue it. They know, however, that the college itself will lay down rules for his behavior, that will serve to guide him into full adult responsibility for his own behavior.

If the child lives at home and attends a local college, parents should give him both the freedom and responsibility that are due his age group. Continue to throw your home open to his friends, maintain your interest in his activities, share his interests insofar as he wishes you to do so. Be slow to criticize, remonstrate, or advise. When you feel you must do any of these things, do so calmly and reasonably, speaking as one adult to another. You still retain your parental authority, but should exercise it only in matters of moment.

The graduate who begins his business career after high school jumps directly into adult living. In his work he will be associating on an equal footing with people of all ages and will be, as a matter of course, held responsible for his own acts and decisions. He should be treated much the same way in the home circle. Now is the time to remember that your child has rights—including the right to make mistakes!

A working child living at home should be required, as a matter of course, to pay for the board, room, and services he receives as a member of the family. Many young persons are outraged at this and feel that to be required to pay for the services they have always received is to be cast out of the family circle. But there are two cogent reasons why such action is just: his parents, after a lifetime of devoted service to him, are clearly entitled now to be relieved of the burden of supporting him; and the young person should learn, from paying out a proper sum for board and lodging, to consider them basic expenses which he must henceforward meet before he can consider spending his earnings on other things. This training in the hard necessities of life is invaluable. The amount contributed will not—probably cannot—be commensurate with the values received; neither should it be so trifling as to be only a token payment. A quarter of his income (after taxes) is a moderate requirement. If the family income is small, a larger sum may be asked. It should be paid promptly and regularly.

Even in families where expenses are no problem, this payment should be required of a working child for his own good. The parent may, if he wishes, bank the amount given and return it intact to the child as a gift upon the occasion of his marriage, but one should not tell the child that one is doing so. Let it come as a delightful surprise at a time when it will be most welcome.

Other than requiring a working child to pay for his own support, one should leave the spending of his wages wholly in the hands of the wage-earner. This is a basic right, one of the tangible rewards of earning one's living. He should spend as he chooses. Even when choosing foolishly, he is learning how to manage his income.

Both the college student and the wage-earner should be granted freedoms in all areas of activity commensurate with their status. Such young people have both the right and the duty to begin to manage their own lives and to accept the responsibility for their own actions. Advise or remonstrate seldom, and only in matters that you consider vital.

Suppose a young man in this group runs into debt, neglects his work, drinks to excess, associates with bad companions? What can a parent do to reform him? Very little. The time for shaping your child's character, training him in the way he should go, is long past. If you have not done so, you have had your chance—and thrown it away. At this point, there is little you can do for him.

Some allowance can be made for this age group. The wine of freedom, when first tasted, is a heady brew. Often a basically sound young person will behave recklessly and foolishly in his early adult years to test out his freedom of action. The best cure in this situation is to let him suffer the consequences of his own foolishness. Debt is a heavy burden, but carrying it for a while teaches a lot. A job lost is a blow to pride from which one also learns. Heavy drinking has an unpleasant aftermath. Associating with bad company brings the loss of the good opinion of good company. Each mistake carries its own punishment, from which the sufferer will learn much about how to manage his life.

The one thing a parent should not do in this situation is to endeavor to spare the child the consequences of his own errors. Let him suffer—and learn.

In the case of a child in college, financed in his education by his parents, the parent has more power. A college student who does not maintain proper grades and manage his social and moral life responsibly should first be warned, then threatened with the withdrawal of financial support. If he does not improve, the threat should be carried out. A college student who fails to take advantage of the opportunities given him should be removed from school.

With either a college child or a wage earner, the parents can watch and pray, remonstrate and advise, encourage, hope, and love. But practically speaking, their authority means little if the child does not choose to acknowledge it. The time has come when, in all areas of living, the child must "do it for himself."

MARRIAGE

Any high school graduate earning enough to support a family, and any girl graduate engaged to such a man, has the right to marry. There may of course be many other considerations such as to make a specific marriage unwise or unsuitable, but young people in this category have fulfilled the basic requirements: they have completed their education and they are self-supporting. Parents of such young adults should recognize their right to seek and find a mate—should, indeed, encourage them to do so.

Many young women marry directly after completing high school. This is certainly better than an earlier marriage, but most thoughtful people feel that a young woman learns much that helps her to be a successful wife by preceding her marriage with a few years' experience in the business world, during which she enjoys a full and varied social life. She then can understand the problems and difficulties of her husband in his capacity of wage-earner, and she settles down more contentedly to the responsibilities of marriage because of the playtime she previously enjoyed.

MARRYING IN COLLEGE

The influx of veterans to college campuses following World War II introduced a new phenomenom to the American college scene: the married college student. Since then, many young people have been eager to combine the duties of marriage and college life. Some have done so successfully; some have not. Some educators approve the change; many do not. The problem appears to be one which must be resolved upon the merits of each individual case. The best discussion of the problem which this writer has seen is an article entitled "Marrying in Haste in College" written by Margaret Meade, the distinguished anthropologist, which appeared in volume II, number 2, of the Columbia University *Forum*. Since this magazine circulates only among graduates of the university, it is not easy to obtain. Anyone who has a personal interest in this problem should certainly make an effort to obtain a copy. The following long quote contains the gist of what Miss Meade so brilliantly says:

Undergraduate marriages have not been a part of American life long enough for us to be certain what their effect will be. But two ominous trends can be noted.

One is the "successful" student marriage, often based on a high-school choice which both sets of parents applauded because it assured an appropriate mate with the right background, and because it made the young people settle down. If not a high-school choice, then a high-school pattern is repeated: finding a girl who will go steady, dating her exclusively, and letting the girl propel the boy toward a career choice which will make early marriage possible.

These young people have no chance to find themselves in college because they have clung to each other so exclusively. They can take little advantage of college as a broadening influence, and they often show less breadth of vision as seniors than they did as freshmen. They marry, either as undergraduates or immediately upon graduation, have children in quick succession and retire to the suburbs to have more children—bulwarking a choice that was made before either was differentiated as a human being. Help from both sets of parents, begun in the undergraduate marriage or after commencement day, perpetuates their immaturity. At thirty they are still immature and dependent, their future mortgaged for twenty or thirty years ahead, neither husband nor wife realizing the promise that a different kind of undergraduate life might have enabled each to fulfill.

Such marriages are not failures, in the ordinary sense. They are simply wasteful of young, intelligent people who might have developed into differentiated and conscious human beings. But with four or five children, the husband firmly tied to a job which he would not dare to leave, any move toward further individual development in either husband or wife is a threat to the whole family. It is safer to read what both agree with (or even not to read at all and simply look at TV together), attend the same clubs,

listen to the same jokes—never for a minute relaxing their possession of each other, just as when they were teen-agers.

Such a marriage is a premature imprisonment of young people,
before they have had a chance to explore their own minds and
the minds of others, in a kind of desperate, devoted symbiosis.
Both had college educations, but the college served only as a place
in which to get a degree and find a mate with the right family
background, a background that subsequently swallowed them up.

The second kind of undergraduate marriage is more tragic.
Here, the marriage is based on the boy's promise and the ex-
pendability of the girl. She, at once or at least as soon as she gets
her bachelor's degree, will go to work at some secondary job to
support her husband while he finishes his degree. She supports
him faithfully and becomes identified in his mind with the family
that has previously supported him, thus underlining his immature
status. As soon as he becomes independent, he leaves her. That
this pattern occurs between young people who seem ideally suited
to each other suggests that it was the period of economic dependency that damaged the marriage relationship, rather than any
intrinsic incompatibility in the original choice.

Both types of mariage, the "successful" and the "unsuccessful,"
emphasize the key issue: the tie between economic responsibility
and marriage in our culture. A man who does not support himself
is not yet a man, and a man who is supported by his wife or lets
his parents support his wife is only too likely to feel he is not a
man. The GI students' success actually supports this position: they
had earned their GI stipend, as men, in their country's service.
With a basic economic independence they could study, accept
extra help from their families, do extra work, and still be good
students and happy husbands and fathers.

There are then, two basic conclusions. One is that under any
circumstances a full student life is incompatible with early commit-
ment and domesticity. The other is that it is incompatible only
under conditions of immaturity. Where the choice has been made
maturely, and where each member of the pair is doing academic
work which deserves full support, complete economic independence should be provided. For other types of student marriage,
economic help should be refused.

This kind of discrimination would remove the usual dangers of
parent-supported, wife-supported, and too-much-work-supported
student marriages. Married students, male and female, making full
use of their opportunities as undergraduates, would have the right
to accept from society this extra time to become more intellectually
competent people. Neither partner would be so tied to a part-time
job that relationships with other students would be impaired. By

the demands of high scholarship, both would be assured of continued growth that comes from association with other high-caliber students as well as with each other.

But even this solution should be approached with caution. Recent psychological studies, especially those of Piaget, have shown how essential and how precious is the intellectual development of the early post-puberty years. It may be that any domesticity takes the edge off the eager, flaming curiosity on which we must depend for the great steps that Man must take, and take quickly, if he and all living things are to continue on this earth.

For further reading material for sub-teens, teen-agers, and their parents, the following books are recommended:

Banahan, the Rev. John S., *Instructions for Mixed Marriage*. Milwaukee, Wis.: The Bruce Publishing Co.

Daniélou, Jean, S.J., *The Bible and the Liturgy*. Notre Dame, Ind.: University of Notre Dame Press.

Flanders, Judy, *Baby-Sitter's Handbook*. Chicago, Ill.: Science Research Associates, Inc.

Ford, John C., S.J., *Man Takes a Drink*. New York, N. Y.: P. J. Kenedy & Sons.

Foy, Felician A., *Ten Commandments for Teen-Agers*. Paterson, N. J.: St. Anthony's Guild Press.

Imbiorski, Rev. Walter, *The New Cana Manual*. Chicago, Ill.: Delaney Publications.

Kelly, Gerald, S.J., *Modern Youth and Chastity*. St. Louis, Mo.: Queen's Work. ..

Stratmann, Francis, O.P., *War and Christianity Today*. Westminster, Md.: The Newman Press.

Highly recommended are the following pamphlets, each costing ten cents, all written by Monsignor J. D. Conway and published by the Ave Maria Press, Notre Dame, Indiana:

Keeping Company
Love and Dating
Modesty, Chastity, and Morals
Engagement
Marriage Outside the Church
Mixed Marriage
Marriage: Catholic and Non-Catholic

23

Fast and Abstinence

Now therefore saith the Lord: "Be converted to me with
all your heart, in fasting . . . " (Joel 2:12).

SPIRITUAL REQUIREMENTS

To fast and abstain on the days appointed is one of the six chief
commandments of the Church. She desires us to fast and abstain on
certain days, not because meat or other foods are evil in themselves,
but because fast and abstinence teach us to control the desires of the
flesh, raise our minds more freely to God, and make satisfaction for
sin. Our Lord Himself set us an example for this by His forty days of
fasting in the wilderness.

Fasting and abstinence are not the same thing. Fasting refers to the
amount of food consumed and the time at which it is taken. Abstinence
is the refraining from eating meat or meat products such as gravy or
soup stock during a given period.

FASTING

A fast day is one on which only one full meal is allowed, to be
taken at noon or in the evening (as one chooses), but two other light
meals may also be taken, the nature and quantity of which is determined by local custom. At the full meal, meat may be taken (unless
the fast day is also a day of abstinence) but it may not be taken at the
lesser meals. In most dioceses of the United States the rule for the
lesser meals is: the amount consumed at the two light meals together
should not be more than the amount eaten at the one full meal. Eating
between meals on a fast day is not permitted. Liquids of all kinds are
allowed between meals, save those so rich as to be considered a food.
Examples: malted milk or thick vegetable soup.

The term "full meal" can be interpreted in its most liberal sense
save for the natural limitations regarding gluttony and temperance. As
long as two hours may be devoted to the consumption of the full meal.

If cocktails and hors d'oeuvres are served immediately preceding, they may be taken and considered part of the meal. A complete seven course meal, including meat, may be eaten if the fast day is not also a day of abstinence. On a day of abstinence, such a meal could be eaten, except for the dishes containing meat or meat products. If candy is passed at the conclusion of a meal or served immediately following it in the drawing room, the candy may be eaten as part of the meal.

The two light meals eaten on a day on which the full meal is so elaborate would preferably consist of considerably less food than the amount eaten at the full meal, although technically it would be permissible to consume the equal of the amount of the full meal. Meat may not be eaten at the two lesser meals.

All Catholics from the ages of twenty-one to fifty-nine are bound to observe the fast days of the Church unless they have been dispensed. Those younger or older are not required to keep the fast. Members of the Armed Forces of the United States on active duty are dispensed from the laws of fast and abstinence except on Ash Wednesday, Good Friday, and the vigil of Christmas. This dispensation applies to members of the soldier's family, if he lives with them, either on or off post.

Pastors are empowered to dispense individual members of their flock from fast and or abstinence for due cause. Anyone who thinks that some circumstance in his life—ill health, pregnancy, very hard work—might permit him to be dispensed should consult his pastor.

ABSTINENCE

A day of abstinence is one on which it is not permitted to eat meat. This means that the following are forbidden: the meat of domestic animals, fowl, and game; by-products of meat, such as kidneys, liver, tripe, brains, meat extract, meat or poultry gravy, sauces and soups made from meat or poultry stock; meat combination dishes, such as pork and beans or spaghetti and meat balls. Permitted are: all fish, including shell fish, and the flesh of cold-blooded animals, such as frog's legs, turtles, and snails; caviar and any kind of fish roe; also allowed is the use of meat fats (lard and drippings) in small amounts, such as can be considered a condiment, rather than the principal ingredient of a dish. Thus an egg fried in bacon drippings is permissible. One may add salt pork fat to clam chowder, or onions that have been sautéed in salt pork fat.

All who have passed their seventh birthday are bound to practice abstinence on the appointed days unless they have been dispensed.

THE DAYS OF FAST AND ABSTINENCE

All Fridays of every year are days of abstinence, to commemorate our Lord's death on Good Friday. The days on which both fast and abstinence are prescribed by the general law of the Church are twenty-nine in number: Ash Wednesday; the Fridays of Lent; the Ember Days; the vigils of Pentecost, the Assumption, All Saints' Day, and Christmas. In actual practice, this number is modified and varied in various localities by the fact that all the bishops of the Church have the power to dispense the faithful of their dioceses from some or all of these days when, in their judgment, it is wise to do so.

In 1952 many of the bishops of the United States, using the provisions of canon law as modified through special faculties granted by the Holy See, published regulations on fast and abstinence for their dioceses which made for uniformity and which are, at the time this material is written (March, 1961), still in effect in many dioceses. The following chart outlines the days of fast and abstinence so set up:

Fast and Abstinence chart

		Age 21 to 59	Age 7 to 21 over 59
Ash Wednesday		No meat; one full meal only	No meat
Lent	On Fridays	No meat; one full meal only	No meat
	On Other Days	Meat at principal meal only; One full meal only	Meat at all meals
Holy Saturday		Meat at principal meal only One full meal only	Meat at all meals
Ember Days*	Wednesdays	Meat at principal meal only; One full meal only	Meat at principal meal only
	Fridays	No meat; one full meal only	No meat
	Saturdays	Meat at principal meal only; One full meal only	Meat at principal meal only
Vigils	of Pentecost	Meat at principal meal only; One full meal only	Meat at principal meal only
	Im. Conception and Dec. 23 or** Dec. 24	No meat; one full meal only	No meat
All Fridays During Year		No meat	No meat

* The Ember Days are: the Wednesdays, Fridays, and Saturdays following December 13, the first Sunday of Lent, Pentecost, and September 14.

** The vigil of Christmas may be observed on either December 23 or 24th, as one chooses.

In 1961, several American bishops further modified the days of fast and abstinence for their dioceses. These changes are extensive, and, since they are a considerable liberalization of former practice, the reasoning which led to their adoption should be discussed: many American theologians feel that the American standard of living is so high and our choice of foods so extensive that a day of fast, for American Catholics, is only a trifling act of self-denial. The obligation to limit slightly the amount of food one eats, to remember to eat meat once only on fast days or to eschew it on days of complete abstinence, is not a real sacrifice, although it may be a nuisance. The period of Lent, some feel, might therefore be better observed by attendance at church services, increased private prayer, reception of Holy Communion, increased acts of charity, reduced social activities, and voluntary denial of some food or habit (smoking, eating candy, drinking alcoholic beverages) such as might be a true sacrifice for the individual.

This is apparently the view of the bishops of Canada, who in 1960 considerably modified the required days of fast and abstinence for the faithful of their dioceses. Three of the American bishops who similarily modified the days of fast and abstinence for their dioceses are the bishops of Buffalo (N. Y.), Ogdensburg (N. Y.), and Portland (Maine). Bishop Daniel J. Feeney of Maine and Bishop James J. Navagh of Ogdensburg have decreed that in their dioceses there will be four days of fast and abstinence: Ash Wednesday, Good Friday, the vigil of the Immaculate Conception, and the vigil of Christmas, the latter to be observed either December 23rd or December 24th. The rules for the diocese of Buffalo are given in the following chart:

DAYS OF FAST AND ABSTINENCE

Approved for the Diocese of Buffalo

	FAST	COMPLETE ABSTINENCE
	Only one full meal; two other meals allowed but together they should not equal another full meal.	No meat; no soup or gravy made from meat.
WHO ARE OBLIGED	All over age of 21 and under 59 years.	All over age of 7 years.
FEBRUARY	Ash Wednesday, Feb. 15.	Fridays, Ash Wednesday, Feb. 15.
MARCH	Good Friday, Mar. 31.	All Fridays except Mar. 17, St. Patrick's Day.
DECEMBER	Thurs., Dec. 7, Vigil of Immaculate Conception.	All Fridays except Dec. 8. Thursday, Dec. 7, Vigil of Immaculate Conception.

ABSTINENCE—On days of COMPLETE ABSTINENCE, no one over 7, unless dispensed or excused, may eat meat at all.

FAST BEFORE RECEIVING HOLY COMMUNION—1. Abstain from solid foods and alcoholic beverages for three hours. 2. Non-alcoholic beverages may be taken up to one hour before receiving Communion. 3. Water does not beak the Eucharistic fast at any time. 4. The sick can consult a priest.

It may be that modifications similar to those in these three dioceses, which so relax the regulations for the Lenten fast, may soon be adopted elsewhere in the United States. The reader should bear in mind that it is his personal obligation at all times to ascertain for himself and those under his care the regulations currently in force in his diocese upon any possible day or period of fast. He may do this through parish announcements or bulletins, or through his diocesan newspaper.

SOME SOCIAL ASPECTS OF FAST AND ABSTINENCE

For Catholics

It is the personal obligation of the individual Catholic who has reached the required age to observe the laws of fast and abstinence. He cannot shift the obligation to another—by saying, for instance, "My wife forgot and served meat at dinner today." Unless the husband himself forgot the day of abstinence, he is not excused. He should have refrained from eating the meat his wife served. In our bounteous land, the food served at any given meal is usually so varied that the diner can eat enough to sustain health, even though abstaining from the principal meat dish. On the other hand, if a mother were through inadvertence to send her ten-year-old son to school with a luncheon of two meat sandwiches and a piece of mince pie, it would be permissible for the child to eat his luncheon. The fact that a growing child would otherwise be obliged to go without food from breakfast to mid-afternoon would be considered a sufficiently grave reason for failing to abstain.

It is the obligation of the Catholic housewife and the non-Catholic wife of a Catholic husband to enable her family easily to observe the days of fast and abstinence by serving food in the permitted quantities on fast days and refraining from serving meat on days of abstinence.

It is the obligation of any Catholic who is chairman of a dinner or luncheon meeting of a club to note the date selected and to determine whether it is a day of abstinence. (A fast day does not create a problem here. On a fast day, it may be presumed to be the duty of individual Catholics to reserve for the time of the meeting the one full meal to which they are entitled and to eat sparingly at the other two meals of the day.) If the date selected is a day of abstinence, the chairman may do one of the following:

a) Change the date of the meeting to another day.

b) For an all-Catholic group, arrange to serve a permissible entree, such as lobster or frogs' legs.

c) For a mixed group, arrange to offer a choice of entrees, one of fish, the other meat.

d) For a mixed group, serve an entree of fish, lobster, or frogs' legs.

The fourth selection of this group is based on the following reasoning: It is sometimes not possible to offer a choice of entrees. In such a case, many non-Catholics would have no objection to eating fish or some other food acceptable to their Catholic brethren. Even if the food selected were not especially palatable to them, many would be willing to eat it, rather than to see their Catholic friends wholly abstain.

In the event that a meal at which meat only is offered is served on a day of abstinence to a mixed gathering, the Catholic club member should observe the laws of abstinence and not eat the meat offered. Remember that most soups, particularly clear soups, are made of meat or poultry stock and may not be eaten.

Entertaining at home for luncheon or dinner on a day of abstinence raises problems for the Catholic hostess. The easiest way of avoiding them is to entertain on another day. If this solution is not possible, the following are suggested:

a) To an all-Catholic group of guests, serve an entree of fish or other permitted food. If soup is served, let it be a fish chowder, fruit soup, or a cream soup made with butter instead of stock.

b) To a religiously mixed group, serve a similar meal, if you feel it would be acceptable.

c) To a religiously mixed group, serve a meat entree to non-Catholic guests and a permissible substitute to Catholic guests.

When employing any of these solutions, the Catholic hostess and members of her family, of course, refrain from eating meat. And a Catholic hostess should never "solve" her problem by serving meat to all.

Exceptions to this rule are rare, but they do exist. Canon law excuses one from abstaining for grave reason. Considerable difference of opinion exists as to what constitutes a grave reason. The following set of circumstances, remote though they are from the lives of most of us, illustrate a case which might constitute a grave reason:

The various ambassadors accredited to our country give a number of formal dinners each season for the President of the United States and other members of the diplomatic corps. The social calendar of Washington is so crowded that the dates upon which various ambassadors may give these dinners are assigned to them and are fairly constant from year to year. Let us suppose that a Catholic ambassador from a Catholic country is assigned a date for one of these dinners which falls upon a Friday.

A dinner which is formal in the true sense of the word follows a strict and inviolable pattern. The menu consists of seven courses: oysters (or clams or caviar), clear soup, fish, meat with vegetables, salad, dessert, fruit. To deviate from this menu in any respect renders the dinner informal.

Thus a problem arises for our mythical Catholic ambassador. As a Catholic, he is obliged to abstain from meat on a day of abstinence. As an ambassador, the representative of his nation, he is obliged to preside at a formal dinner on a day of abstinence. And as the host at this meal, he must eat some of each course served. Such a situation would surely be considered a grave matter, such as to relieve the ambassador and his family from the obligation of abstaining. So, too, his guests who are also Catholic. Since all who were attending would be there in an official capacity, the fulfillment of their official duties would probably be considered sufficient cause to relieve them of the necessity of abstaining.

In actual practice, the Catholic ambassador placed in such a position would probably solve his problem by obtaining a dispensation for this occasion prior to the dinner. But, if one assumes for purposes of illustration that he had neglected to do so, the obligations and responsibilities of the meal, which his position requires him to fulfill, could surely be said to constitute a sufficiently grave reason for failing to abstain.

The election of Mr. Kennedy, our first Catholic president, gives this problem a wider application than it has had heretofore. For him, and for members of his personal and official family who are Catholics, the solution to this problem would perhaps be to obtain prior dispensation from abstaining, applicable to all meals at which they are hosts or guests in an official capacity.

There are other situations in which a Catholic might not observe the law of abstinence for a grave reason, and many shades of opinion among theologians as to what constitutes a grave reason. A common one is the plight of a Catholic who is a guest in a non-Catholic home for a meal on a day of abstinence—a meal at which meat is the principal dish. Assume that his host might be deeply embarassed or grieved by his abstention. Does this constitute a sufficiently grave reason for failing to abstain? Opinions on this matter differ. Some hold that one must always abstain under these circumstances. Others feel that the attitude of the host has bearing in the matter. If he is a man of goodwill, who can be presumed to have offered his guest meat through simple inadvertence, the guest might eat it to spare him embarassment. If he is obviously antagonistic to the Church and might have deliberately served meat to test the strength and sincerity of guest's convictions, the obligation to abstain is clear. About the only general suggestion that can be made concerning possible exceptions to abstaining that arise unexpectedly is this: weigh your obligation against the possible harm to another if you abstain (embarrassment, injured feelings, inconvenience arising from preparing substitute food). Which is graver, or more important? Choose the lesser evil. If in doubt as to the wisdom of your choice, discuss it with your confessor at your next confession, to obtain guidance for similar future occasions.

Bear in mind that one need not be obvious or belligerent about one's abstention. Meals served guests are usually so bounteous that one can eat well while abstaining. When one does so, a well-mannered host should never comment on a guest's failure to eat any specific dish. Should a host so comment, it is usually through an excess of hospitality or a failure to realize that so to do is not well-bred, which is innocent, or through a deliberate attempt to embarass the Catholic, which is not.

There are cases in which abstention is very noticeable. For instance: you are chatting in the garden with a neighbor on Friday. She says, "Don't go. Lunch with me." Then she serves you a meat patty on a roll, some potato chips, a relish and a beverage. The innocence of her act (lack of malice, that is) in serving you such an impromptu meal is obvious. To abstain from the meat would be most noticeable, and might cause her to insist on preparing something else for you. To avoid this embarassment and hustle and bustle, one might eat the meat and say nothing.

For Non-Catholics

The fact that their Catholic acquaintances fast and abstain on certain days creates social problems for the millions of American non-

Catholics well-bred enough to wish never to embarass or inconvenience their fellow-men. For them, the following observances are
suggested:

a) Try to remember that all Fridays of the year are days of abstinence for your Catholic friends. When entertaining on a Friday,
   plan a menu which they can eat freely.

b) If you fail to serve such a menu or entertain impromtu and are
   not prepared to serve such a meal, do not comment if your
   Catholic friends fail to eat some of the food you serve.

c) Remember, it is never good taste to comment upon the amount
   a guest eats, or upon the fact that he fails to eat any one dish.

d) When acting as chairman for a dinner or luncheon meeting of a
   club in which members are of diverse faiths, determine in
   advance whether the day is one upon which Catholic members
   may not eat meat. There are days other than Friday upon which
   a Catholic must abstain. A list of these days is given earlier in
   this chapter. Upon such a day, try to serve an entree that all
   may eat, such as fish, frogs' legs, lobster.

e) If you are entertaining Catholic guests on a day of abstinence,
   have forgotten their obligation to abstain, and have served meat,
   ignore the matter. Do not apologize, offer to prepare something
   else, or express concern as to whether they can dine well without eating the meat. Do not comment on whether they do or
   do not eat it. Such conversations, even though well-meant,
   embarrass your Catholic friend by making him conspicuous.

f) Never urge your Catholic friend to eat a meat dish when he
   appears to wish to abstain.

g) To comment disdainfully upon a Catholic guest's abstinence or
   the requirement of abstinence imposed by his Faith is an expression of ill-will of which no well-bred person would intentionally be guilty. If one indulges in such an expression, one
   should not be surprised if it is resented by the victim of the
   remark.

h) All of the rules above refer to abstinence—that is, to abstaining
   from eating meat on certain days. The Catholic's obligation to
   fast on some days need not be a problem for non-Catholics. As
   Catholics are always allowed one full meal upon a fast day, it
   may be considered their personal obligation to see to it that they
   have reserved the full meal for the social occasion. It is not the
   obligation of the host to serve them a lesser meal. Non-Catholics
   might bear in mind in this connection that Catholics invited to

a tea or cocktail party where hors d'oeuvres are served will, upon a fast day, take only tea or other beverage. Liquids may be taken between meals on a fast day, but solid food may only be eaten at the three regular meals. There is no obligation on the host to take any cognizance of this fact, save by failing to comment upon the fact that the Catholic guest is not taking solid food. Otherwise, the obligation is a personal one which rests only on the Catholic guest.

24

Correct Modes of Address to Those in Religious Life

THE CATHOLIC CLERGY

Written Address	Direct Address	Formal Introduction
The Pope		
His Holiness, the Pope *or* His Holiness, Pope John XXIII	Your Holiness	His Holiness, the Pope
Cardinals		
His Eminence, Francis Cardinal Spellman Archbishop of New York	Your Eminence	His Eminence, Cardinal Spellman
Papal Delegate		
The Most Rev. Egidio Vagnozzi, D.D. Titular Archbishop of Mira Apostolic Delegate	Excellency	His Excellency, the Titular Archbishop of Mira, the Apostolic Delegate
Archbishops		
His Excellency, The Most Rev. Michael Seton, S.T.D. Archbishop of Baltimore	Your Excellency *or* Archbishop Seton	His Excellency, the Archbishop of Baltimore

Written Address	*Direct Address*	*Formal Introduction*

Bishops

His Excellency, the Most Reverend William A. Scully, D.D. Bishop of Albany	Bishop Scully	His Excellency, the Bishop of Albany

Prothonotaries Apostolic, Domestic Prelates, and Vicars General

The Right Rev. Monsignor Gerald Kirwin, P.A. (or V.G.)	Monsignor *or* Monsignor Kirwin	The Right Rev. Monsignor Gerald Kirwin

Papal Chamberlain

The Very Rev. Monsignor John B. Sullivan	Monsignor	The Very Reverend Monsignor John B. Sullivan

Rural Dean

The Very Reverend Eugene Schue, V.F.	Father Schue	The Very Rev. Eugene Schue

Diocesan Priests

The Reverend John Connolly	Father Connolly	The Reverend John Connolly

Religious Priests

The Rev. F. F. Murphy, S.J.*	Father Murphy	The Rev. F. F. Murphy, of The Society of Jesus

Brothers

Brother Donation Joseph, F.S.C.* **	Brother	Brother Donation Joseph, of the Brothers of the Christian Schools

Sisters

Sister Gertrude* **   Sister   Sister Gertrude, of the
                                                    Daughters of Charity
                                                    of St. Vincent de Paul

* Priests and brothers of a religious order, when addressed in writing, have the initials of their order (S.J., O.F.M., C.S.C., etc.) added to their names. Sisters may be so addressed, but need not be.

** Sisters and brothers of a religious order may be addressed as "Venerable Sister," or "Venerable Brother," in writing (as the salutation of a letter) or in formal introduction, but the form is seldom used in the United States today.

When in doubt about how to address any church dignitary whose rank is not here given, consult the Catholic Directory.

NON-CATHOLIC CLERGYMEN

Protestant clergymen of any denomination are properly addressed in writing or in the third person (as in a formal introduction or presentation) as "The Reverend John Black," or "The Reverend Mr. Black," but may not be directly addressed as "Reverend," or even as "Reverend Black." A minister with a scholastic degree (a doctorate) may properly be addressed as "Doctor Black." He is then addressed in writing as "The Reverend John Black, D.D.," or "Litt. D.," or both.

Some Episcopalians address their ministers as "Father Black." Lutherans address their clergymen as "Pastor Black." In all other cases, a minister of any denomination who does not hold a doctor's degree is addressed directly as "Mr. Black."

A Protestant Episcopal Bishop is addressed in writing as "The Right Rev. John Black, D.D., LL.D.," and in direct address as "Bishop Black."

A Methodist Bishop is addressed in writing as "The Very Reverend John Black, D.D., L.L.D.," and directly as "Bishop Black."

A Protestant Episcopal Archdeacon is addressed in writing as "The Venerable John Black, D.D., Archdeacon of Connecticut," and directly as "Archdeacon Black," or "Doctor Black."

A Protestant Episcopal Dean is addressed in writing as "The Very Reverend John Black, D.D., Dean of St. Mark's Cathedral," and directly as "Dean Black" or "Dr. Black."

A Protestant Episcopal Canon is addressed in writing as "The Reverend John Black, D.D., Canon of St. Mark's Cathedral," and directly as "Canon Black," or "Dr. Black."

A Jewish rabbi is addressed, both directly and in writing, as "Rabbi." A rabbi who holds a doctor's degree is addressed in writing as "Rabbi Isaac Fink, D.D.," and is directly addressed either as "Rabbi," or "Doctor."

Index

❖❖❖❖❖

A NOTE ON THE TYPE

IN WHICH THIS BOOK WAS SET

This book is set in Caledonia, a Linotype face created in 1939 by W. A. Dwiggins, which is by far one of the best book types created in the last 50 years. It has a simple, hard-working, feet-on-the-ground quality and can be classed as a modern type face with excellent color and good readability. The designer claims Caledonia was created by putting a little of each of Scotch Roman, Bulmer, Baskerville and Bodoni together and producing a lively crisp-like book type. This book was composed by Progressive Typographers, Inc., York, Pa., printed by the Wickersham Printing Company, of Lancaster, Pa., and bound by Moore and Company of Baltimore. The typography and design of this book are by Howard N. King.